Our Secret Allies
The PEOPLES of RUSSIA

Other Books by Eugene Lyons

LIFE AND DEATH OF SACCO AND VANZETTI

MOSCOW CARROUSEL

ASSIGNMENT IN UTOPIA

THE RED DECADE

OUR UNKNOWN EX-PRESIDENT: A PORTRAIT OF HERBERT HOOVER

Eugene Lyons served as United Press correspondent in Moscow from 1928 to 1934; he has written and lectured extensively on Soviet Russia and world communism. Formerly editor of *The American Mercury*, Mr. Lyons at present is a senior editor of *The Reader's Digest*.

Our Secret Allies
The PEOPLES of RUSSIA

by

EUGENE LYONS

Duell, Sloan and Pearce · *New York*
Little, Brown and Company · *Boston*

DUELL, SLOAN AND PEARCE — LITTLE, BROWN
BOOKS ARE PUBLISHED BY
LITTLE, BROWN AND COMPANY
IN ASSOCIATION WITH
DUELL, SLOAN & PEARCE, INC.

Published simultaneously
in Canada by McClelland and Stewart Limited

PRINTED IN THE UNITED STATES OF AMERICA

Contents

Our Secret Allies
The PEOPLES of RUSSIA

To my grandson
DAVID LYONS HAIMES
in the hope that he will
grow up in a world wholly freed
from totalitarian bondage

I. Death of a Despot

▄▄▄▄▄▄▄▄▄▄▄▄▄▄▄▄▄▄▄▄▄▄▄▄▄▄▄▄▄▄▄▄▄▄▄▄▄▄

1. Jitters in the Kremlin

The collapse and death of Josef Vissarionovich Djugashvilli, self-styled Stalin, in the first week of March, 1953, touched off prodigious discussions of Soviet affairs the world over. Anyone with a claim to special knowledge on matters Russian, however tenuous, was invited to speculate aloud on the succession and its likely effects on Soviet policies. On the odd supposition that one of Stalin's creatures could have voiced private opinions, past speeches of Georgi M. Malenkov were analyzed for clues to his views, and the folds of his physiognomy were searched for clues to his character.

But in the torrents of words poured forth on the occasion, lamentably few were devoted to the people of the Soviet Union. The outside world, as usual, seemed too preoccupied with the rulers, dead and alive, to spare much thought for those over whom they ruled.

In general the assorted experts were content to treat the Russian masses as extras in the drama, leaving them undisturbed and unanalyzed in the passive role of "mourners" assigned to them in the censored Moscow dispatches. The whole stage-managed spectacle of boundless grief — "tear-stained faces," the procession past the catafalque in the Hall of Columns, memorial meetings and obituary poems — was swallowed abroad uncritically.

Without doubt there was a lot of genuine sorrow. Particularly in Moscow, large numbers of people owe their special status and privileges to the *vlast* — a word denoting the whole complex of Soviet institutions, power, and leaders — and Stalin had been its supreme symbol for a quarter of a century. Besides, the death of a mighty ruler can move men to tears — tears that have more to do with the great mystery of mortality than affection for the deceased.

But no intelligent Soviet citizen, we may be sure, took the pageant of formal grief any more seriously than he takes the pageants of formal rejoicing in the seasonal Red Square parades; he is too familiar with the mechanics of synthetic totalitarian emotion. Considering that to abstain might be politically dangerous, the striking fact is that so many millions in the capital did *not* queue up to view the earthly remains of their "Father and Teacher."

Beyond the Soviet realm, however, few questioned the supposed popular love for Stalin and loyalty to his works. Fewer bothered to wonder what was really in the hearts and minds of his subjects. Once again the non-Soviet world went along meekly with the notion that the USSR is a nation like other nations, united on basic things despite differences on specific issues, and therefore reacting as Americans or Frenchmen might react to the passing of their chief of state.

One American correspondent on the scene did acknowledge the importance of the two hundred million human beings in the background. Within a few hours after the funeral, this brave fellow cabled that "Mr. Malenkov and his comrades-at-arms appeared to have the support and enthusiasm of Soviet citizens in all walks of life." The walks of life open to a foreign reporter in Moscow are normally limited to the tourist hotels, foreign embassies, and the censorship office; and the citizen in any walk of life who would openly admit any feeling short of all-out enthusiasm is too far gone in idiocy to count in a poll anyhow. But the correspondent's sweeping fatuity, out-Galluping all opinion pollsters of record, was duly published on the front page of the New York *Times*.

Unlike the outside world, however, Stalin's associates and heirs were enormously concerned about the state of mind of their subjects, including (and perhaps especially) the Communist Party members and other direct participants in the *vlast*. They made this clear enough in all their pronouncements, from the first bulletin reporting the dictator's brain hemorrhage to the orations from the Lenin mausoleum on Red Square, which were all filled with unabashed appeals for "unity" and "vigilance" in the face of "internal enemies," and exhortations to "rally around the party." These were the keynotes of the domestic propaganda, repeated like a litany day after day, and still ringing through the Soviet press, posters, resolutions, and speeches at this writing.

In a statement on the passing of his far-off boss, the head of the American Communist Party, William Z. Foster, declared that the Soviet Union "is thoroughly united." He knew better; so did anyone who read those Moscow bulletins, orations, and editorials. If the country were already thoroughly united, there would be no such clamorous need to *plead* for unity. The beating of the drums of vigilance can be explained only by an acute sense of peril. A party which has been in absolute control for thirty-five years, which has reared a new generation, is scarcely displaying robust self-confidence when it still begs its members and its subjects to rally around it.

The Kremlin's announcements in connection with Stalin's illness and demise will in time be recognized as among the most amazing state papers extant. The most powerful governing clique on earth, in its hour of heartbreak, apparently could not afford to restrict itself to weeping over and eulogizing the lost leader, but felt itself compelled to load medical bulletins with propaganda appeals for popular backing, as if it were a fledgling government afraid of being booted out. The czarist autocracy, upon the death of the monarch, had never felt it necessary to plead for loyalty to his successor; that was something which, perhaps mistakenly, it took for granted.

The very first announcement, along with the report of the stroke, called on party members and the masses to "display the greatest unity and cohesion, staunchness of spirit and vigilance." Vigilance against whom, against what? The Soviet public would know, even if foreigners didn't. One expected the death bulletin, at least, to be a solemn and sorrowful statement of fact without political commercials. Instead, it not only hammered away at the theme of "monolithic unity" — protesting too much — but explained *why* the people should trust and follow the party bosses. It was "sales copy" in support of the "tested leadership," braced with promises of "further improvement" to meet "the material and cultural needs" of all sections of the populace.

The very haste with which the succession government was set up, within twenty-four hours after Stalin's death, suggested jitters. Far from concealing its apprehensions, the ruling group admitted that the ghoulish speed was aimed at "prevention of *razbrod i panika*" — disorder and panic. The phrase was not tossed off casually, being repeated pointedly in the editorial comment in the following days.

What kind of disorder and panic were they so anxious to head off? Why the eagerness to show at once a united front at the top against any challenge? Who was being warned not to try to take advantage of confusions and rivalries? With millions of agents spying on everybody everywhere, the Kremlin surely has its finger on the pulse of national sentiment. It would hardly make such a show of its alarms and trepidations before the world and before its own country unless it thought them well founded.

Another matchless item is worth noting for its telltale quality. Not only the progress of Stalin's fatal illness but the exact treatment administered, even unto the outmoded use of leeches, was made public in minute detail. Clearly the uneasy inheritors were trying to convince their loving people that they were not murdering the dictator, that he was dying a natural death. Millions, we may be sure, remained unconvinced notwithstanding; whispered speculation as to when and how Stalin's end *really* came undoubtedly was widespread. The elimination of Lavrenti Beria, for fifteen years Stalin's head executioner, only four months after the passing of his patron, must have reinforced the suspicions of sinister mysteries and connivings behind the death of the boss.

The Bolshevik hierarchs have often and rightly been described as "the frightened men in the Kremlin." Apparently the death of Stalin raised their chronic fears to panic pitch. Both at home and in the satellite orbits, new security measures were instantly piled upon the stringent normal procedures. Frontier troops were alerted for trouble. In East Germany, local commanders of Soviet forces were instructed not to obey new orders without checking directly with headquarters in Karlshorst, and meanwhile to take into custody the officers bringing such orders.

Though the world gave little thought to the Russian masses, Malenkov and his confreres evidently thought of little else. Demonstratively they closed ranks to discourage hostile moves by those unnamed but ubiquitous "internal enemies." On the one hand they pleaded for trust and support, on the other they boasted of their power to crush all opponents — two seemingly contradictory but psychologically quite consistent expressions of deep insecurity.

2. *The Sickness of Fear*

The fears that obsess the tenants of the Kremlin are, of course, manifold. Besides those common to all tyrants, guilt-ridden by awareness of their own crimes, they labor under special fears unique to revolutionary ruling groups. Their authority has no sanction in tradition, no roots in convention, none of the aura of legitimacy that sustains the inner confidence of hereditary monarchs, for instance. Themselves masters of the insurrectionary technique, the *coup d'état,* the stab in the back, they cannot for a moment escape the dread of such threats to their own survival. Better than anyone else they know that even a relatively small group of "internal enemies," given propitious conditions, can overturn a seemingly impregnable system. Have they not done it themselves?

As individuals, Soviet leaders live in a climate of intrigue and duplicity, even unto murder. They dread the frown of more powerful colleagues that may presage a knock on the door some midnight which for them will have no dawn. They are nervously alert to shifts in the ever unstable balance of competing egos that may suddenly hurl them from the heights. Without exception they have climbed to power over too many corpses of friends and allies to trust anyone or to sleep peacefully.

And collectively they dread the vengeance of the amorphous masses upon whom they have inflicted incalculable hurts and woes. They are in constant terror of those whom they have terrorized. The stench of festering resentment and hatred is ever in their nostrils, no matter how many guards they set to guard other guards in an endless progression.

Those millions of men and women dragging out a tortured existence in concentration camps are in their mental view always: symbol incarnate of thirst for revenge. However innocent these victims may be of the crimes against the state for which they are being punished, would they not seize the chance to make good on the punishments by committing the crimes? Each prisoner, more-over, is the focus of a sullen group beyond the camp or prison — relatives, friends, associates — who have not forgotten or forgiven.

Nor are the fears limited to the uppermost crust of dictatorship. They course through the whole pyramid of power. In a totalitarian society no one holds a post of authority, though it be no more than a minor police job or the chairmanship of a collective farm, by law or natural right or by virtue of personal accomplishments. He holds it in the final analysis largely by the sufferance of his immediate superiors. No place in the pyramid is for keeps, no authority is more than provisional.

For every man political survival depends on someone above him, in an endless chain reaching to the apex. The disgrace or liquida-tion of any official means automatic disaster for dozens or hundreds below. Every contest for power on the upper levels therefore sends tremors of fright through the entire structure. Anxiety is the ele-ment in which officialdom — in the party, the government, the economic setup — has its being.

The higher a man rises, indeed, the more exposed he becomes, so that the wiser among them forswear ambition in exchange for some peace of mind. There are those who actually hide their abilities and pretend mediocrity, if they can, to make themselves a little less conspicuous, less vulnerable. I was friendly with a press censor, an able and affable fellow, whose constant worry was that he might be promoted to head the press department. He intrigued as hard to avoid preferment as his go-getting colleagues did to win it. And he was right. For ultimately, despite himself, he was sent as minister to a Balkan country, only to be recalled and shot soon thereafter.

The scared look, the trembling hand, the masklike face, are the occupational marks of the successful Bolshevik. I have watched officials in important positions, who had a right to be cocky with self-esteem, go pale and tremulous at the sound of a peeved voice on the telephone, or at the prospect of making a trivial decision on their own.

Some years ago I read a report in a British news letter from its agent in Turkey about the Soviet ambassador. This dignitary was a youngish man of the all-Soviet generation, obviously trusted and successful to be holding that vital post. As plenipotentiary of the dominant military nation in that part of the world, he had every right to pride of place. "One might have thought," the agent wrote, "he would be the personification of easy confidence and the most contented of Ankara's ambassadors." But instead he seemed palpably unhappy, morose, without a spark of animation — as if he were "secretly desperately afraid."

It was a shrewd comment. Secret desperation is so close to the surface in nearly all Soviet functionaries, high and low, that a close observer cannot miss it. The bureaucracy, even the portion that has no principled faith in the regime, feels itself part and parcel of the *vlast*, responsible for its sins and fearful of paying the price in some eventual reckoning. It carries the burden of inner guilt for policies and practices of which it does not approve, let alone those of which it does approve.

Men and women in the arts are in no better situation. To write or paint or compose at all, they must serve and flatter the powers that be, and therefore they become psychically a part of the governing class, sharing its sense of guilt. The closer one of them gets to the top in his field, the more he opens himself to observation and suspicion. They live in constant dread that their very talents may betray them into some expression of forbidden truth, some flash of candor, that may sound their death knell. Neither place nor reputation nor brilliant work confers a sense of security. Distinction is too often the prelude to extinction; the one talent that counts in terms of self-preservation is the talent for bending with the political winds.

Scientists and scholars live precariously under the whiplash of the politicians, at the mercy of lickspittles and informers among their own colleagues. Their right to work and their very physical survival depends on changeful party policies and shifting obsessions. Not only has truth been displaced by dogma but dogma itself is an unstable quantity, so that willingness to conform is no guarantee against personal calamity. Pursuits as seemingly remote from politics as astronomy, genetics, linguistics, or thermodynamics must be rated as among the most hazardous of Soviet professions. The prisons and labor camps are crowded with historians, biologists, engineers, and others who unwittingly offended the jealous state in their laboratories or classrooms.

As for the masses, their lives are spun out in a net of harsh decrees, intimidating exhortations, punishments without crime. An unguarded word, a half hour's lateness to work, the arrest of a friend or relative, and the whole edifice of existence may collapse about their ears. Any morning another arbitrary ukase may make millions of them felons by definition, turn their routines of living topsy-turvy, or tear them up by the roots in some mysterious shift of population. They have forgotten the meaning of permanence and inner security. They live on battlefields on the steep flanks of live volcanoes.

Despite its size and military might, the Soviet Union is a sick nation, mortally sick. For the cancer of fear gnaws at its vitals — especially the vitals of its ruling classes. Fear of one another, fear of denunciations, fear of changing party lines and shattering decrees, fear of superiors. But above all, fear of the inchoate, sullen, muttering masses whom the rulers are condemned to dominate and terrorize.

It was this pervasive fear, normally hidden in bluster, that broke through and became audible with the death of Stalin. It was implicit in the sweeping amnesty announced within several weeks, along with a pledge to revise and liberalize the criminal code. It was given melodramatic expression in the freeing of the Kremlin doctors accused of fantastic "medical murders," and especially in the official admission that they had confessed imaginary crimes under third-degree pressures. These moves were followed by a new and loud insistence upon "the inviolability of Soviet law" — a promise, that is to say, of fewer illegal arrests, frame-ups, tortures. At the same time there was another installment of promises, often made but never carried out, to provide more food, housing, clothing, and other consumer goods.

The inheritors were clearly acting to reassure and conciliate the people. They were anxious to create a climate of benevolence which would make it harder for those "internal enemies" to start trouble. Shorn of the awe-inspiring prestige of Stalin, his gang suddenly felt naked and chilled, and began to maneuver for time to consolidate its control.

This impulse, at critical junctures, to placate the masses and win their moral support is highly indicative. It evidences the fact that, for all its engines of physical and moral coercion, the high command of Bolshevism is not indifferent to domestic public opinion. There are supposed experts abroad who regard the Soviet people as entirely a passive, bovine mass of beaten and intimidated people. But this judgment certainly is not shared by the Soviet overlords.

Kremlin moves, immediately after Stalin's passing, to ease the tensions of the cold war, too, can be traced — in a double sense — to misgivings over the temper of the populace. On the one hand, the Malenkov group seemed eager to unload some of its foreign burdens and commitments in order to free its hands for dealing with threats at home and with the struggle for leadership. On the other, it seemed eager to convince its subjects that the new masters would not provoke war. Like people the world over, the Soviet people dread another holocaust; the wounds of the last one are much too fresh and raw. The successors were saying in effect: "You can trust us, brothers. Not only are we relaxing the terror, as you

see, but we are trying to stave off war. What's more, we may
succeed where Stalin failed."

3. "Monolithic Unity"?

The implied derogation of the departed leader — the most astonishing single development after his death — was not accidental, and
it came too quickly to have been an improvisation. A decision to
deflate Stalin, if not a detailed plan to this end, must have taken
shape among his associates long before the last illness. Their attitude toward the dictator, ambiguous from the first, turned subtly
insulting soon thereafter. The funeral oratory and the press fare-
wells were pallid and perfunctory compared to the homage heaped
on the man in life, or compared to the unrestrained eulogies of
Lenin after his death.

Both within and outside the Soviet Union it was taken for
granted that Stalin's survivors would hurry to exploit his authority
to bolster their own, that he would be flamboyantly glorified and
deified. I am aware of no specialist on Russian affairs who did
not foresee the perpetuation of the Stalin cult. Even those of us
who predicted a reversal of some of Stalin's policies and methods
assumed it would be done in his name, just as every violation of
Lenin's precepts had been camouflaged as Leninism brought up to
date.

Instead, Stalin receded rapidly in the official propaganda until,
within a hundred days, the ineffable name had all but faded out
in the Soviet press. Not only did his heirs not choose to lean on
his reputation but they showed themselves anxious to dissociate the
new leadership from Stalinism. A good many observers abroad
took note of this startling fact, of course, but few of them seemed
to fathom its implications.

For a quarter of a century the assumption that the people loved
and adored Stalin had been the keystone fiction in the Kremlin
structure of make-believe. One would suppose that the Malenkovs
and Molotovs, at any rate, believed it or would feel under com-

pulsion to pretend that they did. But their behavior gave little evidence of this. On the contrary, they appeared determined to put distance between themselves and their predecessor, to convince the country that they were not *like* Stalin but *unlike* him, in that they were kindlier, more humane, more respectful of the law, more interested in the needs of the people, more concerned with preventing a showdown with the West.

It is possible that Stalin will yet be deified, perhaps when the remembrance of his infamies has been sufficiently dulled by time. It is less probable, but not entirely impossible, that he will be made the scapegoat for a good deal of the piled-up horrors of the past, and that "Stalinism" will become a term of official abuse on par with "Trotskyism." Certainly in the initial months nearly every important action of the new government implied a repudiation of the departed dictator.

Not merely did the successors proceed to undo much of his work, but they did not bother to invoke his posthumous consent, as they might so readily have done. A number of officials known to have been exceptionally close to Stalin, including his most trusted personal secretary, simply disappeared from public life — and from private life as well, it may be. The rest, having distributed his titles and offices among themselves, did not even claim that it was all in line with Stalin's wishes; if he left a political testament, it has been carefully concealed.

The Malenkov coterie did not hesitate to revise the state and party organs of leadership, which had been revamped with a lot of noisy acclaim by Stalin himself a few months before, at the Nineteenth Party Congress. They did not wait for his remains to be put away before reshuffling the jobs which had been filled under his personal authority. Somewhere in the libraryful of Stalin writings and speeches they could have dug up a quotation or two to give their actions the semblance of his blessing, but evidently they did not consider this either necessary or desirable.

And that was only the beginning. Articles in the party press began to emphasize the idea of collective as against individual leadership, denouncing "the cult of the individual": a left-handed assault on what had been the hallmark of Stalinism. The most extensive amnesty in Soviet history was announced, setting free hundreds of thousands of men, women, and children incarcerated in the Stalin years — their families would have to be grateful to the Almighty for gathering Stalin to His bosom. To leave no margin for doubt that it was a retreat from yesterday's injustice, great numbers who had been arrested while Stalin was alive but not yet tried and convicted were released wholesale. Malenkov was saying almost in so many words that the rights guaranteed by the Stalin Constitution, until then ignored or violated, would be honored now that its principal author was out of the way.

After which came the most resounding slap of all at the memory of the dead boss. The great treason trial already scheduled in connection with the curious "doctors' plot" was canceled out, the victims released and restored to their professional posts, their confessions denounced as products of torture chambers.

The reference, be it noted, was not to petty offenders third-degreed by overzealous policemen, but to eminent men long close to Stalin and his most prominent associates, indicted only a few months earlier with maximum publicity and alleged to have concocted their dastardly crimes as agents of American warmongers. The Order of Lenin had been pinned on the woman who helped frame the accused physicians, including her own ex-husband. Every Soviet child knew that political charges of such gravity could not have been cooked up without the explicit sanction of the deceased leader. In substance he was therefore being accused posthumously of an obscene frame-up. A more forthright insult to Stalin could scarcely be imagined.

During seven successive years "Victory Day," May 9, the anniversary of the German surrender to Moscow, was marked by extravagant tributes to Generalissimo Stalin as a military genius who put Napoleon and Alexander the Great in the shade; his was the main and almost the sole credit for victory. But the eighth anniversary came two months after his demise — and this time his role was slurred over, forgotten. The formal Red Army order of the day pointedly avoided mention of his name. Then, on July 12, came the

fiftieth anniversary of the foundation of the Communist Party —
and Stalin's picture was conspicuously missing in the many pages
devoted to the occasion by the press.

However convinced pro-Soviet foreigners may have been about
the popular love for Stalin, it became clear that his successors put
little stock in it; that, on the contrary, they believed him to be
deeply hated, the despised symbol of an abhorred period. In actions
if not in words they told the masses and their governing elite:
"We know that you detested Stalin, and now want you to know
that we too hated his guts. Please don't blame us for his sins and
crimes. Now that the big bad ogre is dead, we can all breathe
more freely. A new, more decent time has dawned for the peoples
of Russia."

This assuredly is no proof that the new rulers will be any less
ogreish, once their jitters have been quieted and their power solidi-
fied. To suppose that a totalitarian regime can transform itself
from within in the direction of liberalism is to misunderstand the
nature of totalitarianism. Its leaders are trapped by the system and
by their own history. They are not free agents. Beyond a certain
point the relaxation of tension and terror could unleash forces of
incalculable fury.

In thirty-five years of Soviet history there have been several periods
of comparative mildness, when the Kremlin bought time with tokens
of moderation: the Nep years (1921–1928), for instance, and the
several years between the collectivization of agriculture and the
big purges (1933–1936). Each of these proved to be only the prelude to a new tightening of the screws, in accordance with the
Lenin formula of "one step backward and two steps forward." At
this writing the indications are that another such interlude is unfolding. The peoples of Russia will be grateful for the respite, but
they have had their illusions dashed too often and too cruelly in
the past to take a change in political climate at face value. They
are too well schooled by past experience to mistake the phosphores-
cence of propaganda moves for a new dawn of freedom, at least
as long as the terror machine remains intact.

The tacit acknowledgment that the people were sick of Stalin and Stalinism gives the lie to the boast of "monolithic unity." That has again been shown up as totalitarian legerdemain. In conceding that his subjects did not love Stalin after all, the dictatorship in effect has conceded that they have no love for the whole Soviet setup. Malenkov and Company are far too shrewd and too cynical to kid themselves that hatred of the dictator does not express hatred for the way of life he embodied. Better than anyone else they know that unlimited terror and unlimited propaganda can repress but cannot destroy a people's hunger for freedom.

The homicidal contests for power at the pinnacle of the regime, which are always under way, intensified to the point of frenzy by Stalin's death and the power vacuums it created, came to a head even sooner than was generally expected. The façade of unity in the leadership lasted less than four months. The disgrace and liquidation of Beria confirmed that nothing had changed in the pattern of struggle to the death.

In the nature of things the top man in the police establishment is the object of the most concentrated detestation. The very name of Beria — like those of Djerzhinsky, Menzhinsky, Yagoda, and Yezhov before him — became a synonym for fiendish tortures and injustice. In office much longer than any of his predecessors, Beria was hated with a hatred supercharged by time, so that his downfall stirred joy and gloating in nearly two hundred million Soviet hearts. There was a delicate humor in the official reports that his dismissal was greeted with "unanimous approval" throughout the Soviet Union, evoking "prolonged and enthusiastic applause" at mass meetings. On the other hand, Beria was even more conspicuous than Malenkov and the rest in pushing the post-Stalin line of promised moderation. In particular, he had acted swiftly to remove certain officials in Georgia, the Ukraine, and other non-Russian areas who had made themselves odious by their vigor in connection with "Russification" efforts. His elimination therefore tended to deepen the popular skepticism about the whole "softer" line.

Those who accomplished Beria's doom will doubtless present it as another proof of their desire to temper the awful rigors of Stalinism, of which he had been the chief instrument. Each of them is shudderingly aware that when his turn to be liquidated comes it will be greeted with no less joyous and unanimous approval by his worshipful subjects.

4. *Regime versus People*

The attempt to relieve some of the tensions within the Soviet Union was extended also to its satellite states. On orders from Moscow, as part of a concerted revision of policy, its satraps in Red Europe soon after the passing of Stalin began to make placating noises and gestures of good will to their respective populations. Some sedative measures were announced and more were promised. But far from buying tolerance for the communist regimes, these concessions apparently helped provoke latent defiance, which by June, 1953, exploded in acts of open mutiny throughout Eastern Europe: political strikes, riotous demonstrations, and at least in East Germany something approaching full-scale rebellion.

The world had been increasingly persuaded that in the "people's democracies," as in Russia proper, all effective opposition had been squelched. During nearly eight years, "hostile class elements" had been bloodily liquidated, deported, or cowed and driven underground. Only "workers and peasants," the presumptive beneficiaries and supporters of the new dispensation, were left. Parades and demonstrations as impressively monolithic and "enthusiastic" as any staged in Moscow's Red Square became familiar fare in East Berlin, Prague, and the other Red capitals. Pink pilgrims to the new holy lands returned to assure us infidels that despite the flow of fugitives and ever harsher repressions the peoples had made their peace with the puppet regimes. The illusions of essential unity and stability in the satellites promoted by communist propaganda were taking root in the noncommunist part of the world.

Then, with hardly a warning, came the historic explosion. A strike in Pilsen, Czechoslovakia, was followed within two days by the great outbursts in East Berlin. What began as a seemingly orderly protest march in Stalin Allee against the speed-up system in a few plants blossomed within hours into a city-wide and then nationwide strike. Though no one had planned it that way, the Berlin violence was accepted as a signal for revolt. One spark was enough to ignite a conflagration, and soon the fire spread to portions of Poland.

And it was precisely the workers, the supposed foundation element of the communist edifice, who made the uprising. Soviet tanks and troops were thrown against the infuriated masses, after the Red German *Volkspolizei* proved reluctant and unreliable. Dozens were killed and hundreds wounded in the scrimmage, dozens were executed on the spot. Martial law was proclaimed, followed by mass arrests — fifty thousand according to the best estimates — and more death sentences. There were repercussions, in terms of sit-down and slow-down strikes on the one hand and more government concessions on the other, in the rest of Red Europe.

The events are too recent to call for rehearsal in detail here. What needs underlining is that a week earlier not one political observer or specialist would have dared predict the near-revolt which, when it came, seemed natural enough. What seems "impossible" before it happens often appears to have been "inevitable" after it happens. Only a few months before the outbreak of the Russian revolution in 1917 a prominent foreign correspondent in Petrograd warned that the talk of revolution heard abroad was so much wishful-thinking nonsense.

If and when the whole story is told, it will appear that the disorders in the Soviet puppet states were far more extensive than the free world realized. On the basis of my experience in the USSR, I venture to guess that behind nearly every rumor and unauthenticated report of violence in Czechoslovakia, Poland, Hungary, Rumania, and Bulgaria there were occurrences of major importance. We happen to have a peephole in Eastern Germany — our segment of Berlin; consequently the magnitude of the uprisings in that country could not be wholly concealed. Elsewhere we saw developments as through a glass darkly; the Kremlin succeeded in hiding and minimizing the dimensions of the challenge

there, just as it has done for over three decades with respect to
overt resistance in the Soviet Union proper.

The outbreaks were stifled by firing squads and tanks; everywhere the Kremlin proconsuls sought to blunt the edge of discontent with concessions and admissions of "mistakes" and excesses.
All the same, Moscow suffered a terrific defeat. Millions of its
victims have tested their strength and discovered, perhaps to their
own amazement, that the dictatorship is not entirely invulnerable
and invincible. They have taken the measure of their own courage
and the enemy's weak spots, and therefore will never be the same
again.

And the outer world now knows what it had previously merely
suspected. It knows that under the policed surface of seemingly
stable satellites there is a boiling, seething, and ultimately irrepressible mass of resentments, furies, suicidal despairs. The crust of the
Red empire is thinner and more brittle than most of us supposed.
Already the hot lava of revolt is oozing through a thousand cracks
and fissures.

Of all the peoples under the communist yoke, the Germans have
been looked upon as the most submissive and malleable, obedient
to authority and respectful of law and order. Lenin is supposed to
have wisecracked that when German revolutionists want to capture
a railroad station they first buy tickets; a well-known cartoon
showed a ragged German mob marching on the city hall to inquire,
"Where can we get permission to hold a revolution?"

Yet it is in Germany that the first great popular uprising against
Soviet power since the war took place. Entire battalions of the
communist-trained East German military forces refused to leave
their barracks when ordered to repress their recalcitrant countrymen. The memorable pictures of German youth hurling stones at
Soviet tanks, of the Red flag being torn down from the Branden-
burg Gate, of unarmed men and women standing up to the police
and soldiery, remain as thrilling symbols and portents of things to
come.

Perhaps the most significant single incident in the East German
events did not receive the attention it deserved. When demonstrators

in Magdeburg-Neustadt marched on the prison demanding the release of political prisoners, a number of the Russian soldiers guarding the place refused to shoot at the unarmed Germans. Eighteen of the mutineers, among them noncommissioned officers, were put to death a few days later at the military camp in Biederitz.

Subsequently rumors circulated of similar disobedience and executions in other Soviet occupation garrisons. RIA, a Russian *émigré* news agency in Frankfurt, reported: "German workers who were arrested for the part they had taken in the June revolts, and who have now been released, relate that there were many Soviet soldiers in the German jails and that new scores of military personnel are still pouring in. They conclude that Soviet military prisons must be overflowing for otherwise Soviet soldiers would not be sent to German jails." * There may well be an element of exaggeration in these stories, but the Magdeburg-Neustadt episode at any rate is authentic.

This must have sent a chill down the spines of the communist leaders in Moscow. They could not have forgotten that it was just such a refusal of soldiers to shoot unarmed workers — in Petrograd in March, 1917 — that marked the beginning of the end for the Romanoff autocracy. Where a handful of Russians rebelled against shooting at Germans, how many of them under comparable conditions might one day rebel against shooting their own Russian brothers and sisters?

The most serious mistake the free world can make is to assume arbitrarily that the anti-Soviet mood manifest in the satellite countries stops at the frontiers of the Soviet Union. The fact is that explosions of fury as dramatic as those in the satellite states have occurred repeatedly in Soviet Russia; that there the lava of mass disaffection is as hot and potentially explosive as in any of the communist countries outside.

The ever-present fears of the Soviet masters — fully admitted, as we shall see, in the colossal and always expanding machinery of

* The RIA report was published in the July — August, 1953, issue of the *Newsletter* of *Possev,* New York.

repression — are central to the thesis of this book. They are symptoms of complex tensions, particularly those between the rulers and
the ruled, the oligarchy and its victims.

The Russian peoples, some two hundred million of them, are a
vital element in the equation of world affairs today — in my considered view, the decisive element. It can be ignored by the rest of
the world only at its own peril. Foreign policy that disregards the
people, unthinkingly lumping together the regime and its subjects,
is driving blind. Those who discount the people are making a gift
of incalculable value to the Kremlin. They throw away the best
chance of victory over communism without a universal holocaust
or, at worst, of victory in war at a smaller cost in life on both sides.

The fundamental loyalties and aspirations of the Soviet humanity, its stifled hopes and hates, its feeling for the great land it in-
habits and the despotism that holds the land in thrall, must in the
long run spell out destiny for all of us.

Whether the autocrats who took over Stalin's unlimited power
dare launch further adventures in aggression depends in the first
place on their estimate of the morale of the peoples who must do
the fighting and dying. Whether the free portion of mankind can
forge an alliance with those teeming millions over the heads of
their tyrants — the world's best hope of throwing off the communist
incubus — depends in the first place upon *our* estimate of their psychological relation to the Soviet system.

I believe it to be a demonstrable fact that in the USSR a great
gulf yawns between the regime and the people. By this I do not
mean that all the people or even a majority of them are consciously
"opposed" to the rulers. As a British journalist recently put it, "they
do not spend sleepless nights brooding over the iniquities of the
MVD; like all human beings everywhere they take life as they find
it, enjoy it when they can, and keep their reservations to themselves." I mean only that most of them, and I do not exclude the
rank and file of the Communist Party and its secret police, are not
awarely and passionately "for" the regime in the sense that the
American or British peoples are as a matter of course for their
respective ways of life. I mean that psychologically they have not

given their consent and imprimatur to the Soviet way of life, and that as a result they are potentially our allies.

In other countries, people identify themselves with their government. Even in Russia before 1917 they were wont to say, in relation to czarist actions, "*We* have done thus-and-so. . . . *We* have sent an ultimatum to the Kaiser. . . . *We* have made a treaty with Japan. . . ." The Soviet citizen, however, refers to the *vlast* in the third person: "*They* have done thus-and-so. . . . *They* want us to buy bonds. . . . *They* want us to take over Korea. . . . " And the pronoun packs as much contempt as the speaker dares to reveal.

The fifth column for freedom in Soviet Russia, already numbered in millions, can be expanded to scores of millions. Given favorable circumstances, it can be enlarged to embrace nearly the whole population. This is a fact which, if grasped in time and exploited wisely, boldly, and generously, can save the human race — including the portion locked within iron curtains — from a long black night of totalitarian barbarism. I believe that in the Russian peoples we have a weapon more potent than our atomic stock pile. Can we find the wisdom to develop it courageously for our common salvation?

II. The Permanent Civil War

1. The Medicine: Terror

The belief that the peoples of Russia bent their necks meekly to the yoke of Bolshevism is historically false. It is a cruel libel. If there has been one constant in the muffled turbulence of Soviet history from 1917 to date, it is the struggle between the dictators and their subjects — a struggle I propose to trace in this book. There have been periods of reduced hostilities, but never a true armistice, let alone conciliation or peace.

Contrary to misconceptions on this score, both the Italian and the German people accepted their respective brands of totalitarian affliction more quickly, more fully, with less resistance, than the Russians. Neither the Fascist nor the Nazi regimes had to seal their countries as hermetically as do the Kremlin leaders to prevent an exodus of "happy" citizens. Having sojourned in all three police states, Black, Brown, and Red, I can attest that in Italy and Germany the atmosphere was less loaded with a sense of doom, the inhabitants were more friendly to the regime, than in Soviet Russia.

The fairy tale of the Russians' meek resignation to communism does not rhyme with the terrible compulsion the government has been obliged to apply, with the huge slave-labor population, with the chronic Soviet alarms over sabotage and espionage and murder plots. It does not jibe with the suicidal fight of the peasants for their land, with the desperate opposition of workers to the Stakhanovite speed-up system, with the two great tides of emigration (in the first years after the Bolshevik conquest and after the Second

World War), and with other episodes of convulsive mass opposition which I shall deal with in due order.

Let us have one elementary fact clear in mind. Even the most sadistic police state does not murder its citizens wholesale for the fun of it, or confine millions of its subjects in pestiferous camps through arbitrary savagery, or impose, without some provocation, the death penalty for "crimes" which in other countries are unknown or treated as misdemeanors. *These are measures of self-protection by the regime against actual or potential resistance.*

The nature of an ailment can be deduced from the medicines administered. The extent of the Russian peoples' resistance to their Soviet fate can be deduced from the vastness, the ferocity, and the perisistence of the Soviet terror. No government assigns a major portion of its energies and personnel and resources to internal security unless it feels itself utterly insecure.

The political police establishment of the czars — the Okhrana, dreaded in its time and reviled by the outside world — got by with a few thousand officials and operatives. Its communist successors, from the Cheka to the MVD, have needed close to two million, including a huge MVD special army for purely internal operations. This aside from the millions serving as agents, informers and *provocateurs,* willingly or under duress, without formally belonging to the police setup. Every member of the Communist Party and its youth affiliates, the Komsomols and Pioneers, and for that matter every other "loyal" citizen, counts spying and prying and denouncing among his sacred obligations to the enthroned state.

Never before, not even in the world that included Hitler's Germany and Mussolini's Italy, has a state spawned such gigantic organs of surveillance and repression, torture and terror, censorship and intimidation. No government on record has felt itself compelled to invent so many and various "crimes against the state" or to apply the death penalty so extensively as an instrument of governance.

The notorious paragraph 58 of the Soviet criminal code, on "counterrevolution," defines fourteen different categories, each broken down into many subdivisions and most of them punishable

by death at the discretion of secret tribunals. They range from treason, that is to say opposition with arms in hands, to "historical counterrevolution" (point 13), whatever that may mean. In addition
"the highest measure of social defense" — execution — has been decreed from time to time for sins as trivial as the slaughter of a pig,
the theft of a kilogram of grain, the hoarding of copper coins.

As a matter of course the authorities tap the telephones of their
people and open their mail and eavesdrop on their most casual conversation. Every apartment house, office, plant, and subdivision of
a plant, every school, mine, and collective farm, has its appointed
informers. The secret police maintain branch offices or stations on
the premises of the larger factories, mines, farms, universities,
libraries, hotels, railroad stations.

Little agents inform on bigger agents, like vermin on vermin.
Every functionary important enough to rate a secretary or chauf-
feur takes it for granted that these employees are recording not
merely his conduct, contacts, and opinions but his "political mood"
for evaluation by the police. The suspicion that one's spouse or
child, one's best friend or closest associate in work, is on the alert
to report a wayward phrase or facial expression shadows the daily
life of the average Soviet man or woman.

Referring to the engineering school in which he was studying in
the early thirties, Victor Kravchenko wrote in his book *I Chose
Freedom*:

There was at the Institute, as in every Soviet industrial undertaking
or government bureau, a Special Department connected with the GPU.
It was headed by a Comrade Lebed. No one could enter its office, except in a state of terror when summoned for questioning. Few of us
knew what went on behind the grated little window in the steel door.
At the same time few of us were so naive that we did not realize that
every student had his own *dossier* in the Special Department, where
his every word and act, where the very accent of his behavior were
recorded.

To protect the informers and strengthen the network of everyday
espionage, not even the Institute director or the secretary of its Party
Committee was given access to the *dossiers.* The Special Department
had its secret agents in every branch of the Institute and even in the

Party nuclei. But the Party Committee had its own informers in the nuclei, whose indentity was not known to the Special Department. Thus there were spies upon the spies in an intricate pattern that spread a tangible pall of fear.

But that was not all. Besides the Special Department, the GPU agents in the Institute reported directly to its regional headquarters, as a double-check on Lebed and his staff. The City Committee of the Party deployed agents through the nuclei, and the Regional Committee received secret reports from its special people in the City Committee. This interlocking pyramid of surveillance extended to the very top, to the Central Committee of the Party in Moscow and finally to the Politburo headed by Stalin.

Multiple webs of espionage by the Party and of the Party, by the GPU and of the GPU, pooling information at some points, competing at other points, covered Soviet life from top to bottom. We lived in a world swarming with invisible eyes and ears.*

No ruling group in the annals of man has diverted so much of its income, its thought, its man power, to internal security — to its own defense, that is to say, against its subjects. There we have a fair measure of the popular hostility at one end, the sense of menace at the other end. Certainly the number of political prisoners has increased much faster than the membership of the Communist Party.

Scarcely a trace remains of the pre-1917 elements told off for extermination: the upper and middle classes, the old officer cadres, the prerevolutionary intellectuals, the old clergy. Former political formations from extreme right to extreme left have been decapitated and dispersed. Little, indeed, remained even of the founding generation of Bolsheviks after the blood purges of 1936–1938.

And still the reservoirs of "hostile elements" are full to overflowing. Still the official clamor for vigilance and the fevered activities of the punitive agencies show no sign of abating. Soviet speeches, publications, decrees are as raucous as ever with demands that hidden foes be ferreted out, with threats against old and new brands of traitors. Fresh categories of enemies and alien elements are established by definition as fast as the old ones give out.

In the sixteenth year of Bolshevik power an American educator,

* Scribner's, 1947.

the late Eduard C. Lindeman, returned from a Soviet sojourn with the glad news that in the matter of those distressing persecutions the worst was over. "There is stability in contemporary Russia and there is solidarity," he wrote cheerfully. "Revolutionary vigilance tends to relax in all spheres because there is no longer any real danger of counterrevolutionary movements from within." *

His optimism was typical of American liberals at the time. Yet the fiercest persecutions and liquidations, the greatest growth of slave-camp inmates, the most fantastic exposures and demolitions of alleged internal plots to overthrow the regime and murder its leaders, were then in the womb of Soviet history.

On July 19, 1936, in connection with the promulgation of the Stalin Constitution, Walter Duranty informed readers of the New York *Times* that "external enemies are no longer feared and internal enemies have been defeated and scotched, if not totally eliminated." Alas for his timing: Soviet Russia was then on the threshold of its bloodiest period, the era of Moscow purge trials, the Yezhov atrocities, and unprecedented expansion of forced-labor contingents.

That has been the unchanging pattern: the bloody suppression of one million-headed threat to the regime followed by bigger, lustier doses of terror against new "conspiracies" and deviations. From the Soviet government's own shouts of alarm, from the unchecked proliferation of repressive laws and police personnel, the conclusion is inescapable that a hundred new opponents sprout wherever one has been torn up by the roots.

Nor should it be forgotten that propaganda on the Soviet scale is also a species of force. Its deafening din is unceasingly in the ears and on the raw nerves of the people. In textbooks and newspapers, in the movies and on the radio, the slogans of the hour assail their senses. They have no escape, no defense. For they are not allowed the relief of arguing, talking back, asking questions. Even the right to ignore the torrential propaganda is denied them; they are condemned to a lifetime of enthusiasm. Doubts and disagreements must be turned inward to fester in psychic darkness.

* The *New Republic,* March 8, 1933.

The Kremlin is forever promoting what in normal countries is taken for granted: "loyalty" to the existing system. Considerably over a million full-time professional "agitators," trained for their tasks in special schools and served by special trade publications, infest society at every level. The number of these agitators, like the number of concentration camps, grows continually: surely a political paradox. Would these herds of propagandists be needed if the people had indeed become reconciled to communism?

On January 11, 1918, Lenin, commenting on the blood-letting already under way, added: "We are still far from *real* terror, because for the time being we are stronger than they are." They — the foes of the Red oligarchy — surely must have grown stronger with every month and year, since "real" terror has been applied in ever larger and deadlier potions.

Henry Yagoda, head of the GPU at the time, once told an American correspondent, William Reswick: "We are a minority in a vast country. Abolish the GPU and we are through." * That has been the view of all communists, right or left or center. Whatever their inner party differences, they have been at one in their obsessed fear of the people, convinced that any real easement of the terror would mark the end of Soviet dominion. The name of the chief organ of terror has been changed several times; the condition it is intended to deal with has remained unchanged.

2. *Aspects of Resistance*

From the day the Bolsheviks grabbed power in a chaotic and pitifully weakened nation, there has been in effect *a continuous civil war* between the rulers and the ruled. In the initial years it was open and military; since then it has been largely concealed and political, yet perfectly obvious to those who watched with unblurred eyes, and even bloodier than the military phase. Once you grasp this concept of a permanent internal conflict involving the

* *I Lived Revolution*, Regnery, 1952.

entire population, much about Soviet Russia that seems enigmatic
and baffling begins to make sense.

The many millions who have perished in the struggle against the
dictatorship, whether finished off in police dungeons and slave-
labor camps or starved in punitive man-made famine, are the
casualties of that war. So, on the other side, are the thousands of
communists of all degrees who have been assassinated by the populace or shot by political enemies.

The great hordes of inmates of isolators, prison camps, penal colonies, are its prisoners of war.

The special MVD army, estimated at 750,000 men, with its own
air groups, tanks, artillery and communications system, represents
the Kremlin's shock troops and Praetorian Guard in that war. It
is an elite soldiery, far better paid and equipped than the regular
armed forces.

The perennial *chistkas* or purges, the liquidation of this or that
layer of the population "as a class," the abolition of entire "republics" and "autonomous regions," and the recurrent mass exiles are
battles in that war.

The more spectacular episodes of coercion, such as the forced
socialization of farming and the titanic purges in the late thirties
and the postwar purges of returning troops, are major campaigns
in that war.

The incessant thunder of propaganda is the psychological offensive that has become an essential element in modern warfare.

Yes, permanent civil war — that is the reality under all the propagandist pretenses, the key to an understanding of the whole Soviet
scene. Russia has been a nation occupied from within by frightened
conquerors forever uncertain of their tenure.

The outer world has looked upon the sensational Soviet trials
and blood-lettings without comprehending that they are aspects of
the unceasing conflict between a dictatorship and the people. Only
the major demonstration trials — really courts-martial in the civil
war — have made news beyond the Soviet borders. But the process
of purge has been continuous, directed now against one portion of

the populace, now another, intended to dam now one tide of thought or hope, now another.

The regime's war on the peasantry, the basic ingredient of Russia's humanity, has drawn oceans of blood and the end is not yet. The Kremlin's resolve to seal the country against foreigners and Western thought has taken progressively more extreme forms, reaching maniacal heights in the postwar purges of every department of life, from economy to science, music, literature, even circus clowning.

On their side of the barricades, the unarmed masses have responded with every device of open and passive resistance. Necessarily they have resorted to guerrilla methods: sniping, sapping, sabotaging. Great numbers of Soviet functionaries, policemen, communist "activists" and Stakhanovite pace-setters have been killed through the years. Those who lick the boots of officialdom know that they forfeit the trust of their neighbors. In every town and village communist leaders feel themselves engulfed in suspicions and hatreds; they are the satraps of an alien occupying power and the symbol of their authority is not a title or a badge but the ubiquitous revolver.

The tactics of non-co-operation come as naturally to most of the Russian peoples as they did to the masses of India. The refusal of the peasants to sow beyond their own needs, which was their spontaneous response to the outrage of collectivization — and for which they paid with so many lives — exceeded in magnitude anything that India had experienced. But there are myriad less obvious, less overt expressions of the instinct to withhold co-operation which cumulatively, in a country as gigantic as Russia, can harass and debilitate its masters.

Slow-down on the job ("Italian strikes," in Russian slang) and spoilage of goods persist in the face of Draconic laws to discourage idling and laxness. Embezzlement of state funds, pilfering of state goods, distortion of official plans and falsification of state accounts are as common under the Soviets as drinking was under Prohibition in the United States. Such practices are stimulated by the universal poverty, of course. But they also have overtones of protest through acts, of defiance of an odious way of life, as the Kremlin knows full well. Men who would never dream of stealing from a neighbor steal all they can from the socialized economy, as if it were a natural right of the dispossessed. No sense of moral obliquity attaches to sins against the dictatorship.

Exasperated references to a remarkable variety of fraud are standard in Soviet oratory and editorials. Dozens of pages in Malenkov's historic six-hour address at the Nineteenth Party Congress of the Communist Party were devoted to inveighing against thievery, neglect of duty, illicit trade, criminal bookkeeping, and the rest of the familiar inventory of socialist corruptions. Complaints like the following are so commonplace that no one any longer bothers to read them:

"There still exists a dishonest attitude toward work and toward its obligations, embezzlement, theft, and misappropriation of state property and wealth. Various, even leading, workers sometimes endeavor to defraud the state, and permit incorrect information and the submission of untrue reports." *

Examination of a few leading Soviet newspapers for a single month, February 1953, yields morsels like these: *Pravda Ukrainy* — Employees at the Bravilo clothing factory stole 1500 meters of textiles and then, arrested and tried, managed to get acquitted by paying out 50,000 rubles in bribes. *Literaturnaya Gazeta* — A smooth operator named Murlykin held a series of posts, all on forged documents, using each post in turn for large-scale thefts. Moscow *Pravda* — A gang stole watch parts which were assembled for the black-market trade to the tune of a million rubles; two fire engines, of all things, were stolen from the Moscow fire engine works with the help of the senior accountant. Editorial in *Izvestia* — Employees of the central administration of the Ministry of Railroads pilfered a million rubles' worth of goods before being exposed; an official of the Krasnoyarsk Bakery Combine stole 243,000 rubles of foodstuffs in a short period.

Multiply that sort of thing a thousandfold, week after week, month after month, and you get an inkling of the impossible prob-

* *Sovietskoie Gosudarstvo I Pravo*, No. 5, 1950.

lem it imposes on the dictators. Only a meager part of the pillage is ever uncovered, despite legions of informers, inspectors, and investigators. For the most part workers and foremen, administrators and accountants connive to protect one another, sharing the booty in well-established ratios. The morality is that of robbing the robbers. No one who has lived in the shadows of the Kremlin doubts that this epidemic cheating of the government, to which the rulers have to accommodate themselves, has in it elements of conscious mutiny against an exploiting system.*

No less is true of the highly ramified developments of half-legal and illegal "free economy" flourishing within the folds and interstices of the planned economy. A former commercial attaché of the Soviet embassy in Mexico, Kirill Alexeiev, has called it "Russia's underground capitalism." Under the surface, he attests, "there are immense processes that defy the Marxist theories — processes to which the Soviet leaders, like it or not, have to accommodate themselves." **

Black markets of every conceivable type — fed by goods ingeniously siphoned off from factories and warehouses, or produced by private establishments masked as legitimate "artels" — are only the beginning. There is the famous *combinatsie:* a business deal among government agencies but outside the planned channels. Elaborate industrial and scientific "projects" are initiated, merely to provide

---

* The same kinds of indirect resistance, it is interesting to observe, are reported from the satellite countries. Thus George May, who lived in Red Hungary for forty months as correspondent for British and American publications, writes: "Working-class resentments are some of the most significant phenomena in the satellite world. Usually they find expression in anti-communist and anti-Soviet talk. But often they are translated into action. . . . There *is* resistance — shapeless and leaderless but involving thousands of individuals. . . . And when the state demands a full day's work for a day's pay, it is met with cheating on a spectacular scale. There have been literally thousands of 'wage frauds' listed in *Szabad Nép* during the past three years, involving entire factories, industries, and ministries." Much of the spoilage in production, he writes, is "plainly deliberate," and despite Draconian penalties, "sabotage continues undiminished." ("Close-up of a 'Workers' Paradise," *Harper's Magazine,* July, 1953.)

** *Plain Talk,* December, 1949.

extra income for the planners, without any intention of putting the plans into effect. "Tons of these theoretical projects, costing billions of rubles, are gathering dust in a thousand files," to quote Mr. Alexeiev.

Industrial officials vote themselves bonuses for "overproduction" that exists only in juggled records. Scientists and other specialists collect rewards and publicity kudos for "contributions" to Soviet knowledge dug out of prerevolutionary archives or adapted from foreign journals and palmed off as original research. But above all there is the vast diversion of products at the point of origin, or somewhere along the line in distribution. Sometimes entire carloads are declared "spoiled" by inspectors who are in on the game and share the spoils.

In short, in hoodwinking and defrauding the state, the sky is the limit. Many of the esoteric private schemes could never be launched without the collaboration of influential officials in the right government slots. And often, as the press continually points out, the public prosecutors charged with tracking down such crimes are themselves deeply involved.

Corruption in government is no novelty under any system of life. But in a country where everything from a newsstand to the largest industrial trusts is "government," corruption necessarily has political implications. The Soviet regime is not too far from reality in calling it sabotage and counterrevolution. Though the primary motive in spoliation of the state is self-aggrandizement, its inner justification is that the state is the enemy and therefore fair game. It is guerrilla sapping in another, subtler dimension.

And there are endless acts of pure malice against the state, in which loot plays no part. Let no one suppose that there is no fire under the billowing smoke of the Kremlin's outcries about sabotage. The sand in the gears may be an accident — and it may not. The line between inefficiency and purposeful vandalism, between the boredom of disinterest and deliberate damage is not always easy to draw. The high incidence of broken-down machines, flooded mines, disrupted assembly lines, inexplicable explosions in plants, which figure in the Soviet purges and exhibition trials reflect a fundamental apathy on the part of the guilty, even where it is not forth-right sabotage.

It is not stretching actuality, therefore, to include these manifes-tations in the larger pattern of non-co-operation and passive re-sistance. They are part and parcel of the permanent civil war. In that extraordinary contest the opponents have been unevenly matched. So far, inevitably, the people have been worsted. But the regime has not been victorious. Its attitude toward the citizenry, even in its occasional proffers of conciliation, is always conditioned by the fact of the unresolved struggle.

Nor is it farfetched to see in the celebrated Soviet political anec-dotes, in what I have called elsewhere the "stifled laughter" so characteristic of the country, a verbalization of boundless contempt for the Kremlin and its system of values. This *Galgenhumor* — scaffold humor — is immense, ever changing, and ever the same in substance; it has become a sort of folk art, expressing allegorically what cannot be uttered openly. There are thousands of these bitter-sweet jokes; every new event produces a new crop, and those that are especially acute and apt spread instantly throughout the country.

Not one of the anecdotes is favorable to the regime or hostile to its detractors. They are saturated with cynical pessimism about Kremlin promises, derision of its pretensions, scorn for the com-munist way of life. Ask a Soviet citizen how he is getting along and he is as likely as not to answer, *"Luchy chom saftra"* — "Better than tomorrow." . . . "Why," you will be asked, apropos of noth-ing in particular, "is Soviet Russia like a crowded trolley car in motion?" The answer: "Because half the people are sitting" (mean-ing under arrest) "and the other half are trembling." . . . A bright boy has just been congratulated for saying that his "father" is Lenin, father of all Soviet people, and his "mother" is glorious Mother Russia. "And what would you like to be when you grow up?" he is asked; to which he replies promptly, in the anecdote, "An orphan." . . . Variations are endless, but the theme is constant: ridicule and disparagement of the regime.

The nerves of the Soviet hierarchy and its privileged entourage are shot to pieces. Their soul is guilt-ridden; the fearful contrasts between idealistic professions and gory crimes have set up intense inner tensions. The regime has been obscenely brutalized by its long need to be brutish, to the point where it has only one answer to all domestic questions: blood and more blood. A besieged minority in a conquered nation, it sees a threat in every frown, menace in the most innocent criticism, hostile design in every failure of its complicated politico-economic machinery.

3. *The Regime — and Its Subjects*

The dictum of Joseph de Maistre, "Every country has the government it deserves," if taken literally would preclude change. No one can say with assurance to what degree the mass of people under any despotic government are responsible for the sins of their masters.

But long-established dynasties, such as the Hohenzollerns in Germany or the Romanoffs in Russia, did enjoy a certain rapport, a community of viewpoints, with their subjects. They had a solidarity of tradition, habit, prejudices, automatic assumptions — the sense of what Guglielmo Ferrero called "legitimacy." The conduct of the autocrats was normally held within a framework of law and precedent even in its most unjust expressions. Some things just "weren't done." A body of popular customs, in effect popular rights, had been built up which not even the absolute ruler normally dared violate.

The legitimacy of the Soviet regime, however, has never been psychologically accepted by the people. For all its unlimited power — *because* of this very absence of limits — the government in this, its fourth, decade still has about it an aura of the tentative. It is perpetually *on the defensive,* promising, boasting, explaining, and above all, threatening. The unity with their people which legitimate governments take for granted, this one is continually proclaiming. In truth it is thus proclaiming uncertainty of its own status and tenure.

How, indeed, can the Soviet system hope to exact respect for its laws when it is itself a habitual lawbreaker, violating its own constitutions, punishing views and actions today which it permitted and even encouraged yesterday? It can only exact obedience, which is a relationship in another dimension.

The Kremlin regime has been one of *permanent transition*. It has hopped from crisis to crisis in a twilight zone of dictatorial outlawry. There are, to be sure, a good many superficial similarities between the czarist and the communist absolutisms. But the first enjoyed, if not divine sanction, then the sanction of time and immemorial history.

The Kremlin dictatorship is sometimes compared with its Napoleonic prototype. Both marked the climax of libertarian revolutions gone sour in tyranny. One obvious difference, however, is that the little Corsican had a deep sense of legality and order, as witnessed by the Napoleonic Code, whereas the Soviet regime seems wholly devoid of one. A related and more significant difference has been pointed out by Dr. David J. Dallin.

In Russia, he writes, "no genuine reconciliation has taken place between state and community — and above all with the peasantry." Bonaparte's strength lay in a stable civil order. He "could count on the stability of his 'rear' even during operations that took him far away from the borders of France." * There is no equivalent in the Soviet state. The refusal of Red troops to fight for Stalin during the war, the reluctance of millions of Soviet nationals to return home in 1945, the panicky need to isolate the citizenry from foreign ideas did not and could not have occurred under Napoleon.

In the Soviet Union opposition sentiment cannot be channeled through parties and movements, whether above ground or underground. The terror is too colossal and effective for that. It has found expression in elemental explosions involving the whole peasantry, or the whole intelligentsia, or the major armed forces, and on occasion the main part of the ruling minority itself.

The "loyal" and wholly dependable elements in the population, from the Kremlin's vantage point, have been comparatively small and self-interested groups of officials, Stakhanovites and the like;

* The *New Leader,* January 17, 1948.

groups, that is to say, bribed in cash and special privileges and even at that never wholly trusted. There is no large class whose unquestioned allegiance to the regime can be assumed to be automatic and proof against disillusion.

In October, 1947, a social-democratic periodical in New York, *Modern Review,* published a highly revealing article under the title "Voice Out of Russia." Its author could be identified only as "a prominent Soviet specialist," but its authenticity was vouched for by editors counting men of unquestioned integrity like Sidney Hook and Rafael Abramovitch. The vouching was really superfluous for those of us who had lived in the USSR — we knew at once that only someone inside the country and close to its life could have written it.

"Nobody (except a very small privileged group) likes the regime," the anonymous writer declared. "Many abhor it. It continues in power mainly by the prolific terrorism and espionage. Before the war, we estimated that in a party of six one was sure to be an NKVD agent; today that ratio is 1 to 4." Of the workers he wrote that "perhaps 5 percent among them are in favor of the Soviet regime," and "among the peasants you find no supporters of the regime. . . . With the downfall of the Soviet regime the *kolkhozes* will break up spontaneously."

What of the new intelligentsia, that is to say the writer's own class? It contains brilliant specialists, he said, "but few men of general culture" — least of all among the communists, who are paralyzed by party discipline, to the point where "their creative faculties and even receptiveness to new ideas in any domain" are destroyed. As a result, "it is not to the party intelligentsia that the nation owes its achievements," but to "non-party men, among whom I reckon those who, while possessing a membership card (often indispensable for getting or keeping a job), have nothing in common with the communist ideology and morals. . . . Paradoxical as it may seem, the regime is assisted most by people who hate it or at least dislike it. They are capable of creative work precisely because their spirit is not harnessed under a party yoke."

His view rings true. Reading his words I thought I was listening

again to Soviet intellectuals in the 1930's. That is how engineers,
writers, officials who trusted me — some of them outwardly im-
peccable communists — spoke when they felt sure there were no
eavesdroppers. Apparently little has changed in the intervening
years. It is only outside the Soviet Union that I have met the
bland certainty that the Soviet regime is overwhelmingly supported
and even "loved" by its subjects.

Try as they will, the chief spokesmen of the regime seem unable
to conceal their gnawing dreads of "enemies" and of dangerous
ideas. Dark allusions to pervasive menace accompany the very boasts
of monolithic solidarity. "We have no guarantee," said Malenkov
at the Party Congress in October, 1952, "against penetration of
inimical opinions, ideas and attitudes both from the capitalist states
and from groups hostile to the Soviet government *from the inside.*"
Comrade Mikhailov, head of the Komsomols, warned on the same
occasion against "hostile influences" on young people. "Both in cities
and villages," he said, "there are offenders of the rules of socialist
society among our youth. Other boys and girls fall under the influence of religion." That congress, indeed, was notable for its emphasis on more energetic mutual spying and the creation of new
agencies of ideological inspection within the Party.

No two students of Soviet Russia, of course, would agree in
detail as to the extent of loyalty and hostility to the existing system and gradations between these poles prevailing in any section
of the population. Yet it is not without significance that in any
group of recent refugees from the USSR one does find substantial
agreement that the wholly "loyal" category is relatively small, the
wholly hostile elements relatively tremendous. I have read dozens
of books and articles by these fugitives. There were few if any
from which I could not have drawn support for this statement. A
couple of citations must suffice:

Andre Karpinsky, an eminent geologist, wrote in the course of a
book review:

My entire personal experience, together with the testimony of many
former Soviet citizens who escaped from Russia during and after
World War II, leads me to the conclusion that in the main the popula-

tion of the Soviet Union can be considered anti-communist and opposed to the present regime.*

Major Gregory Klimov, who until his defection was an official of the Soviet occupation administration in Eastern Germany, tries to be more specific:

During the 30 years of the Soviet regime at least 30 million people have been subjected to repressive measures on political grounds. As the families of all such people are automatically classified as politically un-reliable, if we assume that each of them has only two relatives, at least 60 million people must be on the blacklist. If 10 million people out of the 30 million died in prison camps, and at least another 10 million are still in the camps, while 10 million have served their time and been released, we get a figure of 80 million people whom the Soviet state has turned into its enemies, or, at least, regards as its enemies. . . . Today it is indubitable that the main class of new Soviet society con-sists of millions of automatic enemies of the Soviet state.**

In the summer of 1949 Dr. Merle Fainsod of Harvard inter-viewed about one hundred Soviet fugitives in Germany and Austria, ranging from ordinary peasants to distinguished intellectuals. He is wisely cautious about drawing definitive conclusions from this sampling, yet asserts that "they seem to give a picture of the Soviet people as a seething mass of anxieties, frustrations, and discontents."

Among former *kolkhozniks,* collectivized farmers, he reports, "there seemed to be general agreement . . . that the *kolkhoz* was a device by which the regime exploited the peasants for its own interests." They loudly denounced official "informers who made it impossible for anyone to speak his mind," and gave him the feeling that village "life is grim and hard." The complaints of workers in the refugee group were extensive: against inadequate pay further reduced by compulsory deductions, against food shortages, bad hous-ing, and the Stakhanovite system, which they described as "a device for raising norms and extracting extra work for the same pay." Workers said that they "had no real freedom to express their grievances" and that the trade-unions "were the creatures of the party and the factory managements."

* New York *Times* Book Review, November 5, 1950.
** *The Terror Machine,* Praeger, 1935.

Former Red soldiers complained of the "special privileges of the officer group," and former officers resented the constant surveillance — "they were not trusted, and . . . had to function in a milieu of constant insecurity and fear." Insecurity and fear, Dr. Fainsod writes, were also the main grievances of Soviet bureaucrats, who "reflected a feeling that the privileges of today might evaporate into the deprivations of a forced labor camp tomorrow." The same grievances were also "strongly expressed by the intellectuals and scientists. . . . It is with intellectuals especially that one senses the tensions generated by enforced conformity and the stifling of the desire for self-expression."

Dr. Fainsod found the younger refugees, those in their early and middle twenties, particularly challenging:

There is a widespread assumption in the non-Soviet world that, since the Soviet regime controls all the instruments of indoctrination which shape the minds of youth, its hold on their loyalty is practically complete. Conversations with young ex-Soviet citizens, school teachers, and others who have had extensive contact with young people in Russia cast some doubt on that assumption. One school teacher who had taught for nearly 25 years in Soviet schools said that the attraction of communist ideology for Soviet youth is greatly exaggerated in the West. . . . Another very intelligent escapee, himself a former Komsomol who had worked professionally with youth groups for many years, insisted that it would be a mistake to assume that all Soviet children came off the Pioneer and Komsomol assembly lines as unthinking and unquestioning tools of the regime. He added that even very young children began to pose embarrassing questions which raised doubts about the official propaganda.*

One need not credit *émigré* opinions in detail to be impressed by their weight in the aggregate. Only for a brief period, in the middle years of the Russo-German war, were the Soviet rulers and the majority of the peoples of Russia more or less reconciled. Patriotism and common danger accomplished what neither force nor propaganda had been able to do. But that short-lived unity, as we shall see in the sections dealing with the war, was imposed by the stupidities and inhumanities of the German invader. It was less a

* "Controls and Tensions in the Soviet Union," *American Political Science Review,* June, 1950.

product of love of the Kremlin than hate of the foreign enemy.

Even that temporary solidarity, moreover, was maintained on terms which confirmed the underlying antagonism and dramatized the failure of the regime to win the population over to its side. The civil strife was not ended. It was merely suspended for the duration. The uneasy armistice was broken as soon as the German menace had been ended, and the great struggle between the regime and its victims was resumed on a larger and more desperate scale.

In his monumental but, alas, unread story of the terror in the earlier Soviet years, *The Guillotine at Work*, the late G. P. Maximoff wrote in the concluding pages:

The gruesomeness of the terror, the unprecedented sweep in the last years — doesn't all that tell that the terror is directed not upon living corpses, not upon submissive slaves, upon men with broken wills and hollowed souls? Only those who have no fear are the objects of intimidation. Only those that do not bend of their own will are made to bend by force, and only those are persecuted who do not submit and who keep on rebelling.

And if in all those years of unrestrained terror the Bolsheviks did not succeed in terrifying the people, if they did not stifle within them the urge to rebel, to protest, that means that the people are still alive, that their will is strong and the drive for freedom and justice is irrepressible. Such a people have a great future and unlimited opportunities. It means that the people cannot be dragged down to degeneration.*

He summed up a great truth, the most important truth about the Russian peoples in their Soviet period. If ever the dictatorship feels it can permanently relax its pressures, we shall have reason to fear that the Russian people may at last have capitulated. As yet there are no signs of any such *rapprochement*. The people have not surrendered, and the ruling clique has gone too far in its depredations, it has evoked too much internal enmity, to risk a genuine compromise. The great duel between the government and the governed must be fought to the bitter end, whether it takes years or decades or generations. Under Leon Trotsky's euphemism of a permanent revolution is the reality of a permanent civil war.

* Published by the Chicago Section of the Alexander Berkman Fund, 1940.

III. The Myth of Soviet Unity

1. An All-embracing Lie

For over thirty-five years the rulers of a great nation, with its total resources at their disposal, have had in their hands the largest, most expertly staffed, scientifically planned, and lavishly financed propaganda machine in all history.

Here was the first government on record — the only government until the advent of its Fascist and Nazi offspring, and again since their demise — that looked upon the control of thought at home and its manipulation abroad as a primary function, with a prior lien on national budget, brains, and energies. In carrying out that function, moreover, it has not been restrained by moral scruples but, to the contrary, has taken pride in The Lie as an instrument of power.

It is perhaps not too remarkable, therefore, that the Kremlin should have succeeded largely in imposing on the world its own version of its own history. No one outside the Red empire, until much too late, felt any responsibility for preventing this imposture — least of all our historians and sociologists, many of whom even joined the droves of foreign gullibles who had taken on the job, gratis, of making all Moscow pretenses stick.

Yet one is moved to marvel at the scope of this propaganda achievement and the daring with which it has been managed. What a magnificent structure of falsehoods, buttressed by deceptions, and camouflaged with delusions!

The major myths of the past evolved through generations or

centuries, growing as trees grow. But the panoplied Soviet myth has been fabricated in our own time, under our very eyes. It hasn't grown but has been deliberately constructed, wings and towers and galleries being added as required and demolished when no longer useful. Events fresh in men's minds have been arbitrarily recast, words and concepts turned inside out, current biographies stood on their heads, annoying witnesses wiped out. Soviet history has been a loose-leaf record, the heroes of one year turned into the villains of the next and vice versa, yesterday's defeats turned into today's victories, the morning's blunders into the evening's strokes of genius.

In *Nineteen Eighty-four* the late George Orwell described how the Ministry of Truth continually revises the past to conform to the needs of Big Brother in the present. The fiction comes close enough to the actuality in Soviet Russia to chill a knowing reader's blood. But in this one respect — that Bolshevik distortions have been forced not only upon the Soviet population but to a striking degree upon the free segment of mankind as well — the Soviet facts are more terrifying than the Orwell fable. Large gobs of the invented propaganda story are believed and treated as solemn fact in the non-Soviet world, even by people who reject the rest of the fabrication, even by men who in the ordinary affairs of life are no fools.

Inside the USSR dissent from the official myth is punished as the crime of crimes; knowledge of the truth is driven into the recesses of men's minds and the crevices of their souls. In the outside world the Kremlin has no such punitive power. But it has taken shrewd advantage of credulity, and of the hungers of our time for pretty illusions. The result is that otherwise well-informed people accept, as if they were unquestioned fact, assumptions about the Soviets that have no relation to reality.

The great Red myth has it that the Bolsheviks under V. I. Lenin — with Stalin and almost Stalin alone at his right hand — over-threw the czarist dynasty in a popular communist insurrection; that they set up a "dictatorship of the proletariat" which in due time, under Stalin, established a "classless society." While certain rotten elements, remnants of the capitalist past and renegades in the new era, opposed "the revolution," the worker and peasant masses embraced and defended it ardently throughout.

This fantasy is official history within the Soviet sphere. And it is credited uncritically by millions outside. Yet it is not only untrue, not merely exaggerated. It is the opposite of the truth, perjurious on every count.

Lenin, Trotsky and their cohorts did not overthrow czarism. What they overthrew was the first democratic society in Russian history, set up after a popular revolution eight months earlier — a revolution that itself was the climax of many generations of struggle, education, preparation, and heroism.

Their Bolshevik "revolution" on November 7, 1917 was nothing of the sort. It was a counterrevolution — not a popular eruption but a sly conspiratorial seizure of power, a *coup d'état,* by a very small minority. Among the valuable assets it appropriated, in fact, was the word "revolution" and the prestige that inhered in the mighty upheaval earlier that year, along with the glamor of those generations of heroic revolutionary background. A handful of able, ruthless, cynical men simply hijacked the revolution from its makers, then applied force and fraud and demagogy to consolidate the theft.

Far from being classless, the society the usurpers fashioned is hierarchical and stratified, with millions of chattel slaves at the bottom and a small group of despotic dictators at the top. It has evolved into a reactionary police state resting on naked force, slave labor and ideological double-talk. Lenin promised that the state would in time "wither away." Only the promise has withered away, along with all the other idealistic and utopian pretensions.

The framework of the myth, the all-embracing lie, is that there is substantial unity between the regime and the people. The claim is that masters and subjects are an indivisible whole. More than any of the other falsehoods, because it is the common element in all of them, this needs to be taken apart if the non-Soviet world is to deal intelligently with the Soviet problem.

2. *It Has Four Faces*

The lie about essential unity has many faces. They contradict one another and are irreconcilable in logic. But in the never-never land of mythology, logic is an outlaw. All the faces have found acceptance, sometimes in the same minds, so that each reinforces the other. At least four variations on the theme can be followed through the symphony of fable:

One: The dictatorship was created by the Russian peoples themselves, who support it fervently and always as the instrument of their hopes and purposes. Such opposition as has arisen from time to time has come from "socially alien elements," usually in league with some foreign government, and has been crushed by the aroused workers, peasants, intelligentsia, and soldiery. Their enthusiastic devotion, in point of fact, is the one constant amidst shifting party lines, slogans, and leaders.

This is the official version, mandatory for everybody at home and for true believers abroad.

Two: The dictatorship was put over on the country by main force and by a handful of fanatics; it has been maintained with an iron hand. But it has been accepted and suffered meekly, unresistingly, by masses who have known nothing better and are incapable of even imagining any alternative — masses, indeed, which crave despotic authority. They bow to their regime submissively as a kind of act of God.

This version is favored abroad alike by liberals and conservatives, by hazy Soviet sympathizers and hazy anticommunists. It is even the solace of some communists in their moments of embarrassment over Kremlin crimes, as Earl Browder, a deposed sachem of American communism, recently confessed in a press interview. "We used to explain away the authoritarian trend of the Communist Party," he sighed, "in terms of Russia's own authoritarian past." * It was my own best consolation during the first year or so

* In interview by Marguerite Higgins, New York *Herald Tribune,* March 22, 1953.

of residence under the hammer and sickle, when my imported enthusiasms were being battered and maimed by the shocking realities around me.

The core of the trouble, according to this theory, is not in communism but in the bizarre Russian person and his national history. Marx and Lenin get all the credit for "achievements" and "progress," while Ivan the Terrible and Nicholas II get all the blame for Soviet inhumanity, chaos, failure, duplicity. Despite the implicit insult to the Russian people, this is the stock in trade of self-anointed "friends of Soviet Russia." And though it is at the extreme remove from the official story, the Kremlin prefers not to dispute it too vigorously. After all, the end product — the assumption of solidarity between the rulers and the subjects — is about the same. The Bolshevik chiefs feel no call to defend the honor of their people.

Recently a few anthropologists have come forward with a "scientific" explanation of this second version. They attribute the alleged Russian preference for absolutism to the national custom of swaddling infants hand and foot. This constraint in the cradle presumably conditions them not merely to tolerate but to relish outer constraints ever after. How the scientists make that fanciful theory jibe with the extension of Soviet communism to unswaddled populations — Czechs and Hungarians, for instance — or with the triumph of similar totalitarian systems in unswaddled countries like Hitler's Germany, remains to be seen.

The idea that people cherish their chains because they were born in captivity is rather cozy for democrats who must somehow reconcile their unnatural affection for a brutal tyranny with a normal dislike of brutality and tyrants. It absolves them neatly from any sense of personal guilt while enjoying the Grand Guignol. Consequently it is standard equipment in communist apologetics.

"Without an ironbound dictatorship," an American writer explained in the twenties, "Russia could not survive, for it is the only thing the Russians understand." He disdained to inquire, of course, why the Bolsheviks had to be more "ironbound" than the most inhumane of the czars. None of the defenders of this viewpoint, in point of fact, gets around to elucidating why the Soviets must use every variety of force and terror to make their victims accept a way of life they crave in any case.

According to Edward Crankshaw, "an absolute dictatorship of some kind was inevitable" after the fall of the Romanoffs, because, forsooth, "a Russian, any Russian, is happier under an autocracy." Why intrude upon his blessed happiness with carping sympathy? Crankshaw admires Russians as individuals; he is aware of elements of greatness in their make-up. But in the mass, as a historic entity, he apparently considers them doomed to eternal oppression. The circumstance that they hate their yoke is in some mystical fashion, Crankshaw avers, no proof that they do not love it: "No matter how deeply the Russian people as a whole may abhor certain aspects of the present regime, they have, to put it crudely, asked for it." * That is crude enough to satisfy any fancier of crudities. Apparently it is something akin to the Freudian death wish. Russians, unlike Britons, are truly happy only when they're truly miserable.

In admitting that the people do abhor "certain aspects" — as anyone who has lived among them must in simple honesty admit — the Crankshaws really box themselves in hopelessly. If the decisive fact is a history of absolutism, why are the aspects abhorred precisely those most familiar in Russian history: the terror, internal passports, feudalistic land tenure and such? One could explain popular hostility to machines, literacy, other *novelties;* but it is, on the contrary, the new varieties of historic wrongs that provoke the most stubborn resistance and the deepest hatreds.

The historical alibi is the loudest note in endless books and articles, some of them anti-Soviet in intent. It can be heard, where it is not spelled out, in the familiar assertion that communism is just czarism with some Marxist sauces. It is what might be called the de Custine fallacy.

Marquis Adolphe de Custine, a Frenchman, spent a few months in St. Petersburg in 1839, almost exclusively among court people and the gentry. It was soon after the Napoleonic wars and the

* *Cracks in the Kremlin Wall,* Knopf, 1951.

Decembrist uprising in 1825 had intensified large social and cultural ferment in Russia. It was a time of significant spiritual and philosophical movements which had in common an emphasis on the dignity and even the divinity of the individual man, a passionate awareness of the grievances and travail of the masses. A great plowing of minds and seeding of ideas was in progress which had already begun to yield a rich harvest in Russian literature, music, theater, science and libertarian movements. Processes were under way which within two decades after his visit brought about the emancipation of the serfs and the enactment of far-reaching social and judicial reforms, the creation of the *zemstvo* and the revitalizing of the *mir*.

Custine must have been peculiarly insulated and insensitive to remain completely blind to this mighty stirring of a nation. He seems to have seen and recorded only the superficials: the abuses, the arrogance of masters and the humility of the plain people. Russians, great and small, he wrote in a dogmatic spirit, were "drunk with slavery." The great reappraisals under way, the literary renaissance, the deep popular sympathy with the men of December who were regarded not as traitors but as heroes — nothing of this sort seems to have come within this man's mental vision. He failed to see, as George F. Kennan has remarked, "the 'other Russia' which was very much there in the age of Nicholas I, though not visible to the Western traveler." The time of Nicholas I, which Custine looked upon without comprehending, was characterized by Alexander Herzen as "an amazing time of outward slavery and inner liberation."

In recent years the Custine diary has been revived, slyly edited to underline parallels with the Soviet abuses, and advertised as proof that Russians have been and must by nature remain slaves who do not really mind being whipped and starved. This provides a convenient salve for the conscience of Westerners annoyed by horrors but determined to do nothing about them.

The Custine fans overlook the obtuse one-sidedness of his findings. They forget that the same sort of reports were made about other peoples who subsequently achieved freedom notwithstanding, in 18th-century France, let us say. Apologists for the Jacobin terror and Napoleon's dictatorship could have cited such reports (and perhaps did) to prove that Gauls were slaves by nature with a peculiar appetite for oppression. A Crankshaw of the period, referring back to Louis XIV and his forebears, could have argued that in France "an absolute dictatorship of some kind was inevitable."

The theory of "once slaves, always slaves" does not stand up in the light of history. What nation does not have in its background a black night of absolutism over a seemingly meek population? Only the most discerning then realized that the inconspicuous freshets of freedom, the tender sproutings of liberty being treated as weeds, were more significant than the pomp of enthroned tyranny. But the partisans of slavery found the theory serviceable in the past, even as they do now in consigning the Russian peoples to eternal subjection. Always it has enabled them to account for a solidarity between masters and slaves that was in truth only skin-deep.

Three: Another variant takes its stance on the principle of non-intervention in the affairs of other nations. Again, as in the Custine matter, it is a principle reserved for the special comfort of the Kremlin. We are told from many directions that it is no damned business of ours how the Soviet leaders deal with "their own" citizens.

Those who proclaim Stalin's — now Malenkov's, tomorrow someone else's — divine right to behave as he pleases toward his subjects were not quite so sure about Hitler's right to do what he pleased with his Germans or Jews. They have been especially emphatic in denying Chiang Kai-shek's right to do what he wished with "his own" Chinese.

Ironically, those who consider the *status quo* in the Soviet Union as sacred and untouchable are usually the very people who itch to demolish the *status quo* elsewhere. Freda Kirchwey, editor of *The Nation,* spoke for them all when she wrote: "We must accept revolution as the dominant, inescapable fact of our time. . . . We must become, and quickly, the *sponsor of revolution,* helping the people of the world to win all that communism promises or provides — plus liberty. . . ." *

But how about accepting the fact of revolution against the established order in the Soviet sphere? How about helping its peoples to win what Lenin and his successors promised and failed to deliver — especially liberty? Why should American sponsorship of aspirations to freedom stop cold at the iron curtains? She neither raises nor answers such questions.

The hands-off-Russia principle was sharply enunciated in 1948 by the very prototype of the postwar liberal, Justice William O. Douglas. In a widely praised speech he said at one point: "It is of course the right of the Russian people to have such form of government as they choose. We, the democrats, will be the first to defend that right. When confined within their borders, their totalitarian regime is their concern, not ours."

The supposition that a totalitarian setup represents "the choice" of its subjects is remarkable enough. More remarkable, in the name of democracy the statement enters a cold-blooded disclaimer of "concern" for evil provided it is confined in a particular set of frontiers. It washes its hands of the Russians and their sorrows, their aspirations, their human dignity, on technical sovereignty grounds. It makes the untenable political assumption that evil on that scale, evil nurtured as a base for world dominion, *can* be confined within its own borders. This despite three decades of proof to the contrary.

Such neutrality vis-à-vis the Red tyranny is particularly strange in the light of Justice Douglas's books and talks on the Middle East in the last few years. In that area, it appears, he is a hot partisan of the masses against their exploiters, who for some reason do not share the Kremlin's privilege of maltreating "their own." He has urged forthright and vigorous American intervention on the side of the people against the ruling groups, and frontiers be hanged.

Suppose an accredited liberal, a decade earlier, had insisted that the Nazis had the right to sadistic social experiments in their own

* *The Nation,* January 28, 1950.

country; more, that *as democrats* we would be the first to defend that right. He would have been called to order by outraged fellow liberals. Douglas and his kind seem unaware that before 1917 liberals as a matter of course took the side of the Russian masses against the autocracy. They did not allow technicalities to inhibit their sympathies or angers and they found ways to make the autocrats conscious of them.

Four: Perhaps the most irrational face of all, with respect to the myth of Soviet unity, is the contention that it doesn't matter — that we must act *as if* the regime and the people were one and indivisible, regardless of the facts. It is less a face than a grimace. The Kremlin is making war on the free world in the name of its whole population, it asserts, so why bother finding out whether it has the consent of the population?

A crude expression of this point of view appeared in papers all over the country in February, 1953, in a column by an able and well-meaning journalist. Rather disdainfully he dismissed all differentiations between "good" and "bad" Russians, between Russians and communists, between loyal and disloyal communists, as a parlor game for intellectuals. For "emotionally soft Americans." Emotionally hard Americans must avoid such subtleties and go on the wild guess that "any Russian is the enemy."

This is not the first time that political confusion has preened itself as toughness. German leaders who survived the war realize today that in Russia they could have saved hundreds of thousands of German lives, and possibly avoided defeat in the East, had Hitler not insisted that "any Russian is the enemy." Hitler, we now know, disdained those who sought to make allies of the Russians as "emotionally soft." Yet Red troops deserted and surrendered en masse as long as they believed the Germans would distinguish between the communist minority and the rest of the country. The despised Russians, upon discovering that they were all "the enemy," rallied around the Kremlin and licked the emotionally hard Nazis.

"Our concern," the columnist wrote, "is to avert another universal war if we can and to be ready to fight to victory if we

cannot." Agreed. But why is that inconsistent with fifth columns
of freedom and political sappers behind the iron curtains? Both in
averting war or in winning war, are we not better off with friends
in the adversary's empire? The toughness that cuts off its strategic
nose to spite its face, I dare suggest, is neither logical nor mature.
Softness, as mankind's teachers have tried to convey, may have a
strength of its own, even in terms of expediency. Thomas Paine
wrote: "He who would make his liberty secure must guard his
enemy from oppression," but he was an emotional softie.

To concede a solidarity in the Soviet camp that does not exist,
to reject allies out of hand, amounts to giving the Kremlin a valuable victory by default. It repeats the Hitler mistake of turning
millions of Russian allies into implacable enemies. Though our
potential friends in the USSR were a handful, we would have no
alternative in common sense but to enlist them on our side of the
struggle.

These, in brief, are some of the faces of the great Soviet myth
of a monolithic society. In one aspect it is presented as the product
of a revolutionary people; in another, as the very opposite — the
product of racial meekness devoid of rebellious instincts, and actual
preference for despotism. But the resulting picture, as a practical
matter, is almost the same. The picture of a society which the rest
of the world must accept as fully unified and integrated, without
meaningful internal rifts, without tensions worth exploring and
exploiting.

In February, 1947, a pro-Soviet journalist, Edgar Snow, wrote a
series of articles in the *Saturday Evening Post* defending Moscow's
postwar aggressions and general mischief-making under the familiar
propaganda disguise of "explaining" them. One of the articles was
called "How It Looks to Ivan Ivanovich," meaning the average
Soviet citizen. Lo and behold! it turned out that to Ivan "it" looked
precisely as it did to Stalin, not merely in a general way but in
detail. Not only did Ivan see the complex world picture exactly as
the Kremlin did (or more accurately, as the Kremlin pretended to
see it) but he justified Soviet policies in approximately the same

language as *Pravda, Izvestia* and the *Daily Worker*. Mr. Snow, of course, offered no proofs of this miraculous identity of all views and thoughts as between a sophisticated Politburo and an average subject; he simply took it for granted.

To anyone halfway acquainted with the real Ivan's automatic skepticism with respect both to the conduct and the propaganda of his political overlords, it seemed a bizarre performance.* But do not all free-world journalists and statesmen make the same arbitrary assumption of Soviet unity every time they talk of "the Russians," whether in praise or in blame, when they have reference to the Soviet regime? Are they not supinely conforming with the central myth manufactured by the pro-Kremlin crowd?

The maintenance and strengthening of this myth is of life-and-death importance to the Soviets. By the same token its exposure and demolition is of life-and-death importance to the non-Soviet world. Already the Kremlin has won too many facile victories, at home and in the international arena, by using the prestige of presumptive inner strength and solidarity, by making us swallow the biggest of its Big Lies.

No one disputes the influence of a people's history and traditions upon its present and future. Of course communism in Russia or China or Guatemala will be colored by the total experience of its population, just as democracies in different settings develop their native accents of behavior and institutions. But this does not mean that an absolutism of long duration can be succeeded only by another and preferably worse absolutism ad infinitum. There are crises in a people's development when minor themes in the symphony of their history suddenly become dominant, when the long persecuted and defeated strains in its tradition finally conquer and prevail.

The belief that Russia and oppression are inseparable Siamese

* Since then the *Saturday Evening Post* has made handsome amends for the strange Snow series, in editorials and articles delineating the great conflict between Soviet regime and people, such as "In Defense of the Russian People" by Alexander Barmine, September 4, 1948, and "Terror in the Kremlin" by Ellsworth Raymond, August 15, 1953.

twins has no validity in logic or in the historical experience of the rest of mankind. Millions of Russians have died to disprove this defeatist assumption. The fact that their struggle has *not yet* succeeded proves exactly nothing about the future.

IV. Russia before 1917

1. The Distorted Image

Immediately after Stalin had been consigned to the embalmers, his successors graciously opened the doors of their slaughterhouse to a batch of small-town American editors. The belief that a brief visit to a totalitarian capital can provide insights into the country's real nature is a piece of journalistic folklore. On the whole the reports of the editors were about par for tourists in a strange land: some keen observations imbedded in a sticky mess of irrelevant trivia.

Among the most perspicacious in the lot, judging by a series of articles she wrote, was a Pennsylvania newspaperwoman, Mrs. Jane S. McIlvaine. Her description of the externals of Moscow life was hardly appetizing. She ended one installment, however, with a gratuitous slap — not at the Soviet dictatorship but at the prerevolutionary Russia.

"The Russian people are proud," she wrote. "In spite of current conditions the communists never fail to point out, and Western observers agree, that life is less hard than it was under the czars. The Russians never forget this." *

How did the estimable lady discover that "life is less hard" than before Bolshevism? Or that "Russians never forget this"? Did the particular Westerners who agreed with the communists on this verdict have direct knowledge of the *ancien régime,* or were they echoing a standardized propaganda line, even as Mrs. McIlvaine echoes their echo?

* New York *Journal-American,* April 14, 1953.

Not many things about Russia are beyond dispute. But one of them is that life under the old dispensation, for all its hardships, was freer and more tolerable than under the new. By contrast with the Sovietized country, the pre-1917 Russia was a veritable haven of contentment. The very Russians who devoted their best years to fighting czarism, thousands of whom are still alive and vocal in our midst, are the first to concede this. Whatever yardstick of measurement is used — political, cultural, spiritual, even economic — czarism stacks up as humanly more attractive. Given a choice based on fact rather than fable, only the mentally defective with a relish for punishment would prefer the present system.

In blandly assuming that the Soviet Union, for all its brutalities and self-evident wretchedness, is an improvement over what it displaced, tourists merely accept one of the propaganda clichés. They are in good (or at any rate numerous) company. That assumption is part of the mental furniture of so-called liberal historians and pundits the world over. Probably the outstanding Soviet achievement has been its success in blackening the character of the historic Russia.

There was plenty of black in it, to be sure, before the propaganda artists set to work. But they have managed to ink out important white areas and to turn all shades of gray into a uniform jet black. Their job was made much easier precisely because Russia *was* backward, reactionary, and disfigured by running social sores, as compared with any modern democratic nation. But the comparison is with the Soviet Union, and that is an entirely different matter.

One does not have to perfume the past to recognize that the old order — in all things but one, namely the growth of heavy industry — was indubitably superior to the new. Its political, intellectual, moral and spiritual climate was infinitely more wholesome and hopeful than that now prevailing. Even in its darkest periods, such as the reigns of Nicholas I and Alexander III, Russia was not remotely like the total tyranny it is today. Relatively at least, the life of the mind was strong and creative, conscience was untrammeled, the self-respect of the individual and his rights under law were better safeguarded.

These statements will, no doubt, lift some eyebrows. The notion that Russia, until the advent of Bolshevism, was a dark and savage land of slaves and nihilists, the knout and the Okhrana, has been so rigidly riveted by repetition that it does not easily yield to argument.

There is poverty, ignorance, and oppression in both Russias, old and new, but the differences in degree tell the story. Before 1917, open dissent from the official ideology was not only possible but fashionable; social and philosophical ideas were continually and ardently explored; two-way cultural intercourse with the West was wide and unbroken; simple subsistence was taken for granted by the overwhelming mass of people and especially (except in time of famine) by the peasantry; a vigorous opposition press and an array of opposition parties were in being; the frontiers were comparatively open for Russians to leave and foreigners to enter; the families of political emigrants carrying on violent antigovernment agitation abroad were not molested.

Merely to list a few such things is to point up the contrast with Soviet conditions. A Soviet citizen magically transported backward in time to 1913 or even 1900 would find personal freedoms and political liberties that are unthinkable in his present setting. He would find evil and injustice — but also that they were recognized as such and that it was possible to protest, to fight, to organize for change.

A number of circumstances have conspired to fix a distorted image of the old Russia on the mental retina of mankind. The most important of these, of course, was the large element of truth in the grim portrait of Russia with its low living standards, censorship, pogroms, secret police, and Siberian exile system. In addition, the Western world drew its limited and selective concepts of Russia from sources which had this in common: that for high-minded reasons they were all intent upon exhibiting the country in the worst possible light.

The first of these was Russian literature, which was to an extraordinary degree a literature of protest and exposure, using all the wiles of art to indict the *status quo* and nourish a spirit of revolt. It was as if mankind were to judge America almost exclusively upon the evidence of Upton Sinclair's *The Jungle,* Steinbeck's *The Grapes of Wrath,* and the like. Second, there was the flaming anti-czarist propaganda of Russian liberals and revolutionists, at home and in emigration. Finally, there were the writings and lectures of hundreds of zealous foreign champions of the Russian revolutionary movements.

I do not suggest that these sources were false, but only that taken together they presented an exaggerated, one-sided picture. They necessarily showed only the seamy side of the national garment. Our contemporary world, inured to large-scale horror and callous to mass sorrows, can scarcely remember how sensitive public opinion was before World War I to the misdeeds of the Russian autocracy; how those lurid tales of Siberia haunted the conscience which today remains untouched by a hundred Siberias. The liberal nineteenth-century rationalism of Europe and America could not make peace with an autocratic, socially retarded Russia. The totalitarianized liberalism of today, alas, readily comes to terms with the new autocracy.

And thus it happened that the image of a completely savage nation, a stagnant pool of backwardness, was indelibly impressed upon the world. Then came 1917, hailed almost universally on trust alone as the dawn of a bright new era. Anything, it was assumed, would be an improvement on the past. The excesses of the revolution seemed purified by the sins of the deposed rulers and classes.

The new masters made the most of this alibi. As the Bolshevik tragedy unreeled, its crimes seemed less barbaric when posed against a background of total barbarism under the czars. The more bloody the Red regime became, indeed, the more constrained were its defenders to deepen the colors of that background. The need to blame everything distasteful upon the Romanoff legacy amounted to a psychological compulsion. Somehow, for the traveler committed to the Soviet "experiment," even the bleak steppes and the tundra spelled the past, while any magnificent scenery seemed hand-tooled by the experimenters.

Communists knew how to take advantage of these circumstances. They concealed from the world the worst aspects of their regime and attributed the rest to the past. The "nevertheless" school of apologetics prospered. Past blemishes became a sufficient alibi for present cancers. Whatever evil the Kremlin compounded, whatever indignities it heaped on the people, its partisans were ready with "Nevertheless, it's not as bad as in the dark past." And there have been few to challenge this inanity.

Break down a statement like Mrs. McIlvaine's, and you discover that it rests primarily on two elements of presumptive progress under the Soviets: economic expansion and "literacy." The economic gains are treated as ends in themselves, unrelated to security or happiness, economic freedoms, or the dignity of labor. And literacy, similarly, is treated as an absolute good in itself, without reference to the newly literate's access to truth, or to education in the deeper sense of minds liberated from ignorance.

2. Genius of the Russian People

In their joyous transports over new smokestacks, the hallelujah shouters ignore the fact that the innovations have not improved or enriched the life of the masses but, on the contrary, have made existence more servile and more onerous.

But even on the dehumanized plane their judgment is warped. For it rests on the false premise that Russia before the Five-Year-Planners was an industrial desert. The truth is that while the country entered the industrial race very late, it made remarkable progress, at a speed greater than that of some West European nations. Its enormous resources and population, plus the available experience of the rest of the world, made this inevitable.

Ironically, it was Lenin, in his book on Russian capitalism written in 1899, who emphasized the terrific tempo of the "technical revolution" then under way. He aligned statistics to prove that industry was expanding faster in Russia than in any European country, and in some instances faster than in the United States. That, in fact, was the basis of his argument that a working class was emerging large and robust enough to support a proletarian revolution.

By 1912 Russia was second only to the United States in total railroad mileage. General industrial production increased from 6,177,-800,000 rubles in 1912 to 7,357,800,000 rubles in 1913 — a rate of expansion of 19.1 per cent for the year. This compares not unfavorably with the average annual accretion claimed for the Five-Year Plans. When quality factors and dependability of the statistics are taken into consideration, the natural industrial growth was greater than under the Soviets. There is no reason for doubting that the arc of progress would have continued at the same rate of acceleration without revolution — and without the enormities and mass slaughters that marked the process under the Soviets.

A normal industrial revolution had been under way for fifty years. In the decades preceding the war of 1914 that revolution was hectic in its velocity. Coal production, four million tons in 1890, reached thirty-five million in 1913, and additional ten million were imported to meet the surge of industrial demand. Textile mills in 1913 consumed over three times as much cotton as in 1890, half of it grown in Russia. The same general picture held true for iron and copper, sugar and machinery, scores of other products. At that pace, as Manya Gordon put it, the country "would have been in the year 1939 industrially very near the point actually reached by the Soviet Union" — this despite the serious interruptions of the Russo–Japanese war, the 1905 revolution and the First World War.*

Igor Sikorsky, who ought to know, has written that "aeronautical science and industry in Russia before 1914 were at par with America in that period. Several world records were established by airplanes designed and produced in Russia at that time." Russian-made locomotives and railroad cars were among the best in Europe; high-grade automobiles, motorcycles and bicycles were being manufactured.

Nor were the growing ranks of industrial workers mere exploited robots, in effect state helots, as they are today. Labor's awareness of its rights and its powers was greater by far than in

* *Workers Before and After Lenin,* Dutton, 1941.

the corresponding stage of industrialization in any other country. "Every increase in the size of the industrial plant and the number of employes," Manya Gordon attested, "registered a corresponding increase in strikes. In other words, the workers were always conscious of their right to a share of the increase in profits. . . . In the large plants employing more than 1,000 workers, the number of strikes in 1905 was more than twice the entire labor force: in other words, they struck more than twice a year." This is not exactly the record of a hopelessly cowed and backward proletariat.

The history of protective labor legislation in Russia goes back as far as 1741. In 1785 a law was passed establishing a ten-hour day and six-day week in all trades. It was not well enforced and in time withered on the vine of statutes. All the same it is noteworthy even as a portent when we recall that the ten-hour day did not appear in Europe and the United States until a century later.

A Russian law of June 1, 1882 — which *was* enforced — forbade work in factories by children under twelve, and limited work for children of fifteen or under to eight hours in two four-hour shifts. Night work was forbidden for all minors. In France at that time child labor of twelve hours a day was legal. While other countries outdistanced Russia in labor legislation by 1917, it was still incomparably more progressive than under the Soviets.

Now to return to the matter of literacy. In the old Russia, reading and writing had a profound meaning, since they opened up horizons of mental enlightenment. They provided access to a world of stimulating, many-sided Russian and foreign books; to a varied and (again relatively) free domestic and foreign press; to empires of knowledge and beauty. Mere literacy today, by contrast, simply gives the Kremlin a readier channel for mesmerizing minds with official lies. The concern of all totalitarian societies with teaching their subjects to read is hardly an expression of a benign interest in education. It is functional. What would be the advantage of a state monopoly of printing presses if the people remained illiterate?

But even in its most elementary sense, as a material skill rather than a passport to an ampler mental life, the facts in the old Russia were not as bad as Soviet distortion has made them out. The census of 1897 showed 51 per cent of men and 22 per cent of women literates in European Russia. In the 1920 census (before the Soviet drive for literacy had started) those percentages rose to 82 and 47. That is a far remove from the total illiteracy implied by communist boasts. In the normal course of events, had there been no revolution, literacy in Russia would probably have reached the level of Western Europe by the end of the 1920's if not sooner. There was a great recession in the early Soviet years, due to civil war and general dislocations. The boastful communist percentages of increase take that new low as their base, rather than prewar figures.

The goal of universal elementary education loomed on the Russian horizon when war and revolution intervened. The compulsory schooling law of 1910 was geared to embrace the entire population by 1922.

For over a century before the Bolsheviks appeared on the scene, Russia had taken deep pride in its great universities, which were a match for the world's best in quality if not in quantity. "Russian scholarship before the revolution reached the very highest standard," the late Sir Bernard Pares wrote in 1942. Contradicting the fable that university education was only for the rich and the nobility, he added that "the number of places filled by sons of the peasantry was far greater than anything that was dreamed of at Oxford or Cambridge before the present century." Under the law, in the last decades of czarism, 15 per cent of university students were on scholarships provided by the state; another 15 to 20 per cent were supported by private endowments. Close to one half the student body, in short, comprised young men and women too poor to pay their own tuitions.

The quality of education, moreover, was not only incomparably higher than under the Soviets but higher than in most other countries. Its essence was free inquiry — even in sociology, economics and government — to the constant despair of the autocracy. None of the doctrines of social and political reform could be kept out of the curriculum or the classroom, so that the institutions of higher education became the very seedbeds of subversion and revolution.

Anyone who has known the prerevolutionary generation will probably confirm that the educated Russian, by and large, was better educated than the average-educated West European or American. The Russian faculties were self-governing along democratic lines, and autonomous student organizations of every conceivable type flourished despite all that a reactionary officialdom could do to frustrate them.

The Russian intelligentsia was a unique phenomenon. Because of the handicaps imposed by the government, intellectual freedom — amounting at times to license — was exercised with a peculiar zest. "This intelligentsia," Helen Iswolsky wrote, "was something more than a cultured elite: it has been compared to a religious order in that it was austere, ascetic, and disinterested. Its representatives were not content to preach their doctrines: they sought to apply them." *

There were few ivory towers in Russia. Education, culture, carried with them moral responsibilities: an impulse to "rediscover the secret soul of the common people," to heal their wounds. That impulse was behind the strong political movement of populism, whose adherents "went to the people," literally, not only to teach but humbly to learn. Social discussion and disputation between Marxists and SR's, between Mensheviks and Bolsheviks, Westernizers and Slavophils, were not a platonic parlor pastime. They were suffused by a sense of destiny, related to the creation of a better country.

To be sure, writers and thinkers had a hard time of it. But the crucial fact is that they were never frightened or silenced. What they could not say forthrightly they said elliptically, and their audiences understood them perfectly. New ideas from the outer world had free entry: the first translation of Karl Marx's *Das Kapital,* in 1872, was into Russian, fourteen years before it appeared in English, and it was freely available in all bookshops and libraries. Independent monthlies like *Vestnik Yevropy* and *Russkoye Bogatstvo* were outspoken and progressive.

No, the old Russia was no more an intellectual than an economic

* *Soul of Russia,* Sheed & Ward, 1943.

Sahara. The best proof of this, in common sense, is in its towering achievements in letters, the arts, science. These are implicit in names that have transcended the boundaries of Russia to become part of the wealth of civilized mankind — names like Pushkin, Gogol, Turgeniev, Dostoievsky, Tolstoy, Chekhov, Merezhkovsky, Gorki in literature; Tchaikovsky, Glinka, Rimski-Korsakov, Scriabin, Rachmaninoff, Prokofiev in music; Repin in painting; Stanislavsky and Nemirovich-Danchenko in theater; Mendeleyev in chemistry; Metchnikov in medicine; Pavlov in psychology; Struve in astronomy; Bakunin and Kropotkin and yes, Lenin, in social theory. The whole world drew inspiration from Russian literature, the Moscow Art Theater, Russian ballet. A vulgar Soviet boastfulness in recent years, claiming Russian priority for all inventions from the safety pin to radio, has drawn the ridicule it merits. This, however, should not blind us to the truth that many of the claims are justified and that Russia did make vital contributions to science and invention.

A national culture of this order could not have come to fruition in a human vacuum. Its roots are in the genius of the Russian people. That the renaissance could have taken place at all was proof of the psychological freedom which existed side by side with political tyranny and in the final analysis overshadowed that tyranny.

"In my first visit to Russia in 1905," Henry W. Nevison wrote, "I perceived a freedom of social intercourse and general behavior greater and more pleasurable than in our country." Another British observer, Sir Maurice Baring, wrote before the revolution: "There is no country in the world where the individual enjoys so great a measure of personal liberty, where the 'liberté de mœurs' is so great, as in Russia; where the individual man can do as he pleases with so little interference or criticism on the part of his neighbors, where there is so little moral censorship, where liberty of abstract thought or esthetic production is so great. . . ."

We live in a time when nations and people are measured only by political and economic criteria. But these cannot gauge the influence of social liberties, moral tolerance, creative freedoms, which, at least until the rise of the modern total state, often found significant expression even in despotically ruled countries. Russia is the case in point.

If proof were needed that the Russians are a gifted people, it could be discerned in the rapidity with which they assimilated the cultural idioms of Western Europe and refashioned them in their own image. The very fact that the end products were in turn absorbed by the West, becoming an integral part of our civilized heritage, cancels out the exaggerations about Russia's Asiatic and Byzantine qualities. Where are the Asiatic and Byzantine books, poems, symphonies, and scientific discoveries that fit so readily and completely into the Western mind?

3. Serf, Not Slave

The central confusion, in appraising Russia, is the tendency to look upon a historical time lag as if it were a quality in the nature of the people. From the fact of obstructed and retarded development, too many have deduced that the nation is made of different human stuff and incapable of developing. Historical misfortunes, like the long subjection to the Mongols, are mistaken for attributes of the Russian character.

One of the most perceptive students of Russia, Thomas Masaryk, the first president of Czechoslovakia, alluded to this fundamental error when he wrote that "Russia has preserved the childhood of Europe. . . . Russia does not differ essentially from Europe, but Russia is not yet essentially one with Europe."

"There existed a vigorous and independent democratic tradition in the Slavic civilizations of former centuries," Father Edmund A. Walsh writes in *Total Empire*. "Autonomous republics such as Pskov and Novgorod were city-states as jealous and assertive of their freedom as was ever Ghent, Venice, or Florence. The court of Yaroslav at Novgorod saw true popular assemblies of free men, the *Vecha,* determining the character of their political institutions six hundred years before the Mayflower reached Plymouth; its Declaration of Independence was drawn up seven centuries before the Philadelphia masterpiece of Thomas Jefferson, and was much shorter, too: 'If the Prince is bad, into the mud with him.' "

The free Cossacks of Zaparozhie in the southwest had a species of military democracy in the sixteenth and seventeenth centuries. Various communal arrangements in the cultivation of the land effective in those times were decidedly democratic for this period. On the whole the country was keeping pace with, and in many respects was far in advance of, Europe. If it had not been for the Genghis Khan conquest in 1223 and Mongolian domination until 1480 and the political trauma they inflicted, Russian history might well have paralleled that of the rest of Europe.

Serfdom was one of the main effects of the historic backsliding and in turn the chief cause of the long retardation. It was evolved only through the sixteenth and seventeenth centuries, just when Western Europe was throwing off the shackles of feudalism. But it differed from ordinary feudalism in one vital respect: it was never fully accepted by Russian society or the serfs themselves as a fixed and divinely sanctioned institution. Always it was regarded as something *imposed* from above, as a piece of legislation that could be repealed even as it had been promulgated. Though it was to last until 1861, until the day before Abraham Lincoln assumed the Presidency, it was not regarded as a permanent way of life but as a thing to be argued about, rebelled against, tinkered with. In its heart the nation did not acknowledge serfdom as sacrosanct.

Maurice Baring, who knew Russia intimately, could write in 1914: "The peasants never, through nearly two centuries of slavery, lost sight of the fact that this legislation was only a temporary makeshift, a stroke of opportunism. Moreover, they kept hold of the idea that the land was theirs; that the land belonged to the people who tilled it. . . ." * Unlike the French or German serfs, they did not think of themselves as slaves by the law of nature but as captives by the laws of man, and therefore never resigned themselves fully to their status. The Russian historian I. Ignatovich wrote that "Serfdom did not make the peasants timid, submissive

* *The Mainsprings of Russia,* Nelson & Sons, 1914.

slaves. In various ways, beginning with individual cases of disobedience and ending with formidable mass movements, putting
government on its mettle, they protested against serfdom."

A Russian proverb familiar in feudal times ran: "The peasant
owns the land to which he has applied his plough, his scythe, and
his ax." It bespoke a psychological rejection of the institution of
serfdom. Certainly no other feudalism was marked by such continuous resistance. Aside from great uprisings like those of Pugachev
and Stenka Razin, the statistics of localized rebellions must be reckoned in hundreds. Evidences of the mutinous temper abound in
Russian literature and folklore. Runaway serfs were almost an integral part of the system, sanctioned by national opinion if not by
national law; these fugitives even played a pioneering role in opening up frontier areas to colonization. Most important, there was
never a time when strong voices, in the intelligentsia and in the
government itself, were not raised against serfdom. Yet the theory
that the Russian people have no taste for liberty rests primarily
upon the long period of peasant subjection.

The vital truth is that the value of the person was never discounted in Russia as it was in other slave civilizations. The peasant
in bondage might be treated like a chattel but he was never written
off as a different species of animal from his feudal master. Both
were equal in the sight of God. Pushkin, the national poet, Dostoievsky pointed out, "was the first to understand that the Russian
is no slave, in spite of century-old slavery."

A deep respect for the individual, indeed, was the common denom-
inator of Russian moral perceptions, from Saint Sergius of Rado-
nezh to Count Leo Tolstoy. Even when expressed by atheists and
iconoclasts, it was informed by a Christian sense of the importance
of the person.

A consciousness of the travail of what would today be called the
common man, and of his right to personal happiness, was the most
familiar note in Russian thought. "I do not want the happiness
which is bestowed on me," the nineteenth-century critic Vissarion
Belinsky exclaimed, "if I am not previously reassured as to the fate
of my brothers. . . . The destiny of the subject, of the individual,

is more important than the destiny of the whole world." It is generally recognized that this high estimate of people as people was the essence of Tolstoy's genius. There is less general realization that, despite the vast differences between the two men, it was no less basic in Dostoievsky's outlook.

In *The Brothers Karamazov* it is Alyosha who speaks for the author. There is a scene in which Ivan puts a question to his brother Alyosha: Supposing he were engaged in work involving the happiness of all mankind, "but it was essential and inevitable to torture to death only one tiny creature — that baby beating its breast with its fist, for instance." Would he consent to that sacrifice? "No, I wouldn't consent," said Alyosha softly. The fate of an individual, of one helpless child, took precedence over everything else!

The Russian revolutionary movement was with minor exceptions grounded in the primacy of the person. The fact that the exceptions came into the ascendancy with the triumph of Bolshevism does not alter this truth. The late Nicholas Berdiaev often emphasized that even in its most extreme manifestations the Russian revolutionary movement still retained a religious impulse.

The assumption that Bolshevism somehow expresses dominant Russian trends does not bear serious examination. Its contempt for the person, its readiness to torture that innocent baby for the sake of unborn generations, is a reversal and repudiation of age-old Russian attitudes. The distinctive quality of Russian socialist doctrines, as against the juiceless European Marxism, was precisely its preoccupation with the happiness of the individual rather than mechanical revisions of institutions.

The famous utterance of Alexander Radistchev — "My soul is smitten with the suffering of man" — became the motto of the whole agitation for peasant emancipation and political reform. That bearded giant Michael Bakunin, who prophetically denounced Marxism as a path to slavery, was certainly less European, closer to the essential Russia, than either the Bolshevik or Menshevik leaders. The same may be said of the agrarian mutualism of Kropotkin. Alexander Herzen, an *émigré* well versed in European socialist thought a century ago, advocated a specifically Russian brand of socialism, based on the *mir,* or peasant commune.

A remarkably democratic institution of ancient Russian origin, this *mir* in its political aspects had a good deal in common with the New England town meeting. Its vitality is indicated by the fact that it persisted to a large extent even during serfdom. The heads of all peasant households in a village voted and argued as equals in deciding common problems and in settling disputes.

On the economic side the *mir* was a collective enterprise; but in contrast with the socialized society projected by Marx and his followers, it was highly personalized, voluntary, and respectful of individual preferences. Its members enjoyed the right, usually by a two-thirds vote, of disbanding in favor of other types of land cultivation. It was precisely this voluntary element which attracted Herzen and led him to reject conventional socialist doctrine. It is significant that the Social Revolutionary Party, whose socialism was agrarian and geared to the personalism of the *mir,* was numerically Russia's largest.

"The law has allowed the *mir* a considerable amount of self-government," Stepniak wrote in 1888 in his celebrated book *The Russian Peasantry.* "The *mir* forms a microcosm, a small world of its own. With the Russian *mir* the law is nowhere, the conscience everywhere. . . . It is the personification of the living law speaking through the collective voice of the country."

And the eminent British journalist, William T. Stead, that same year gave it as his view, in *The Truth About Russia,* that: "The life of Russia is not in the Senate, in the country house or the barracks. The life of Russia is in the peasants' hut. . . . The first thing that strikes an Englishman is the absolutely republican, democratic character of the government of the Russian villages (*mir*) . . . Every member of the Russian village seems to regard it as his natural right as a member of the *mir* to exercise all the prerogatives of legislation and sovereignty."

An American student of that country, William English Walling, writing in 1908, declared in *Russia's Message:*

"The history of the Russian peasantry has been that of an unending series of revolts. . . . The peasant is a democrat in everything, and a socialist in regard to the land: he is almost without race prejudice and he is liberal and even independent in his religious views. . . . The hundred thousand villages where the mass of the Russian people live are in their spiritual affairs so many little immemorial republics. At the present moment, as at the earliest dawn of history, they are ruled by a pure spirit of democracy not only in political but in economic affairs. . . . "

No doubt these men, though speaking of what they had seen with their own eyes, overstated the case. It was then the liberal fashion to idealize the Russian peasant and his *mir*. After all discounts are made, however, what remains is still far removed from the society of meek slaves which is the premise of most present-day judgment of Russia before and after the revolution. It is hard to find in the *mir* the roots of the *kolkhoz* and other Soviet institutions.

The glib statement that communism is a peculiarly Russian visitation rests, in the final analysis, simply on the accident that it first came to power in Russia. These postwar years have demonstrated with tragic certainty that the affliction can be imposed no less successfully on Poles and Czechs, on Germans and Chinese. It is quite unlikely that in a free vote, given a real choice among various political parties, the Russian peoples would give the communists as large a share of the total ballots as the peoples of Italy and France regularly give them. Can we forget how the blood-purge trials, with their rites of abject confession, were reported as uniquely Russian? How reporters invoked Dostoievsky and alleged practices of the Orthodox Church confessional to explain it all? Since then, alas, we have witnessed the same sort of trials, complete with self-accusation and confession, in Eastern and Central Europe — with Americans on occasion in the role of confessors.

A stronger case, indeed, can be made out for the claim that Soviet communism is a negation of things primordially Russian. Bolshevism, Helen Iswolsky summed up in her brilliant little book, "is an *imported* teaching based on Western materialism.

Lenin did not seek to realize Russia's spiritual mission of love and brotherhood. He brought to Russia the system created by the German socialist Marx, who in turn had been influenced by the German philosopher Hegel and by the German atheist school of thought. In the practical sphere, Lenin had yet another teacher. As he himself admits in his writing, he applied in his revolutionary action the methods of the Prussian General von Clausewitz, the inventor of total war."

"Militant communism," she continued, "was not inspired by that desire for collective solidarity, that *sobornost,* realized by the Russian masses in the *mir* and in the church. It was formulated, as the Bolshevist theorists clearly state, according to the principles of class hatred with the resulting class conflict. Nowhere in Russian cultural and spiritual history do we find an ideology informed by hatred." *

There is a superficial resemblance, of course, between the methods of the communists and czarist practices. But the same family resemblance holds true for all oppressive political systems. Bolshevism might just as convincingly be treated as deriving from Prussian autocracy or the ancient Pharaohs. The Nazi and Fascist dictatorships and a number of existing dictatorships are close enough to the Bolshevik pattern without benefit of the czarist background. There are endless derivative forms and details common to the Soviet and the pre-1917 government, as there were in Mussolini's regime and that of the Borgias. But in its whole, as a philosophy of life and governance, Bolshevism is a new and modern phenomenon. Not only is it not peculiarly Russian but its whole spirit is peculiarly unRussian and at points anti-Russian. There were a few Russians, like Nechayev, who propounded amoral ideas of the kind that the Bolsheviks practice, but there have been any number of non-Russians of the same mentality, and not necessarily typical for their race or nation. The Machiavellianism of the Kremlin is no more Russian than the Nechayevism of the Hitler regime was Italian.

Reducing millenniums of national history to formulas is a futile business, even if I had the erudition to undertake it. Without being

* *Soul of Russia,* Sheed & Ward, 1943.

dogmatic about it, therefore, I venture to suggest that Russian communism is not a continuation of the past but a tragic break with
that past. The dominant Russian obsessions were clearly with the
private conscience or soul, with the happiness and self-respect of
the individual — in short, they were humanitarian, personalized,
compassionate. They have been renounced and insulted by the Bolshevik usurpers. Perhaps it would be more just to say that the
present regime represents a reaction against Russia rather than a
confirmation of the Russian genius.

4. Duma and Zemstvo

Those who seek alibis for the Kremlin rummage through all of
Russian history, and pick up what they need from Ivan the Terrible, Peter the Great, and Nicholas I. Why do they normally slur
over the decades immediately preceding the revolution? The answer, I think, is that it is simply easier to trace alleged continuity
between the reign of Ivan or Peter and the reign of Lenin and
Stalin than between the thirty years before and the thirty years
after the Bolshevik seizure of power. The pre-1917 generation saw
an enormous amount of political and social progress, which the
communists, far from continuing, reversed and destroyed.

Common sense tells us that the abortive revolution of 1905 is
a better index to Russian aspirations here and now than, let us say,
the crimes of Ivan the Terrible. The 1905 uprising began with a
general strike, mutinies of sailors, seizures of big estates by land-
hungry peasants. It was definitely a revolution from below, ex-
pressive of the whole nation. The modern constitution and the
pledges of reform granted by the frightened dynasty were in direct
response to pressures from the people, in line with popular demands.

The constitution was whittled away and the pledges were in
large measure repudiated in the later reaction. Had the promises
exacted been kept, the people would have enjoyed political liberty
and full rights of citizenship not too far removed from those under
other constitutional monarchies. And despite the reaction, the

twelve years between the two revolutions provided a substantial base for peaceful democratic evolution.

Though the electoral and franchise laws were stacked in favor of the upper and owning classes, the democratic and revolutionary parties in the aggregate won an overwhelming majority of the Duma seats. The powers of the Duma were continually restricted, but it was by no means wholly impotent. It retained enough control of the country's purse strings to obtain concessions from the government and on occasion to force out unpopular ministers. The Duma was a great forum. Its debates — amazingly vigorous and courageous, not merely critical of the *status quo* but often boldly revolutionary — were published in the leading newspapers. Lenin in Switzerland wrote speeches delivered by his Bolshevik deputies. In the course of the budget debate in 1913, the liberal deputy Alexandrov had no hesitancy in speaking words like these:

"Gentlemen, it is said that each nation deserves the government it has. I don't believe this and consider it a prejudice, a historic falsehood. I think, gentlemen of the State Duma, that the Russian people, the great Russian people, are superior to their government. The present government is not worthy of its people."

The press reported that these remarks drew "prolonged applause on the Left and some parts of the Left Center; cheers." The immunity of the legislators was not violated.

The press, to be sure, was not free in the British and American sense. But all the liberal groupings had legal papers and periodicals of their own, and even the most extreme factions and parties managed to express their views in print. While most liberal papers flourished, few of their reactionary competitors could subsist without government subsidies. A number of satiric journals needled the authorities mercilessly. A Menshevik monthly, *Nasha Zarya,* was published from 1910 till the outbreak of war. Several Bolshevik monthlies were in existence, and in 1912 — called "the high point of the darkest reaction" — a Bolshevik daily, *Pravda,* was established in St. Petersburg, edited by Molotov.

By the time 1917 rolled around, the Russian people had behind them a tradition of a hundred years of revolutionary thought and

action. At the turn of the twentieth century Russian protestant politics were predominantly left, with the Social Revolutionaries and
the Social Democrats in the lead, and committed not only to far-
reaching social change but to overthrow of the monarchy. There
was an increasingly powerful trade-union movement, vigorous
peasant organizations and student societies, legal and otherwise.

Agriculture was still burdened by remnants of feudal practices.
All the same, by 1916 small holdings of 135 acres or less comprised
71 per cent of the cultivated area; excluding forest holdings, this
percentage rises to over 80. Individual peasants owned 82 per cent
of all cattle and 86 per cent of all horses. "The peasant," Baring
wrote, "not only tills the arable land but he owns the greater part
of it. . . . Scientific agriculture is being widely taught at the present
moment in Russia. Agricultural colleges are spreading, and the
number of agricultural students is every day increasing." *

In one respect at least Russian agriculture led the rest of the
world, namely agricultural co-operatives of every type. In the last
years of the Romanoff era, some ten million peasants belonged to
co-operative credit associations, and there were over twenty thousand consumer co-operatives with over six million members —
more than in Great Britain, Germany, France, Italy, Switzerland,
and Denmark combined. A Carnegie Foundation report published
in 1929 declared:

"No other country possessed co-operative organizations as broad
in scope and affecting the interests of so many classes of the population. Conceived for the benefit and welfare of the great masses,
it possessed all the force of a new and original democratic ideal,
breadth of organization, business ability and social vision."

This instinct for common action, from the emancipation in 1861
to the advent of Lenin, does not jibe with the tall tale of a peasantry resisting Soviet collectivization because of some intrinsic "sel-
fishness." It opposed collectivization and continues to abhor the
kolkhoz — not because it is a co-operative enterprise but because
it is just state peonage garnished with cynical co-operative verbiage.
The deadly hostility of the Russian peasant is directed against the

* The Mainsprings of Russia.

loss of economic freedom, which to him resides in true ownership of land, whether individually or in voluntary communities of equals.

Speaking at a conference of the Central Executive Committee in June, 1928, Stalin said: "We have no colonies; credit or loans they [the capitalist world] do not give us; consequently our basis must be taxing the peasantry." He regarded the tillers of the soil, in other words, as a sort of internal colony to be exploited to the limit; when taxation amounting to confiscation failed to work, the scheme of collectivization was hatched. There we have the heart of the conflict between the peasantry and the Kremlin, rather than in some native peasant incapacity for mutual action in freedom.

A political institution that served as a school in self-rule was the zemstvo, or local and provincial administration, brought into being in 1864. The temptation is to exaggerate its democratic character, so many writers have done so before me. Elected by the taxpaying population, the zemstvos were on the whole controlled by the gentry. But they became increasingly imbued with a liberal and progressive spirit, to the point where the central authorities came to look upon them as hotbeds of subversion. The leadership fell largely to the more socially minded and liberal landowners and intellectuals, who brought a real Russian zeal to the promotion of local medical aid, road building, home crafts, mutual life and fire insurance — and above all the education of the masses. Half a century of zemstvo effort produced notable results not alone in material improvements but in fostering impulses to self-government and mutual help.

5 Justice under the Double Eagle

Now let us consider briefly the administration of justice in the old Russia. This is of critical importance, against the backdrop of purges and slave camps which are the hallmarks of the Soviet state.

Siberia became the lurid symbol of the cruelties of the old regime. It is not my intention to "debunk" that symbol. Those who today justify czarist political terror by reference to Red Terror are in no better moral position (except as to degree) than Kremlin apologists who excuse Red outrages by invoking outrages in the past. Realism demands, however, that two vital truths be underlined.

One: With the reforms of 1864 Russia acquired a judicial system superior to most in the West — except with regard to political crimes. It had trial by jury and a bar remarkable for its elevated moral and intellectual standards. Judges were appointed for life and thereupon became independent, subject neither to removal nor transfer to other places against their will.

So far as ordinary crimes are concerned, Russia was governed by codified laws which not even the most headstrong of the last czars dared violate. Punishments were humane even by modern reform standards. The death penalty had been abolished as early as 1741 for all crimes except murder or attempted murder of the imperial family. It was extended to cover all political assassination only after the rise of the terrorists and the actual murder of Alexander II.

Two: The handling of political crimes, while unfair by the standards set in Russia's own practice in ordinary offenses, was incomparably more just than under the Soviets. Indeed, there is really no basis for comparison, the contrast is so great. There were no juries in such cases, but only a panel of judges. Jury trials for "politicals" were abolished, it is worth noting, because the juries had proved remarkably lenient to enemies of the monarchy.

But even political trials were open and reported accurately in the press. Evidence was meticulously examined by men who took their judicial robes very seriously. The most successful and respected lawyers did not hesitate to defend the accused, from political assassins down; many of them, in point of fact, built national reputations and popularity upon spirited defense of revolutionists. Far from confessing to lies in the Soviet manner of the future, the accused proudly confessed to the truth (if they were guilty) and turned the courtrooms into forums to arouse the masses. Under the guise of defense arguments, the lawyers unbosomed themselves of eloquent indictments of the government and social evils — propaganda that appeared in the press as privileged matter and often was circulated in huge editions in pamphlet form.

Not one of the moral obscenities of judicial practice under the Soviets — torture, the hostage system, the mock public trial, the star-chamber trial — can be equated with specifically Russian practices. Some of these methods, as a matter of fact, were common in West European states long after their eradication in Russia. In 1802, when torture to extract evidence was legal procedure in some parts of Europe, Czar Alexander I, in the course of a ukase prohibiting the evil, decreed that "the very word 'torture,' which confers shame and disgrace upon humanity, be forever effaced from the memory of the people." Under the laws of 1864, prosecutors not only had the right to stop a prosecution if they became convinced of the defendant's innocence, it was their duty to do so. Far from sharing the guilt of the accused as in Soviet practice, relatives could not be compelled to testify, and if they chose to give evidence did so without oath, to permit them greater leeway.

In extent the political persecution was not small — it only seems strangely small today because we have become unhappily accustomed to counting political victims in millions. The shock of surprise, as one examines the old Russian statistics, is therefore a measure of the present terror rather than a proof of past benevolence. The decade of 1906–1916 was sufficiently blood-soaked for its time.

According to figures provided by Andrei Vishinsky, who would not be likely to underestimate knowingly, there were in 1913 only 32,000 convicts at hard labor, including ordinary criminals. This was at the peak of the prewar reaction. About 25,000 were exiled to Siberia in the first ten years of this century, and 27,000 more between 1911 and 1914.

In the 1880's George Kennan (great-uncle of his namesake, our former ambassador to Moscow) made his historic investigation of the Siberian exile system. Not only was he permitted to do so but St. Petersburg gave him full co-operation. He returned to America to condemn what he had seen, in writing and speeches, with unflagging passion. Yet he acknowledged that "the number of political offenders is much smaller than it is generally supposed to be." He estimated the yearly score of political exile between 1879 and and 1884 at 150. The totals increased rapidly after the turn of the century and in particular in the aftermath of the 1905 uprising.

The most extreme estimates came from Prince Peter Kropotkin, in his effort to awaken the conscience of mankind. He gave the number of inmates of all Russian prisons at the time he was writing, 1909, as 181,000 and the number of exiles as 74,000, plus some 30,000 more then believed in process of transportation. The totals covered offenders of all categories, with ordinary criminals constituting a majority of convicts and "politicals" a majority of exiles. Considering that the Throne and established society were being seriously threatened, even the Kropotkin statistics now seem unimpressive.

In the entire reign of Alexander II, from 1855 to 1881, there was only one execution. A man named Karakosov was hanged for an attempt on the czar's life. In the following twenty-seven years, which saw the emergence of assassination and the bomb as political weapons, 114 were put to death: an average of about four a year. Not until 1906 did the annual toll of the hangman begin to run into hundreds, with a record 1139 in the first postrevolutionary year of 1907. It then fell off to 73 in 1911 and 126 in 1912. A few hundred more should probably be added for prisoners killed while "trying to escape" and not reckoned in the formal statistics.

These are the hard figures behind the impassioned protests the world over, Russia included. This was the notorious Russian White Terror which made the world shudder, and led Count Tolstoy to publish his famous *I Cannot Be Silent*. It is no slur on the noble emotions of the time to remark that the whole White Terror did not equal in sheer volume a month of the Red Terror.

The treatment of political prisoners, of course, was mild, almost idyllic, as against their fate under communism. Though vindictively punished by the regime, such offenders were universally respected. They were rarely placed together with criminals and enjoyed a great many privileges which made existence tolerable, both in prison and exile. For many a Russian, exile was a time of intensive reading, writing, and even revolutionary agitation. It was in Siberia that Lenin wrote his book *The Development of Capitalism in Russia*, one of a libraryful of revolutionary tracts composed by many others in the enforced isolation and leisure.

The exiles were usually joined by their families and lived a relatively normal life despite the harsh surroundings. They were in constant correspondence with their friends and political comrades in Russia and abroad. Those who had money or received help from outside — and committess for the succor of political prisoners collected money throughout the liberal world — often went in for hunting, fishing, and other sports. Lenin, Trotsky, and Stalin were among the ardent huntsmen in their exile years.

Reading the memoirs of exiles is today an interesting experience, against the awareness of Soviet concentration-camp purgatories. Nadezhda Krupskaya, recounting her own and Lenin's routine in Siberia, might be talking of a middle-class winter vacation. One of her letters to a relative does have a tragic note: the maid has just walked out on her, Mrs. Lenin reports, and she has been obliged to do her own housework; but she expected to hire another in a few days. One is struck by the intense intellectual life the exiles led, and by the ease with which they returned to civilization when the spirit moved them.

No stigma attached to political punishment. The victim even acquired a certain social glamor — he was a warrior for freedom who wore his service stripes proudly. Partisans of the monarchy not infrequently expressed admiration for the "political" and salved their conscience by helping him. The police agent and the informer, by contrast, were despised pariahs; no self-respecting Russian, regardless of his political sentiments, cared to shake hands with an informer.

As for the common people, they never confounded political prisoners with criminals and, if anything, held them in special esteem. Russians avoided words like "convict" or "exile" in talking of political offenders, referring to them as "unfortunates" or even, among the educated, as "passion-bearers" — a term earlier applied to religious mystics who withdrew from the workaday world.

Along the Siberian roads used by exile convoys and escaping prisoners, the peasants often put milk, kvass and bread on their window sills for "unfortunates" who might be running away.

"Among the Russian revolutionists," Kennan wrote, "I met some
of the best, the bravest, and most generous types of manhood and
womanhood that I have ever known. I am linked to them by the
ties of sympathy, humanity, or friendship, but I wish that I were
bound to them by the tie of kindred blood."

Those who *were* tied to them by blood felt for the most part
as the American did. The political fugitive from prison or the
police readily found helping hands, food, hiding places. Though
they may not have thought of it in such literary terms, the Russians by and large considered him a champion of the people. There
were no official efforts, as today, to smear opponents of the established order as "wreckers," "enemies of the people," and "mad
dogs." Both the official and the popular attitudes scarcely fit into
the picture of a benighted land inhabited by savages who craved
the whip of Asiatic despotism — the slanderous picture exhibited
by nearly all foreign champions of the Kremlin.

A more generous appraisal, and closer to the truth, though not
the whole truth, was given by President Woodrow Wilson on
April 2, 1917, about three weeks after the overthrow of the Romanoff dynasty:

"Russia was known by those who knew it best to have been
always in fact democratic at heart, in all the vital habits of her
thought, in all the intimate relationships of her people that spoke
their natural instincts, their habitual attitudes towards life. The
autocracy that crowned the summit of her political structure, long
as it stood and terrible as was the reality of its power, was not
in fact Russian in origin, character, or purpose. . . . The great
generous Russian people have been added in all their native maj-
esty and might to the forces that are fighting in the world, for
justice and for peace. Here is a fit partner for a League of Honor."

Before the end of that year that vision of Woodrow Wilson had
dimmed, but his judgment is still valid.

And thereafter, let it be remembered in simple justice, the most eloquent and persistent protests against the horrors that ensued came not from Western democrats but from Russians, both inside the country and in the dispersion of the emigration. By and large the West either watched the Soviet depredations with equanimity or cheered them with insane enthusiasm. Only the Russians themselves continued to inveigh against the whole wicked system without pause, and to warn tirelessly against its menace to all mankind. This assuredly would not have been the case if Bolshevism were deeply Russian and congenial to the spirit of its people.

From his prison cell, in 1918, Patriarch Tikhon, having excommunicated all communists, issued a proclamation excoriating the new rulers in words of fire:

"It is not enough that you have stained the hands of the Russian people with the blood of their brethren. You have instigated the people to open, shameless robbery. You have befogged their conscience and stilled their concept of sin. But, under whatever name you may disguise an evil deed, murder, violence, and plunder will always remain crimes and deeds of evil clamoring to Heaven for vengeance. Yes, we are living through a dreadful time under your domination, and it will be long before it fades from the hearts of the people, where it has dimmed the image of God, and impressed that of the Beast."

There, rather than in anything that has been said by Lenin, Trotsky, Stalin, or Malenkov, is the authentic voice of Russia, true not only to the essence of its past — but of its future no less.

V. Triumph of Counterrevolution

1. Armed Insurrection

An important ingredient in the fictitious version of Soviet history put over on a gullible world, as already indicated, is the claim that what transpired in the night of November 6–7, 1917, was a great people's revolution. The "proletariat," yearning for communism, supposedly rose in majestic might and drove the bourgeois money-changers out of its temples.

This has been so long and so often repeated that the average mortal may be forgiven for swallowing the nonsense. But there is little excuse for men who pretend to be moderately well informed. The truth is a matter of record, even of contemporary Bolshevik record. Scores of books setting forth the unadorned facts are in the libraries. Many of the key actors in the tragedy are still alive outside the USSR.

A more accurate understanding of what actually happened is indispensable — to strip the Leninist clique of its revolutionary glamor and, more important at the present time, to absolve the Russian people of blood guilt.

The Bolsheviks were the smallest of the Russian radical groups, not so much a party as the nucleus of a party, mostly head without body. Launched at the turn of the century, they claimed twenty-five thousand members when the Romanoff society caved in, but probably had about fifteen thousand. In the Putilov factory in Petrograd, a stronghold of radicalism, employing some thirty thousand men and women, there were only thirty Bolsheviks.

But they represented a movement which scoffed at numbers and frankly despised the multitudes. Lenin always sneered at the obsession of competing radical organizations with their "mass base." When conditions were ripe, he would rely upon "uprising as an art" to take over. "Give us an organization of revolutionaries," he used to say, "and we will turn Russia upside down."

In his view revolution was not a popular surge in the romantic tradition. It was a *Putsch* by a small, disciplined elite, unencumbered by democratic or sentimental scruples. The job, as Leninists saw it, was not for word-logged amateurs. It was for ruthless professional rebels working in "rigorous secrecy," prepared "to use any ruse, cunning, unlawful method, evasion, concealment of truth." They certainly lived up to this formula in full measure.

For Bolsheviks the masses were so much raw stuff for processing. The people as such had no inherent rights, least of all the right to choose between alternative social systems. Their hopes, greeds, and angers were motive power to be channeled in the way an engineer channels electric power.

"Only scoundrels and imbeciles," Lenin would explain in 1919, "can think that the proletariat must first win a majority in elections conducted under the bourgeois yoke. . . ." When the advanced portion (meaning those who obeyed him) had sufficient "striking forces" it must "conquer the power of the state, and then use the power of the state, that is, the dictatorship of the proletariat, as an instrument of its class in order *to gain the sympathy of the majority of the toilers.*" *

Lenin thus did not bother to pretend that he already had the sympathy of "the toilers" when he conquered power. First you hijack control, then you make them like it: except for the revolutionary jargon, it was the strong-arm code of gangsterdom. The Bolsheviks had left it to others to "go to the people," to lead strikes, to stir up the sluggish peasant, and finally to overthrow the old regime. Meanwhile Lenin perfected his conspiratorial organization to exploit the upheaval he saw coming.

The Bolshevik seizure of power in Petrograd was accomplished,

* *Collected Works,* XVI, 336.

in Lenin's words, by "an amazingly small number," enjoying no mandate except the theory that no mandates were necessary. The actual forces involved were about twenty thousand soldiers, sailors and workers' Red Guards; this in a city of over a million. Even these minor contingents of armed men were pathetically duped, having not the remotest notion of the real purposes for which they were being manipulated. In their own minds they were certain that they were striking out for freedom, equality, justice, and other goals which their puppet masters regarded as emotional garbage.

The supposed upsurge of sentiment for "proletarian dictatorship" and communism is a subsequent invention. In the crucial months of 1917 the Bolsheviks mentioned such notions publicly only to deny them in wrath. Lenin's real objectives were carefully concealed from the Red Guards who dispersed the helpless Provisional Government under Alexander Kerensky, from the left wing of the Social Revolutionaries who supported the coup, and even from the rank-and-file Bolsheviks. He angrily denied that his communists had any communist intentions.

The historic tide that had toppled over the throne was running wild. All the rotted dams of law and social accommodation were smashed. The more moderate socialist and democratic elements sought to curb the flood. Only Lenin and some of his associates — not all by any means — chose to ride the tide.

The nation was hungry, divided, leaderless, racked by epidemics and brigandage. Production was all but paralyzed. War-weary troops were deserting the front and spreading like lava over the country. Peasants were seizing and dividing the coveted land. Workers in some places were grabbing control of factories and mines. The hungry were breaking into larders, wine cellars and warehouses. Along came the Bolsheviks — of whom the masses had scarcely heard — and urged them to do what they were already doing in any case.

Everybody promised peace and land. But the moderates promised it for tomorrow, when an elected parliament would lay down the rules. The Leninists cynically outbid them. "Take what you want," they shouted; "take it now, including peace." No hint was dropped of the price that would be exacted for those permissions once the flood was tamed and its energies harnessed.

The Bolshevik membership swelled to several hundred thousand in eight months. Few of the new adherents had any inkling of the implications of communism, world revolution, and the rest. Such things were for the insiders, the elite, not the ragged rabble. For them a slogan: "Bread and peace!" — neither of which they would receive for years to come — that and outlets for angry incoherent impulses.

The death knell of czarism had caught the Bolshevik leaders by surprise, unprepared, bewildered. On the day the dynasty collapsed, Lenin and Zinoviev learned of it from the newspapers in Switzerland, Trotsky and Bukharin from the newspapers in New York. Stalin was among the lesser figures scattered in exile colonies within Russia.

Lenin and a batch of his disciples reached Petrograd on April 16, 1917, having crossed Germany in a sealed train by arrangement with the Kaiser's government: a calculated injection of poison into the Russian blood stream. Trotsky arrived a month later. Others straggled in from remote corners of the Russian empire.

Beyond a determination to capture supreme authority by hook or crook and a Machiavellian code of conduct, they had no plan. The focused will of Lenin was plan enough. Into the confusions of the period he brought his clear head, his passionate sense of destiny, and his genius for exploiting the weaknesses of opponents and of the masses. For their doubts, their inclination to compromise with larger groups, he excoriated his followers as dolts and cowards. He drove them willy-nilly to undertake a *Putsch* which most of them denounced until the last hour, and many even after its initial successes, as a mad adventure.

Among top leaders, Trotsky was one of the few who supported Lenin's insurrectionary scheme without reservations. As for Stalin, in the words of a participant in those events, he seemed a "gray spot which flickered and left no trace." Grayness was the wily Georgian's shield as he hovered in the background, ready to lead the adventure or turn against it, depending on how it all worked out.

The soviet — the council of workers', peasants', and soldiers' deputies — was not a Bolshevik creation. It had been developed in the revolution of 1905 and arose again spontaneously in 1917. With the more moderate and democratic groups concentrating on the Provisional Government, the Soviets tended to attract the more impatient and demagogic spokesmen. The Leninists easily infiltrated the Petrograd and Moscow Soviets until they had a majority; in most provincial Soviets they were minorities. Thus the Bolsheviks obtained a potent instrument, which Lenin used in the way that countless communist "fronts" were destined to be used all over the world.

In raising the cry of "All Power to the Soviets!" the Bolsheviks gave it a populist and even democratic ring. Their propaganda gave no indication of the one-party monopoly to come. On the contrary, it was baited with democratic pledges, couched in the vocabulary of freedom. Specifically, they denied as foul bourgeois lies the charge that they intended to impose communism on the country. In the preparatory months Lenin repeatedly warned against "totalitarian power," "a standing army set apart from the people," and the rest of the things he was determined to inflict on Russia. As Father Edmund A. Walsh has written: "What was promised to the Russian people should do credit to Thomas Jefferson and the framers of the Magna Charta."

"We uphold the principle of election," Lenin proclaimed, "the right to recall any official any time. . . . The idea that it is necessary to direct the state through officials appointed from above is basically false, undemocratic, Caesaristic, or is in the nature of a Blanquist adventure. . . . In a free country the people is governed by those who are elected for the purpose."

This was the burden of Bolshevik talk in the months before their coup and for a brief spell after — until their grip on the nation was secured. As for something called communism, Lenin laughed and fumed at enemies who said he planned to destroy the fundamental system of private ownership. To what lengths those bourgeois gentry go in maligning the tribunes of the people!

In the weeks when he was working out the details of the "armed insurrection" (*that*, not "revolution," was what he called it in missives to associates), Lenin declared: "The vital matter is not the expropriation of capitalist property. We shall readily substitute for expropriation the collection of just taxes." His party, he said, had no intention "to deprive the business-owner of a single penny of his money. It is necessary to lay great stress on this fact. . . ." It was indeed: the peasantry, 85 per cent of the population, would have been frightened out of its wits by any portent of nationalization.

The point is not simply that the Bolsheviks were lying; that would hardly be worth space at this late date. The point is that the Bolsheviks *had* to lie, and that the content of their lies was dictated by a realistic awareness of what the people wanted and did not want.

They knew that the population, the working people included, had no desire for expropriation or communism, for proletarian terror or world revolution. What it did crave was inventoried by Lenin himself in the promises he made. They are spelled out in every issue of the *Pravda* of those months, under the editorship of Molotov and Stalin: promises of freedom, civil liberties, the secret ballot, a Constituent Assembly, even-handed justice, the right to strike, the right to secede from the union; above all, immediate peace.

Knowing as we do today the bottomless contempt of the Lenin crowd for such rights and freedoms, it should be clear that they offered them only because it represented their shrewd estimate of the basic popular aspirations. There we have a sufficient answer to those who prate of a special Russian relish for the swaddlings of absolutism.

2. Rule-or-Ruin Strategy

The very idea of a Russian proletariat, in whose name the new despotism was soon to be proclaimed, was in the main a piece of duplicity. The proletarians were so few as to be negligible. Four years later, on December 25, 1921, when he could tell the truth with impunity, Lenin would taunt his followers in this connection:

"Comrades say that they are the representatives of the Communist Party, of the trade unions, of the proletariat. We beg your pardon on that score. What is a proletariat? It is a class which is occupied in big industry. But where is your industry? What sort of proletariat is it? The industrial proletariat . . . has been dislocated, has ceased to exist as a proletariat. . . the proletariat vanished."

In short, the dictatorship of a class which was negligible when it supposedly assumed total sovereignty, and was nonexistent a few years after the assumption!

Nearly all his close associates were terrified by the wildness of Lenin's bluffs, though for the most part they obeyed his orders. They knew that his trumped-up government represented nothing and nobody and were terrified by the chaotic forces around them. That was why they urged the enlistment of partners in the enterprise, pleading with their leader to invite other socialist parties, at least, to form a coalition. On the morrow of the seizure of power Lenin allowed negotiations to be started, but only as another tactic of deception: "a diplomatic move to divert attention from military operations," as recorded in the secret minutes.

Soon after the successful *Putsch,* five members of Lenin's Central Committee resigned in protest against his high-handed policies. Among them were Gregory Zinoviev, who was to reign for years over the Communist International, and Alexei Rykov, who in 1924 would succeed Lenin as premier — both of them were fated to be murdered by Stalin in 1936–1937. In deserting their brand-new regime, these men declared:

"We cannot accept responsibility for the disastrous policy of the Central Committee, carried out against the will of an enormous majority of the proletariat and soldiers, who are eager to see the rapid end of the bloodshed between the different political parties of the democracy. . . . We cannot calmly look on while the policy of the chiefs of the Central Committee leads towards the loss of the fruits of victory and the crushing of the proletariat."

Out of their own mouths we thus have the admission that the Leninist setup was not an expression of popular will but a rule-or-ruin defiance of the people. All five, and others who resigned, were soon back in the fold, but their warnings remained true and prophetic.

In pulling off the insurrection, the Leninist party at first kept itself carefully in the background. It let its false front, the Petrograd Soviet, hold the foreground, through a Military Revolutionary Committee briefly headed at the outset not by a Bolshevik, but by a Social Revolutionary stooge, one Lazimir.

The Leninists, in fact, claimed that they were not revolting at all, but acting in the nick of time to head off a revolt by others! The trick, according to Lenin, was "to lay not only the blame but also the initiative at the door of the adversary." So he invented and advertised an imaginary plot to restore the monarchy through a military coup. As the night of the *Putsch* came nearer, the Bolshevik howls about the nefarious plotters grew louder. This maneuver too — ascribing to the victim what you are about to do to him — was to become familiar to mankind, in such episodes as Stalin's invasion of Finland to block an imaginary Finnish invasion of Soviet Russia.

A more obscene record of complex deceit can hardly be found in all the annals of demagogy. The Hitler Nazis, when their day came, were paragons of candor by contrast. They did not need to beguile the German people with visions of freedom, justice, and electoral mandates, and they acted in their own name on the basis of their own program. The Bolshevik lies and disguises, if rightly comprehended, amount to a compliment to the Russian people.

The executive committee of the All-Russian Council of peasant delegates reacted to the Leninist coup with a passionate manifesto. "The Revolution is perishing!" it began, then went on to say: "Innumerable are the disasters which this outbreak spells for Russia, formidable is the crime against the people and the Revolution on the part of those who have started the uprising and sown discord in the country." The Bolsheviks, it charged, were "starting a civil war and usurping power, at the very moment when the Provisional Government, obeying the will of the peasants, was completing the draft of the law regarding the transfer of all land to the land committees, and at a time when only three weeks remained before the convocation of the Constituent Assembly, the only authorized ruling body of Russia."

When the extent of the deception became apparent, soon after the seizure of power, some of the staunchest Bolsheviks and fellow travelers — Krassin, Vorovsky, Kamenev, Maxim Gorki — assailed Lenin as a mad gambler hell-bent for disaster. They did not disturb his monumental calm. The gifted novelist of the working class, Gorki, wrote in *Novaya Zhizn,* his own newspaper, two weeks after the Bolshevik usurpation:

Blind fanatics and unscrupulous adventurers are rushing headlong toward "social revolution" — as a matter of fact it is the road to anarchy and ruin of the proletariat and the revolution. Along this road Lenin and his aides think it is possible to commit all crimes, such as the bloody fight in Petrograd, the devastation of Moscow, the annulment of freedom of speech, the senseless arrests. . . .

The working class must not allow adventurers and madmen to thrust upon the proletariat the responsibility for the disgraceful, senseless and bloody crimes for which not Lenin but the proletariat will have to account.

Day after day Gorki protested against the unfolding terror, begged his Bolshevik friends to come to their senses, reminded them of their promises. He wrote better than he knew. His ultimate capitulation to the "adventurers and madmen" did not cancel out the wisdom of his earlier insights. Not just the proletariat but all of Russia, especially the lowly plain folk who inhabit Gorki's masterpieces, paid — and are still paying — in blood, suffering, and monstrous spiritual humiliations for a regime not of their making.

But the impassioned warnings and protests by men like Gorki, men who were wholeheartedly on the side of "the revolution," were soon squelched, with the suppresion of all but the government newspapers and the arrest of the most articulate champions of decency.

The Bolsheviks did not, as careless historians and journalists are in the habit of saying, "free Russia." On the contrary, it was a revolutionary Russia that freed the Bolsheviks from their exiles, their prison cells, their underground lairs, enabling them to choke the revolution. Their *Putsch* was not an extension of the dominant revolutionary trends and traditions of the preceding century but a reversal and rejection of the main revolutionary motifs. They did not free, but rather enslaved, the young Russia, which Lenin himself had called "the freest country in the world."

3. Lenin Spits on Russia

The hopes of self-government unleashed by the fall of czarism were centered on a Constituent Assembly, a democratic parliament. Its first task would be to draw up a democratic constitution embodying a bill of rights.

Lenin and his followers, of course, jumped on that band wagon too, noisily, raucously, outshouting and outbidding everyone else. They posed not merely as advocates of the parliament but as its only true friends. Endlessly the Petrograd *Pravda,* their mouthpiece, pounded the slogan, "Long live the Constituent Assembly, the Master of the Russian Land!" They accused the other parties of delaying the elections, while doing their utmost to compound the chaos that was causing the delays. Of the four master slogans launched by the captive Petrograd Soviet, the last read: "An honest and prompt convocation of the Constituent Assembly."

What if the voting went against them? The Bolsheviks piously pledged themselves to abide by the popular verdict.

"As a democratic government," *Pravda* asserted on the morrow of Lenin's *Putsch,* "we cannot disregard the decision of the people, even if we do not agree with it. If the peasants follow the Social Revolutionaries farther, even if they give that party a majority in the Constituent Assembly, we shall say: So be it."

In the first weeks Lenin did not feel strong enough to renege on the most conspicuous of his pre-*Putsch* promises, though privately he swore in anger over the annoying necessity of holding the elections, which had already been set. He did not delude himself about the insufficiency of his popular backing. But he had not the remotest intention of allowing an elected legislature to function. By the time the voting was concluded and the deputies foregathered, he figured, he would have enough military leverage in his hands to deal with the business.

The balloting began on November 25, eighteen days after the Bolshevik expropriation of the government, and continued until December 9. The peasants and a large part of the rest of the population did choose to follow the Social Revolutionaries. In view of the prevailing disorders and confusions, the fact that thirty-six million citizens voted — in the part of the country normal enough to hold elections — is a revealing commentary on Russian democratic instincts.

In most of the great centers of population the election was conducted under Bolshevik auspices. Yet twenty-seven of the thirty-six million votes cast went to other parties; the Social Revolutionaries received twenty-one million or about 58 per cent, Lenin's lists drew nine million, or about 25 per cent. Of the 707 deputies chosen, 370 were Social Revolutionaries, 175 Bolsheviks, the rest divided among the Mensheviks and other groups. Nine million votes, a quarter of the ballots cast, was a formidable showing, of course; in Petrograd, Moscow, and a few other large cities, moreover, the Bolsheviks scored a majority. But the elections, it must be borne in mind, occurred under conditions heavily weighted in Lenin's favor. The urban masses were still under the influence of those glowingly democratic pre-*Putsch* slogans; the romantic-revolutionary prestige of the Petrograd Soviet and the Red Guards was on the Bolshevik side; *de facto* power was already in Bolshevik hands; great numbers of conservative and reactionary citizens abstained from voting, either on principle or because of their defeatist state of mind. Despite all these factors, Lenin's party received less than half as many votes as the only other well organized party, the Social Revolutionaries. As David Shub summed it up in his biography of Lenin:

"The Russian people, in the freest election in their history, voted for moderate socialism as against Lenin and against the bourgeoisie." *

Here was a clear-cut and massive repudiation of the Leninists only a few weeks after they had seized the reins of government and long before the full horror of their dictatorial and terrorist program had been grasped. It annihilated any lingering illusions that the Bolsheviks had acted for the "toiling masses," let alone the people generally. Never again would either Lenin or his successors risk anything remotely resembling a free vote on their government as a whole or on any aspect of its policies, either by the entire electorate or by its supposedly favored segment, the industrial workers.

The election results provided a clean-cut test of Lenin's democratic pretensions — of the "So be it" in the *Pravda* pledge. The nation did not have long to wait for the test. Popular enthusiasm for the Assembly was at a high pitch. This, after all, was the democratic government of which generations had dreamed. The repudiation of the communist usurpers in the voting was a strong element in the general fervor. What a couple of Petrogard regiments and the Red Guards had done on November 7, the voters presumably had undone a few weeks later.

Lenin knew that if the elected parliament survived, his imposed regime would not. He set in motion a vast and skillful propaganda campaign against the majority party and against the Assembly itself. In factories and military barracks, however, his agitators met with resentment and even open hostility.

In one plant Commissar Smirnov, a top-ranking Bolshevik, hinted at the use of force to kill the parliament. The Constituent Assembly, he charged, was "full of bourgeois superstition and . . . counterrevolutionary tendency." A workman named Shmakov gave

* *Lenin, a Biography,* Doubleday, 1948. Many of the quotations in this and the next chapter are drawn from Mr. Shub's brilliant book, and I wish gratefully to acknowledge my indebtedness.

the answer for most of his factory-mates. "No, comrade Bolsheviks," he exclaimed, "you are ruining the rights of all who elected
this Constituent Assembly. You must remember that this forcible
dissolution will never be forgotten or forgiven by the Russian
people or the Russian proletariat." Commissar Nikolai Krylenko
sought to turn the Semionovsky regiment against the scheduled
meeting. He was interrupted with shouts of "Down with the
Soviets! Long live the Constituent Assembly!" and barely escaped
from the barracks without a beating.

Instinctively the average man sensed that the Assembly was his
last defense against encroaching despotism. But its very popularity
hardened Lenin in his plan to crush this defense with one swift
blow. "We cannot depend on the Russian peasant," he admitted
wryly. "He is likely to join the other side." * He was referring, of
course, to the overwhelmingly peasant make-up of the armed forces.
He felt that he could not depend on Petrograd troops, who shared
the mood of the capital, or on Russians at all.

Accordingly he decided to by-pass the local troops. Instead he
imported a division of Lettish sharpshooters, a contingent less
infected by the deepening anti-Bolshevik sentiment in Petrograd
and likely to be less squeamish about shooting down its residents.
(Actually even some of the Letts refused to shoot and were quickly
disarmed in punishment.) At the same time Lenin deployed the
most trustworthy of the Baltic Fleet sailors through the capital, and
stationed a number of its warships in the Neva, their guns trained
on the Tauride Palace, where the Assembly was to meet on January 18, 1918. He was ready to make his historic comment on the
democratic nonsense and bourgeois superstitions.

On the morning of January 18 massive columns of unarmed
workers and students marched from different parts of the city
toward the center to greet their new parliament, under banners
proclaiming faith in democracy. As they proceeded, thousands more
joined the procession, making it as genuine a demonstration of
popular feelings as that city had ever witnessed. But as the procession approached the Tauride Palace, their path was blocked by the

* Trotsky, *On Lenin*, p. 93.

Lettish sharpshooters, who opened fire without warning. About a hundred of the demonstrators were killed, hundreds were wounded, the rest dispersed in panic.

With this bloody overture, the Constituent Assembly, embodiment of a vision that had been Russia's for a century, gathered in the afternoon for its first — and last — session. The elected deputies found the corridors patrolled by Letts, Red Guards, and sailors in a derisive and insulting temper. They found the galleries packed by noisy, drunken, jeering communists; admission tickets had been managed solely by Lenin's police.

The Social Revolutionary leader, Victor Chernov, was elected president but could barely make himself heard above the hurricane of catcalls and whistling. Toward evening Lenin arrived to survey his handiwork. He sprawled himself contemptuously on the stairs leading to the rostrum and winked wickedly as his hand-picked soldiers and sailors guffawed and banged the floor with their rifle butts. At one point he stretched out on a bench and pretended to go to sleep to underline his disdain for the proceedings, to the utter delight of his rowdy henchmen.

The Bolshevik faction presented a "program" which in effect was an ultimatum calling for the Assembly to turn over its power to the Soviets and commit suicide. It was of course voted down, whereupon Lenin's deputies left the hall in a body. Amidst the organized pandemonium Chernov managed to present and obtain passage of a basic land reform bill, providing for the orderly distribution of land to all peasants. Gruff sailors repeatedly intruded on the platform, pulled at Chernov's coattails and threatened to turn out the lights if he did not wind up the meeting.

When the session was adjourned toward dawn everyone knew that it would never reopen. The first and only genuine expression of the people's will after the revolution was wiped out in cynicism and violence. The more optimistic deputies, who returned to the Tauride Palace next day, found its doors locked and sealed and guarded against the people, with artillery and machine guns.

The doom of the revolution too was sealed. A sinister tyranny, despising the people in whose name it had taken control, was in the saddle. Gorki wrote a fitting epitaph for the murdered revolution:

> Yesterday the streets of Petrograd and Moscow resounded with shouts of "Long live the Constituent Assembly!" For giving vent to these sentiments the peaceful paraders were shot down by the "People's Government."
>
> On January 19 the Constituent Assembly expired — until the advent of happier days — its death foreboding new suffering for the martyred country and for the masses of people. . . . It can be resurrected only through a new alignment of forces, only if the masses of the people will come to their senses and soberly realize the impasse to which their own ignorance, cleverly used by a handful of madmen, has brought them.

The maddest of the madmen was only amused by this kind of rhetoric. He valued one Lettish riflemen above all the humanitarian intellectuals put together. Underlying his strategy was a bottomless contempt for the masses whom he was "saving" from the dangers of democratic procedure, and a contempt no less for his native land. To former comrades who complained about his recklessness with the life and happiness of the country he had replied:

"It isn't a question of Russia at all, gentlemen. *I spit on Russia.* . . . This is merely one phase through which we must pass on the way to a world revolution." *

Russia, in other words, was expendable: a battered beachhead for the conquest of world dominion. It was the sacrificial goat on the altar of international revolution.

Russia wiped the spit and tears and blood from its eyes and prepared to resume its centuries-old struggle for liberty. Its great revolution had been stolen by a gang of political highwaymen. If Lenin, in his sovereign scorn of the Russian peoples, thought they would submit meekly, he was mistaken. The cruelest and most desperate civil war in all history was under way. It would be fought with every instrument of resistance, from guns and explosives to sabotage and non-co-operation. Though its casualties have run into tens of millions, it is still going on. The one certainty is that it will not

* G. Solomon, *Sredi Krasnikh,* Paris, 1930, quoted in *Lenin, a Biography,* by David Shub.

altogether cease until the hopes symbolized by the murdered Constituent Assembly are triumphant.

It should be noted that many of the hundreds of big and little uprisings during the three years of military civil strife were conducted under the banner of the one-day Constituent Assembly. The whole episode of January 18–19, 1918, has been expunged from the official Soviet histories. But its memory has been passed down to its sons and daughters by the generation that witnessed the atrocity.

VI. Wellhead of Terror

1. The Unsheathed Sword

The reign of Bolshevism began with a decree abolishing capital punishment — and an orgy of executions. The decree was adopted on November 8, 1917, by the same session of the All-Russian Congress of Soviets which established the Council of People's Commissars (Sovnarkom) with Lenin as chairman, the first Soviet Government. The Sovnarkom, at a meeting from which Lenin was absent, then specifically abolished the death penalty for desertion at the front.

When Lenin learned of this last action he was furious. He raged at his colleagues for giving in to what he once called the "intelligentsia-bred prejudice" against taking life. Did these dolts expect that without exuberant killing they could hold a nation that detested them? In this initial period, Trotsky was to write later, "Lenin at every opportunity kept hammering into our heads that terror was unavoidable." * The Father of Bolshevism could ease off on these educational exertions after a time; the few in his entourage who were inclined to blood nausea did not long survive in his government.

As for Trotsky's own leonine head, it needed no hammering on this score. He had plenty of the homicidal urge which seems to go with revolutionary self-righteousness. The circumstance that his skull was eventually cracked with an alpenstock by a Stalin assassin should not blind us to this truth. "As for us," Trotsky declared in

* *On Lenin,* pp. 101–105.

1920, "we were never concerned with the Kantian-priestly and vegetarian-Quaker prattle about the 'sacredness of human life' " — thus justifying his own murder to come.

The Sovnarkom and Soviet decrees were born of politics, of course, not compassion, and in any case were stillborn. Executions were being publicly totaled while the law was theoretically in force, and the carnage rose to frenzied heights as popular opposition and organized military challenge grew. Soon enough it won for the Soviet chieftains — Lenin, Trotsky, Zinoviev, Djerzhinsky and the rest — a place in the select company of history's mass killers that counts Caligula, Genghis Khan, Tamerlane, Hassan ben Sabbah, and Fouquier-Tinville.

A new and deeply odious vocabulary of blood lust, a sort of slaughterhouse slang touched with mordant humor, was evolved: "To put against the wall . . . to dispatch to Dukhonin's staff . . . to apply the iron . . . to liquidate." Not until much later, when the regime took on a veneer of legal forms, did the death penalty come to be styled "the highest measure of social defense."

The hostage system — murder of innocents at random to avenge real or imagined attacks on the new rulers — was not a Bolshevik invention, but the Bolsheviks carried it to unprecedented lengths. "One person out of ten will be shot, whether guilty or not," an early warning said. The ratio was rapidly stepped up. Within less than a year a local Cheka, in Ostrogozhsk, announced its intention "to annihilate hundreds for the life of one communist, and tens of thousands for attempts made upon the life of the leaders." This was not rhetoric. Ultimately Stalin would shoot scores of thousands for the assassination of one Politburo member, Sergei Kirov.

A young Social Revolutionary who was Commissar of Justice in Lenin's short-lived coalition cabinet, Dr. I. Steinberg, has called the hostage horror "the arithmetic of insanity and cowardice," practiced by a "dictatorship of panic." * For all that bluster and bravado, it was animal fear, a sense of being hemmed in by crowding hatreds, that drove the usurpers to make bullets their main argument. Only five weeks after taking power they set up the Extraordinary Com-

* *Terror and Violence in Revolution,* Rowohlt Verlag, Berlin, 1931.

mission for Combatting Counterrevolution. Under the fanatic Pole, Felix Djerzhinsky, it began immediately to carve its dread initials — Che Ka — on the naked and writhing body of Russia.

In his first talk to subordinates Djerzhinsky made his government's intentions plain enough. "We have no need for justice now," he told them. "Now we have need for a battle to the death. I propose, I demand, the initiation of the revolutionary sword which will put an end to all counterrevolutionaries." The sword then unsheathed was never returned to its scabbard, for there was never an end to what the regime called the counterrevolutionaries. It was wielded like a butcher knife.

A spare, ascetic man with a wispy beard, thin of lip and cold of eye, a dash of the pervertedly aesthetic in his psychic make-up, Djerzhinsky was inaccessible to human emotion. He signaled the murder of thousands as casually as he flipped the ash from his cigarette. Legends of his cruelty are legion and are repeated in Bolshevik folklore, not in reproof but in eulogy.

Once, at a committee meeting, Lenin passed a note to his executioner inquiring how many "vicious counterrevolutionaries" he had in local custody. "About 1500," the Cheka chief scribbled under the query. Lenin read, nodded, put a tiny cross near the figure and returned the scrap of paper to Djerzhinsky. That night all the fifteen hundred were shot. But it was a slight misunderstanding. The cross mark, as his secretary later explained, was Lenin's habitual way of indicating that he had read and noted a memorandum.*

The pattern of ferocity set by the demonic Pole became the exalted standard of "Bolshevik firmness" for the new regime. To be able to kill wholesale without a tremor of pity or remorse became the proud boast of every Chekist, and "Chekist" in turn the highest compliment in the Soviet jargon.

Among the Soviet journalists I came to know in the 1930's there was one who had been a Cheka officer in Odessa and seemed under an inner compulsion to talk about his bloody acts. He yielded to it when under the spell of vodka, which was often, and there was in his boastfulness more of hysteria than of pride. "We were

* Iks (A. Naglovsky), *Krasnaya Vozhdi,* No. 61, pp. 441–442.

short of lead," he would say, "so I'd line up the prisoners in such a way that I could kill ten or a dozen with a single bullet, right through a neat row of hearts! Or we cracked their windpipes with two fingers — like this! It takes practice. Ekh, those were the days. . . ."

If Djerzhinsky was the technician of terror, Lenin was its theoretician. His faith in blood and iron never faltered. His scorn for the squeamish was blistering. Is our dictatorship a "jellyfish" or "a thing of iron," he would chide his commissars.

One night, Dr. Steinberg (now living in New York) recalls, he decided to complain to Lenin about new reports of ghastly mass executions in the prisons. He knocked on the door of the Smolny Institute room where the leaders were in conference. Trotsky came to the door. "I must talk to Lenin right away," Dr. Steinberg said. "It's terribly urgent." Soon Lenin came out, rubbing the smoke from his eyes.

"Comrade Lenin," the Commissar of Justice began heatedly, "your Djerzhinsky is shooting hundreds out of hand, innocent people, shooting them illegally. . . ."

Lenin looked at him with a mocking smile and shook his beard in annoyance. "And for *that,* Dr. Steinberg, you interrupt an important meeting!" He slammed the door in the young man's face.

The Muscovite legend has it that the Red Terror was merely the "answer" to its White counterpart. Actually it had been foreseen and justified in advance by the Leninist brethren. In their thinking it had always been the essence of proletarian dictatorship. In practice it was applied not only to Whites or to any other special segment but to the people as such. "There must be submission to the armed vanguard," Lenin wrote, until "people will grow accustomed to observing the elementary conditions of social existence without force and without subjection. . . . During the period when the proletariat still needs the state, it does not require it in the interests of freedom, but in the interests of crushing its antagonists."

For Lenin, terror was a complex organ to be played with an ear for nuance. He considered the French model too crude. "The guillotine," he lectured his underlings, "only terrorized, it broke down *active* resistance. . . . We have to break down passive resistance, which doubtless is the most harmful and dangerous one."

Besides imprisonment and death, he proposed a calculated use of hunger and forced labor: "The grain monopoly, the ration card and universal labor are in the hands of the Proletarian State. . . . Those means when applied to capitalists, to the rich, and *to the workers,* will furnish power unprecedented in the annals of history. . . . The Soviets will introduce the work book for the rich and gradually for the whole population."

Twenty years later, a decree by Stalin on New Year's Day of 1939 did in fact introduce the compulsory work book, the so-called "labor passport," for the whole population. It was the final turn of the screw in the feudalization of the workers.

From the day he took over to the day he died, insistence on blood and more blood ran through Lenin's utterance: "We want to transform the state into an institution of violence. . . . We want to organize violence in the interests of the people. . . . We shall be ruthless toward our enemies as well as toward all hesitant and noxious elements in our midst."

Formulas like "hesitant and noxious elements" embraced every man and woman who might oppose the new regime, and that meant virtually the whole population. The fable that Lenin, in contrast to Stalin, was a benevolent idealist who loved mankind is made of whole cloth. Compassion was equally alien to both their natures. *In the final analysis only men with a twisted urge to mass killing reach out for theories that demand and justify mass killing.*

Lenin's thirst for blood, the regime's thirst, grew with indulgence and was inflamed by the very resistance it provoked, until it became a fearsome intoxication. "From now on," *Pravda* announced early in the struggle, "the hymn of the working class must be a hymn of hate and revenge. . . . No fear, no hesitation, but hate and revenge!" And a manifesto in mid-February said: "Enemy agents, speculators, plunderers, hooligans, counterrevolutionary agitators, German spies, must be shot on the spot." In ordering formation of labor battalions drawn from the upper and middle classes, the instructions said flatly: "Those showing resistance must be shot."

When protests against the blood madness were voiced abroad, Lenin released an open letter to American workers: "The British bourgeoisie," he declared, "have forgotten their year 1649, the French their 1795. The terror was just and justified when the bourgeoisie used it for the liberation of the chains of feudalism. Now the terror is criminal and cruel when the workers and poor peasants use it against the bourgeoisie."

He was being disingenuous. Lenin knew well enough that those who were revolted by his cruelties were no less revolted by the cruelties of other dictators in other ages. He knew, too, that the foreign protests came not alone from "the bourgeoisie" but from labor unions, socialists, and individual workers, and that all of them were aware that the terror was being applied not *by* but *against* Russia's workers and poor peasants.

Beyond Moscow and Petrograd, little Lenins aped the leader. In Briansk the death penalty was decreed for drunkenness; in Viatka for "leaving the house after 8 P.M."; in many cities for theft, anti-government leaflets, hoarding of food, a hundred other new crimes. The Cheka in one area ordered "shooting without warning" of persons congregating on the streets, and in another various misdemeanors were ordered punished by drowning "with a stone on the neck in the river Dniester."

"Iron order . . . iron power . . . iron discipline" became the clichés of Leninist rhetoric, with never a note of pity or spiritual grace to cushion the impact. The flabby, genderless Zinoviev reigned as boss of Petrograd after the government moved to the Kremlin in Moscow. At a soldier's meeting he shouted in his high-pitched voice: "The bourgeoisie killed individuals; we kill whole classes!"

In the course of a report to a neighborhood Soviet in September, 1918, Zinoviev called for the extermination of ten million: "We must win over to our side 90 million of the 100 million inhabitants of Russia under the Soviets. As for the rest, we have nothing to say to them; they must be annihilated." * History proved his estimate too modest.

* Petrograd *Severnaya Kommuna,* September 18, 1918.

On August 8, 1918, *Pravda* issued a directive that was echoed and improved upon throughout the land: "Stand up against the wall all those who agitate against the Soviet power. Ten bullets for everyone who raises a hand against it." Meanwhile Lenin egged on the murder bands with verbose lectures on "applying compulsion in such a manner as not to desecrate the slogan of proletarian dictatorship with the practice of a jellylike power." Jellylike was his favorite sneer word for those who still shrank from finishing off their friends and comrades of yesterday.

One of the top Chekists, a Comrade Latsis, edited a kind of house organ for the slaughterhouses, the *Weekly Cheka*. From time to time it published production figures — so many thousands imprisoned, so many thousands shot — but mainly it was devoted to whipping up the labor morale of the killers. "Enough of this long, sterile and vain talk about Red Terror," Latsis wrote. "It is time, while it is not yet too late, to carry out by deed and not by word, a ruthless and strictly organized mass terror."

While it is not yet too late. That was a recurring and revealing idea.

The consciousness of weakness, of a desperate minority position, is mirrored in everything the Bolsheviks did and said. Repeatedly Lenin and his cohorts expressed amazement that they had not yet been crushed by the multitudes of their enraged victims. They were themselves astonished by the efficacy of demagogy braced with lead. It seemed to justify the contempt for the people with which they had started.

Every policeman, every armed guard, every Chekist, became a law unto himself and dealt out death arbitrarily. The hideous principle that it is better to kill thousands of innocents than risk the escape of one guilty person was made official dogma. With "anti-Soviet agitation" and "suspicious origin" recognized as capital offenses, who was safe? Hordes of men, women and children were rounded up almost at random as hostages, to await death for anti-Soviet actions not yet committed by others.

The first of the housing crises to plague the new regime was lack of space for prisoners. Frequently prisoners were shot en masse to make room for new arrivals. Construction of prisons was to remain a large item in the Soviet building plans.

2. *Orgy of Bloodletting*

Many thick volumes would not begin to tell the story of the Red Terror. Dozens of them have already been written. Here I can hope only to suggest the temper of the terror and its awesome range *as a measure of the resistance met by the Bolshevik regime.*

Murder, massacre, and pillage were no less horrifying in scale and brutality on the part of most of the regime's opponents. The anti-Jewish pogroms, in particular by reactionary Ukrainian armies, added one of the bloodiest chapters to the tragedy of this people. Every burst of blood lust on one side ignited a larger one on the other side, in a chain reaction that piled White atrocities upon Red, and Red upon White.

But between these extremes there were anti-Soviet movements which ruled out cruelty for cruelty's sake. The moderate socialists and reform parties — those who had made the revolution and whom the Bolsheviks had dispossessed — did not join in the sadistic orgies. *Lenin and his crowd must be equated with the worst, not the best, of their opponents.* They, almost alone among the teeming terrorists, made brutality a sacred principle of their creed. Only the Reds added insult to injury by decking their savagery with the raiment of a universal world-saving mission.

In the nature of the case, the workers and peasants, being the most numerous classes, provided the most victims. The pretense that these classes backed the new rulers is vulgar fatuity. "The proletarian layer which actually governed Russia in that year [1918], carrying out all the policies and constituting our power," Lenin would explain much later, "was very thin." As for the peasantry, its opposition was so nearly unanimous that the government hardly bothered to conceal it.

"The kulak cherishes a fierce hatred of the Soviet government," Lenin declared in August, 1918. But "kulak," the name for the better-off peasant, was in fact a propagandist euphemism for any peasant resisting the new regime. That fierce hatred was all but total in the countryside.

As the fingers of hunger tightened on the throat of the urban population, the government in effect declared war on the tillers of the soil. In the spring of 1918 the Moscow and Petrograd Soviets were ordered "to mobilize 10,000 workers, to arm them and equip them for a campaign for the conquest of wheat from the rapacious and monopolists." The reference, in simple truth, was to the overwhelming majority of the peasants. Other cities and towns similarly equipped armed expeditions against the village populations.

Wartime weapons were still abundant. The villagers defended themselves. Women and even children joined their men in fighting the invaders. In the course of four months, according to official Soviet data, the "food army" lost 7309 men in killed and wounded out of a total of 36,500 sent against the peasants. The village casualties were vastly greater. Everywhere there were pitched battles and dozens of villages were put to the torch.

The system of requisitions of grain and other foods degenerated into forcible confiscations. Though they resisted heroically, the peasants were no match for the city marauders and in most cases were slaughtered like so many sheep. The countryside ran with blood. The city brigades plundered and killed and sometimes raped in the name of the dictatorship. Requisitions under "war communism" became a hated synonym for plain robbery. But Lenin's talent for rationalizing any crime was equal to the saturnalia of violence he had unleashed against the peasantry. "That we brought civil war to the village," he wrote in the course of a polemic with the German socialist Kautsky, who had protested against the terror, "is something we hold as a merit." *

At least that phase of the civil strife, he thus conceded, was deliberately provoked — *brought to the village* — in line with class-war theory. But the village, it must never be forgotten, was Russia — 85 per cent of it peasant and most of the rest so recently urbanized that their emotions were rooted there. Left to themselves, the

* *Collected Works*, XV, 507.

Leninists knew, the peasants would have starved the regime into submission. Indeed, despite the murder brigades and arson, passive peasant resistance did in the end force the government into the compromise of Nep, the New Economic Policy.

Nor was the hunt for food limited to the countryside. Armed bands, often self-appointed, raided city homes in a search for "hoarders." Ostensibly aimed at the rich, this offensive spared no one found in possession of a little extra bread or cabbage or potatoes. Since money at the time could not buy food, the victims most often were workers with relatives in the villages. Not infrequently the "hoarders" were shot on the spot and the loot divided among the raiders. In the cities, too, the frontiers between official and unofficial brigandry were extremely vague.

Months before White forces of czarist restoration had become a threat, the Bolsheviks faced bitter hostility among the very people — at any rate the very kind of people — who had helped them into power. The Petrograd regiments whose neutrality or active aid made possible the November *Putsch* became so restive that Lenin had them disarmed. The revolutionary sailors, pride and mainstay of the commissars, began to pass resolutions demanding their abdication and the erasure of edicts limiting freedom of press and assemblage.

The Sovnarkom shrewdly began to build up its Praetorian Guard of foreign mercenaries: Letts, Chinese, German and Austrian prisoners of war. These represented Lenin's first line of defense in the initial years — a fact which has been completely blotted out of the official Soviet histories.

In April, 1918, a conference of factory workers, claiming to speak for a hundred thousand Petrograd proletarians, formally demanded the resignation of the Soviet government. The demand was supported by the union of railway workers and other labor groups. Usually their resolutions specified that the governing authority be returned to the suppressed Constituent Assembly.

The only democratic faction to back Lenin's *coup d'état,* the left wing of the Social Revolutionaries, was quickly disillusioned. The make-believe of coalition faded out. Thereafter these Social Revolutionaries led all the rest in spirited resistance to the dictatorship, at cruel cost in life.

On July 6, 1918, one of their adherents shot the new German ambassador, Count Mirbach, in protest against the separate Russo-German peace of Brest-Litovsk. The spontaneous uprising which was to be touched off by this act of terror did not materialize. With the support of dissident Red soldiers and Cheka troops, however, the Left Social Revolutionaries did capture the Moscow Telegraph Building. They took head-executioner Djerzhinsky prisoner. But Lenin, relying primarily on his Lettish guards, soon had the capital safely in his hands again. Subsequently, leading Bolsheviks admitted that they had thought their game was up and were awaiting the arrest of the Sovnarkom. But the rebels failed to follow up their momentary advantage and were themselves arrested.

Had there been an equivalent for Lenin on the other side, a leader with the necessary force of character and some talent for strategy, the new regime could have been unseated as easily as the Provisional Government had been. There was no such personality. Besides, the anti-Bolshevik radicals were hobbled by the hesitancies, the respect for life, the scruples inherent in their democratic ideals.

Vilification of the desperate masses and ever stronger doses of lead, these were the Kremlin's answers to the tidal wave of discontent. The blood bacchanalia, already raging wherever the Soviets were in control, shed the last semblance of restraint after August 30, 1918.

On that day a student in Petrograd assassinated the head of the regional Cheka, Uritsky. A few hours later, in Moscow, Dora Kaplan shot and wounded Lenin. In a statement before her execution this woman said that she had been a terrorist against the old regime and was pursuing the same tactics against the new despots. She had decided to kill Lenin as "a traitor to the revolution," citing the suppression of the Constituent Assembly as his major act of treachery.

These individual acts set off an orgy of official bloodletting that was to establish a new historical record of bestiality. In the Bolshevik stronghold of Kronstadt, 500 prisoners were dragged from their

dungeons and mowed down by firing squads. In Petrograd, 512
hostages were shot in a few days. Hundreds of innocents were similarly murdered at random in other cities. A telegram to all local
Soviets from Moscow prescribed stern action:

"Done with weakness! Done with sentimental considerations!
All Social Revolutionaries have to be arrested at once. A large number of hostages have to be taken from the bourgeoisie and the officers; at the slightest provocation or attempt at resistance or a move
among the White Guards' adherents, mass executions have to take
place without fail."

The redoubtable Latsis announced: "We are exterminating the
bourgeoisie as a class. Don't look for incriminating evidence. . . .
The first questions you should put to the arrested persons are: To
what class does he belong, what is his origin, what was his education, and what is his profession? These should determine the fate
of the accused. This is the essence of the Red Terror."

On the morning after the attempt on Lenin's life the Moscow
Pravda demanded extermination of "all those who are harmful to
the revolution. . . . The counterrevolution, this vicious mad dog,
must be destroyed once and for all." And in Petrograd the *Red
Gazette* wrote after Uritsky's funeral: "For the death of our champion thousands of our enemies will have to pay with their lives. . . ."
Kill so many, it urged, that the enemies "will choke themselves
with their own blood." Every other Soviet sheet played fiendish
variations on the same theme.

In the course of a discussion in a Moscow factory a workman
made a contribution that reveals the hysteria of the time. Speakers
had mentioned the kind of questions to be put to suspected enemies.
Whereupon the workman rose and declared — "heatedly," as the
Soviet reporter recorded — "Why even ask those questions? I'll just
walk into his house and look into his pots. If there is meat in them,
then he is an enemy of the people and should be stood up against
the wall."

A formal "Order about Hostages" commanded the rounding up
of people from the bourgeoisie and officer ranks to be held in
reserve for "mass executions" at the faintest show of opposition in

the locality. "Not the slightest wavering should be tolerated" in
carrying out this directive, it warned.

Enemies of the people . . . bourgeoisie . . . White Guardists . . .
kulaks . . . noxious elements. . . . These were categories without definition or boundaries. In practice they meant torture and death for
anyone who resisted or might conceivably resist the dictatorship.
Whatever it may have been in theory, in practice Lenin's regime
"evolved into *a system of self-defense of a small minority against
their own people* — a system which has never been surpassed by any
tyranny at any time in the world's history." This was the verdict,
in 1922, of Paul Miliukov, one of Russia's exiled democratic leaders.*

3. Civil War: Military Phase

Under slogans directed against the right, the regime in fact concentrated on demolishing its critics of the left. These it feared, with
good reason, more than all the monarchists and reactionaries put
together. Djerzhinsky's prisons were soon crammed with men and
women celebrated in Russian revolutionary annals. Czarist generals willing to take orders from Trotsky had more chance of saving their skins and fattening their bones than non-Bolshevik veterans of the long fight against the old order.

I have already touched on the abortive Social Revolutionary rebellion in July, 1918. At about the same time the famous left terrorist, Boris Savinkov, led an insurrection in the Yaroslav district,
a hundred and fifty miles from Moscow. At first it went his way.
The Red detachments were worsted in skirmishes and Yaroslav
fell to Savinkov. Then German prisoners in the area were induced
to join the Reds and the scales were turned. A guarantee of immunity for prisoners was the central condition of the surrender,
but more than four hundred of Savinkov's officers and men were
promptly executed.

In Moscow an anarchist club was raided. In the ensuing battle
many of the defenders died and the survivors were swallowed by

* *Russia Today and Tomorrow,* Macmillan, 1922.

the prisons. Although the aged Prince Peter Kropotkin was invited to return to his native land, and treated as an honored guest, his followers were packed into the fetid dungeons along with Tolstoyans and other varieties of anarchists. When Kropotkin died, in 1921, his daughter, Princess Alexandra, succeeded in wresting permission from Djerzhinsky for anarchists in Moscow prisons to attend the funeral. They were released on their word of honor to return — a word not one of them violated. The spectacle of these ragged, emaciated ghosts marching silently behind the coffin is one that Moscow did not quickly forget.

These are random episodes. Its newspapers outlawed, its leaders hounded unto death, the anti-Bolsehvik left never had a chance. It was remarkably lacking in dynamic personalities. More and more of its survivors were driven to the periphery, where Soviet control was still sketchy, and a few of them succeeded in generating armed oppositions. A committee of deputies of the strangled Constituent Assembly mobilized a "People's Army," which, however, never affected the course of the civil conflict.

Those of the better-known socialist and democratic spokesmen who were not killed or incarcerated fled the country. They were part of the huge Russian emigration of those years, perhaps 1,500,-000 people, which must be rated as part of the over-all opposition. While the outlawed classes — the wealthy, czarist officers, landowners, and such — predominated, the escapees also included the cream of the democratic parties. The foremost intellectuals and bearers of Russian culture, too, fled by the thousand: writers like Bunin, Kuprin, Andreyev, Merezhkovsky, Balmont, Artzibashev; painters like Repin, Korovin, Yakovlev; composers like Rachmaninoff, Glazunov, Grechaninov, Stravinsky; scientists, opera singers, even chess-masters like Alekhine and Bogoliubov.

Of the pre-1917 revolutionary generations, only a handful of superannuated veterans of the czarist political prisons were permitted to live with their melodramatic memories. Considered harmless, they were gathered in a kind of old folks' home, on the former Sheremetiev estate about fifty kilometers from Moscow.

I visited that home many years later. Among the pensioners I

found legendary heroes and heroines of the revolutionary saga —
people like Vera Figner, Michael Frolenko, Elizaveta Kovalskaya.
The ordinary Soviet citizen did not even supect that these historic
figures were still among the living. Children read about the martyrdom of Vera Figner in their schoolbooks, but were not permitted
to know that she was still alive and among them. Because these
veterans all opposed Lenin's dictatorship, the Kremlin rarely mentioned their existence.

Vera Figner, who had been involved in the assassination of Alexander II, was eighty-four when I met her, and still beautiful. After
observing me for a few hours and exchanging some casual words,
she apparently decided I could be trusted. So she took me for a
stroll in the woods. She spoke in a stilted English which she had
taught herself in the isolation of her forty years' imprisonment in
Schluesselburg Fortress.

At the time, I could not quote her, but now she is dead. She
spoke more in sorrow than in bitterness. The Bolsheviks, she said,
had betrayed every hope and principle for which she and her comrades had fought; they had instituted an absolutism more cruel
than any in the past. She who had helped kill a czar now talked
with a touch of nostalgia of the rights, the legal protections, the
leeway for political struggle under the old regime. The people, she
said, had been defeated but some day would win their freedom.
The indictment of czarism in her famous autobiography is tame
compared with the indictment of its successor I heard that day
from Vera Figner's lips.

The Leninist device of equating all non-Bolshevik radicals with
White Guards, capitalists, landlords — the celebrated "amalgam"
tactic that still serves the Kremlin's purposes — was perfected in the
civil war period. Punitive measures against such political absurdi-
ties as Menshevik-Whites, kulak-anarchists, bourgeois-Social Revolutionists, disguised the truth that all socialist, democratic, and
moderate forces were fighting the new regime.

At home this semantic trickery deepened the confusion in which
Lenin maneuvered with supreme skill. Abroad it blinded liberal
sympathizers with the Russian revolution to the fact that the Soviets

were at war with the people and parties which had prepared and carried out the revolution. These foreigners cheered for the executioners of the revolution under the tragic impression that they were on the side of the revolutionary angels.

To this day there is a lamentable tendency to view the civil struggle of 1918–1920 as a two-way contest between "revolutionaries," meaning the Bolsheviks, and "counterrevolutionaries." In this instance, too, history has been written by the victors. But it was in truth a bizarrely complex contest among the most diverse groupings — monarchist, socialist, national-separatist of endless denominations; Reds, Whites, Greens, in myriad shadings — fighting each other in shifting patterns of alliance and betrayal.

In *The Days of the Turbins,* a truly great play by the late Mikhail Bulgakov reflecting this period, the Reds do not even figure in the action, except as off-stage noises in the final scene. The military contest against which the story develops is not between Reds and Whites, but between two anti-Soviet armies, Russian and Ukrainian-nationalist. Its picture of the czarist past, incidentally, is at the farthest remove from the caricature since then spread by communist propaganda. Bulgakov drew the czarist officers sympathetically, as high-minded and cultured patriots motivated by a profound love for their country and its people.

The confusions were further compounded by freebooting movements under ambitious individual generals and politicians. Meanwhile the Germans were overrunning the Ukraine and cutting deep into the flesh of the North Caucasus; there were guerrilla formations fighting at once against the Germans, the Reds, and Russian Whites. Superimposed on the military chaos were the several Allied interventions, in the Murmansk-Archangel area, the Caucasus, the Far East. Then there were some forty thousand Czech prisoners of war, their ranks swelled by peasant and worker volunteers, fighting in the Ural region.

What all of them had in common was their detestation of the communist regime. Had any substantial portion of these disparate elements been able to pool their strength under disciplined command, the Soviet government could not have survived its first year. But Trotsky's armies were able to deal with them piecemeal, often exploiting their fierce mutual enmities. With the new and old capitals in their hands, holding the core of Russia through all-out terror, the new masters could throw their military potential against any point on the compass where the danger was most urgent. Comparatively small Soviet armies, reinforced by mercenaries from the stranded German and Austrian war prisoners, braced by a sprinkling of fanatic Bolsheviks, often led by able czarist officers in Trotsky's pay, achieved the near miracle of defeating a whole spectrum of enemies.

To suggest the complexity of the struggle we need but look at the Makhno Insurrectionary Army of 1919, locked in contest at various times and often at the same time with the Don Cossacks, White armies under Generals Denikin and Wrangel, and of course the Red Army. In the over-all civil war it was a minor segment, surpassed in importance by a dozen other armies and leaders, but it will serve to underline the extraordinary confusions and contradictions of the time.

Nestor Makhno was a colorful self-trained guerrilla chieftain who called himself an anarchist. He drew to himself the boldest and most desperate of the Ukrainian peasants hating the old order and the new alike. Under a black flag, the Makhno forces swept into the vacuum left by retreat of the Germans from the Ukraine after the fall of the Kaiser. Lenin and Trotsky were content to let Makhno battle Ukrainian nationalists, but refused to give him support that might have been decisive. However, when a rightist offensive was undertaken by one Grigoriev, Moscow asked Makhno to deal with it, which he did expeditiously. Meanwhile the Whites under Denikin, their numbers swelling with new adherents as they moved northward, collided with the anarchist strength.

Perhaps underestimating the Denikin potential, Trotsky helped open the Makhno front to him in the Grishin sector, in the hope that the two forces would annihilate each other. Having thus been enabled to outflank Makhno, Denikin's troops moved so swiftly that Moscow itself seemed doomed. In less than four months he

was master of Crimea, the North Caucasus, the Don, a large part
of the Volga region and the southern reaches of Great Russia
itself. Had there been no serious harassments behind his lines,
Denikin might have written finis to the Bolshevik chapter in Russian history, as was generally expected. But the Makhno contingent, reorganized in his rear, sapped Denikin's strength. It provided
the balance of pressure that enabled Trotsky to turn back that
White tide. Soon Denikin's forces rolled back to the Black Sea
as fast as they had advanced.

The remnants of his beaten soldiery were forged into a new
White army headed by General Wrangel. A solemn compact was
now entered into between the Kremlin and Makhno for joint operations against Wrangel. No sooner, however, had the White
leader been licked, than Lenin tore the compact into shreds. He
hunted down his anarchist "allies" to the last man, shooting its
officers and wreaking vengeance even on their families in the
Ukrainian villages.

As for the Allied intervention, the key fact is that it was on an
ineffectual scale, lackadaisical and wholly un-co-ordinated. Soviet-
angled outcries, then and since, have magnified that episode out of
all proportion to reality. The Allies did not have their hearts in the
undertaking. Everywhere and always they gave too little and gave
it too late and at the wrong places; they seemed positively determined to avoid accomplishing their supposed mission. In the sum
total of the nation's fighting in the civil-war period, the foreign
share was negligible, and in the aggregate resistance to Bolshevism
it was nil.

How much wretchedness and horror — not only the brutalities
of the Soviets but those of Mussolini and Hitler, and the Second
World War itself — might have been avoided had Bolshevism
been stopped then and there! The fact that the world still has a
guilt complex over the intervention is a triumph of communist
propaganda. Only Churchill among statesmen has had the moral
gumption to say that the crime, so far as humanity is concerned,
was not the sending of Allied troops but the pusillanimity which
doomed the expeditions to failure. For a later and comparable ex-

ample of futility one thinks of the halfhearted and self-defeating
"aid" given to Chiang Kai-shek against Chinese communism after
the last war.

We have been conditioned to think of the intervention in Russia
"against the revolution." It was, or at any rate could have been, an
intervention *for* the people's revolution, against the gang which
had crushed the democratic hopes symbolized by the Constituent
Assembly. It is curious and revealing that the same kind of people
who demanded intervention against Franco in defense of Spanish
democracy think it would have been criminal to intervene effec-
tively against Lenin in defense of Russian democracy. Dr. Fedor
Bohatirchuk, a Soviet refugee now on the faculty of the University
of Ottawa, writes: "The Soviets were so weak that only a little help
from outside . . . would have been necessary to throw off the
usurpers." Like millions of others in his country, he finds it hard
to forgive the failure of the democracies to give them more than
token help in the decisive hours.

President Wilson's moral authority was still dominant, and it
was used as a brake on genuine intervention. Except for the British
action in the Baku oil region, the meager Allied forces were holding actions in a few scattered spots rather than true military enterprises. The handful of American troops hardly fired a shot, and
in the Far East they served to nullify the Japanese invaders of
Siberia. The whole business was more show than reality, more useful to Lenin as a propaganda bonanza than hurtful as a military
threat. Its propaganda potential, indeed, has increased with the
passing of time; an *unsuccessful* intervention has no friends.

The one major foreign challenge to the Soviets was the Polish
invasion, and that, of course, was cold aggression rather than intervention, with territorial aggrandizement as its announced aim.
And it came when the White waves had been forced back, leaving
the Red Army free to deal with it. Moreover, because it was obviously an *anti-Russian* venture, the Polish attack rallied the battered
patriotic spirits of stricken Russia. The momentum of the counter-
attack carried the Red troops to the very gates of Warsaw before
its vitality ebbed.

For more than three decades the Kremlin has gotten away with the specious theory that its terror had been "forced" upon the regime by White Guard attacks and foreign invasions. Both the ideology and the techniques of the Red Terror, however, were unfolded before the civil war had jelled as a real military contest, and before a single Allied soldier had set foot on Russian soil. The Cheka, symbol and instrument of the terror, was in full operation less than two months after the Leninist *Putsch*. Freedom of press and assembly had been largely obliterated even earlier. The democratically elected municipal administrations were killed by arbitrary decree in December, 1917, and the freely elected Constituent Assembly was wiped out a month later.

Mass resistance and the counterterror of the government were bloodiest in the interior provinces, a thousand miles from the nearest interventionist. Some of the most savage repression, including the Kronstadt blood bath, took place after the military oppositions had been defeated. Moreover, the terror was not abandoned after the military phase of the civil struggle was definitively over; it reached its homicidal peaks after 1928, with Stalin's accession to absolute power. By then, of course, the alibis of White and foreign menace had become ancient history.

The Bolshevik dictatorship never had the moral consent of the Russian people. Wanton demagogy and wanton bloodletting without measure succeeded in conquering those people despite their heroic defense. The tortured years of internal military struggle stand as confutation of the belief abroad that the masses yielded readily to the Bolshevik whip. The failure of their resistance must not obscure for us its extraordinary dimensions and sacrificial passion.

VII. People's Rebellion — and Stalemate

1. *The Grass-Roots Struggle*

The end of organized conflict found the nation in a mood, not of exultation but of despair. The great masses felt themselves vanquished, not victorious. The victors were the communists, not the people. The government took on the coloration and psychology of an armed occupation, which was to remain its unique character ever after.

Formal accounts of the military phase of the struggle necessarily emphasize organized battles, campaigns, armies. A few names of leaders dominate the history: Yudenich, Kolchak, Petliura, Wrangel, and so on. But the broader conflict, sometimes woven into the military operations and more often independent of them, took place on what Americans would call the grass-roots level.

It was a chaotic, tumultuous, often suicidal tangle of resistance in towns and the countryside, in single villages and single factories. There are no statistics to convey its dimensions, diversity, and convulsive force. There is no way, apart from the novelist's art, to convey the nature of this diffused violence of a people's war under and around the more systematic hostilities.

The notion that one fragment of the Russian humanity, the workers, was exempted from the reign of terror is a figment of oratory. From the outset the new rulers thundered against the "scoundrels" who "cling to the traditions of capitalism . . . who strive to retain high wages." The quoted words are Lenin's. Strikes, which became epidemic, were increasingly treated as acts of rebellion. Often they took the form of general abstention from work; men and women simply stopped showing up at their benches. Some found it more remunerative to join raiding parties; others returned to the villages whence they had sprung, to share the somber fate of the peasantry.

In the explosive resentments with which the Cheka and sometimes the Red Army itself had continually to deal, Lenin professed to see an anarchic frame of mind: "hatred and distrust on the part of the masses toward everything connected with the state," as he put it. But his party *was* the state. However he might generalize the growing distrust and opposition, they were specifically directed against his regime.

"We see the entire country," Lenin said, "swept with the fire of counterrevolutionary uprisings that are financed by the British-French imperialists." According to the precise Latsis there were 245 uprisings in 1918 and 99 in the first seven months of 1919, in the restricted territory under Soviet rule. The figures were arbitrary, of course; had he counted minor outbreaks, his total would have mounted to thousands. To suppose that more than a few could have been inspired by foreign gold is nonsensical.

They were a continuous, desperate, but futile expression of an all but unanimous popular rebellion. Some frank remarks by Mikhail Frunze, as head of the Turkestan Command, reveal more than he intended. Frunze, who would one day succeed Trotsky as War Commissar, was talking only of the guerrilla fighters in his area, the so-called *basmatchi,* but his words were valid for anti-Bolshevik partisans everywhere. The *basmatchi,* he said, counted "hundreds and thousands whom the [communist] authorities had hurt and offended." He went on to concede that the Red Army had needlessly terrorized and looted local inhabitants: These "defenders of the working people and the revolution" had in fact acted as "an instrument of violence against them."

This does not mean that all the anti-Bolsheviks were welcomed either. Gradually, in the words of the Kadet leader, Miliukov, "the military anti-Bolshevist movement degenerated into a purely reactionary movement." As between the Whites and the Reds, the city workers did tend to regard the Reds as the lesser evil, and the peasants did fear the return of the landlords as much as they hated the brigandage of Soviet power.

In a vague elemental fashion the temper of the nation remained revolutionary. The masses wanted a new order without communism and repressions, without czars and feudal lords, one that they translated into personal rather than political terms: land, jobs, food, immunity to arbitrary arrests and imposts. They were caught between a Red and a White Terror, each feeding on the other, each outdoing the other in barbaric fury. Whichever side won, the people lost.

In the area under its dominion, the Soviet regime wrestled with unceasing opposition. The years 1919 and 1920 saw waves of strikes that overflowed into the violence of 1921. Economic in form, they were political in content and (correctly from its own vantage point) the dictatorship treated them as insurrections. What the workers demanded was first of all bread: better wages, the right to private trade with the villages, the removal of police cordons that kept peasants and their food supplies out of the towns. But always they demanded also civil rights, freedom for their labor unions and an end to the terror.

The strike in the Putilov factory in early 1919 still remained in popular memory ten years later, when I visited Leningrad. An old workman told me how he and his benchmates, coming out of a mass meeting in the plant, were fired upon by Cheka riflemen; how a memorial meeting for the victims next day was broken up with further casualties; how Red troops were quartered in the factory until the crisis subsided.

Detailed eyewitness accounts of the incredible slaughter with which a strike in Astrakhan, involving most of the local industries, was crushed in March, 1919, have come down to us. A certain Silin, who was present, wrote:

Ten thousand workers peacefully assembled at a gigantic rally were discussing the distressing material situation. Soon the meeting was surrounded by machine gunners, sailors and grenade throwers. The refusal of the workers to disperse was met with a volley of machine guns aimed

directly at the compact human mass of workers and by the deafening
explosion of hand grenades.

The mass of workers wavered, shrunk back and fell back in awe-
stricken silence. The rattling of the machine guns smothered the groans
of the wounded and the agonized cries of the mortally stricken
victims. . . .

According to Silin, "no less than 2,000 victims were snatched
from the ranks of the workers" that day. Forty-eight hours later
the local authorities received their orders from Moscow, over the
signature of Trotsky himself: *"Give no quarter!"* That meant instant death for hundreds of the strikers in Cheka cellars. The burial
squads could not keep up with the firing squads; hundreds of
bodies, weighted with stones, were thrown into the Caspian Sea.
The Cheka instituted a house-to-house search for ringleaders. When
it did not find the men, their womenfolk were shot. The massacre
lasted for five days, until no family in Astrakhan was without a
loss, and repressions continued long after the survivors were back at
work. Estimates of the dead were as high as four thousand.

The dictatorship of the proletariat had given the country a
sample of how it proposed to deal with recalcitrant proletarians.

Peasant outbreaks were on an even more sanguinary scale. One
of the most appalling acts in that tragedy was played out in the
province of Tambov in November, 1919. It began, as did most of
these agrarian troubles, with the refusal of peasants to surrender
their last stores of grain — food for their families and seed for the
coming season. Red Army artillery was used to raze disobedient
villages. Peasants were flogged in public. In Spassk, ten peasants
and a priest were executed in full view of the inhabitants as a
warning. In Morshansk, eight wounded peasants were forced to
dig their own graves, then buried alive. Deaths on both sides ran
to hundreds before the province was "pacified."

Momentarily alarmed by its own excess, the Soviets again decreed an end to capital punishment as of January 15, 1920. Ironically, executions that year surpassed those of the preceding year.
Tipped off that the decree was coming, Cheka officials hastened
to shoot prisoners wholesale before the deadline. They need not

have worried about losing their prey. On May 24 the decree was rescinded and murder was resumed on a "legal" basis.

In abandoning cities to anti-Soviet forces, the Reds as a matter of routine killed the political prisoners and hostages in their custody. The Whites did the same when they, in turn, were forced to retreat. Cities and towns changed hands a dozen times in those years, each transfer of control marked by a new installment of horror. Not until civil war came to Spain did the world see barbarous and hysterical fratricide on this order.

By the beginning of 1921, Lenin had all of Russia in his grip, except for the more remote areas of Siberia, Central Asia, and Georgia, where a socialist government was in power. But it was precisely in that year that he harvested the calamitous crops of his "war communism.'

In industrial regions, as many as 50 per cent of the workers had either ceased to go to the factories and mines or had run away to their native villages. The regime set up special committees to combat "labor deserters." These proceeded to apply the familiar pressures of roundup, arrests, shootings. Meanwhile peasant resistance grew more violent, in the measure that their surplus grain was exhausted and the specter of starvation emerged more starkly. Knowing that their crops would be expropriated, the farmers had stopped planting beyond their own needs. The cultivated area declined to 62 per cent of the prewar total and the yield in 1920 was little more than a third of the prewar figure.

The whole country was swarming with the the so-called *bezprizorni,* the homeless "wild" children. Already there were millions of them, and new millions would be added by the gruesome famine of 1921–1922. Some of them were as young as four and five years. These fantastic droves of displaced children, dirt-crusted and ragged and diseased, turned into predatory animal creatures, foraging for food, robbing, murdering. There are no words in any language to describe the phantasmagoric horror of these armies of little derelicts, infesting the country like a dreadful parasitic growth.

As late as 1928, the *bezprizorni* were still very much in evidence, even in Moscow. People regarded them with a mixture of fear, disgust, and pity. The high mortality rate took care of the problem in part. Efforts of the authorities to concentrate them in special homes and camps barely affected the larger problem, though many thousands were salvaged; a few were even to become persons of influence in Soviet society. For the rest, these orphans of terror and hunger were exterminated by wholesale shooting.

2. *Revolt in Kronstadt*

It is against this background of cumulative tragedy, of universal bloodshed and encroaching hunger, that the climactic episode of Kronstadt must be viewed to be understood. Kronstadt was the symbol of the final bankruptcy of the revolution. It is no accident that in the libraries of sycophantic writings about the glorious "new Russia" Kronstadt, if mentioned at all, is glossed over with a few official lies. It is the ghastliest of the skeletons in the Soviet governments's ample closets and in many ways the most significant.

An island naval fortress on the Gulf of Finland, close to Petrograd, Kronstadt had become almost a synonym for Bolshevism. Sailors had always been among the most militant of the rebellious Russian minority. They had played a role in the 1905 revolution, dress rehearsal for 1917, as those who have seen Eisenstein's motion picture *Potiomkin* will remember.

Kronstadt sailors were among Lenin's most effective supporters in the seizure of power, in capturing the Winter Palace, in policing the capital when the Petrogad garrisons turned surly, in suppressing the Constituent Assembly. So there is historical drama in the fact that the pent-up discontents of the country should come to a head precisely in this bastion of Bolshevism.

The sailors on the battleships in the Kronstadt harbor, in its garrisons, were in the final analysis peasants and workers in uniform. The conduct of the government they had helped to set up had been corroding their enthusiasm. Outraged workers in nearby

Petrograd came to know that they could find sanctuary in the naval town.

It was in the local Soviet and in the Communist Party of Kronstadt that the spirit of insurgence first found expression, and from there spread to the naval and civilian population. The official propaganda subsequently invented czarist generals and foreign agents to mask its own guilt, but there is not even a remote excuse for doubt that the Kronstadt affair was primarily an insurrection within the Bolshevik elite itself.

The deepening despairs focused in this spot reached a climax with a mass meeting of fifteen thousand sailors and workers on March 1, 1921. Aware of the dangerous situation, Lenin had sent several of his best people, among them Michael Kalinin, "president" of the Soviet Union, to take part in the proceedings.

One after another members of the Kronstadt Soviet, Red naval officers, sailors from the ranks, detailed their grievances, in effect the grievances of the whole country. They told of murder in their villages, shootings in their cities, persecutions of revolutionists, even of communists, who dared oppose the dictatorship in the slightest degree. When Kalinin tried to speak, he was shouted down.

"Comrades," one of the nameless sailors exclaimed, "look around you and you will see that we have fallen into a terrible mire. We were pulled into this mire by a group of communist bureaucrats, who under the mask of communism have feathered their nest in our republic. I myself was a communist, and I call on you, comrades, to drive out these false communists who set worker against peasant and peasant against worker. Enough shooting of our brothers!"

The resolution adopted by this great meeting refutes the later charges that the Kronstadters were planning an armed uprising. Its language was temperate, though it left no doubt about the profound hatred for the Soviet rulers. "In view of the fact that the present Soviets do not express the will of the workers and peasants," it began, the crews of the First and Second Squadrons of the Baltic Fleet petitioned for immediate changes.

Chief among these was the demand for "new elections by secret

ballot, the pre-election campaign to have full freedom of agitation."
Then the resolution went on to demand freedom of speech, press,
and assembly "for workers and peasants, for anarchists and left
socialist parties"; liberation of political prisoners; restoration of the
peasants' rights to the products of their labor; in short, the fulfillment of the promises of the revolution.

Four days later the Kronstadt sailors established a small committee, chiefly composed of communists, which assumed control of
the town, the fortress, the ships. Moscow accepted the challenge. It
determined to treat the petition as a mutiny and, if necessary, to
provoke a battle to the death.

Trotsky issued an ultimatum. He ignored the complaints and
demands, giving the insurgents only a choice between "uncondi-
tional surrender" and the prospect of being shot "like partridges."
When the Kronstadt committee refused to yield unless their major
demands were met, Trotsky assigned General Tukhachevsky —
the same Tukhachevsky who was destined to be executed by Stalin
— to take Kronstadt by force.

Zinoviev, the Petrograd boss, proclaimed a state of seige in his
city. He disarmed the local garrisons and confined them to barracks, deploying reliable Red military cadets on bridges and at all
approaches to the city. People congregating on the streets, he ordered, were to be shot without warning. He knew, as did the whole
country, that the former capital, cradle of the revolution, was ripe
for revolt. Despite his precaution, hundreds of Petrograd workers
crossed the ice to join the Kronstadters.

Tukhachevsky marched on the naval town with 60,000 picked
men. Ardent young cadets provided the spearhead of his forces and
tough Cheka troops brought up the rear, ready to shoot Red Army
men who might flinch from attacking the heroes of Kronstadt. Several regiments at nearby Oranienbaum, indeed, refused to join the
offensive; they were promptly disarmed by the Cheka and every
fifth man in the ranks was shot. Several hundred top party people
were rushed from Moscow to the battlefield to prop up the morale
of the attackers.

The siege began with an aerial bombardment at 6:45 P.M. on March 6. This was followed by an artillery barrage. Then the troops advanced across the ice. The sailors answered with fire from the fort and from their ships.

Tukhachevsky later declared that in all the years of war and civil war he had not witnessed carnage such as he overseered at Kronstadt. "It was not a battle," he said, "it was an inferno. . . . The sailors fought like wild beasts. I cannot understand where they found the might for such rage. Each house where they were located had to be taken by storm."

By March 16, though the residential portion had been captured, the battered fortress was still holding out. That day the fortress was stormed and on March 17 Tukhachevsky could report to Trotsky that the job was finished. Kronstadt was a place of death. Eighteen thousand of the rebels, it was estimated, had been killed; thousands of the government troops paid with their lives. Hundreds of those taken prisoner were executed by the Cheka, hundreds more sent to prisons and concentration camps, where, no doubt, a few survivors linger to this day.

On the evening when the first bombs fell on Kronstadt, its revolutionary committee addressed a radio message to the world. It read:

"The first shot has thundered. But the entire world knows of it. The bloody Field Marshal Trotsky who stands up to the waist in fraternal blood of the workers was the first to open fire against revolutionary Kronstadt, which rebelled against the government of the communists in order to re-establish the real power of the Soviets. We will rise or fall under the ruins of Kronstadt, fighting for the bloodstained cause of the laboring people. Long live the power of the Soviets! Long live the world socialist revolution!"

The eighteen thousand who died were too optimistic in supposing that their message would reach the world's ears and heart. Those to whom they appealed — the radicals and liberals and supposed friends of the Russian revolution — were too engrossed in worship of Lenin's and Trotsky's "new Russia" to give a thought to the martyrdom of its makers; too thrilled by an abstraction called revolution to bother about the torments of mere human beings. Already they had been hypnotized by the Soviet propaganda. "The revolution can do no wrong . . ." and that was that.

In the standard apologetics for the Kremlin gang the Kronstadt drama is hurriedly dismissed in embarrassment. But its meaning is decisive in the comprehension of Russia's history in our century. The victims had been the staunchest partisans of the Bolshevik *coup d'état*. The Soviet leaders hastened to befoul their memory with the familiar charges of reaction and foreign collaboration, but assuredly they were revolutionists, even communists.

Their massacre signalized the rupture of the last natural bond between the regime and the sons of the people. The last link of the Leninized Soviets with the revolutionary history and tradition of the country was snapped. What remained was a thing alien and hated and cancerous. The totalitarian state had triumphed. Again the people realized that *their Russia was a nation occupied by an internal enemy.*

The occupying power was ill at ease, deeply afraid. Sitting athwart the devastated and blood-drenched land, the last challenge to their suzerainty crushed, the dictators yet were more frightened than at any time since they had taken over. What the men in the Kremlin dreaded was no longer a concrete foe, since all organized opposition had been overcome, but an indefinable process of dissolution.

In the spring of 1921 Lenin therefore offered a far-reaching compromise to the conquered country. War communism, he conceded, had been a terrible blunder:

"The defeat we suffered . . . on the economic front was more serious than that we had ever before suffered when fighting against Kolchak, Denikin and Pilsudski. The system of distribution in the villages and the immediate application of communist methods in the towns held back our productive forces and caused the great economic and political crisis we met in the spring of 1921."

He was ready to make concessions to every element in the population. They were not, it should be emphasized, concessions in the political domain. The government's grip would not be relaxed, the terror would not be tempered by common sense, let alone mercy. The Cheka, under the revised name of GPU, would continue to be a government within the government.

The retreat announced was solely in the economic sphere. As the price for retaining a monopoly of power, the regime gave up part of its monopoly of economic life. The New Economic Policy, Nep, restored private capitalist enterprise first of all in agriculture, then in small business both at the production and distribution ends. The government retained nationalized control of all big industry, transport, communications, banking: the "commanding heights" of economic life, as the phrase of the time had it.

Lenin and his associates did not attempt to paint the changes as a victory. They spoke of them candidly and sadly as a tactical retreat, with a new strategic advance to come when the country had regained some of its strength. Russia would be allowed to put some flesh on its bones before being subjected to another socialist operation. Even on the economic front Nep was not peace but an uneasy truce, with the government sniping at private traders and systematically harassing private manufacture. Capitalist enterprise, though again legal, was denounced and derided in the official propaganda as a parasitic growth and the entrepreneur was made the butt of ridicule and planned hate.

On the political front, the dictatorship ceded little enough. It gave up none of its monopoly of power, put away none of its instruments of terror. Sporadic eruptions of violence in town and village were crushed with the familiar brutality; arrests continued; prisons and prison camps multiplied. Yet the six years of Nep were the nearest the country came to a normal existence in the whole Soviet period.

What needs underlining in the context of this book is that the Bolshevik retreat was made neither willingly nor graciously. *Nep was a victory for the people, wrenched from the dictators by main force.* It was paid for in mountains of corpses in Petrograd, Astrakhan, Tambov, Kronstadt, a thousand other places. It was a compromise exacted from surly conquerors — not by Kolchak, Denikin, Skoropadsky, Wrangel, and the rest, but by the mass of workers, peasants, soldiers, sailors, and intellectuals. Their victory would be lost again in the attrition of the continuing contest, but its import in judging the Russian peoples cannot be exaggerated.

3. The Great Famine

The grudging compromise came too late to save the country from the disaster of famine that had been building up since 1917. The policies of plunder in relation to the countryside had destroyed all incentives to planting and wiped out the reserves which the Russian farmer traditionally stored up against years of blight.

The Soviet regime of course cannot be held responsible for the drought that struck the most vital food-growing areas of the country. Famines had been a recurrent feature in the country's tragic history. But the Kremlin must shoulder blame for the helplessness of the peasantry in meeting the calamity, and therefore for its magnitude. In the past, it was some time before a ruined harvest turned into famine. Now hunger had the right of way immediately.

Victor Kravchenko, who was a boy at the time, recalls the catastrophe in these words:

In the summer of 1921 the famine was in full tide, and with it the brother of famine — epidemic typhus. They were to take many millions of lives before running their gruesome course. After the long years of war and civil strife, we faced hunger in its most elementary and cruel forms. The drought was centered in the Volga regions but its skeleton fingers reached out grimly beyond the Dnieper. The area of most intense famine coincided in a general way with the area of most intense civil war; it was as if the soil were revolting against its long diet of blood.

There are no words to describe the suffering and horror. Men eyed every living thing — horses, dogs, cats, house pets — with greedy despair. The cattle that were not slaughtered died of starvation and were consumed despite official warnings against pestilence. Trees were stripped of their bark which was brewed for "tea" or "soup." Untanned leather was chewed for sustenance. Fields were picked bare of every last stalk of straw and blade of grass. Stories of peasants eating their own dead became more frequent; and unhappily they were often true. . . . Death —

bloated, cadaverous, ugly death — was the commonplace fact in our lives. All of us were too deeply concerned with our own survival to notice or, at bottom, to care about the others.*

Lenin's approach to the mounting disaster was, as always, strictly political. The food supplies in government warehouses, he announced, would be applied to keep alive people in production; the distribution of provisions must become "an instrumentality of politics, used with the view of cutting down the number of those who are not absolutely necessary, to spur on those who are really needed." "If in the year of 1920 we had thirty-eight millions kept up by the state," he declared cold-bloodedly, "we have by now succeeded in cutting down this figure to eight millions." What happened to the thirty millions stricken from the ration lists did not much trouble him.

The famine, in its sinister way, operated to reinforce the totalitarian authority of the state. A half-starved people might revolt, but an all-starved people lacked the physical stamina even for protest. Men and women reduced to eating field mice and chewing clay, reduced in many places to cannibalism, watching their children swell up and die, had no margin of spirit left to quarrel with those in power. It is not hunger but the fear of hunger that brings on revolution.

The intervention of American charity, through the American Relief Administration under Herbert Hoover, mitigated the horrors of the famine. Without doubt it saved millions from death. But over five million perished, according to the official estimate. Foreign observers on the scene have given much higher figures. But no figure can compass the whole tragedy. Millions of the survivors were debilitated and crippled for life. New swarms of homeless children were added to the hordes left by the dislocations of civil war and war communism.

One shrinks from cold arithmetic in dealing with suffering on the Russian scale. The human mind can grasp the horror of one

* *I Chose Freedom.*

man, woman, or child in torture but it is numbed into indifference by statistics in millions. Yet it must be stated for the record that at least twelve million lives were destroyed from 1917 to 1924 by fratricidal wars, punitive expeditions, executions, assassinations, and famine.

The remaining islands of independence in the Far East, Moslem Central Asia, and the Caucasus were sunk, one after another, in the sea of Soviet domination. Doughty little Georgia put up a brave fight. Its socialist government was overthrown by an invading Red Army. A dark, dour, and pock-marked commissar sprung from its own soil, Joseph Stalin, came down to command the "pacification." His native land thus had the first direct sampling of the sadistic butchery he would in due time inflict on the whole nation.

Two years later a full-scale political insurrection in Georgia was stamped out under command of a foreign communist, the bloodthirsty little Bela Kun, who had headed a short-lived Soviet regime in Hungary. Kun is credited with murdering at least four thousand, mainly socialists and disillusioned communists. He delighted in decorating trees and lamp posts with the bodies of his victims. Within a dozen years he would himself be murdered by a Georgian, by Stalin.

And thus, outwardly at least, the Russian peoples were subjugated. Bled white by four years of war with Germany in which they had lost millions of lives, their economy in ruins, starved and half naked, their waning energies dissipated in a welter of political and moral divisions, they knuckled under to the one disciplined, coherent, ably led and fanatically ruthless minority in their midst.

Lenin died in January, 1924. The consoling belief among the Russian emigres scattered in foreign lands and also at home that the regime might collapse with the passing of its founder proved to be a delusion. The dictatorship was firmly in the saddle. The people were too weak from their long ordeal, too eager for a respite of stability, to take advantage of the opportunity.

For about six years, roughly until 1927, the truce between government and subjects signalized by the start of Nep prevailed. The GPU was never idle; its empire of surveillance and repressions, isolators and labor colonies, spying and shooting, grew. But relatively, as against the four initial years, the terror subsided.

The revival of private production in industry, restoration of private trading, and especially the abandonment of food requisitions, brought a rapid improvement in living conditions. A series of splendid harvests dulled the aching memories of famine. Before long Soviet citizens would speak of the Nep years as the "good old days," just as during the Nep period they had spoken of the czarist past as "the good old days."

A fierce struggle for leadership had begun within the dictatorship even before the paralyzed Lenin breathed his last. Stalin and Trotsky were the principal contenders and the entire ruling shift was torn by this strife. For the masses this meant a breathing spell. When the masters fight among themselves, the slaves can relax a bit. Stalin came out on top, gathering into his fists more power than any czar had ever exercised. The nightmare foreseen by Count Leo Tolstoy — despotism with a telephone, despotism armed with the might of modern science that is to say — had come true.

The iron logic of the dictatorship principle is wondrous to behold. First, the Communist Party usurped the right to speak for "the people." To make the lie stick it had to suppress all people's rights. Then a small group within the party began to speak and act for the whole organization. To make its authority stick, it had to limit the rights and initiative of the party membership. Finally, one man arrogated the sole right to speak and act for the group, removing his more intractable colleagues and terrorizing the rest into abject obedience. Rule by an elite degenerated, inexorably, to rule by a single and absolute dictator.

VIII. Stalin Makes War on Russia

1. Martial Law

Having routed the left or Trotskyist opposition, Stalin took over, as booty, the main features of its program: all-out industrialization and socialization at home, militant revolutionary strategy abroad. These he exaggerated and vulgarized as he did everything he touched. In the name of the very policies he had fought and defeated, he soon turned viciously on Bukharin, Rykov, Tomsky, and the rest of his allies against Trotsky. They surrendered without giving battle.

Now, sole master, Stalin was ready for the second great offensive against the Russian people: for "socialism" in one mad leap. It was launched in late 1928, and hit its frenzied stride in 1929 — the year Stalin called *perelom,* or the great "break" with the past.

On the whole the masses and the party had sided with Stalin, or more exactly, with the moderates, against Trotsky. Nep had been a relatively relaxed time and people yearned to make a permanent abode of that historical halfway house. They were sick and tired of world revolution and new revolutions at home. The former War Commissar seemed the more zealous revolutionary and internationalist and hence more likely to disturb the settled tenor of existence. Stalin had associated himself with Bukharin, who was actually advising the peasantry to "enrich itself"; with Tomsky, who was popular among industrial workers; with others of their kind. In fighting the fire-eating champion of "permanent revolution," Stalin had voiced the fatigue and despair of a nation fed up with sacrifices.

The nation learned its mistake soon enough, as the Georgian proceeded to out-left the left. He smashed the worried truce of Nep and projected the breath-taking Five-Year Plan of Reconstruction, including collectivization of agriculture.

In its outward forms the Plan seemed merely a too ambitious economic enterprise. Actually it was a device for accomplishing far-reaching social changes at breakneck speed. It implied the elimination of some classes in the population and a reshuffling of all classes, without the slightest regard for the pain and death involved. Before the process ran its pitiless course, it would take even greater toll in blood, suffering, and bitterness than Lenin's war communism. The wounds it inflicted suppurate to this day.

I could not realize, when I reached Moscow in February, 1928, that the moment was pregnant with history. For one thing, I was too much under the spell of the illusions typical of young American liberals with respect to the Great Experiment for calm assessment. For another, it is likely that even Stalin's closest colleagues could not yet gauge the full measure of the abominations he was charting. No one had as yet grasped the man's satanic capacity for violence.

For six years I was destined to observe a transformation that made Russia as different from the country bequeathed by Lenin as both of them were from the pre-1917 Russia. The story of those agonized years has been told in many books, but almost always in terms of economics and politics. Here I must try to recapitulate it in terms of its essence, which was *a war of internal conquest,* a Homeric struggle between an all-powerful dictatorshp and a desperately hostile population.

Stalin's offensive opened with swift and fatal blows at the counterfeit capitalism of Nep, and ended with the imposition of state feudalism in both farming and industry. In the process all the sorry remnants of popular influences and institutions — such as trade-unions, production artels, co-operatives, independent agriculture, creative movements in the arts — were either killed off or subjected to the state. The last vestiges of civil freedoms were erased.

Until then the communist elite of about a million did, in an indirect and refracted fashion, reflect the people from whom it was drawn. It served as a link of sorts with the masses. Now the link was broken. With inner discussion finally snuffed out, the party too became an inert instrument of one man's will, carrying out policies it had no part in shaping.

By 1934, when I departed from Russia, nothing was left of the high mood of dedication, traces of which I had still found among communists when I arrived. The very vocabulary of idealism had been outlawed. "Equality" and "compassion" had become dirty words, lampooned as bourgeois romanticism. Excessive concern for the people, their needs, or sensibilities, was punished as "rotten liberalism." It was a time when the verbal camouflage was peeled from arbitrary power. Terror was no longer explained away as a sad necessity. It was used starkly, arrogantly, and glorified as "human engineering." Among those who wielded power there developed a grotesque pride in the "Bolshevik firmness" and "Leninist courage" that could torture and kill millions without sentimental self-reproach, so that officials sometimes even exaggerated the number of victims. If starving a million took Bolshevik daring, did not starving five million prove that daring fivefold?

The offensive was directed, at various times or at the same time, against the "technical intelligentsia": engineers, technicians, scientists, the educated generally; against the industrial proletariat; against the peasantry; against the Communist Party itself. Its operations were reported to the outside world through "demonstration trials," industrial charts and statistics, figures on "socialized" acreage, edicts in effect chaining the worker to his machine and the farmer to the soil.

Its most ghastly piece of strategy was the man-made famine of 1932–1933. Its most sinister and enduring by-product was the institution of slave labor in conditions that made ordinary chattel slavery, ancient or modern, seem benign by comparison. An intensive attack on "superstition," meaning religion, was an inevitable part of the undertaking: The harried individual must be denied a spiritual sanctuary beyond the reach of the state. And everything that was creatively unconventional in the arts, the cultural sanctuary of the more sensitive citizen, was driven underground for the same reason.

Having watched the incredible spectacle at close range, I am convinced that even Stalin had not planned to go to quite the inhuman lengths he ultimately did go. Had his victims been more co-operative, which is to say submissive, their fate no doubt would have been milder. It was the great popular resistance, ranging from the most violent to the wholly passive, that drove him to pile horror upon horror. His determination to make the people malleable to his purposes, to break their spirit, met obstacles which could be blasted from his path only with limitless "Bolshevik firmness."

Sympathy for the battered and bleeding Russian people should, in justice to their human dignity, be matched with a sense of their heroic obduracy in an uneven struggle. Few have noted that the Kremlin's attack on each of the main groupings — the intelligentsia, the workers, the peasants, and finally the party and government bureaucracy (in the superpurges of 1936–1938) — was in some measure *provoked* by its hostility.

In writing about the first of the "show trials" of engineers and scientists, at a time when its impact was still fresh on my mind, I said: "The Shakhty men were pilloried not merely for their own misdeeds, but for the crimes of the whole embittered, rebellious intelligentsia." * It *was* bitter and mutinous. The picture of vast sabotage and plotting projected by the regime was largely a phantasmagoria of its panic — but not entirely. There were real saboteurs among the specters, though they were not necessarily the ones brought to trial. There was, more important, the unplanned sabotage that derives from apathy and contempt for the state as employer.

Some at least of the confessions extracted by torture had threads of truth woven into the fabric of police invention. The fact is that the educated classes had never wholly surrendered, that they felt themselves the exploited captives of a hostile power. For the more daring and more despairing among them, bedevilment of the

* *Assignment in Utopia,* by Eugene Lyons, Harcourt, Brace, 1937.

enemy was a matter of secret honor and secret pride. More than once, in telling me about the hopeless chaos in their plants or offices, engineers and plant directors were not quite successful in keeping the gloating note out of their voices.

The same held true for great masses of workers, though their tactics of harassment were certainly less conscious. The government's endless complaints about laziness, idling, alcoholism, malingering, absenteeism, and general lack of labor discipline had plenty to feed upon. These allegations against workers were the proletarian equivalent of the sabotage charges against engineers and planners.

If one tenth of the Kremlin's nagging accusations were justified, then the Soviet workers were indeed a shiftless and recalcitrant lot. They seemed remarkably disinterested in "their own" factories, mines, and offices, while remaining unreasonably interested in wages, work conditions, and food supplies. They hit the trail of rumor in search of better jobs, and, failing to find them, quickly followed the glimmers of hope in some other direction.

In industry as a whole, by official count, the turnover of labor often passed 100 per cent annually; in a great many enterprises it was close to 100 per cent a month. Millions of haggard men and women turned migratory, overloading the railroads and tying production into knots. They were voting with their feet against the new industrial order.

From the viewpoint of the employing state, the torrent of decrees aimed at disciplining labor made sense. They amounted to military measures in an undeclared war.

As for the peasantry, it was virtually on strike. In the Leninist era the growers of food had tested their muscles and tasted a degree of victory. Now they rebelled the more boldly against feeding the urban population for rubles that could not buy manufactured goods. They found ingenious devices for frustrating the government's seasonal "grain collections," ostensibly purchases but in reality thinly disguised requisitions. Millions of farm families saw no point in planting and harvesting more than they needed for themselves.

Food lines everywhere were therefore growing longer and uglier. The situation was aggravated by a partial crop failure in 1928–1929 in Southern Russia. Grain mobilization was not going well, and, as always when this happened, the collectors resorted to strong-arm tactics and the peasants responded in kind. Moscow ordered what it called euphemistically "extraordinary measures," amounting to forcible confiscation. GPU troops were sent into the more intractable regions to halt leakage of foodstuffs through private channels. Government agents were ordered to meet their grain quotas by *any* means, and many of them paid with their lives for trying.

The official legend is of a peasantry divided between the mass of poor and the minority of well-to-do exploiters or "kulaks." Actually the countryside, with the negligible exception of some *batraks* or landless peasants, was a solid bloc against the state impositions. The "kulak resistance" that figured in government propaganda was really peasant resistance. Reports of local uprisings in the Kuban, the Ukraine, and other sections spread through Moscow. From all sections came news of local or visiting state representatives waylaid and murdered. At one point a rare official admission placed the murdered communists at five hundred; we could easily surmise that the number of so-called "kulak agents" summarily shot in retaliation must therefore have run into thousands.

Arson, a traditional weapon of village vengeance, was epidemic. Warehouses, clubs, Soviet buildings, other places symbolizing the *vlast* were burned down wholesale, and Army or GPU forces "pacified" the offending areas with lead. Great numbers of peasants, lured by reports of city jobs, abandoned the land and swelled the gypsy hordes moving across the land from nowhere to nowhere like hunger-crazed animal herds.

Disaffection was rife also among officials of the party, the government, the economic institutions. The job of slave driver and prison warden is not always a pleasant one. In the earlier years more squeamish members of the proletariat of power — party functionaries, administrators, police officials, and so on — could at least rationalize their dirty chores with clean idealistic professions. With the advent of Stalin that consolation was denied them.

Again, as in the case of the technical intelligentsia, there were molehills of fact under the mountains of wild fancy thrown up by the police to justify the great purges. The rarefied air where bureaucracy had its being was stirred by subversive grumblings and whisperings. The humiliation of their once revered leaders, the Trotskys and the Bukharins, and the loss of the last margins of inner-party democracy, offended the self-esteem of the elite. My own contacts, in the nature of the case, were chiefly in the elite area, and there, I can testify, hatred of Stalin and his associates was as palpable as the fear they inspired.

Taken together, these expressions of non-co-operation on every level of Soviet life were crowding the dictatorship into a cul-de-sac. It must either make far-reaching concessions to a recalcitrant people or crush it utterly, release the screws or tighten them to the limit. It had either to fill hungry mouths or shut them up by force. Given Stalin's nature, his choice was preordained.

He proceeded to impose what was in effect economic as well as political *martial law*. Every turn of the screws, by deepening resentments and evoking new varieties of resistance, made another turn inevitable. What one of my colleagues called Russia's "iron age" was under way: the harshest, hungriest, most terror-ridden age in all the tragic history of the country.

2. The "Disfranchised Ones"

The headlong revision of every aspect of life was conducted with the drum beating, the deadly urgency, and especially the total disdain for casualties, characteristic of war. It was conducted under the banners of "class war" and reported in martial terms. "The industrialization," Victor Serge, a disillusioned French communist who witnessed the events, was to write, "is directed like a march through conquered territory. . . . The collectivization is like installing an army in a conquered land, according to the worst rigors of war."

Campaigns and battles were fought on the bread front, the steel front, the antireligious front. Fortresses of the old order were razed, citadels of the *bourgeoisie* were stormed. Garden variety tyranny was explained in terms of military discipline. Hated industrial pacesetters became "shock troops." But above all, swarming "class enemies" were outsmarted, overpowered, exterminated. In social areas where no such enemies existed, they were arbitrarily *invented* — how else could they be defeated in a class war?

The first of these enemies to be extirpated were the Nepmen, the new *bourgeoisie* of private shopkeepers, artisans, small manufacturers, well-to-do professionals. It had come into being since 1921 and was a group unique in history: a large middle class without a past or a future, without roots or a culture of its own, without public respect or much self-respect.

Though entirely within the law, it was eternally molested and ridiculed. A class of pariahs who, paradoxically, were the only moneyed, well-fed, well-clad people in a wretchedly run-down country. Because it had risen quickly out of the chaos and was at bottom uncertain of its tenure, it tended to be *nouveau riche* with a vengeance, crude, loud, and profiteering, as if eager to make the most of its uncertain lease on life.

The obliteration of this class having been decided upon, it would have been kinder to carry it out by a forthright decree. But for some esoteric reason the Kremlin preferred to strangle Nepmen "legally." It arrested them by the tens of thousands for alleged violation of laws or on farfetched counterrevolutionary charges. The main agent of demolition, however, was the tax collector, empowered to review earnings and profits from the year one and to impose punitive retroactive taxes. The inspectors swooped down on the victim and inventoried his business and personal assets, down to the kitchen utensils and his extra pair of shoes. When the back taxes and penalties were estimated, they always turned out a shade larger than the victim's total possessions. Accordingly he was stripped of all his earthly belongings, his home included, and in most cases shipped by cattle car to Siberia or some other exile area for good measure.

Whatever the devices used, the last of the private stores and workshops and pushcart hucksters were eliminated by the end of 1928. The names of personal owners on shop fronts and restaurants gave way to synthetic government names like Mosselprom 8 and Mosselprom 17. The harshest parts of the country, its Arctic reaches and Central Asian deserts and Siberian timber empires, had their first lush contingents of forced labor. Aside from the scrubby bazaars where people sold pitiful personal effects displayed on soiled newspapers, about the only private enterprise remaining was represented by the teeming prostitutes, many of them teen-age girls, on the main city streets.

This sort of summary does not even suggest the human tragedy of the "liquidation." Hundreds of thousands of men, women, and children who only yesterday lived better than their neighbors were suddenly reduced to absolute destitution. All former Nepmen and their dependents, even if they evaded exile, were officially "declassed." This meant that they were rated as *lishentsi*, "disfranchised ones," and as such deprived of normal human rights and legal status.

The *lishentsi*, curiously, remain largely an unknown phenomenon to the non-Soviet world. Somehow their ordeal has not registered on the minds of foreign journalists and scholars, viewing the USSR through a haze of statistics. There were millions of them, as degraded and helpless as the untouchables in India. They had no right to jobs except in the lowest or "black" grades of manual labor, no right to rations, hospital care, or living space under controlled rents. Their children were barred in effect from schools and the armed forces.

Their name derived from the fact that in every community special electoral commissions drew up lists of citizens entitled to vote for members of the local Soviet. Though an empty privilege, voting being a farce, it was one cherished beyond wealth or honors. Because those excluded became the *lishentsi*, in effect told off for a lingering outlaw death.

The principal cause for disfranchisement was faulty "social origin," meaning that the unfortunates (or their parents or grandparents) had been aristocrats, priests, businessmen, shopkeepers, czarist officers, prosperous peasants, and the like. Now Nepmen and the children of Nepmen were put into this persecuted category, despite the fact that Nep had been a legitimate Soviet way of life while it lasted. Rarely in history had the crime of being born in the "wrong" family been so cruelly punished. The sins of the fathers were visited upon the children in the name of Marx. Even today, though the *lishentsi* principle no longer prevails, the stain of improper "social origin" is under the Soviets all but ineradicable.

Hundreds of thousands of "former people," *bivshiye,* the leftovers of the prerevolutionary upper classes, petty traders, members of former socialist and democratic parties or idealistic movements, had lost themselves in the Soviet world. The fact that they were alive meant that they had found employment in some corner of the government economy. They thought themselves safely forgotten. Great numbers of younger people had simply lied about their families, converting wealthy or ecclesiastical or merchant forebears into respectable workers and peasants.

Their unspeakable audacity in having survived was suddenly remembered. A veritable pogrom was whipped up against "class enemy elements" who might be "hiding" in government offices, banks, schools, museums. A lot of them, having come from shopkeeping or peddling backgrounds, had naturally gravitated to the distribution branches of socialized economy; this was true in particular of the large Jewish population. The order of the day was to ferret out such "formers" and "drive them out of Soviet life."

No one dared raise the question of how the victims would live — that would be foul bourgeois sentimentality. When I raised the question myself, a press official shrugged in impatience. "Why should they remain alive?" he countered. The fellow had what it takes to be a good Stalinist, though the ungrateful Stalin had him shot a few years later.

"A thousand incidents crowd to my mind," I wrote of this mass atrocity after leaving Russia. "A meek old man who had been bookkeeper in a government office for many years now cast out as a class enemy. A young teacher dismissed because her father had been a shopkeeper. A student in the technical school thrown out for 'concealing his social origin' by claiming descent from a poor peasant when, as a matter of fact, his father had owned four cows. 'Nests of former people' uncovered in museums and libraries, or research institutions: broken-down middle-aged or elderly people suddenly hounded from their jobs solely because of their 'social origin.'" *

A sharp increase in street beggary was among the immediate effects of these pogroms. The whining professional mendicant was a familiar enough part of the urban scene; so was the tattered peasant family sprawled on the sidewalk and begging for alms. Far more pathetic was the new crop: mostly old men and women, with something of dignity and breeding in their looks despite threadbare clothes, heads bowed in shame as they timidly stretched out their hands.

3. Breaking the Intelligentsia

Coincident with the crushing of Nep came the assault on the intelligentsia, which in Russian usage embraced brain workers of every type. The first "big story" I covered, a few months after reaching the Soviet capital, was the signal for attack. It was the first of the great "demonstration trials" which, year after year, were to bewilder the world with spectacles of men confessing unbelievable crimes and debasing themselves for the glory of the Kremlin.

"Trial," with its connotation of justice, is a strange name for these political circuses. The guilt of the accused is assumed to have been established in the preliminary investigations. The prosecution comes into "court" with a sheaf of confessions. The idea is merely to demonstrate the heinous nature of the crime as theatrically as an omnipotent dictatorship can contrive. The accused are selected as carefully as actors in the casting of a play. There would be less mystification about "why they confess" if the world realized that *only those who confess* are ever brought into the limelight of these public exhibitions. The rest are dealt with in darkness.

* *Assignment in Utopia.*

But the system has not yet been perfected in May, 1928. In this first of the blood trials — the so-called Shakhty case — a few of the victims still tried to save shreds of honor, a few tried to repudiate portions of the confessions extorted in GPU interrogations.

Fifty-three engineers and technicians from the coal industry in the Shakhty region were brought into the garish ballroom of the former Nobles' Club, now the House of Trade Unions. Before microphones, under klieg lights, they told a fantastic tale of plotting with former mine owners in emigration to ruin the industry. All were found guilty, of course, but only eleven were sentenced to death, the kind of leniency that would become increasingly rare in later years.

Though my eyes were still glazed with pro-Soviet illusions, the experience left me with a sickish feeling. Too often in the course of the trial, an unguarded word or outcry from a prisoner had given hints of sinister processes behind the scenes; the shadowy torture chambers kept intruding despite all the state could do to keep them out of sight. "I came increasingly to feel the demonstration trial as a hoax," I would write in due time — "not merely on the outside world which received it naïvely as a species of justice, but a hoax on the Russian masses themselves who were being offered a lightning rod to divert their resentments."

The offer was spurned. Hundreds of mass meetings of workers passed resolutions thanking the government for having caught and punished the villains. But the Kremlin must have known, since even a naïve foreign reporter knew it, that the people were skeptical. In an ambiguous phrase or a politically off-color joke, or in the embarrassed silences when the Shakhty trial was mentioned, Soviet citizens betrayed their doubts — or their cynical certainties.

Despite the removal of the self-confessed culprits, production troubles in the coal industry got worse. In the Shakhty district itself, ironically, output took a nose dive, as was only to be expected with its technical personnel arrested or paralyzed by fear.

The big push against the educated continued for nearly four years. Men and women whose only sin was that they had learned their technical professions before the revolution waited in agony for the nocturnal knock on the door. A popular comedian, Vladimir Khenkin, had a sure-fire "gag" which convulsed Moscow audiences. "One night," he said with a straight face, in his monologue, "I heard a vigorous knock at my door. *So I took my little suitcase and went to open the door.*" He paused for the guffaws and they always came, though there were many who winced and only pretended to laugh. He was alluding to the simple fact (incredible to anyone outside Russia) that prerevolutionary intellectuals usually had a few things packed in a satchel in case of sudden arrest!

Gory posters inscribed "Death to Wreckers!" or bearing the one grim word *Rasstrel!* — "Shoot!" — filled the land, and every engineer, every production specialist, however clean his conscience, knew that he was the target. Since it was in sore need of technical brains for its Five-Year Plan, the Kremlin could hardly have wished to eliminate all these people. Its purpose was to cow them into submission, to break their spirit.

The ambitious industrial plans unfolded noisily. Huge new factories, foundries, chemical plants, a thousand other projects rose all over the Soviet map. Miles of leaky barracks and *zemlyanki,* primitive dugouts in the ground, served as homes for millions of new workers, fresh from their villages, and for the rapidly expanding armies of slave laborers. The thunderous cry for speed and more speed drowned out the groans of the hungry, the overworked, the homesick.

As was only natural in a country without technological experience or trained labor forces, trying to crowd a generation of normal expansion into a few hectic years, monumental blunders were made. Structures collapsed. Plants fitted with the latest American and German machinery somehow stalled. Plain incompetence, faulty planning, and bureaucratic red tape no doubt accounted for most of these things.

But the Kremlin chose to see the hand of plotters and saboteurs in every mishap and failure. Nor was it content until a few miserable people had been bullied and tortured into confessing guilt and been imprisoned or shot. It became a sort of ritual of propitiation. But the more engineers and administrators were liquidated, the more badly things went, so that yet more of them had to be arrested and executed, in an endless vicious circle.

When conditions in any department of national life grew scandalously bad, one could expect the presentation of some scapegoats, luridly trimmed. By the autumn of 1930 the food situation was catastrophic; meat in particular had all but disappeared in the cities. This was clearly one of the effects of peasant resistance to being socialized. But the Kremlin had to save face by uncovering a spectacular plot in the food industries.

Thirty-odd foreign correspondents were on a government-sponsored junket down the Volga River. We had just visited Rostov when the shocking news exploded. On September 22 the press announced that the glorious GPU had smoked out another "counterrevolutionary society," and forty-eight culprits were under arrest. Conveniently the saboteurs were headed by a member of the meat trust, a Professor Alexander Riazantzev, and his confederates were all professors, agronomists and administrators connected with food trusts.

The next day the press was loud with synthetic popular "demands" that the scoundrels be shot forthwith. The factory resolutions had only the word of the GPU to go upon, except the towering fact that the country's food supplies were indeed depleted, rotted, hopelessly inadequate and expensive. By September 24, only two days after the plot had been announced, the government had yielded to the "demands." It announced that all forty-eight had already been shot. Forty-eight ghosts rode with us for the rest of the trip down the Volga. I wrote a mock dispatch which did not endear me to the authorities. It began: "The Kremlin today moved to solve the acute meat shortage by slaughtering 48 officials of food industries."

The frenzy of engineer baiting reached a pitch of planned hysteria in another and even more bizarrely melodramatic show trial at the end of 1930. For some reason it caught the imagination of the outside world, which reported it in immense detail day after day. But how were readers abroad, who could not know that truth and justice are not even involved in this kind of exhibition, to judge the weird proceedings?

In the grayish dusk of November 25, half a million workers from Moscow factories and offices marched through the snows past the former Nobles' Club, chanting two words: *Rasstrel! Smert!* — "Shoot!" and "Death!" They marched because they had been commanded to march, under banners reading: "Death to the agents of imperialism!" "Shoot the wreckers!" "No mercy to class enemies!" Similar hate parades were staged at the end of the workday in all other cities. The same tom-tom of "Death! Death!" pulsed through endless editorials, radio harangues, and billboard posters. The enthroned state was sparing no trick of ballyhoo to inflame hatreds, to give the masses an outlet for their bottled-up angers.

Within the Nobles' Club, in the ballroom hung with many blazing chandeliers, eight scholarly looking men sat in two neat rows in a prisoner's box on a high stage. Hundreds of privileged spectators jammed the chamber as for a carnival, and about seventy-five domestic and Soviet reporters occupied the front rows of seats at the foot of the stage. The podium was cluttered with klieg lights and microphones. Andrei Vishinsky was the presiding judge — his debut in the Soviet limelight — and the tense little prosecutor, Nikolai Krylenko, appropriately in hunting costume, his clean-shaven bullet-head gleaming, was in command.

All of us heard the baying under the windows. The eight lonely figures in the prisoners' pen were the least villainous looking of mortals. The thought that all the gigantic nationwide excitement was focused on them seemed grotesque. Several of them wore neat professional beards and pince-nez. They shuffled papers and made copious notes, as though waiting their turn to address some scientific conference. At their head, the alleged ringleader, was Dr. Leonid Ramzin, a thermodynamic engineer, a mild little man in his early forties, clean-shaven and with the manner of a pedagogue. In due time each of them was to contribute his prearranged portion to the outline of the plot, and sure enough, they spoke in the precise academic tones one expected.

Two weeks earlier the press had published the indictment. It unveiled as startling a picture as any government had ever presented to an incredulous world. An underground "Industrial Party" comprising thousands of Soviet engineers and official planners, it charged, had worked for years with the connivance of the General Staffs of a dozen nations to overthrow the Soviet regime. Its activities allegedly involved such names as Poincaré, Briand, Colonel T. E. Lawrence of Arabia fame, and Sir Henry Deterding abroad; and men in key places in the Five-Year Plan at home. By undermining Soviet industry the ground was to be prepared for a sudden foreign attack under the leadership of France. Even a slate of the new government to take over when the Soviets fell was supposedly drawn up.

Here was a complete alibi for the industrial dislocations, the lags in fiulfilment of the Plan, and above all the lack of food and the awful living conditions.

The eight men pleaded guilty, of course. Under the whiplashing of the sadistic Krylenko they lacerated themselves without mercy. If one defendant made an obviously absurd statement, the others hastened to correct him. Judges, prosecutors, defense lawyers and the accused seemed intent upon the same job: to convince the country that the fantasy was true, that a hostile world and enemies inside the USSR were responsible for the mounting trouble and terror. Ramzin and four others were condemned to death, the rest drew prison terms. Two days later the death sentences were commuted to ten years' imprisonment.

The case against them, for all their vehement self-accusation, was pathetically flimsy. Any tyro of a defense attorney in a free court could have made the state look like the liar it was. There was not a scrap of evidence aside from self-incrimination. The whole plot, it seemed to nearly all the foreign observers, was "sewn with white thread," as the Russian phrase has it. Some of the stitches came apart. For instance, the slate of the succession government included the names of two men who had long been dead at the time it was presumably drawn up, one of the corpses being scheduled to become Premier, no less. Not that it mattered, since the slip-up was uncovered abroad and was not revealed to the Soviet audience.

Again, as in the Shakhty case, the hardest thing to find was a Russian who had swallowed the story. Even the press department official who urged me to write a book on the case, strictly within the framework of the frame-up, couldn't repress a cynical smile. He was doing his duty.

But the artificial thunder of vengeance rolled through the country long after the trial was over. The posters continued to bawl *Rasstrel!* The trial had been little more than a perverted morality play, a symbol awkwardly fashioned. With popular bitterness and disillusion over the wonders of industrialization growing, Stalin was saying through this mumbo jumbo: "Now you see why you're suffering. It's all the fault of the capitalist nations, plotting with traitors in our midst! Destroying your factories, spoiling your food, flooding your mines, selling out to your *émigré* capitalists and landlords!"

Obediently the masses shouted *Rasstrel!*, even as they had marched obediently under prefabricated banners the day the trial started. But they saw through the fraud, of that I had no doubt. Their knowledge was a secret they read in one another's eyes, a secret they whispered, when they could no longer contain themselves, to the few whom they trusted.

Their own lives had become a cruel treadmill, ten hours a day for five days, with a rest day on the sixth. But the rest days were staggered, so that no one day was a holiday for all or even for all members of a family. Their Sundays were thus obliterated, as part of the campaign to liquidate God. At the same time incredible laws, each harsher than its predecessor, were promulgated to end the fluidity of labor and eradicate its easygoing and apathetic ways. Meanwhile, in the countryside the most pitiless campaign of all, to strip the toilers of their land ownership, was in progress.

The workers and peasants, no less than the technical intelligentsia, were being "engineered" to the rigid totalitarian pattern.

IX. Conquest of the Workers and Peasants

1. Worker into Serf

A small minority, chiefly communists too young to be totally corrupted by cynicism, embraced the Five-Year Plan (announced in 1929) with fanatic zeal. Its enthusiasm was real and deep, fired by a vision of material plenitude in a true socialistic society around the corner. But the official claim that this enthusiasm was shared by the masses, or even "the proletarians," was a cruel lie. A lie refuted by mountains of corpses, millions of deportees and prisoners, piles of decrees whose undisguised purpose was to *force* unwilling men to labor.

The overwhelming mass of Russians received the Plan with knowing skepticism or sullen indifference. Their folk intuition, made keener by repeated disappointment, told them they were being earmarked for yet bigger and better "sacrifices." Watching the communists stoke their altar fires, the plain people had no doubt who would fry.

In the beginning of course there was a certain amount of diffused hope, if only because wretched millions craved an excuse for hope. The timetable feature was comforting: The five years would pass, then perhaps surcease from pressures and enough to eat. As those years wore on, however, the hope grew dimmer and in the end it expired in the swamps of blood and forced labor.

The planners made the psychological mistake of meticulously

detailing the great improvements in daily existence which would accrue. The buying power of the ruble, they said, would appreciate by one fifth, real wages by two thirds; the cost of living would decline 14 per cent, people would eat 27.7 per cent more meat, 72 per cent more eggs, and so on. For the ordinary mortal this was the heart of the Plan, besides being one phase they could check without benefit of statisticians. It was the phase, alas, utterly forgotten in the noisy shuffle of later boasts. To allude to it, as I discovered, was considered an "unfriendly" act. The Kremlin would have been wiser to restrain its hosanna singers who were only sharpening the cutting edge of disillusionment.

The exertions of these years were *by* the people, but neither *for* nor *of* the people. The masses did not go along willingly. They were driven by threats and hideous punishments, mobilized and deployed like so many conscripts. They were not Stalin's allies but his captive foes. The ever more overt forms of coercion required to "discipline" them were the measure of their essential disobedience.

Almost at the outset rationing of food and clothes was introduced. A reminder of hardships a decade before, its connotations were alarming. The ruble fell precipitously — from four down to one hundred per dollar in about three years. Prices skyrocketed, making the higher wages a swindle. Some essential products disappeared entirely, all were in tragically short supply. Only families in the highest income brackets could resort to the flourishing black markets. As in a city besieged, food became the one absorbing subject, obsessing all minds.

The last pretenses that industrial workers were a favored class were jettisoned, as hours of work were stretched, production schedules stepped up, freedom of movement for labor all but ended. What had survived of "old-fashioned" concepts of trade-unionism, which was precious little, was now expunged. The symbol of this crucial defeat of the workers — and they counted it a defeat — was the liquidation, as a right deviationist, of their last champion in the hierarchy, Mikhail Tomsky. In due time he was driven to suicide.

The trade-unions, as set up by Lenin and administered by Tomsky until 1928, were intended in theory at least to give labor some

protection against management, even if management was the government. A representative of the trade-union was part of the "triangle,"
along with management and the party, which administered a given
enterprise. Stalin canceled out all such liberal nonsense. Being the
"owners" of industry, why should workmen require safeguards
against *themselves?* The triangle was dismantled. A single director
designated by the center took its place. Backed by a secret police
unit on the premises, he exercised more power than any capitalist
boss in history. He could deprive an employe not alone of his job, but
of his ration card and "living space." In the final analysis he could
starve a worker's whole family into submission.

The old comedy of "negotiations" on wages and work norms was
abandoned. Such things were thereafter arbitrarily decided by the
state. The general job of labor unions was the same as that of other
branches of the government: to carry out orders originating elsewhere. Its specific job was to extract the most work for the least pay.
Sergo Ordzhonikidze, Commissar of Heavy Industry, explained the
Stalinist view of wages bluntly enough in addressing a conference:

"As directors, administrative officials, and experts, you must personally occupy yourselves with wages in all their concrete details
and not leave to anyone this most important matter. *Wages are the
most powerful weapon in your hands.*"

The "anyone" who must not be permitted to interfere was the
worker. The weapon was the threat of hunger. Everything is fair
in war.

The workers retaliated in the only way open to them: They
dragged their feet. They engaged in what Thorstein Veblen called
"conscientious withdrawal of efficiency." Their resistance was expressed in ingenious slow-up, confusion, absenteeism, pilfering,
wrecked machinery and spoiled goods. The Kremlin dealt with
them, not by improving conditions but by improving its punitive
laws.

From 1930 on, new labor decrees hit the workers before they had
recovered from preceding blows. The authorities put into effect
what was a barely disguised conscription of labor. The ration card
was club enough for bludgeoning reluctant men and women into

unpleasant jobs in unpleasant places. Workers were forbidden to change employment without written consent of the management.

In the summer of 1931, Stalin finally resorted to payment on the basis of piecework. It was then that "equality," of income or any other variety, suddenly became a heinous political sin. At the same time other techniques for squeezing more work out of its industrial serfs were developed by the state.

"Shock brigades," or pacesetters, were generated in every factory, mine, office, and construction job, usually with the communists taking the lead. *Udarniki,* as the brigadiers were called, became a kind of labor aristocracy, rewarded by more food, priority on deficit products, better living quarters. So-called "socialist competition" between enterprises and between departments in one plant, was developed, again with material bonuses for the winners. Finally, the Stakhanovite movement — a Soviet exaggeration of the Taylor speed-up principle — was inaugurated, and the press began to boast of "proletarian millionaires" who had achieved that proud status by their extraordinary productivity.

While eulogized on the factory walls and in the press, the brigadiers and Stakhanovites were regarded with murderous hate by the other 99 per cent of the working class. Jealousy of their privileges was part of the story. More important was the realization that the production standards set by the eager beavers tended to become the norms for everybody, with reduction of payment per unit accordingly. Small wonder that the more zealous speed-up champions were afraid for their lives; many of them were murdered.

The one device for raising labor output that would have been genuinely effective was sufficient food for the workers and their dependents. But this was beyond the power of a state simultaneously engaged in conquering the peasantry. Yet the Kremlin made brutal use even of the food shortages. The hungrier the worker, the more exciting the carrot dangled out of reach. On December 4, 1932, food supplies and other necessities were placed under the control of the factory management. Stalin made no bones about the purpose: "in order to strengthen the power of directors," the announcement specified.

By the end of the same month, "internal passports" were instituted. Their effect was to chain people to their jobs and areas of residence almost as firmly as feudal serfs were tied to the soil. Domestic passports had been one of the execrated nuisances of life under the *ancien régime,* and roundly lambasted in earlier Bolshevik literature. But the Soviet version was incomparably more drastic. Unauthorized absence from your home for seventy-two hours, or sojourn elsewhere for more than seventy-two hours, was reported to the police and punishable by forced labor.

Ultimately a worse visitation was put into practice. That was the "labor book" which Lenin had recommended as more effective than the guillotine. It came at the end of 1938 as part of a package labeled "Measures for Improving Labor Discipline" that brought together and amplified in the direction of greater stringency the measures promulgated in preceding years. It included the incredible provisions imposing forced-labor and prison terms for lateness of twenty minutes or more, and for other kinds of "absenteeism." Factory directors who might be squeamish in reporting the "criminals" and public prosecutors too lax in imposing punishment were ruled as sharing the offender's guilt and subject to stiff penalties.

The package was the logical climax of a process that began in the *Piatiletka* period. The outrages against the once glorified "ruling class," the proletarians, were not kept in the shadows. They were always announced amidst thunderous propaganda that added insult to injury by pretending that the victims had "demanded" these "reforms" and were grateful for them.

A nauseating hypocrisy has been standard in Soviet procedure. Thus a manual of labor laws published in 1940 begins with a lecture on the fine freedoms enjoyed by Soviet workers compared with their exploited brothers under capitalism. Then follows a compilation of the most obnoxious antilabor regulations to which any supposedly "free" working class has ever been subjected.

According to these laws, billed as glorious achievements, anyone who left his job twenty minutes too soon or stretched his lunch hour to that extent must forthwith be brought before the People's Tribunal, there to be sentenced to six months of "correctional labor," meaning a 25 per cent reduction in earnings. Should the culprit repeat the offense, he must go to prison. Regulations of shocking severity are listed for transport workers. According to paragraph 59/3 of the Criminal Code, a railway man can be sentenced to ten years' imprisonment if his lateness caused economic loss to the state or an upset in the timetable. If his absenteeism is coupled with "bad intent," the penalty can be death by shooting. Paragraph 84/4, dating back to June 1, 1932, provides that damage or loss of tools and materials, if due to a worker's negligence, must be refunded fivefold, the money being taken out of his wages.

To suppose that the Russian toilers *like* such laws and the virtual enslavement it suggests is to libel not only Russians but the human race. Those who still contend that "the workers," at any rate, are devoted to the Soviet regime would be cured of their error by a perusal of Soviet labor legislation.

Labor's traditional weapon of self-defense, the strike, had been snatched from its hands in the early Soviet years. It was never restored, being dealt with by the regime as insurrection. Nevertheless, strikes there were; usually spontaneous and undirected actions of the sit-down and slow-up types under the spur of hunger and anger. Rumors reached us in Moscow of strikes bloodily crushed in various parts of the country. Not until recent years, when eyewitnesses of those events among fugitives from the Soviet Union began to tell their stories, did I learn that those rumors had not overdrawn the picture.

For instance, I am told by a former resident of Kharkov that in the spring of 1931 the tens of thousands of workers in the city's great locomotive factory could no longer bear their lot. One day they dropped work, held mass meetings, passed resolutions demanding better working conditions and more political elbowroom. GPU troops arrived to show them who was master.

Two years later the approximately fifteen hundred workers in an Odessa jute factory, mostly women, staged a sit-down strike. They elected a factory committee and a delegation to place their grievances before the city Soviet. Though sparked by food shortages, the demands went far beyond the economic, including entreaties for greater personal freedom. Russian strikes traditionally had carried strong political overtones.

The answer of the Odessa Soviet came swiftly. Strikebreakers were sent to displace the regular workers, and when their entry was barred, militia and GPU soldiery surrounded the plant. The workers refused to surrender despite this military encirclement. Thereupon the armed forces broke down the doors and entered with guns blazing. About eighty workers, nearly all women, were killed. Then the alleged ringleaders were hauled away, never to be seen again.

Such episodes are reported from virtually every industrial area. Under the sloganeered surface of industrial life were smoldering resentments which found vent continually in gross or subtle types of non-co-operation. Despite the piled-up punitive decrees, workers remained mutinous. For all the terror, the most familiar words in the economic news of the period were *proriv* — "breakdown" — and *uzkie miesta* — "narrow places" or bottlenecks — in production.

The workers were beaten, beaten utterly. The fantasy that it was "their" dictatorship became good for a bitter laugh wherever they foregathered. I was interested in a report by a Frenchman who found himself, after the last war, working in a Soviet coal mine. Though the period was different, the state of mind he attested was familiar to me. Upon his return to France, he told of talks with fellow miners.

"I tried to explain to them," he said, "what the Soviet Union meant to workers of the world. 'You don't seem to realize that you ought to love your country. The Soviet Union is known all over the world as the workers' paradise.' They laughed. They said I was trying to be funny; said they didn't know what to admire more — the cleverness of the people who fooled the workers of the world or the stupidity of the workers of the world. Till my last day at the mine, they kidded me about the workers' world. Every time we had reason to complain about some injustice or hardship on the job, they used to say: 'Well, what do you expect? It's your paradise, isn't it?'" *

*The magazine *politics,* Spring, 1948.

2. *War on the Peasantry*

A miasma of fear spread over the entire country. The sound of the Black Raven, as Russians called the police wagon, rolling over the cobbles after midnight sent a chill through men's veins. Laconic announcements of executions, in fine type among the miscellaneous news items, became so familiar that they lost their power to move people. On a battlefield one gets used to the litter of corpses.

Under the censorship rules we could cable anything that was in the Soviet press. How many official murders a correspondent reported therefore depended on his energy in hunting up items in the papers. A German colleague, having subscribed to a batch of provincial papers and engaged extra secretaries, was able to write dispatches about hundreds shot when less industrious reporters wrote of mere dozens or scores. And we all knew of course that only a tithe of the aggregate executions ever got into print.

On a day when I had totaled over forty executions in the morning newspapers — speculators, saboteurs, kulaks, priests — I asked a Moscow acquaintance who was reading the same papers whether there was any exciting news. He glanced through *Pravda* again and shrugged: "No, nothing important."

"Nothing important? Just count the death sentences in Novorossisk, Krasnodar, Rostov — "

"Oh that!" he smiled wryly. *That* was no longer news.

Those finished off with a shot at the base of the head were luckier than the others — soon millions taken together — who were sent to slow death in the proliferating concentration camps. And the victims, it should be borne in mind, were either suspected or guilty of blocking the regime and its works. However trifling the offenses, however disproportionate the punishments, here was continuing evidence of elemental opposition. If the Kremlin's purpose was to intimidate its subjects by shocking examples of the risks of insubordination, it must have been convinced that a spirit of rebellion was abroad to undertake intimidation on such a monstrous scale.

* * *

The cities and towns were oases of peace compared to the villages, where collectivization was being imposed. There the description of the process as "war" ceased to be a figure of speech. It was real war, war of aggression, against a population larger than Germany's. The defenders were unarmed and unorganized, so their defeat was a foregone conclusion. Yet they never wholly capitulated.

The fact that the government has been obliged periodically to renew hostilities against the peasants would indicate that they never accepted their conquest as final. Most of them were to judge the war that came in 1941, and are sure to judge any major disturbance in the future, primarily in terms of their hope of liberation from the yoke put on their necks in the early thirties. They did not resist the aggression in the name of "democracy" or any other political abstraction; they were fighting very concretely for their farms and their human status as owners of land.

Despite all that has been written about collectivization, the magnitude of its malevolence has not been conveyed to the world. The word has a disarming ring, giving no inkling of the enormities it covered. One must reach back into the history of great conquests with fire and sword for some sense of its dimensions and ferocity. Russian agriculture was "reformed" in about the way that the Golden Horde of Genghis Khan reformed the continent it ravaged, or conquistadores reformed the Indians they subjugated.

To call collectivization an "agrarian revolution" is sheer irony. It was not an eruption from below, like the seizure of land after the fall of czardom in 1917, but an imposition from above. It was no more a revolution than the expropriation of Jews in Nazi Germany. A powerful dictatorship used its social machinery, vast police forces, and at times its armies to rob the peasantry of land, animals and implements — and especially of the remaining personal and economic freedom. No, it was not a revolution but a conquest of the larger half of a country's population.

Foreign observers in the capital were first sharply alerted to the spreading catastrophe by a curious event. In the late summer months of 1929, families from the German regions on the Volga, in Crimea and elsewhere began to arrive in Moscow on all trains. They came with their bedding and household effects — under the strange delusion that they would be allowed to migrate to Canada. Most of them, having sold their farms and other possessions, had enough cash to buy shelter in peasant cottages on the outskirts of Moscow, sometimes twenty and more in a small room. Perhaps five thousand persons reached the city before the government could choke off the exodus at its points of origin.

These people were descendants of the Germans, mainly Mennonites, given asylum in Russia by Catherine the Great. Through all the generations they had kept their language and bits of their racial culture. On the whole they were more efficient and more prosperous than their Russian neighbors. Somehow, as the pressures of collectivization began, the rumor spread among them that they would be allowed to leave the country. This mirage of a new life in the Western hemisphere was too exciting to resist.

Ordinarily the authorities would have crushed this demonstration of basic hostility — and that is what it amounted to — as it was crushing other forms of recalcitrance. But the German embassy, on instructions from Berlin, interested itself in the affair, and resident correspondents were watching it as sheer human drama. The Kremlin therefore thought it best to show some restraint. A few hundred emigration visas were actually issued; the rest of the refugees were gradually sent "home" in tight-packed and stinking boxcars. Reports had it that most of the cars were shunted to the northern forest areas, where labor was needed.

These Germans were a pathetic, bedraggled and bewildered lot when their mirage faded out. Yet they seemed to some of us a heartening symbol and portent. The dream of a freer and ampler life that had moved them filled the hearts of all Soviet peasants in varying degrees, whatever their race. The episode gave us a glimpse of the terror that had already gripped the countryside, but also an indication of *the stubborn antagonism the regime was meeting.*

Despite all that the government could do to stop them, tens of thousands of other peasant families, laden with bundles, flocked to the cities. The Moscow stations began to look like encampments of desperate refugees from a flood or an earthquake, and the same must have been true in all the larger centers. As their supplies gave out, the unfortunates took to begging for a crust of bread on the streets and from door to door.

Hundreds were dragged from trains. The railroads demanded special travel permits. Yet the flow of escapees continued. Rather than submit to being collectivized, these families simply abandoned everything and fled. Additional guards and bloodhounds were posted on the western frontiers to block the wild scramble of fugitives crossing into Rumania, Poland, the Baltic countries. Great numbers perished in the attempt. Finland had to protest officially against the influx of refugees from Soviet Karelia. Had the borders been open, there is little doubt that millions would have fled their native land.

The first draft of the *Piatiletka* set 10 per cent of the peasantry as the portion to be collectivized, and the final draft raised it to 20 per cent. How much duress would be needed to reach that goal may be deduced from that fact that voluntary collectivization had been accepted during twelve years by only 2 per cent. But in the intoxication of the effort the sights were arbitrarily raised to 50 per cent, and in the main grain-growing regions, to 100 per cent.

On December 27, 1929, Stalin issued the slogan of "liquidation of the kulaks as a class." It amounted to a declaration of war on the whole farming population. Before the revolution, the word *kulak* — meaning "fist" — had been applied to the very small group of well-to-do peasants who owned flour mills, lent money at usurious rates, and were in fact a hard-fisted breed. Now the word was redefined to cover any peasant who owned two cows or the equivalent, and in practice it was stretched to cover anyone who insisted on holding on to his own parcel of land. Opponents of collectivization so utterly destitute that the label wouldn't stick were called "kulak agents."

Stalin's slogan amounted to an imperious command to smash and disperse between five and ten million peasant men, women, and children as quickly and rapaciously as possible, in order to help the others recognize the virtues of sinking their private farms in government-owned estates called *kolkhozes*. These were not, as apologists disingenuously pretend, agrarian "co-operatives" but state "collectives" in which the individual had no more direct role than the worker in a state factory.

Sixty-five days elapsed between the launching of the liquidation slogan and the order on March 2, 1930, calling a halt to the lawlessness it touched off. The ruthless campaign had begun months before December 27 and was to continue for years after March 2. But the brutalities reached their peak in those nine weeks. Raw force had rarely been applied so shockingly even in Russia. Hell broke loose in seventy thousand villages:

A population as large as all of Switzerland's or Denmark's was stripped clean of all their belongings — not alone their land and homes and cattle and tools, but often their last clothes and food and household utensils — and driven out of their villages. They were herded with bayonets at railroad stations, packed indiscriminately into cattle cars, and dumped weeks later in the lumber regions of the frozen North, the deserts of Central Asia, wherever labor was needed, to live or die. Some of the human wreckage was merely flung beyond the limits of their former villages, without shelter or food in those winter months, to start life anew if they could on land too barren to have been cultivated in the past.

Tens of thousand died of exposure, starvation and epidemic diseases while being transported, and no one dared guess at the death rate in the wilderness where the liquidated population was dispersed. Locomotives dragged their loads of agony from every part of the nation under armed guards and when the human debris had been emptied, jogged back for more. Thousands of bewildered refugees, panic fear in their eyes, flocked to the cities, where they were once more corralled, stuffed into disease-ridden cars, and hauled away to the dumps. . . . The spectacle of peasants being led by soldiers with drawn revolvers through the streets even of Moscow was too commonplace to win more than a casual glance from the crowds on the sidewalks.*

For those who saw "liquidation of the kulaks" at close range, the phrase is freighted with horror. Most upsetting was the awareness

* *Assignment in Utopia.*

that the colossal calamity was not a natural phenomenon but *man-made* — that it could be stopped by a word of command from one man. I wrote: "It was as if, in the midst of a terrible volcanic erup-tion, one were to catch sight of someone turning a crank that kept the lava pouring over men and towns." The impression was macabre.

The "war on superstition" was intensified during collectivization and, indeed, became one of the instruments of assault. Priests and deacons and the more notoriously pious folk were treated as kulaks; churches were turned into granaries, storehouses, libraries; church bells were melted down for scrap metal.

3. The Peasants Fight Back

Let no one underestimate the fury of the peasant reaction. Collec-tivization officials were afraid to venture out in the dark, and for all their caution hundreds of them were killed. Men and women slated for deportation often managed to set fire to their homes and grain. Brigades arriving to remove bells and icons from churches sometimes found believers armed with sticks and pitchforks ready to prevent the sacrilege. Red Army and GPU troops were ever on the move putting down riots.

The most startling act of sabotage, and the most hurtful to the national economy, was the slaughter of farm animals. By 1929 the losses of the civil war period had been made up; there were more domestic animals than in 1916. Now the peasants hurried to kill their horses, cattle, and sheep rather than relinquish them to the state. The death penalty was decreed for such action: the life of a man or woman for the life of a pig. But by the end of the Five-Year Plan the country had lost half of its cattle and horses, two thirds of its sheep and goats, two fifths of its pigs. Much of the food difficul-ties and actual famine can be traced to that desperate gesture of defiance.

Destruction of the same kind deprived agriculture of a large part of its farm implements. The peasants might not be able to prevent seizure of their land and persons, but at least they could wipe out their possessions. They were applying to the invading regime the very "scorched earth" policy they would be asked a dozen years later to apply to the invading Germans.

When the pressures were eased up, more than half the families that had "voluntarily" joined collectives promptly resigned. But at a somewhat slower pace the process of coercion continued, and by 1932 close to 80 per cent of the national acreage had been feudalized.

One significant victory the resistance did extract from its conquerors: Collectivized peasants were allowed to cultivate a tiny plot, normally a half-hectare garden near their cottages, and to own a few fowl and farm animals on a private basis. Output on those individual plots has been dramatically higher than on the *kolkhoz* land; their produce has been the mainstay of the limited free market in food which the Kremlin, again reluctantly, was constrained to legalize in order to keep the industrial centers from starving. Twice as many cows and pigs have been reared on the individual garden plots than on the huge collectives.

In many areas the popular opposition was so strong that the aggressor state chose not to make fine distinctions between the guilty and the innocent, but whipped entire villages and agrarian towns. It fell to my lot, accidentally, to apprise the world of one such "collective" chastisement, and it will serve as prototype for its species:

In January, 1933, all inhabitants of three Cossack towns in the Kuban, North Caucasus — some forty thousand men, women, and children, young and old, sick and sound — were rounded up, herded into waiting cattle cars, and shipped to the Arctic reaches. By chance I got hold of the Kuban newspaper which told the tale under banner headlines, sparing no ugly details, with the apparent intent of terrifying the rest of the region. When I tried to cable the story, the censors turned thumbs down. But it happened that I was soon out in Berlin for a vacation, and I decided to risk writing the story there. It made sensational reading all over the world. For a few weeks it was touch and go whether I would be readmitted to the Soviet Union.

By that time, of course, I had long been ejected from the category of "friendly" correspondents. In my own attitude toward communism in practice, the terrible sixty-five days were decisive. My last defenses against total disillusionment collapsed. I could no longer evade the choice that had been plaguing me from the first: the choice between the regime and the people. During collectivization I cast my lot, emotionally, with the masses against their tormentors.

Nor was I alone in this. Other foreigners who, for one or another subjective reason, were determined to remain "loyal" to the Kremlin turned against it under the impact of collectivization. Yet others, whose commitments to the regime were more deeply rooted, needed further shock treatment. It came, hideously, in the shape of a great famine.

Concealed from the non-Soviet world at the time, denied for years by the Kremlin and its foreign apologists, the famine of the winter of 1932–1933 has since then been officially admitted. Only its extent is still in dispute. The *Times* correspondent — who had been out front in denying the disaster while it was under way — placed the deaths at four million, though most estimates were higher. Soviet spokesmen in *boastful* moments claimed seven millions.

What makes this famine unique in history is that it was man-made, deliberately planned to chastise and humble forty or fifty million citizens. Having put on the harness of collectivization, the peasants chose to sabotage the new system. They planted and harvested barely enough for themselves. That was their instinctive, spontaneous answer to the outrages they had suffered: the most extensive example of mass non-co-operation in all history.

But they had underrated the savagery of the enemy. The Kremlin saw what was coming; even reporters in their Moscow isolation could see it coming. Grain happened to be cheap in the world market, so that a few million dollars diverted from other foreign trade could have prevented the calamity. But Stalin decided to seize the whole harvest from the recalcitrant peasants by force, leaving them to starve. Every bloated baby belly, every cadaver that cluttered the highways, was his purposeful doing. It was an act of war as surely as if he had killed those millions by gunfire or poison gas.

I resist the temptation to recount the incalculable tragedy. Death and sorrow of such proportions cannot be put into words in any case. There were authenticated reports of cannibalism. In Ukrainian, Central Asian and Caucasian cities, wagons went from door to door to collect the night's corpses. The American engineer who directed the building of the Stalingrad tractor plant, the late Jack Calder, came to Moscow after a sojourn in Central Asia; he told us of roads lined on both sides with frozen bodies, like so many logs. Refugees from the stricken regions concentrated on Moscow and other centers.

The distribution of deaths by hunger was geographically in direct proportion to the "success" of the collectivization campaign. Though weather conditions were not optimal, neither were they of the kind that normally causes famine. The catastrophe was the direct consequence of the policy of the government, which could have headed it off but refused to do so. Then, to save face for its glorious Five-Year Plan, it denounced reports of the famine as capitalist propaganda and rejected all proffers of foreign relief measures.

In 1937 the regular ten-year census of Soviet population was taken. Its findings were suppressed, because it revealed between twenty and twenty-five million fewer people than had been promised by official statistical forecasts. Allowing for errors in the forecast and for a drastic decline in birth rate due to the hardships of the decade, it is still a fair estimate that between ten and fifteen millions, the majority peasants, were killed off by Stalin's great offensive.

Roughly as many more were in mobile slave contingents, exiled to shift for themselves in the most rigorous areas of the country, and in the fast expanding forced-labor camps. Those saintly Fabians Sidney and Beatrice Webb, in their declining years, were moved to write a two-volume book glorifying the Soviet system as a "new civilization." They stated that a million "kulak" families had been deported — among peasants that meant from five to six million people. Since the Webbs put the best face they could on Soviet atrocities, we may be sure the figure was actually much larger. No one can estimate how many tens of thousands died in transit and in their new habitats. The survivors provided the basic pool of forced labor that was to grow into a gigantic slave system.

Only people ignorant of such staggering realities can continue honestly to suppose that the Soviet masses and the Soviet regime

are one and indivisible. Collectivization, more than any other major
aspect of Soviet history, left indelible marks on popular sentiment.
It is, even today, the main ingredient in the enduring blood feud
between the dictators and their subjects.

Even those who find it possible to justify the incalculable tragedy
in terms of historic necessity must recognize that it was in effect a
war between the regime and the people. With respect to both industrialization and collectivization, Isaac Deutscher, for instance,
writes: "The terror matched the resistance which those policies
encountered. Only with scorpions could tens of millions be driven
into collective farms, multitudes be shifted to new industrial sites,
and the vast majority of people forced to toil in misery and suppress
in silence the fury evoked by the privileges of a minority." *

* *Russia: What Next?* Oxford, 1953.

X. The Kremlin's Prisoners of War

1. Dark Side of the Moon

When historians draw a line under the nightmare of Russia's Bolshevik interlude, it is safe to guess that they will mark slave labor as its most repulsive and uniquely Soviet feature. Among the achievements of Stalin's initial Five-Year Plan, the rise of systematic, institutionalized forced labor is surely the most impressive and the most characteristic. Factories and foundries are everywhere in the world: Russia was ripe for them and would have had them under any political tutelage. The Bolshevik ingredient in the brew of industrialization is large-scale forced labor. So typical has it become of communism in practice that it is introduced immediately in every country taken over by the Soviet Union. According to data gathered by Roger N. Baldwin, a lifelong champion of civil liberties, there are probably already as many slave laborers in Red China as in Red Russia; 100,000 of the 300,000 industrial workers in Bulgaria are slaves laboring at bayonet point.[*]

Great prison camps and isolated penal colonies for political enemies and "socially dangerous elements" came into being with the birth of the Soviet epoch. The former island monastery beyond the Arctic Circle, Solovki, was among the first and remains among the most notorious concentration camps. Until Stalin's time, however, these places were simply punitive; their convict labor was not an end in itself but a by-product, as in other countries.

Beginning with the late twenties, conventional convict labor

[*] *A New Slavery,* edited by Roger N. Baldwin, Oceana, 1953.

evolved into planned slave labor. It ceased to be an extra and became an essential and indispensable part of the national structure, like slavery in ancient Greece and Rome or in our South before emancipation.

Were the arrests and deportation of vast numbers related to an advance plan for mobilizing an abundance of the cheapest possible labor? Did the slave system, rather, grow up as a consequence of the sudden availability of millions of prisoners and exiles? This is a riddle that will probably remain without answer. We know only that the great mass liquidations — of *lishentsi,* Nepmen, technicians, intellectuals, recalcitrant workers, and finally hostile peasants — made the secret police the master of more working hands than any of the industrial commissariats commanded. Before long this tremendous manpower was being deployed to do the dirtiest, the most dangerous, the most urgent jobs, in particular those in the remoter areas of Siberia, the Far North and Central Asia.

This labor supply was channeled to road, harbor, and canal buildings; to gold and coal mining in the most inaccessible regions; to cutting and processing timber, draining swamps, cutting peat. But as the numbers swelled, they were injected into almost all industries. They were set to making shoes for the army and furniture for the bureaucracy, canning fish and meat for the general market. Besides carrying out immense economic tasks assigned to it specifically, the GPU (later NKVD, then MVD, but always the same organization under the shifting initials) began to lease its surplus labor to regular state trusts on a contract basis. In nearly all the large new undertakings, slave contingents thus worked side by side with free labor but under guard, with the secret police pocketing their wages. This, plus profits on its own enterprises, tended to make the whole Red Terror self-supporting.

For those of us who have lived under the hammer and sickle, the need to "prove" that there is slave labor in the USSR is frustrating. It is as if someone who lived in the United States in the thirties were asked to "prove" that there was a depression. Inside the Soviet Union, not even the deaf, dumb, and blind could remain unaware of a condition that blanketed the entire nation and directly or indirectly

impinged on the life of every inhabitant. There could be dispute as to
the precise dimensions of the system in a given year, but not as to
its vastness and inhumanity.

The haze of doubt around the subject is the calculated product of
communist propaganda. People who were content with reasonable
evidence of slavery in Abyssinia or the Belgian Congo, who credited
the reports of Nazi gas chambers, become strangely skeptical and
cautious when faced with overwhelming testimony to Soviet slavery.
They want photographs, maps, exact numbers. They counter with
inanities about chain gangs in Georgia and prisoners in Spain, as if a
pimple in one place somehow canceled out a cancer elsewhere.

One night a few years back I was on the air in the role of attorney
for defense of a book, on a radio program cast in the form of a trial.
The book before the bar was about Stalin's concentration camps,
written in blood by an escaped victim and overflowing with blood-
chilling horror. With the author present, his eyes still haunted by
excruciating memories, I did perhaps grow a bit emotional in con-
demning the Soviet slave system. Whereupon the "judge," a popular
literary critic, admonished me in a finger-wagging tone not to forget
that we have chain gangs and prison labor in the United States
too!

The trouble has not been with the quality of the available evidence but with the psychic resistance of the outside world. It had
been so conditioned to think of the Soviets in roseate terms of social
experiment, socialism, a new world, that it shied away from threats
to its heart-warming illusions.

Actually, few aspects of affairs in our tormented generation have
been so copiously described and documented. Though forced labor
is the ugliest skeleton in the Kremlin closets, the closet doors are
made of glass. Eyewitness accounts — in thousands of affidavits, articles, books — have been given by men and women who emerged
alive from the purgatory. Since the war's end, there is not a great
Western city without its quota of former Red slaves, all burning with
a desire to "tell the West." Hundreds of them are in New York,
London, Paris, Berlin. In the United States, Germany, and other

countries there are today societies of former Soviet political prisoners which despite their poverty publish journals filled with intimate memoirs of their ghastly experiences.

The late Professor John Dewey, reviewing the most complete study of the subject — *Forced Labor in Soviet Russia,* by David J. Dallin and Boris I. Nicolaevsky* — wrote: "It may be doubted whether any story of human degradation has ever been more fully or more accurately told in so short a time after its occurrence, and this in spite of the iron curtain." A summary of the more important published materials, in the Dallin-Nicolaevsky book, fills ten octavo pages. And that was in 1947. Since then there has been a deluge of personal accounts of the slave camps.

At least half a million Soviet citizens remained in the West after the last war, despite all pressures to drive them home, and every one of them is familiar with the essential facts. Close to a million and a half Poles were forcibly deported to the Soviet Union after Hitler and Stalin had divided the living body of Poland in September, 1939. Most of them were scattered through the slave-labor camps and colonies. Hundreds of thousands died there; some fifteen thousand Polish officers were slaughtered outright in Katyn Forest and other abattoirs; most of those released in the amnesty exacted by General Sikorsky after Hitler's invasion of the USSR ended in a Sovietized Poland and enforced silence. But at least one hundred thousand "graduates" of the Red slave system wound up in the free West.

Their exile government took a vast number of depositions which, in the aggregate, provided a complete, detailed, and indubitable picture. Students therefore have no dearth of authentic and intimate data. A dreadfully vivid distillation of that evidence was published in book form as *The Dark Side of the Moon,* with a foreword by T. S. Eliot.

No, only people outside Russia so hopelessly committed to Kremlin worship that they are impervious to reality can still raise questions about the existence or the satanic nature of the slave system. The mystery is not in the Soviet camps. The mystery is in the

* Yale University Press, 1947.

callous indifference of free men in the face of the clear and horrifying record.*

While denying this skeleton, or wrapping it in verbal veils about "corrective penology," the Kremlin itself indirectly concedes the magnitude of its slave empire. The system is simply too huge to be hidden. Its dimensions can be estimated from the economic assignments openly turned over to the secret police.

In 1932 an American engineer in Moscow with a penchant for industrial statistics was able to calculate with certainty the employment of a few million forced laborers. He merely estimated the labor forces on undertakings officially announced as under the aegis of the GPU — such as the White Sea–Baltic Canal, the Moska–Volga Canal, the laying of a parallel line of trans-Siberian rails, etc. But a secret document of 1941 removed the need for guessing. It was a breakdown of the current economic plan prepared only for the eyes of Soviet leaders, a book of 750 pages, which fell into German hands during the war and passed into Allied hands afterward.

The plan lists gigantic industrial enterprises, from timbering and harbor construction to mining and manufacturing, under direct control of the NKVD, which is to say within the slave-labor system. It becomes clear that not one of the economic trusts or commissariats even came close to the NKVD in scope of operations, capital investments, and products. Almost one fifth of all capital construction, for instance, was earmarked for the slave masters. The NKVD emerges from the compilation as the main center of heavy industrial production and close to a monopoly of heavy transport construction. Mining of gold and other non-ferrous metals appears to be largely a slave operation. Coal mining in newly opened fields in harsh regions, like

* The American Federation of Labor deserves credit for initiating and pushing a proposal that the UN investigate forced labor. Under this pressure, the United Nations Economic and Social Council finally, in 1951, undertook the inquiry, jointly with the International Labor Organization, under the chairmanship of Sir Ramaswami Mudaliar of India. Its report, made public in June, 1953, of course confirmed beyond doubt the existence of slavery on a huge scale in the USSR. But, to avoid "irritating" the sensitive slave masters in the Kremlin, discussion of the findings was discreetly postponed.

Vorkuta in the Far North and the Khabarovsk Territory in the Far East, was assigned to the police administrations.

How many millions of men were required to carry out the NKVD plans? Here estimates range up to twenty millions. Former inmates of camps in Kolyma, a vast slave area, put the prisoners in that region alone at about two million. Arthur Koestler has used the figure of seventeen million, Victor Kravchenko twenty million, Brooks Atkinson (after a Moscow sojourn as New York *Times* correspondent) between ten and fifteen million. Dallin and Nicolaevsky, taking all the data on hand in 1947 into their reckoning, came up with an estimate of fourteen million.

Part of the dissonance derives from the fact that there are various grades of slave labor, so that the totals depend on whether all types are counted. Besides the forthright barbed-wire enclosures — "the camps of death" in the prisoners' vocabulary — more loosely organized forced-labor colonies and special penal settlements exist. Then there are exile regions where the prisoners do not live in camps.

Moreover, the slave population is not stable. The death rate is so high that at times the total falls sharply, until new slave seizures replenish the supply. In the camps of death the common mortality rate is 12 per cent — which means the extinction of all the slaves within eight years. Confinement in the worst of the camps, in Northern Siberia and the Soviet Far East, on the edge of the polar deserts of eternal ice and snow, is rightly regarded as equivalent to a death sentence. During and since the last war, the slave population has been enlarged by millions of Japanese and German war prisoners (with the consent, to our eternal shame, of Mr. Roosevelt and Mr. Churchill), and then by deportees from Poland, the Baltic countries, Czechoslovakia and the rest of the new Soviet empire. Thus the totals rise and fall.

A little elementary analysis reveals that the figures are even more startling than appears on the surface. Fifteen million, to take an intermediate estimate, is 7.5 per cent of the country's population of two hundred million. But only about 10 per cent are women, so that we are really dealing with 13.5 per cent of the entire male population. Furthermore, the very young, the very old, and the infirm do not qualify for slave labor. What is involved in actuality, counting both workers and peasants, is *more than 20 per cent of the effective male labor forces of a great country!* In the light of that extraordinary fact, a statement such as the following by Dr. Dallin becomes entirely credible:

> Whatever the actual number of workers under the forced labor system may be, it is equivalent to the population of a country like Yugoslavia or Czechoslovakia, or the Argentine, and it is certainly not less than the population of Australia. *The number of people subject to forced labor is not less and is probably greater than the total number of industrial workers at liberty in Russia.*

But the arithmetical game in dealing with such an enormity is at bottom nauseating. As if the tragedy and the horror would be any more tolerable if there were only five or eight instead of twenty million slaves! The issue is not the precise size but the character of the institution, and that is beyond the capacity of language or emotion to compass in full. The millions already swallowed and digested by the slave system are incomparably greater than those going through the nightmare at any point in time.

2. *Cross Section of a Nation*

People who have survived both Soviet and Nazi concentration camps (and several of them have written their stories) reluctantly admit that the Soviet brand is more horrible. At their worst, the Brown-Red choice is between a quick death in a gas chamber and a protracted death by overwork, undernourishment, and filthy living conditions. That is what Mikhail Rozanov, a Soviet economist now in the West, meant in his book *The Conquerors of the White Spots* when he spoke of "the Bolshevik Auschwitzes where nature and exhaustion replace gas and crematoria." That is what Dr. Julius Margolin, a Zionist from Poland who spent five years in Soviet captivity, meant when he wrote that "the Soviet camps are the biggest death factories in world history."

There are no words in any language to convey adequately the agonies of the great herds of suffering humanity, in dirty tatters, vermin-ridden, chronically hungry, wracked with scurvy, toiling from dawn to dusk in the "white spots," that is, the most remote and brutal parts of the empire. A French journalist who made an intensive study of Soviet forced labor, David Rousset, has tried to sum up "the concentration camp man":

He is nightmarishly typical. He is hungry, sick and afraid. He lives in wooden barracks, or under a tent, or in earth caves. His fate is locked between barbed wire barricades, beneath observation towers. Under constant threat of dogs and rifles, he works far beyond the power of his muscles. Given neither means nor time to wash, he wears foul rags. He is awakened before dawn; at night, having returned exhausted from work, he stands in an interminable line, near a hospital lacking medicaments. In the middle of the night, in every kind of weather, he is aroused by blows to unload freight cars. This is a faithful condensation of hundreds of reports — and thousands of such reports exist.*

But Rousset, like all who try to express the grim reality, is clearly frustrated. His summation is necessarily of the surface, the physical torment, whereas the essence is in the crushing of human personality, the humiliation of the divine in man, which only another Dante could convey. Here and there one comes close to this chilling human essence in the best of the personal reports on the Soviet camps: in George Kitchin's *Prisoner of the OGPU,* in *I Speak for the Silent,* by V. Tchernavin, *Tell the West!* by Jerzy Gliksman, and especially in *The Dark Side of the Moon* and that little masterpiece of distilled horror by Elinor Lipper, *Eleven Years in Soviet Prison Camps.*

I have talked to men just returned from the hell of the slave camps. They found themselves tongue-tied, in despair of ever making the uninitiated begin to understand. They were like soldiers who have seen the uttermost in war horror on a battlefield and know that never, hard as they may try, can they make others com-

*New York *Times,* February 28, 1950; abridged from *Le Figaro Littéraire,* Paris.

prehend their memories. But I did read bits of their dreadful secret in the tremor of their limbs and the terror in their eyes.

One need only read *Uncle Tom's Cabin* and one of the Soviet slave books together to see that conventional chattel slavery was a mild and benevolent thing compared with what has evolved in the "homeland of socialism." The Negro slave lived in the same world with the freemen, he had a family and a body of minor rights granted by custom and the conscience of his owners; he was cared for as horses and swine are cared for because he had a dollar value. But the concentration-camp slave is cut off from the community of the living, stripped of all human and animal value, severed from his family, beaten and starved and neglected because it is cheaper for the state to replace him than to care for him.

The typical Soviet forced laborer is not only a slave but a convict, in the world's worst plague spots, in conditions sadistically calculated to erase the awareness of having belonged to the human race. In most cases he is forbidden to write or receive letters, or even to apprise his loved ones of his whereabouts. If husband and wife, father and son, close friends, are convicted together, the state carefully puts them in widely separated camps. Should fellow prisoners become too friendly, they are deliberately dispersed. The isolation is as complete, physically and morally, as sadistic ingenuity can contrive.

The distinction between criminal and political offenders that was traditional under czarism was wiped out by the Soviets. Not only are "undesirable" poets and priests put into the same barracks with murderers, thieves, and degenerates but the ordinary criminals are given preferential treatment and a free hand in piling their persecution on top of the state's persecution. Women political prisoners, if they are young enough to tempt the criminals or the guards, usually have only a choice between becoming the "camp wife" of a few or the object of rape by all the cutthroats on the camp grounds.

Food is doled out so that it will sustain a flicker of life and no more — and this only on condition that the slave fulfill the steep labor "norm." In many camps the only way the "politicals" can retain their pitiful bread ration is to swallow it quickly, before the criminals snatch it from them. Refusal to work is punishable by death, and so is failure to accomplish more than 30 per cent of the established "norm" of production. To talk back to a guard or straggle in the line of march to and from camp is often the shortest road to eternity.

The most shocking fact about the Soviet slave system is that the world has not been shocked. Its heart has been numbed by surcease of horror, its mind addled by the apologetics of paid agents and muddled "liberals" of the totalitarian brands. Soviet slavery has yet to find its William Lloyd Garrisons and John Browns. There are no antislavery societies dedicated to arousing the conscience of mankind. And while this indifference prevails, free men share the guilt for what transpires behind the iron curtains.

In July, 1909, Prince Peter Kropotkin published in London his pamphlet on the plight of political prisoners in his native land, under the title *The Terror in Russia*. It was released to the public with a prefatory note by a Parliamentary Committee. Kropotkin documented his charges that there were 74,000 exiles in the frozen North and Siberia; that executions at the peak of the terror ran as high as 60 to 90 a month; that the prison population, including ordinary criminals, had risen from 85,000 in 1905 to 181,-000 four years later.

Liberal and humanitarian opinion in England was outraged. The pamphlet went through many editions. There were passionate protests in the House of Commons and the press heaped coals of fire on the St. Petersburg government. Yet how picayune was the terror exposed by Kropotkin when measured by the Bolshevik scale!

Today the prisoners and exiles must be counted by the millions, executions by the tens of thousands. The prerevolutionary exiles lived in relative freedom; they could read, write, study, correspond with the outer world, and escaped almost at will. Today the banished are herded in diseased and filthy camps, hermetically sealed off from the world, and worked pitilessly till they drop in their tracks; escape is practically unthinkable.

But there are no protests, no outcries of outrage. And the perpetrators of the obscenities are accepted as equals in international society — including United Nations commissions dealing with "human rights." Worse, self-styled liberals find pretty words to camouflage the hell on earth. A Professor Henry Pratt Fairchild defends the Kremlin's "corrective labor." A Corliss Lamont finds it in his heart to write that under the Soviets "unemployment is unconstitutional" — ignoring the fact that that largest group of "employed" are slaves. Louis Fischer, in his pro-Soviet period, now behind him, could write that "the GPU is not only an intelligence service and militia — it is a vast industrial organization and a big educational institution."

Construction of the White Sea – Baltic Canal, as most informed people know by now, was one of the most horrible of the slave-labor enterprises. As many as 200,000 prisoners, of whom probably less than 10 per cent were ordinary criminals, worked in indescribably brutal conditions; tens of thousands froze and died in the process. But how does a respectable American writer, one Joseph Barnes, deal with this mass atrocity? He characterized it as "One of those massive and frenzied undertakings with which the Bolsheviks keep their own brand of Boy Scout public passion alive and quick in Russia — the reforming of thieves in the construction of a canal between the Baltic and the White Seas." *

The wickedest of the horror areas is Magadan. In 1944 it was visited by a party of Americans, headed by the then Vice-President of the United States, Henry A. Wallace, chaperoned by Owen Lattimore. Mr. Wallace returned to shout hallelujah for "pioneering" in Magadan, which he put on par with the American pioneers of the West. And Lattimore wrote even more glowingly of life in that prison land. "There has probably never been a more orderly phase of pioneering," he reported in the *National Geographic,* "than the opening up of Russia's Far North under the Soviets."

Mr. Wallace, as he has belatedly conceded, was a naïve and confused victim of his monitors. But Lattimore, an expert on matters Soviet, should have known that Magadan and all Kolyma were

* Book-of-the-Month Club *News,* October, 1945.

peopled almost exclusively by slaves and their overseers; that the "industrialists" who were his hosts were officials of *Gulag,* the slave administration. Yet he wrote that Magadan is "part of the domain of a remarkable concern, Dalstroi (Far Northern Construction Company), which can be roughly compared to a combination of Hudson's Bay Company and TVA." His readers had no inkling that the "concern" was a subdivision of the dread NKVD and its "pioneers" all prisoners.

Elinor Lipper, a remarkable Swiss woman who was in Magadan at the time and watched the Americans happily admiring the wonders of its graveyards, lived to write of Lattimore's amazing report:

"Who would be willing to take the responsibility of such statements as this if someday the camps of Kolyma are thrown open to the inspection of the whole world, as the camps of Dachau and Auschwitz were opened? Would these words bear repetition when the mounds of frozen corpses under the snow are one day disinterred to testify to what the Soviet Union really is?" *

The largest and most brutal slave system in human history was the crowning achievement of Stalin's offensive against the Russian people. The victims represent a true cross section of those people, both as to social origins and ethnic composition. Basically they are workers and peasants, as any big slice of a nation's population is bound to be; but they contain contingents of intellectuals, artists, priests and other religious people; everything from Moscow professors to Kirghiz nomads, from disgraced top-shelf communists and Red Army generals to primitive Samoyeds. Apart from their physical isolation, these unfortunates are Russia — good, bad, and indifferent. Their fundamental attitudes can differ from those of the nation at large only in degree.

Having admitted that such a large segment of its subjects is so bitterly opposed to the regime that it must be surrounded by guards and police dogs, the Kremlin has in substance admitted that it rules over a vanquished and hostile country. In the final analysis the slaves are made of the same human material as the rest of the population:

* *The Reader's Digest,* June, 1951.

the ex-slaves and tomorrow's slaves. They represent one end of a spectrum from deadly hostility to loyalty. Those at the other end, those completely devoted to the regime, cannot be any larger numerically — and in between are just gradations of enmity to the Kremlin.

In the permanent civil war, as I have already suggested, the slave population are the prisoners of war. Political considerations aside, the dismantling of a system which bulks so enormously in the over-all national economy is no longer possible, short of a complete revolution in the existing order. An occasional amnesty may release a few hundred thousand or a million captives, but replenishment of the labor supply has become an inescapable necessity for the state's survival. The slave-labor establishment is by this time one of the primary foundations of the whole Soviet edifice.

It is a foundation permeated by hate of the conquerors and hunger for revenge. That hate and that hunger radiate far beyond its confines to the tens of millions of relatives and friends of the victims and to the Russian peoples at large, who are deeply ashamed of the new slavery.

XI. The Great Carnage

1. Release of Pressures

The Stalin Constitution of 1936, still touted by its acolytes as "the most democratic in the world," is at bottom a swindle, especially so with respect to its provisions for civil rights. The document was a dead letter from the hour of its birth, and most of its authors were dead authors soon thereafter; many of them, in fact, were liquidated before their handiwork was formally adopted.

All the same, the constitution is significant as a commentary on the peoples it is supposed to govern. Even in *rigor mortis,* the document was a promissory note. Conceived in a transition period when the dictatorship sought to quiet its public with soothing syrups, the things it promised deserve attention. For they represent the Kremlin's best judgment as to *what its subjects really want,* and Kremlin views on this matter are likely to be accurate.

The promise of ice cream and candy to a child, rather than spinach and castor oil, is a fairly reliable estimate of what the child prefers. Stalin and his cohorts would scarcely have gone to the trouble of promising falsely gifts which the people didn't want or have any use for. On paper at least, the populace was offered a large measure of personal freedom. Not esoteric counterfeits for masses craving Asiatic despotism, but the basic freedoms enjoyed by the citizens of conventional democracies.

Article 125 states that "citizens of the USSR are guaranteed by law: freedom of speech; freedom of the press; freedom of assembly, including the holding of mass meetings; freedom of street processions and demonstrations." Article 127 prescribes the "inviola-bility of the person," and Article 128 "the inviolability of the homes of citizens and privacy of correspondence."

The political sections outline rights and procedures which are democratic in outer appearance, at any rate: universal suffrage for all who reach the age of eighteen irrespective of sex, race and pre-vious class status; the direct and secret ballot; direct recall of elected officials. The catch, of course, is that only one political party is permitted to exist. But this stark limitation is blurred at the edges by references to candidates drawn from mass organizations like trade-unions, co-operatives, youth and cultural societies.

Communist dogma made it difficult for the regime to offer much in the way of personal rights in the economic area. Nevertheless, the constitution does make such pledges as it can within the limi-tations. It states that "the law permits the small private economy of individual peasants and artisans based on their personal labor . . . the right of citizens to personal ownership of their incomes from work and of their savings . . . the right of inheritance of per-sonal property. . . ." The peasants are told that "every household in a collective farm has for its personal use a small plot of land attached to the dwelling and, as its personal property, a subsidiary establishment on the plot, a dwelling house, livestock, poultry and minor agricultural implements."

I am not suggesting that these provisions have any intrinsic value. The political and economic concessions are hemmed in by reservations, and the civil liberties have been honored in the total breach. Yet it seems to me revealing that the Kremlin should have resorted to lies of that particular order — that a fiendish oligarchy considered it prudent to give *lip service* to fundamental, garden variety freedoms.

Neither the Italian nor the German dictators, be it remembered, ever felt constrained to make such promises and pretenses. On the contrary, they were frankly contemptuous of ordinary democracy, on the apparent assumption that their respective peoples had no relish for outmoded bourgeois gadgets like free speech, press, as-semblage and demonstration. *Among the subjects of modern totali-*

tarian states, only the Russian peoples have to be beguiled from time to time with a vision of individual freedom.

Lenin, as we have seen, offered a Constituent Assembly and the whole gamut of democratic processes even while plotting to impose his dictatorship. He promised the bread of liberty and delivered stones of tyranny. But nineteen years later that dictatorship, to placate the populace for a while, once more evoked the mirage of freedom.

It is no accident that in the crisis of the German war, the Soviet peoples were again encouraged to believe that, come victory, they would at last be granted the liberties repeatedly dangled before their bruised eyes. And it is no accident that in March, 1953, with the death of Stalin, his successors hastened to exhibit those moldering promissory notes. Said Malenkov, speaking over Stalin's corpse:

"The workers, collective farm peasants and intelligentsia can work calmly and confidently, knowing that the Soviet Government will solicitously and incessantly guard the rights written in the Stalin Constitution."

The implications of such words and gestures, from Lenin to Malenkov, are crystal clear. Though foreign experts insist that Russians neither understand nor desire what we in the West recognize as freedom, the Kremlin experts repeatedly attest their conviction that this is precisely what their subjects do yearn for. Their gestures are empty, their promises unkept. Which does not alter the fact that in the opinion of the dictatorship itself the Russian masses aspire to simple political and economic rights.

The framing of the "most democratic constitution" began in the aftermath of famine, collectivization, and tense disaffections. It was one of the symptoms of a policy of general easement. By 1934 Stalin and his cohorts realized that they had brought the country close to the limits of endurance, that the moment for releasing the screws was at hand.

Rumblings of revolt could be heard even close to the seats of power, even in Stalin's personal household. Whether his wife, Nadezhda Alleluieva, died by his hand or her own is not clear, but that the immediate cause of her death was her outspoken protests against mounting tragedy is certain. Nadezhda Krupskaya, widow of Lenin, too, was demanding an end to atrocities. These were signs of the intolerable strains. Communists of every degree, including top-echelon military men, were whispering fearfully that the Boss was going too far; some of them no doubt explored ways and means, at least conversationally, of halting the madness. What grains of fact there were in the subsequent police fantasies about plots to unseat and liquidate Stalin dated back to these years of mutinous grumbling.

All of this was perfectly well known to Stalin. He released some of the pressures before the bursting point — and bided his time to deal with the mutineers, actual or potential. A bumper crop helped cover up the wounds of famine. The tide of terror receded perceptibly and glad anticipation of "better times" rippled through the communist rank and file, touching the mood of the whole country. An unwonted affability on the part of the dictator, who began smiling into cameras and talking of the "happy life" ahead, stirred a revival of hope, which the constitution was expected to confirm. Not only were a good many former Oppositionists allowed to return from exile after eating humble pie, but a few of them were given important posts.

The main focus of this tendency to conciliation was Sergei Kirov, a Politburo member, boss of the Leningrad Region, and widely looked upon as Stalin's heir apparent. Not that Kirov was in the slightest measure a sentimentalist. He had been second to none in ruthlessness during the tough years. His comparative "liberalism" flowed not from the heart but from the head. He came to believe that the regime might even strengthen its grip if it softened its methods.

Lenin, on his deathbed, had warned the party to avoid the fatal mistake of the Jacobins in the French Revolution who destroyed one another. Until the end of 1934, indeed, it was considered axiomatic that no important Bolshevik, whatever his sins, could be subjected to capital punishment. There had been a few grim exceptions to the rule. A GPU agent named Blumkin, set to spy on Trotsky, ended up a Trotskyist. He carried a letter from the deposed leader to Karl Radek, who promptly denounced him to the police. Blumkin was executed. In 1932 Stalin spoke up for the execution of one Riutin, a leading communist caught circulating an anti-Stalin document. The suggestion still seemed so outrageous that Stalin did not push it.

Kirov showed a certain daring in defending Lenin's advice on this issue. Increasingly he became the spokesman within the hierarchy for moderation, reflecting a great body of sentiment in the party and its leadership. The time seemed propitious for "democratic" shadow play, if only to gain friends abroad as a counterweight to Hitler's anti-Soviet bluster. Without committing himself, Stalin allowed this tendency to deepen. It had the warm support of Maxim Gorki, by now part of Stalin's intimate entourage.

Discontents were everywhere. Among young people and students in particular they were finding expression in vague allusions to "acts of heroism" and a new interest in the romantics of the terrorist underground in czarist days. Wherever uncovered, young people's clubs and even tea parties were brutally exterminated. That the tea parties were not always innocent is attested by Kravchenko, then a student himself. He has described one such gathering and its overtones of a vague, poetic, but clearly revolutionary temper. Kirov and those who supported him were inclined to the belief that only milder policies could head off more serious developments. His popularity in the party grew. At a party congress in February, 1934, he was cheered almost as long as Stalin himself and a lot more sincerely — something that Stalin could not easily forgive.

Just when the mood of conciliation was at its peak, Kirov was assassinated. He was shot to death in the corridor outside his office in the Smolny building, Leningrad, by a young communist named Nikolayev.

No political crime in all recorded history has been more hysterically avenged. The word "purge" was raised to a new dimension of sadism and Stalin leaped to first place among the bloodiest rulers in the memory of mankind. Within a few weeks barely a trace remained of the "softer" drift. Indeed, it was as if Stalin had waited for the signal to erase all delusions of liberalism and to erase all those who might conceivably challenge his despotic power. The very leaders who had prattled about "broader bases for the *vlast*" and coming closer to the masses, now in sheer fright outshouted the rest in clamoring for death blows to "the enemy."

2. Cure by Bleeding

To this day the truth about Nikolayev's revolver shot — the shot that spelled death for tens of thousands and new miseries for millions — is not fully known. The assassin was an unstable, nervous young man. For some time he had been recording his distressed thoughts in a diary, selected passages of which were subsequently to be circulated among Kremlin insiders. The entire diary, if ever it is exhumed from the archives, should provide a startling picture of the true state of mind of Soviet youth at the very time it was presumably galvanized by enthusiasm for Stalin's offensive.

Enough has been divulged through the years, however, to provide a fairly consistent outline of what occurred. The most telltale fact that became known quickly was that the Leningrad NKVD, whose chief job was to protect Kirov's life, had been suspiciously lax. It was intimately aware of Nikolayev's thoughts; the young man had talked to "friends" who reported his every word. Yet nothing was done to isolate him; and one of these "friends" helped him obtain the gun. On the crucial evening of December 4, 1934, Nikolayev found it strangely easy to enter the normally heavily guarded Smolny and to loiter for a long time in the corridor outside Kirov's conference room.

Under Soviet conditions such negligence could not have been fortuitous. The top Leningrad secret police officials ultimately tried and convicted for their negligence got away with amazingly mild sentences. Poor Nikolayev thought he was acting alone; he would challenge the country to rise against the tyrants by killing one of them, like revolutionists of old. But his hand was guided by the secret agents who encircled him. Behind them was the sinister

Henry Yagoda, head of the NKVD and among Stalin's most intimate associates. Was Yagoda merely carrying out the instructions of his master? This suspicion, which seemed farfetched when first advanced, seems close to a certainty in the perspective of time.

Stalin rushed to Leningrad on receiving the news of the killing of the rising competitor for his toga of power. He took personal charge of the investigation. More than a hundred political prisoners were immediately dragged out of their dungeons and shot. The public announcement identified them as "White Guard agents" of foreign countries, suggesting that Nikolayev was the tool of external foes. But soon the foreign ramifications were soft-pedaled and the whole affair was transformed into an inner-party plot. Nikolayev and thirteen alleged confederates were killed off without benefit of public trial.

Stalin's strategy soon came into clear focus. He would use the elimination of Kirov as an excuse for eliminating all his real and imagined enemies! A year of hysterical propaganda, arrests, and liquidations — 1935 — proved to be only a mild introduction to the great carnage carried out in 1936–1938.

The initial move was the arrest of Zinoviev, Kamenev, and ninety-five other formerly notable Bolsheviks, brought from their offices, their prison cells, and exile points. They were all convicted, behind closed doors, of "moral responsibility" for the dissident sentiments that had resulted in Kirov's death. They were given prison sentences, but ultimately nearly all of them were retried and condemned to death, or shot without the formality of a retrial. Other former Oppositionists were rounded up in batches of five thousand — there was nothing miserly in the scale of a Stalin butchery — and killed without so much as charges being lodged against them.

This new terror set off a series of linked accusations that served the regime as an alibi for destroying literally tens of thousands of communists, among them nearly all the remaining founders of the Soviet state. Each batch, before being hauled to the abattoirs, inculpated another batch, and thus forged an endless chain of death.

The official blood lust did not confine itself to the political arena. Real or potential "enemies" were ferreted out in the armed forces,

annihilating nearly the whole of the High Command, and liqui-
dating some thirty thousand officers, more than two thirds of the
higher officers' corps. Before the climactic orgy was over, the heads
of nine of the eleven "autonomous republics" were either executed
or driven to suicide. All but three or four of the top Soviet diplomats — and precisely the three or four who had not been Bolsheviks
in 1917 — were killed off. Among the executed or "missing" were
the top men in the "triumphant" fulfillment of the Five-Year Plan.
Industrial directors, leading scientists, great writers and critics —
all, all officially murdered or hounded to self-destruction or mysteriously missing.

Then, to cap the obscene climax, the ranks of the executioners
and interrogators themselves were cut down by the sickle of terror.
The highest officials of the NKVD, including the chief architect of
Stalin's homicidal apparatus, Yagoda, fell before the firing squads.
The new head of the secret service, Nikolai Yezhov, was put in
charge of the carnage in its later and worst stages and himself "disappeared" after he had dispatched several dozens of thousands to
eternity and several hundreds of thousands to slave camps. One report had it that Yezhov was confined in a madhouse, a raving
lunatic.

Foreign correspondents during the two-year period calculated
more than five thousand formal executions announced in the press.
But their tally did not include thousands more recorded only in the
provincial press. Besides, for every execution that made the papers,
dozens and scores were never publicly reported. An estimate of fifty
thousand executions gives the Kremlin the benefit of a large margin of doubt.

This wholesale butchery was merely the smaller aspect of the
total tragedy that compassed the humiliation of once great men and
women, a mighty wave of suicides, moral degradations which left
the world aghast. Systematically Stalin besmirched the records of
those who had led the Bolshevik *coup d'état,* won the civil war,
made the Five-Year Plans. He turned them all into "mad dogs,"
spies for foreign intelligence services, actual or would-be assassins.

If a hundredth part of Stalin's charges were true, then Bolshevism would be one of the filthiest enterprises in human history. Not satisfied with just taking their lives, he forced most of the principal victims to make public "confessions" of incredible crimes and grovel in the mud at his feet. In a series of demonstration trials, the notorious Moscow Blood Trials, the Fathers of the Revolution called themselves dirty names, admitted impossible and mutually contradictory crimes, and glorified the name of the monster who was putting them through these macabre paces.

Of the cumulative Grand Guignol of the great purges, the outside world saw only a few carefully staged shadow shows in the publicized open trials. It saw men with records of revolutionary heroism, great economists and political leaders, reduced to stuttering imbecility. Hardened criminals behave more nobly on the threshold of death. The tradition in which these men spent their younger years was rich with the legendry of defiance in the face of hopeless odds, contempt for death. It was a tradition in which accused men turned courtrooms into forums to indict oppressors.

We shall never know in detail the terrible pressures which crushed the spirit of these men and made them abject doormats for the bloodied boots of Stalin. Certainly the coercion was different for different victims. The subtle theory that some of them humbled themselves and murdered their own reputations as a "service to the party" has been given wide credence by Arthur Koestler's great novel, *Darkness at Noon*. I for one doubt it. By 1936–1938 there were few illusions left among prominent communists and probably no shreds of loyalty to "the party."

Indeed, that they suffered abysmal disillusionment, to the point of disgust with the results of their own lifework, would be a more tenable explanation. Men will accept martyrdom for ideals that seem to them all-important; they will die a hundred deaths rather than renounce their faith in God, or their belief that the sign of the cross should be made with two rather than three fingers. But martyrdom seems silly when the ideals have foundered, when faith is no more. People of the caliber of the Bukharins, the Rykovs, the Piatakovs could be induced to lie and demean themselves precisely because the whole business had ceased to matter. Their self-degradation seemed trivial in the context of the degradation of the revolution. It became a gesture of utter contempt.

It is likely that they surrendered readily to a combination of promises and threats: promises that their lives would be spared, threats that their wives and children and close friends would be tortured and exterminated if they refused to "co-operate" by playing assigned roles in the tragicomedy of trials and confessions. A strategically placed former Soviet official who was close to the secret police, Alexander Orlov, has confirmed this in detail. The hope of a reprieve for their families, he has revealed, was the clinching factor in extorting the capitulation of Zinoviev, Kamenev, Rykov, Piatakov, Sokolnikov and most of the other great Soviet figures brought into the limelight.*

Only seven out of the dozens involved in the three principal Moscow trials were allowed to live. The rest were shot in a day or two after the curtains went down on the demonstrations. Those to whom Stalin had given his personal pledge that they would not be murdered were usually the first to be dispatched. In between trials, the country and a gaping world were treated to the news of the liquidation of eight top marshals and generals in one clip, among them Marshal Tukhachevsky. Of the seven outstanding military figures who signed their death warrant — after a court-martial that never took place — five were themselves executed, among them the famous General Blucher who, under the *nom de guerre* of General Galen, had helped Chiang Kai-shek come to power in China. When the grisly tally was complete, five of the country's nine marshals were dead, along with 13 of its 19 army commanders, 57 of its 85 corps commanders, 110 of its 195 division commanders, 220 of its 406 regimental commanders.

Suicide accounted for Tomsky, long head of the trade-unions; for Gamarnik, a Deputy Commissar of War; for several of the presidents of autonomous Soviet republics. Execution without trial ended Abel Yenukidze, a childhood friend of Stalin and one of his few intimates until the very day of his arrest; Karakhan, the Armenian who was long Assistant Commissar of Foreign Affairs;

* Series of articles in *Life,* April 6–27, 1953.

Budu Mdivani, another boyhood associate of Stalin; and hundreds of others. Only those sufficiently familiar with Soviet history to recognize such names can savor the full horror of the protracted bloodletting.

The outside world, as I said, was chiefly aware of the trials, with their bewildering pattern of self-accusation, shocking treachery, and devious lies. There was the fascination of ultimate nightmare about the proceedings. But this stage-managed segment was an insignificant fraction of the over-all purge. It diverted attention from the main business; it cut off the view of the thousandfold greater crimes in the background, as the managers of the nightmare intended.

The result was that the true extent of the carnage and terror has never been grasped by mankind. Perhaps it was too vast and bewildering ever to be grasped. "Russia was a battlefield strewn with corpses, blotched with gigantic enclosures where millions of wretched 'war prisoners' toiled, suffered and died," one refugee wrote. Of the 138 members and alternates of the Central Committee of the party, only a score or so remained at liberty; the rest were killed, imprisoned, or demoted. Of the 757 members of the *Tzik,* theoretically the Soviet "parliament," only a few dozen survived.

But concentrating on such identifiable victims tends to obscure the larger reality. Actually the whole population was affected. In the ruling party, 1,800,000 members and candidates were stripped of their communist status, more than half the total, and usually that meant anything from exile and concentration camp to death. At least eight million more were subjected to liquidation, implying anything from loss of their jobs to loss of their lives. A purge of some ten million men and women staggers the imagination. Including their families and close friends, whose lives were shaken up and often wrecked, we come close to a third or a half of the entire population! And in truth no one escaped the tragedy, living amidst the thunderous fears and threats and uncertainties of the time. Undoubtedly millions who did not actually pass through the purge process remained maimed in mind and spirit by the sheer waiting and dreading.

In simple fairness to a cruelly martyred people, it should be made clear that not all "confessed," not all surrendered. Only the shabby side of the tragedy was exposed to the eyes of the world. Those who died meanly had the klieglights playing on their humiliation. But we shall never know how many tens of thousands died bravely and defiantly. After all, only those who agreed to confess and degrade themselves were ever brought into the public arena. Certainly Stalin would not have missed the chance to parade a beaten Tukhachevsky, Yenukidze, Blucher, or others of their towering importance in the limelight had they lent themselves to it. The vast number of suicides in itself bespeaks a vast reservoir of self-respect.

Terror is a stale and frail word to describe the extraordinary slaughter. It was an extension of war — a conqueror consolidating his position by unlimited killing and unlimited intimidation of potential rebels against his authority. Had death and destruction on that gigantic scale been brought by an invader, this would have been clear. Only the circumstance that they were imposed from within, by domestic conquerors, conceals the reality.

The unhappy Nikolayev, confiding his hatred of the regime to a notebook, dreaming of an assassination that would arouse Russia to action, as he hoped, attains a symbolic stature. He was too young to have known anything but life under the Soviets, as a product of the new system, its schools, its Komsomols, its ruling party. In a crude and desperate way he was Russia, the repressed but unconquered Russia reasserting its age-old aspirations. Had he been willing to play a rehearsed part in a public trial, blaming others and expressing contrition, he would not have been shot so quickly without a public trial.

In Nikolayev the Stalinists doubtless saw a portent of their ultimate doom. They did not spill oceans of blood just for amusement. They had a compelling purpose. They wanted to wash out, if they could, the unorganized yet formidable resistance taking shape among the people and mirrored throughout the system of Soviet power.

XII. The Acid Test of War

1. Appeal to Patriotism

From the first hour of the invasion the situation was catastrophic. Along a fifteen-hundred mile front from the White to the Black Seas the Germans were pushing forward at blitz speed, engulfing entire Red armies and capturing mountains of munitions and supplies.

Soviet divisions were melting away, running off in chaotic spills of retreat eastward and surrender westward. Even far behind the fronts in some sectors, military formations were crumbling, disintegrating in anticipatory spasms of fear and disgust. The invaders could not build barbed-wire enclosures fast enough to contain the hordes of prisoners and deserters — it was hard to tell which were which because the defense was so halfhearted, the line between voluntary and involuntary surrender so nebulous.

Fearful of disclosing the full extent of the debacle, the Kremlin communiqués were recklessly optimistic, filled with resounding generalities about stubborn resistance, German armies smashed, enemy tank units wiped out. But the people noted that these mythical triumphs took place at points deeper and deeper within the country and were not fooled. A population long conditioned to total censorship seems to develop a sixth sense for the facts under the propaganda.

Not until July 3, 1941, twelve days after the start of the war and the flooding calamity, did the late Joseph Stalin, chief architect of the shattered Moscow-Berlin alliance, address his subjects. The de-

lay was ominous. It meant, as most people realized, that the hierarchs were pondering what to say and how to say it. As the news
of disaster poured into their crenelated, triply guarded citadel they
were assessing the state of mind of the populace.

By the twelfth day they presumably knew the worst, and Stalin's
broadcast reflected that knowledge. The interval had been long
enough to reveal the fatal flaw in the Red war machine, its lack of
a robust will to fight. More important, it had been long enough to
give the dictators a terrifying sense of the mood of the masses.

Stalin's long-suffering subjects were bewildered, frightened, sullen — but also curiously exhilarated and hopeful. The long stalemate between regime and people had apparently been broken at last
by an external blow, and now anything might happen. The walls
of the prison house called the Soviet Union seemed to be caving in.
Men and women read unspoken and tremulous secrets in one another's eyes. *Could it be that the liberation from Bolshevism, like
its imposition twenty-four years before, was coming through war?*

Many eyewitness descriptions of those first days and weeks have
been given to the world since the war's end by Soviet nationals
now self-exiled in the West. Though they differ on details they
agree on the substance. They agree that there was no upwelling of
patriotic emotion or resentment against the alien intruder, that there
were no spontaneous demonstrations, no surge of volunteers such
as had marked the outbreak of war with Germany under Nicholas
the Last in 1914. There was only amorphous panic streaked with
vague elations.

Rarely in the years of his supreme power had Stalin talked directly to the country. His swarthy image was everywhere, in litho-
graph and plaster of Paris, in stone and metal. But his living voice
was virtually unknown. Now its rasping monotonous sound, with
its thick Gruzin (Georgian) accent, seemed the voice of a stranger.
He spoke, those who heard him agree, hesitantly, tremulously,
stumbling on words and pausing often to wet his throat, conveying
the distinct impression of a man scared and embarrassed. And what
he was saying, too, seemed strange to the millions in factories and
mines, on farms and in offices, in army barracks and encampments,

who paused to listen. Somehow it was like an echo from an incredibly far-off and outlawed past.

Stalin, it was instantly clear, had decided to forego the ritual phrases, the clichés of communist double-talk. He was uttering in deadly earnest words that until then had been heard publicly only in derision — words like freedom and democracy and fatherland. He was appealing to sentiments long ago driven into the underground of men's hearts.

"A grave danger hangs over our fatherland," he said. "The aim of this war against the fascist oppressor is to help all the peoples of Europe who are groaning under the heel of German Fascism . . . In this war we shall have faithful allies in the peoples of Europe and America. . . . Our war for the freedom of our fatherland will merge with the struggle of the peoples of Europe and America for their independence, for democratic freedoms. . . . Brothers and sisters, I address myself to you, my friends!"

Less than two weeks earlier the nations now lauded as stout allies, as the very hope of Russia's survival, had been assailed as democratic jackals, plutocratic warmongers, degenerate capitalists. For refusing to submit to a peace dictated by Hitler, they had been denounced as bloodthirsty imperialists. So now, through their confused astonishment, his listeners had a feeling of walls tumbling, their long isolation from the body of mankind giving way. A worker in a Moscow plant, as later recounted in a book by a fugitive, whispered: "The Boss must be in a hell of a pickle to call us 'brothers and sisters.'" A hope of emancipation stirred in the nation's breast.

Stalin expressed gratitude to President Roosevelt and Prime Minister Churchill — the top villains in thousands of Soviet editorials and speeches in the preceding twenty-two months — for their pledges of solidarity against the German aggressor. Though he ended the address with a reference to the banner of "the Party of Lenin and Stalin," it was as far removed from a typical communist speech as his audience had heard for over two decades. Its keynotes were simple patriotism, love of country.

Again, as in the glorious time of resistance to the Napoleonic invasion, Stalin urged, the people must fight "a national war of liberation"; they must make supreme sacrifices for "the imperishable image of Russia." Deliberately he was addressing himself to the heart and soul of the historic Russia, touching gingerly upon the Soviet interlude, as if it were a minor theme in the vast symphony of the nation's career.

This speech was duly reported in the press of the outside world, where its summons to "scorch the earth" in retreating before the enemy was given major attention. But its dramatic political implications were entirely missed. The peoples of Russia, however, understood these to the full. They knew that Stalin was saying, "Though you do not like me and my fellow dictators, this is not the moment for settling scores. Don't fight *for* me, fight *despite* me." They sensed, too, in his ample references to the democratic allies and defense of freedom against Nazi savagery, an implied promise of freedom and democracy for themselves if the war were won.

For nearly a quarter of a century the Soviet dictatorship had been molding the old generation of Russians and rearing a new one in its own grim image. Toward this end it had applied its monopoly of force — the physical force that breaks bodies and the propaganda force that maims spirits — continually, ruthlessly, without scruples.

No corner of the individual citizen's life and mind had been overlooked in a gigantic enterprise in "human engineering," as it was officially called. Millions who would not or could not be engineered had been systematically broken on the rack and destroyed. Entire classes of the population had been liquidated. Every instrument of communication and indoctrination, the press, schools, radio, shop meetings, mass organizations, had been brought to bear on the task of softening and kneading minds.

As a vital part of this job, the Russian past had been in part buried, for the rest distorted, maligned and ridiculed. The country's pre-Bolshevik achievements were largely concealed, while its many faults were blown up into monstrous crimes, its traditions reduced to laughable superstitions. Its religion especially was condemned and persecuted. The real dawn of history was dated 1917, with everything that had gone before treated as darkness upon the face of the deep.

Presumably a new "Soviet man," hand-tooled product of the communist era, had displaced the historic Russian. This presumption was widely credited abroad, in particular among the gullible educated of the West, some of whom, in fact, wrote solemn treatises on the brand-new human being fashioned by the Bolshevik designers of souls.

Then, on the morning of June 22, 1941, came the first great test of this portentous handiwork.

One would suppose that in the hour of crisis the Kremlin would as a matter of course summon its engineered Soviet men to a crusade in defense of the new society, of the communist civilization, the collectivized farms and socialized industries. One expected Stalin and his brethren to invoke the haloed names of Marx and Lenin, to muster the phalanxes of their Soviet organizations, the Red trade-unions, the local and regional Soviets. Here, finally, was the payoff on more than twenty years of indoctrination, on the regiments of trained agitators, the new education, the parrot press, the acres of posters, the great anti-God campaigns, the familiar communist slogans and symbols.

But amazingly, they did nothing of the sort. The celebrated "Soviet man," that faceless and godless robot, might never have been. He was snubbed utterly. Instead, the dictators appealed to the insulted past and its maligned leaders, exhorting the people to revive the spirit and attitudes that had defeated Napoleon's Grand Army more than a century before! The communist years were barely mentioned, the communist boasts and promises discreetly forgotten. The word "socialism" was all but expunged from the propaganda lexicon.

Let no one suppose that this extraordinary behavior was merely an impulsive concession under the pressures of initial defeat. On the contrary, it was a calculated policy, a deliberate and — for the Kremlin — humiliating retreat from the official ideology. It was to endure for years: specifically, until the time when victory over the

Germans seemed assured and reconciliation with the masses therefore no longer an urgent necessity. With every month it was to become more forthright, rather than less so, in restoring old Russian values — and old native values in the Ukraine and other areas as well — and brushing aside the values of the Soviet period.

2. Retreat from Bolshevism

In Soviet history there had been other reluctant retreats from dogma at critical junctures, to appease the people and divert their angers. The best known, of course, was Lenin's promulgation of the New Economic Policy (Nep) in 1921, ending the period of so-called war communism. But none of them was as far-reaching, as complete and galling a defeat for the Soviet leadership as this virtual repudiation of Sovietism in 1941.

The deeply national note struck by Stalin set the tone for all the speeches, editorials, posters, songs, movies, and plays of the subsequent war years. The familiar Soviet formulas and stereotypes were swept out of sight to make place for prerevolutionary concepts and precepts. There was no longer room for "the proletariat," for classes generally, in a propaganda geared to blood, soil, national unity, and national greatness.

In his second broadcast, on November 7, Stalin repeated that note more clearly and loudly. Between the two speeches, the Germans had overrun a territory containing about one third of the Soviet population and had gathered in more than three million prisoners. Leningrad was besieged and the enemy was hammering at the gateways to Moscow. Though he spoke on the anniversary of the Bolshevik seizure of power, from the ledge of the Lenin mausoleum on Red Square, Stalin had little to say about Lenin or Bolshevism. He did recall the failure of foreign invaders in the first years of the Red regime but the emphasis was on the centuries-wide panorama of history. And he concluded with a sentence startling to Soviet ears:

"Let the images of our great ancestors — Alexander Nevsky,

Dmitri Donskoy, Kuzma Minin, Dmitri Pozharsky, Alexander Suvorov, Mikhail Kutuzov — inspire you in this war!"

This was an astronomic distance from the ritual perorations of prewar days, from the "Long live the Party of Lenin and Stalin," from the routine salutes to world revolution. The names Stalin carefully selected for symbolic invocation, spanning centuries of Russian glory, pointedly bypassed any revolutionary, let alone Marxist, figures of the past. Before long even Ivan the Terrible, favorite whipping boy in the denigration of czarist times, was being played up as a hero and model for Soviet warriors; the leading film director, Serge Eisenstein, was assigned to glorify his memory in a picture cycle.

Igor Gouzenko, the code clerk in Ottowa who exposed the Soviet spy ring in Canada, was to write of the war period: "The words 'communism' and 'Soviet' disappeared. Instead, everything was spoken of as 'Russian.' Marxism was forgotten. Communism-versus-Fascism was forgotten. Everything carried the 'Defend Russia!' theme." *

All that was recent, Soviet, communist, was tactfully muted where it could not be expunged. The very name of Stalin was mentioned as sparingly as possible. Not once in the blood-soaked years did he visit the fighting fronts, as Roosevelt and Churchill and Hitler were doing; it was taken for granted that Stalin's personal appearance among the troops would be of very doubtful morale value. His "genius," endlessly trumpeted in the publicity abroad, was muffled in the propaganda at home.

Traditional military titles, from marshals, generals, and admirals down, were restored and soon gaudy epaulettes — redolent of the *ancien régime* — appeared on the shoulders of officers. The demonstrative return to the past, as a matter of fact, was especially vigorous in the military orbit, for understandable reasons. The system of political commissars attached to and in effect superior to regular officers was abolished; and item by item all other "socialist" and "revolutionary" customs and institutions were dispensed with,

* *The Iron Curtain,* Dutton, 1948.

while formations and practices with strong historical associations were restored.

The Cossack divisions, suppressed and execrated by the revolution, were again constituted, as well as special Guards divisions, some of them bearing names famous in czarist annals. Newly minted medals and orders were no longer named after Soviet deities but after personages of the Romanoff era. The new Orders of Suvorov and Kutuzov tended to outshine the Order of Lenin.

"All the songs of the prewar period, about the 'Leader,' the 'proletariat,' and similar eyewash, had been swept out of the army as though by the mighty incantation of a magician," a former Red Army officer recounts. "Instead, the genuine Russian marching songs conquered the soldiers' hearts. Even quite unmusical fellows bawled them out, simply because they were now again allowed to sing about neighing steeds, old mothers, and young beauties. The magician in the Kremlin realized that such things were closer to the soldiers' hearts than Karl Marx's beard." *

Most indicative of all, religion was made not merely legal but almost respectable. Church bells, long silenced, rang out once more, even over the radio. Church dignitaries, from the new Patriarch down, took to the microphone to plead for the war effort in the name of the God whom the Kremlin had tried so hard to "abolish." Stalin and lesser leaders received the church heads formally and with a maximum of publicity. This new tolerance was capped by the formal legalization of the Orthodox hierarchy; the fact that it was obviously under the heel of the government was itself, conveniently, a parallel with the past.

The surge of nationalism affected every phrase of the country's life. With the Bolshevik penchant for going the limit, the new patriotism was played with all stops out. The ubiquitous agitators, disciplined as ever, pushed the new line of slogans as briskly and as crudely as they had the old. To derogate a czar or a czarist general now became as dangerous as it would have been only a few years ago to praise him. As for the heroes in the communist pan-

* *The Terror Machine,* by Gregory Klimov.

theon, people gladly took their cue from Stalin — the less mention the better.

The formal dissolution of the Communist International midway in the war was accepted by the world as a move to reassure and placate the democracies, and no doubt that was one of its purposes. But its larger and more immediate objective, wholly missed by foreign commentators, was domestic. It was another act in the unfolding drama of propitiation of the masses. It was the Kremlin's way of suggesting that it was through at last with the nonsense of world revolution and would hereafter be dedicated solely to national interests. The abandonment of the *Internationale* as the national anthem, and its substitution with a frankly Russian anthem, spelled out this thought beyond danger of misunderstanding. The slogan "Proletarians of all countries, unite!" disappeared from the front page of *Pravda*.

The retreat from Sovietism was mirrored in the Russian literature of the period, from sketches in the daily papers to novels and plays. In a police state under conditions of absolute censorship the written word is the most reliable index to official policy; every piece of printed matter is a direct or tangential expression of government purposes. A perceptive student of Soviet literary trends residing in New York, Vera Alexandrovna, was able to write:

> In plays and novels and poems, communists appear to be receding into the background while ordinary Russians, sometimes Russians not entirely sympathetic to the communists, take the foreground. Even when the heroes are communists, it is the Russian in them rather than the political person which stands out. Of the former standardized passion for world revolt, there is scarcely a trace and the clichés about industrialization and "Soviet achievements" are fewer and less insistent. Above all, one senses a love for the common folk, the folk who are fighting and suffering, that is far removed from the ritual phrases about workers and peasants, from the cynical disregard of the individual characteristic of the recent past. There is a sort of return to the people in recent literature, tinged with a feeling of guilt for years of neglect.*

Normally under the Soviets, writers had to be driven to follow

* The *American Mercury*, March, 1943.

a new line in literature with directives, threats, and sometimes actual arrests and exiles. But not this time. Once the ideological restraints were relaxed, writers fairly rushed to voice the love of folk and country which had been bottled up in their souls for a quarter of a century. There was a flowering of sentiments long repressed.

Constantine Simonov, who was later to emerge as a kind of writer-laureate of the dictatorship, had the keenest ear of all for his masters' voice. He found it politic now to celebrate, in a poem, the "land of villages which our fathers knew, with simple crosses on their Russian graves." Novelists like Leonid Leonov and Gladkov, whose reputations rested on books glorifying communism and the new Soviet men, suddenly discovered other heroes worthy of their talents — noncommunists, just Russians, concerned with individual rather than exclusively social problems. Many writers, in fact, were destined to pay dearly after the war — when the ideological strait jackets were restored — for the telltale enthusiasm and speed with which they had jettisoned Soviet themes for traditional human material.

The United States Office of War Information and other such agencies of the democratic allies purported to see in the eventual ardor of the Russian people in fighting the Germans an obvious proof of "loyalty to the Soviets" and to Generalissimo Stalin personally. They chose to interpret every Russian victory over the enemy as devotion to communism. At the core of this delusion, of course, was plain ignorance. But it was deftly encouraged and buttressed by Soviet sympathizers and outright communists operating in the OWI, BBC, and other such propaganda agencies. To this day pro-Soviet publicists cite the heroic showing of the Russian people in the war as conclusive evidence of their support of the Kremlin regime.

But inside the Soviet Union this delusion was shared by neither the government nor the governed. There, the fighting spirit that in time displaced the early apathy and defeatism was recognized and approved as old-fashioned patriotism, unrelated to the Soviet epoch and even hostile to that epoch. Again and again Stalin frankly told foreign visitors that the Russian people were not fighting for him, Stalin, or for the communist system, but only for their fatherland. To judge from their published reports, not one of these foreigners — Harry Hopkins, Lord Beaverbrook, and others — grasped that he was listening to a political confession of major importance. They were inclined to dismiss as playful modesty what was in truth an aggrieved admission.

The moral of the story needs to be underlined for its pertinence to the present international picture. *Under the impact of the German invasion Stalin and his satraps in effect disowned the Bolshevik revolution.* They fell back helter-skelter upon the pre–1917 legitimacies they had long labored to defile and erase. In word and deed they acknowledged that despite two and a half decades of total terror and indoctrination they had failed dismally to "sell" communism and the Soviet way of life to their subjects. In the time of supreme test they were pleading with the population to accept them as Russian rather than communist leaders, as national patriots rather than international conspirators.

The substantial repudiation of Soviet ideology and world-revolutionary goals was, of course, a cynical lie. At closed meetings of trusted comrades there was no concealment of the fact that it was all a strategy of expediency, to be canceled out at the first opportunity. Despite the sham interment of the International, special academies of revolution for both Oriental and Occidental communists functioned at full throttle, and insiders were continually cautioned not to take the retreat from Leninist internationalism at face value.

But it was a strategy forced upon the Soviet regime by the real sentiments of the Russian peoples, by the palpable failure to eradicate the historic Russia. In this lies the importance of the fact to mankind at the present crossroads in world affairs.

3. *Freedom through Defeat*

To explain the magnitude of the initial defeats, the Kremlin and its foreign press agents spread a number of claims which a world

too eager to believe swallowed uncritically. They said that the Soviets had been caught helplessly unawares; that the country was
unmobilized and relaxed; that the attackers disposed of greatly pre-
ponderant forces. These claims were in part exaggerations, for the
rest inventions. A decade and more later such alibis were still passing muster as historical fact.

Was the Kremlin really caught off guard?

As early as December 18, 1940, Hitler's Operation Barbarossa, his
plan for the conquest of Soviet Russia, had been circulated among
top generals and advisers. Its translation into plans and military
deployments, involving a multitude of details and thousands of big
and little officials, began without delay. The prodigious shifts of
armed forces and the creation of specialized agencies for the occupation and economic exploitation of Russian territories made leak-
proof secrecy impossible. With every week the coming offensive
was less of a secret, if only because so many highly placed Germans
were engaged in despairing efforts to prevent what they considered
a mad adventure foredoomed to failure.

It is too much to believe, therefore, that Stalin had no inkling
of what was on foot. Allied intelligence knew everything but the
precise date; both London and Washington conveyed urgent warnings to Moscow. The notion that Soviet intelligence was not
equally well informed is a strain on credulity. We now know what
might have been assumed then: that Soviet agents were spread
through the Nazi establishment on all levels. In Tokyo, a vital center
of German diplomatic preparations for the impending attack, a
Soviet spy, the amazing Richard Sorge, served as press attaché of
the Germany Embassy and enjoyed the full confidence of the German Ambassador. Before his execution by the Japanese, Sorge revealed that he had been able to apprise the Kremlin of Hitler's
projected double-cross at least thirty-three days before it occurred.

"Any Soviet General Staff officer would laugh outright if anyone were to tell him that Germany's attack on the Soviet Union
took the Kremlin by surprise," Major Klimov declares. "And with
justice, for no other regime in the world is so well informed on the
situation in neighboring countries as is the Kremlin. . . . Weeks be-

fore the start of the fighting on the Soviet-German front many citizens in the Soviet Union heard the British radio reporting the transfer of 170 German divisions to the eastern frontier of the Reich. And did the innocent children in the Kremlin have cotton-wool in their ears?" *

The angry Soviet denials of tensions between the two capitals amounted to indirect confirmation of the things denied. Two weeks before the blow fell, Stalin for the first time assumed the title of Premier, surely a sign that he expected dramatic developments. Demonstrative gestures of Soviet loyalty to Hitler, such as recognition of a pro-Nazi government in Iraq and expulsion of the anti-Nazi Yugoslav diplomats, were eleventh-hour measures to delay or head off the approaching German onslaught.

In line with Operation Barbarossa, *Wehrmacht* forces began to concentrate on the eastern edges of the swollen Reich, making necessary troop movements too massive to be concealed. At the same time reconnaissance flights over Soviet soil became bolder and more numerous. A formal protest lodged by the Soviet Foreign Office listed eighty such German violations of frontiers between March 27 and April 18.

Against this background, we are asked to believe that a naïve Stalin discounted the mighty activities on his threshold as innocent maneuvers; that the dictator who trusted no one else chose perversely to trust Hitler, of all people. The theory is touching but makes no sense.

Actually, a hidden mobilization of Red forces under the guise of maneuvers began many months before the invasion. Divisions in the Kiev area moved to the frontier zones in early June. The circumstance that the *Luftwaffe* demolished thousands of Soviet planes on the ground in the first days of the war points to the extent of air force concentrations in border regions. Possibly the Politburo did not expect the Nazi attack to come as soon as it did. To the last the Kremlin may have hoped that the calamity could still be averted. But the idea that the invasion was not expected at all does not survive analysis.

* *The Terror Machine.*

Were Soviet military forces inferior to those Germany brought to bear in its offensive?

The answer given by German military leaders is almost unanimous, and it is in the negative. In his book based on interrogations of German officers after the war, *The German Generals Talk,* Lidell Hart writes: "Hitler embarked on the invasion of Russia in the face of knowledge that his forces would be fewer than those opposing him at the outset, and were bound to be increasingly outnumbered if the campaign were to be prolonged."

About four months before the invasion, according to Hart, General Keitel estimated that the 121 divisions Germany could muster would face 155 Soviet divisions deployed in Western Russia. "Rundstedt's Southern Army Group," Hart declares, "had to perform its part with a handicap of marked inferiority of strength, especially in armor — the most essential element. Kleist told me his panzer army, which formed Rundstedt's spearhead, comprised only 600 tanks." He quotes Kleist as saying: "This will probably seem incredible to you, but it is all we could assemble after the return of the division from Greece. Budenny's army group, facing us on the south, had some 2,400 tanks."

Yet this very army of Budenny, with a four-to-one advantage in armor, was thoroughly smashed, netting the Germans some 700,-000 prisoners. After its defeat at Darnitza, about ten miles from Kiev, the Budenny force in its headlong rout abandoned some 40,000 motor vehicles of all types.

No other nation, and that includes Nazi Germany, had put as huge a part of its budget into preparations for war as the Soviet Union. The country had been starved and exploited without restraint in the name of military vitality. The three Five-Year Plans were first of all defense undertakings; consumer goods, including food beyond bare subsistence, were sacrificed to production for national security. No other country had boasted so loudly of its military prowess and its capactiy not only to meet any challenge but to fight it beyond the Soviet borders on the challenger's soil.

During the twenty-two months of neutrality the Kremlin could observe and analyze German blitzkrieg techniques. Soviet admirers, indeed, justified the Stalin-Hitler pact as a wily stratagem to gain time for further arming and training. After the messy Soviet aggression against Finland, there was sufficient time to correct weaknesses in the Red Army structure.

No, the Soviet military debacle was not due to inferior forces. It was not the flight of an unarmed mass from overwhelming attackers, but the rout of a well-equipped and numerically superior force. The total Soviet territory overrun before the Germans were stopped was several times as large as France. This means that had Russia been only the size of France, or even twice as big, it would have been completely swallowed up. As Boris Shub points out in his fine book, *The Choice,** this conclusively answers the pro-Soviet historians who contrast the fighting spirit of the Reds with the "decadence" of the French. The turn of the tide came when the defenders in effect ceased to be "Reds" and became Russians — a change, as we shall see, for which Hitler rather than Stalin deserves chief credit.

Are the Soviet defeats and retreats to be explained perhaps by intrinsic defects in Russians as warriors? The magnificent showing made by the Red armies from Stalingrad forward gives us a sufficient answer. In addition, the experience of World War I is pertinent.

Russia entered the conflict in 1914 with a tragic inferiority in equipment, transportation, and productivity as compared with the Central Powers. As against Germany's 381 batteries of artillery, for instance, it had only 60. A year after the start of the war, nearly a third of the Russian troops were being sent to the fronts without rifles.

Yet Russia scored dramatic victories in the first half of the war. It struck deep into East Prussia, imposing upon Germany a diversion of forces which probably saved France from summary defeat. "And note especially," Marshal Foch told a New York *Times* correspondent in March, 1919, "that if France was not wiped off the map of Europe, we owe it first of all to Russia." The 1916 offensive by General Brusilov in Bukhovina and Galicia doubtless saved

* Duell, Sloan & Pearce, 1950.

Italy; over 300,000 Austro-German prisoners were taken in an action described by a member of the British General Staff as "one of the finest feats of arms of the whole war." * The world has somehow forgotten that the czarist armies, before the collapse at home, took 2,200,000 prisoners and 3,850 guns in thirty months, compared with 360,000 prisoners and 1,500 guns taken by all the Entente Powers in fifty-one months.

Standard Soviet apologetics has it that under Stalin the people fought brilliantly and heroically, whereas they had made a pitiful showing under the czar. So far as the first half of the Nazi-Soviet war is concerned, the truth is exactly the reverse. By the end of 1917, after three and a half years of exhausting conflict that included ten months of revolutionary chaos on the Russian side, the Germans had not captured a single important city in Russia proper. In the first two years of the more recent conflict, however, the Germans were in possession of Western Russia up to the environs of Moscow, all of White Russia, the Ukraine and the North Caucasus, an area embracing a dozen major cities.

For all their grievances against the Romanoff autocracy, the Russian people fought more enthusiastically and successfully in World War I than in the initial years of World War II. There was never, in the earlier war, any mass desertion or any defeatism, except toward the end under the impact of total defeat.

The stunning defeats of 1941–1943 cannot, of course, be attributed to any one set of reasons. The havoc wrought in the officers' corps by the wild purge bleedings of a few years before had not yet been fully repaired; anger and fear enfeebled the military leadership from the highest to the lowest echelons. Distrustful of its field commanders, the Kremlin insisted upon blind fulfillment of its orders, without a decent margin for decisions and initiative in action — and the orders were often slow in coming through because of panic and confusion at the uppermost levels.

It is likely, too, that the deployment of forces and supplies had been predicated on all-out offensive, should a conflict with Germany become inescapable, rather than defense. Supplies were too

* *Encyclopaedia Britannica,* Vol. I, p. 59.

close to the frontiers and fell at once into the hands of the invaders. Besides, the Politburo was collecting dividends on its own glorification of the military prowess of Hitler. For nearly two years it had hailed every Nazi victory over the "decadent capitalist imperialists," throwing an aura of invincibility around the German war machine. It could hardly expect self-confidence in the Red ranks when yesterday's ally literally overnight became the enemy.

More important than all these factors, however, was the fundamental disinterest in the contest on the part of the population, the widespread reluctance to fight for an unpopular and generally hated political system, the burgeoning dream of *freedom through defeat*. The mood of the military forces reflected the defeatist temper of the Russian peoples as a whole. The people, as Major Klimov states, "had no desire whatever to defend the Politburo," regarding the war "as an opportunity to free themselves of the hated conditions of the existing regime." More than that: Many "genuinely welcomed the war! Secretly they thought of it as a European crusade against Bolshevism. That is a paradox, and very few people in Europe suspected its existence. . . ." And his report is one to which nearly all escapees subscribe, with merely variations in tone and emphasis.

4. *The Unknown Internal War*

In his revelatory broadcast of July 3, Joseph Stalin made statements of another order that might have been examined with profit — but weren't — by his democratic associates in the struggle: statements that threw into sharp relief the wretched morale of his country.

Even since 1936–1938, the period of the terrible blood purges and the imbecile Moscow trials, a shocked world had been lectured by Sovieteering "liberals" to the effect that the carnage was justified by the emergency. They explained that the Kremlin, menaced by Nazi and Nipponese ambitions, had to act swiftly and ruthlessly against the enemy within. Accordingly it murdered a whole gen-

eration of Soviet leaders — the generation that had made the Bolshevik revolution — and with them at least fifty thousand assorted
officials, diplomats, professors, engineers, administrators. Accordingly, it destroyed its leading marshals, generals, and admirals
as part of a liquidation of three fourths of its officers' corps, some
thirty thousand men, by demotion, exile and firing squad.

For the benefit of the squeamish, the apologists were ready to
concede that the therapeutic bloodletting was perhaps too drastic,
that the heaps of corpses did deface the landscape of their dreamland. But after all, they exulted, the actual and potential fifth
column was no more — Soviet Russia alone among nations was
without that handicap.

But now Stalin himself, in the second week of the war, showed
himself deeply alarmed by domestic menace from teeming traitors,
saboteurs, diversionists, foreign agents, and the other varieties of
the genus fifth columnist. "There must be no room in our ranks,"
he warned, "for whimperers and cowards, for panic-mongers and
deserters."

His well-schooled audience needed no glossary, knowing that
whimperers and panic-mongers were those who dared give voice
to discontents, cowards and deserters were those who had no wish
to fight for the Soviet way of life. From the moment the Germans
struck, press and radio had howled hysterically that the country
was crawling with spies and traitors. Far from having wiped out
fifth columns, it now appeared, the sanguinary years had caused
them to multiply and flourish.

The official howling was certainly not without justification. If
opposition to the Soviet regime and the hope of turning the foreign
war into a civil war for liberation be defined as treason, the incidence of sedition assuredly was enormously high in the USSR.
The fact is that the Kremlin was obliged from the outset to fight
a war on two fronts — against the Germans and against the enemy
at home.

Only the first of these struggles was reported; the internal war,
though it absorbed a huge portion of the Kremlin's energies and
took heavy toll in casualties, did not figure in the military com-

muniqués. Its ravages have become known in recent years primarily through the testimony of Soviet escapees. A brief but graphic account, for example, has been given by Kravchenko:

A long time before, an NKVD friend had told me that in case of war all "dangerous elements" would be stamped out. In every village, town and city long blacklists were ready: hundreds of thousands would be taken into custody. He had not exaggerated. The liquidation of "internal enemies" was, in sober fact, the only part of the war effort that worked quickly and efficiently in the first terrible phase of the struggle. It was a purge of the rear in accordance with an elaborate advance plan, as ordered by Stalin himself.

Several years later, in America, I was to hear the amazing nonsense — apparently accepted even by intelligent Americans — that "there was no fifth column in Russia" because the blood purges had wisely eradicated all "traitors" in advance. . . . I could only marvel at the success of this childish propaganda, evidently exported by Moscow.

I say "exported" because inside Russia the government took the very opposite tack. It insisted that our nation was rotten with fifth columnists. From the first day the press, radio and speechmakers howled for the lives of teeming internal enemies, spies, disorganizers, rumor-mongers, saboteurs, fascist agents. And the NKVD followed up the howling with mass arrests and executions. In the initial period, at least, we had the impression that the Kremlin was no less frightened of its own subjects than of the invaders.

We had no fifth column in the sense of pro-Germans or traitors — this *despite* the blood purges. But we did have millions of patriots who hated the Stalinist despotism and all its evil works. To that extent the fright of the ruling clique was justified.

The savagery of collectivization, the man-made famine of 1932–33, the gargantuan cruelties of the purge years had all left deep scars. There was hardly a family that had not suffered casualties in the regime's offensive against the masses. Stalin and his associates were not worried about our loyalty to Russia; they were worried, and with good reason, about our loyalty *to themselves*. Perhaps, in their nightmares, they saw twenty million slaves suddenly crashing through prison walls and barbed-wire enclosures in a multitudinous stampede of hatred and vengeance, in a floodtide of destruction. . . .

In any case, ruthless suppression of potential opposition took first place in the government's plans. It took precedence over measures of military defense. Soviet citizens of German origin, no matter how remote the taint, were arrested almost to the last man. The whole population of the Volga German Republic, nearly half a million men, women and children, was driven out of the region it had inhabited since the time of Catherine the Great and disappeared through Siberia and the Far East. Next came the turn of Poles, Balts and many other nationals who had not been bothered before the war. The isolators and forced-labor stockades bulged with additional millions. Our rulers behaved like a frightened wolf-pack.

Several days after the outbreak of the war, "military tribunals" were set up in Moscow, headed by the former president of the City Court, Comrade Vasnev. Branch offices of this new agency of terror mushroomed throughout the capital and its suburbs. The same was true in every other city. All the pores of Soviet life were blanketed by this organization, vested with extraordinary powers to arrest, to try in secret, to mete out death. There were special railway tribunals, river transport tribunals, Army tribunals — a nationwide army of witch-hunters under NKVD specialists, charged with the noble task of squelching discontent. Clearly the regime was in a state of panic.

Why this febrile fear of what Stalin called "disorganizers of the rear," Kravchenko asks, in a country supposedly cleansed of traitors with oceans of blood? Listening to the dictator's warnings, he knew, as did all Soviet listeners, that the Kremlin was girding for that war on the internal front. He continues:

It became widely known in Moscow communist circles that as the enemy rolled closer to Moscow thousands of men and women who had been in prisons or labor camps for many years were summarily shot. They were the more prominent political prisoners of the Left — Socialists, Bukharinists, Social Revolutionaries, Anarchists, ex-communists. They were the people whom the Kremlin dreaded most because, in case of a revolution, they might offer leadership to inchoate masses. Again that nightmare of twenty million slaves bursting their chains. . . .

It was no secret that the machinery of military mobilization, too, was used to destroy those of little faith in the Soviet regime. NKVD *dossiers* were turned inside out. Lists of suspects — border cases where arrest seemed unnecessary — were in the hands of every neighborhood draft commission. Those told off for speedy extermination were promptly inducted and rushed with little or no preparation to the most dangerous sectors of the fighting fronts. It was a kind of left-handed purge.

The magnitude of the terror inside Russia cannot be overstated. It amounted to a war within the war.*

And thus began what would be, as far as the world beyond the borders of the USSR was concerned, the unknown internal war. As always, the Politburo combined raw force with the force of propaganda — on the one hand a virtual renunciation of communist ideology in favor of orthodox patriotism, on the other a vastly expanded terror.

Endlessly the population was warned, exhorted and threatened. Lurid posters enjoined everlasting mutual spying and reporting. Daily the press chronicled arrests and executions by way of intimidating the public at large. Nazi Germany was content to prohibit listening to foreign broadcasts; but the Soviets took no such chances — they confiscated all private radios, allowing only collective receivers to be tuned to the domestic stations. The spectacle of trucks piled high with radio receivers gathered in house-to-house collections was another striking outward sign of the regime's dread of German propaganda and its small faith in the loyalty of its subjects.

The exile and dispersal of the Volga Germans to which Kravchenko alludes was one of the most dramatic single acts of repression. The Volga German "republic" was one of the theoretically "independent" and "autonomous" states of the Soviet Union: proud examples of the "ethnic democracy" that figured so prominently in the hymns to Stalin sung by pious foreign disciples. For about two centuries they had been as isolated from their country of origin as any other Russians along the Volga, though they had retained their racial and linguistic identity. In the Soviet years they had been "engineered" through indoctrination and force as intensively as the rest of the population. But Stalin had so little faith in the efficacy of this process that he would not risk their presence a thousand miles from the oncoming German armies. Not even the communists among the Volga Germans were exempted from the order of liquidation.

* *I Chose Freedom.*

A technical word, liquidation, which does not begin to convey the tragedy of the event. Nearly half a million men, women, and children whose only sin was that they spoke German were torn up by the roots from their cherished ancestral homes on the great river, packed into foul cattle cars and dumped in inhospitable areas beyond the Urals. It was an act of war, directed not against the foreign but against the domestic enemy of a doubly besieged regime.

Neither force nor propaganda would have succeeded in defeating the people in the internal struggle had not the Hitlerites chosen blindly, drunkenly, stupidly, to save the Soviet dictatorship by driving the citizenry to rally in despair around its hated masters.

XIII. How Hitler Saved Stalin

1. Bread and Salt

The wartime orgy of terror gave the measure of the Kremlin's fears. This, however, does not imply that the fears were the figments of jittery nerves. On the contrary, they derived from long and keen awareness of the extent of popular disaffection, and were further sharpened by the dictators' sense of guilt in relation to their victims. For two decades the rulers had lived in the shadows of looming retribution.

To a government with multitudinous eyes and ears it had been no secret that millions were praying for war as the best chance, perhaps the only chance, to throw off their shackles. Back in the thirties I had myself heard a simple peasant say, "When the Germans come we'll get our land back." To him "the Germans" meant foreigners generally. Again and again, in discussing the possibility of war, intelligent Russians had told me that the Kremlin would not risk putting arms in the hands of the people in a general mobilization, except as a last resort.

It was, I am convinced, the government's chronic dread of the populace under war conditions, more than any other single factor, that had motivated the alliance with Nazi Germany and the anxious appeasements of the Brown barbarians thereafter. Stalin and his associates were prepared for large-scale opposition, defection, and desertion if war came.

The reality surpassed their forebodings. The immense numbers of prisoners corralled by the Germans reflected a lack of fighting morale. According to secret German documents uncovered after the collapse of the *Reich,* over two million Soviet prisoners were taken in five districts between June 29 and October 18, as follows: 320,000 in the Bialostok-Minsk pocket, 300,000 in the battle of Smolensk, 103,000 in the Uman battle, 665,000 in the Kiev area, and 665,000 more in the Bryansk and Vyazma battles. The listing, of course, does not include those taken in smaller actions on the vast front in the same three-and-a-half-month period.

The Red forces, it should be remembered, were fighting on their own territory against an unprovoked invader, normally a guarantee of keen battle morale. They were on terrain wide open to rapid retreat. Can there be any doubt that these millions preferred capture to continuing the fight? Certainly Stalin had no such doubt. That was why he issued his notorious edict, unprecedented in modern times, that all Soviet captives were to be regarded as deserters.

Of a piece with the mass surrenders, and even more amazing to the Germans, was the friendly spirit in which they were welcomed by the populace, and its eagerness to co-operate. Isaac Deutscher, a historian whose approach is basically pro-Soviet, has stated: "A minority was certainly sullen and bitter; and . . . this could not have been an insignificant minority." That is a charitable understatement.

A German journalist who has written extensively about the Eastern campaigns, Jurgen Thorwald, refers to "the real joy with which the population everywhere received the advancing German soldiers; the words of greeting, the first church services in twenty years." Drawing on reports by German officers who had been on the scene, he describes streets in towns on the path of the conquerors garlanded with flowers, house-fronts displaying crudely lettered placards of welcome, villagers turning out en masse to greet their German liberators.*

Too much has probably been made of the nationalist sentiment of White Russians, Ukrainians and other ethnically non-Russian peoples in explaining this cordial reception. No doubt this played a large part in the total picture, but how large no one can pretend to estimate. Non-Russian *émigrés* from the Soviet Union who today

*Wen Sie Verderben Wollen, Steingruben-Verlag, Germany, 1952.

attribute the pro-German attitude solely to racial feelings are indulging in political guesswork. They ignore the fact that the invaders found a no less friendly welcome in purely Great Russian areas: in the Smolensk, Vyazma and Bryansk regions, for instance. They forget that the armies which fought with so little appetite and surrendered so heartily were largely composed of Great Russians.

Wallace Carroll, writing about the same subject in *Life,* probably came close to a balanced judgment: "In the Ukraine the spirit of nationalism further heightened the antipathy to Stalin's regime, *though the nature of the regime itself remained always the greatest source of discontent.*" * In every part of the Russian empire there were — and there are — particular local grievances, ethnic, historical and so on. But these are secondary, reinforcing the common and general opposition to the communist despotism as such. It would be a mistake to give more weight to the particular than to the general.

In the first months of the invasion, entire Red regiments and even armies gave up without offering genuine resistance. In many instances Soviet prisoners pleaded for the privilege of turning their guns against the Soviets. A popular witticism had it that the most important weapon of a Red warrior was the white handkerchief.

Desertion in another dimension was represented by the tens of thousands of men of military age who went into hiding, in cellars and forests and friendly peasant huts, to avoid conscription. The practice was especially widespread in the more western portions of the country, where the early arrival of the enemy could be expected to end quickly the ordeal of concealment. Dr. Leo Dudin, a Russian journalist now living in America, who was in Kiev when the conquerors entered, writes:

On the main street, the Kreshatik, the Germans were greeted with flowers. The scene was later frequently shown in German newsreels. On the very next day the streets were crowded with cheerful people, among whom men of military age were very much in evidence. They had until now been in hiding to escape mobilization. You cannot imagine how large was the number of such "slackers." In Kiev alone they came to thousands, and in comparing notes with others I was convinced that

* "It Takes a Russian to Beat a Russian," *Life,* December 19, 1949.

Kiev was typical. This mass evasion of service, I am sure, had no parallel anywhere else in the world.

I was myself among those hiding out. I was then an instructor in the Kiev university and was ordered to Tashkent with the rest of our faculty. But I managed to conceal myself for two months, at the constant risk of arrest and shooting, in order to extricate myself from the Soviet power. What the Germans would bring for me I neither knew nor thought about. In my apartment two others, engineers, were also hiding. To our sorrow and peril the Germans halted for a long time about fifteen kilometers from the city.

But do not make the mistake of thinking that these men hid out of cowardice. They were not saving their skins but rather risking them out of hatred for the regime. The same men were ready enough later to fight *against* the Soviets under General Vlassov and in the German ranks. Take my own younger brother. He hid himself to keep out of the Red Army, but subsequently joined the Vlassov movement and won several decorations, including the Iron Cross, for exceptional bravery in battle.*

The peasants everywhere met the *Wehrmacht* with the traditional offering of bread and salt in spontaneous ceremonies of hospitality. By the thousand, civilians flocked to volunteer for noncombatant tasks under the invaders; they enlisted willingly, in this short-lived honeymoon phase, for shipment to Germany in labor contingents.

A refugee from the Soviets, now in Argentina, has written to me:

The people in our city were overjoyed to see the Germans, their liberators, coming. I state this as a fact, based on the experience of my brother, who was among 130 workers in an electric plant; my wife, who was among about 100 workers in a gun factory; and myself, one of fifteen teachers in a school.

People were embracing and kissing each other as on great holidays. There were nine families in our courtyard, among them one communist. The communist looked a bit worried, the rest seemed on their first genuine holiday in years. The Germans came on October 8th. By the 9th the town had a gala look. People were on the streets in their best clothes. I know that the same happened in every town and every

---

* From a letter to the author, quoted with permission.

village. . . . Soldiers from the fleeing Red Army trucks jumped off and begged the inhabitants for civilian clothes.

This exile was writing in response to my question, and his answer is typical of those I received from former Soviet citizens in Germany and America. In a magnificent recent novel by Mikhail Soloviev, *When the Gods Are Silent,** there is a scene well worth summarizing in this context. Though it is fiction, I know directly from the author that it is faithfully transcribed from reality as he had himself observed it repeatedly — in Mglin, a town of twenty-five thousand in Orlov province, for instance.

The main character, Mark Surov, finds himself in such a Mglin just as it is being invested by the Germans. For some days the people had been in hiding, uncertain which side of the front they were on. Only when it was clear that the town had fallen to the Germans did they begin "to venture out cautiously." The arrival of enemy troops "was disturbing, yet it was somehow reassuring." Gradually a crowd gathered outside the church turned into a grain warehouse:

At last someone broke the doors open and they flocked in. A minute or two later the sound of the church bell beat over the town, ringing clearly in the still air, for the artillery had died down, and there was only an occasional gunshot. The sound of the bell seemed to bring the place to life.

Mark mingled with the people. He was astonished to see that Jewish inhabitants, too, were joining heartily. One young Jew to whom he spoke, alluding to what awaits his kind at the hands of the Nazis, shrugged it off angrily. The Germans, the young man said, were "civilized Europeans," the anti-Semitic tales were silly propaganda . . . An old man in a military tunic was haranguing the townsmen:

Crossing himself with a great sweep of his hand, he declared, "Well, citizens, the Bolsheviks have fled from our town. They burned down half our houses before they left, but not all, thank God! God grant they forget the way back to us!" Many people in the crowd followed his example and crossed themselves, while he continued: "The Germans

* McKay, 1953.

have driven out the Bolshevik murderers. We must thank them for coming and liberating us from Stalin. Let's give them a good welcome."

By the time a German motorcar on caterpillar tracks rolled up, the people had formed a line — "the Germans like good order." The old man stood at its head, holding a dish on which was a loaf of bread covered with an embroidered towel.

2. *German Testimony*

The testimony of Russian exiles is amply corroborated by both overt and covert German reports from occupied areas, some of these a matter of record in the proceedings of the Nuremberg war-guilt trials. It is supported by statements from German officers questioned after the war. Not only did millions of Stalin's troops decline to die for him, putting up only token resistance, but civilians everywhere were frankly anxious to take the invaders to their hearts as liberators.

A long top-secret report from occupied Russia, dated October 24, 1942, signed by Dr. Otto Braeutigam, an official of the *Reich* Ministry of the East, is available in full in the Nuremberg records. It says in part:

Were the war being conducted only for the smashing of Bolshevism, then it would have been decided long ago in our favor, for, as all experiences of this war have confirmed, Bolshevism is hated to the utmost by the Eastern peoples, above all by the great mass of peasants. . . . In the Soviet Union we found on our arrival a population weary of Bolshevism, which waited longingly for new slogans holding out the promise of a better future for them. It was Germany's duty to find such slogans but they remained unuttered.

The population greeted us with joy as liberators, and placed themselves at our disposal willingly and freely with body and life. Wherever Ukrainians, Russians, White Ruthenians and members of the Baltic peoples enlisted in the German Wehrmacht or in the police they proved themselves and fought excellently almost without exception. . . .

He went on to explain the opportunity that the universal friendliness presented, reiterated proposals he had made previously for meeting popular hopes halfway — especially the restoration of private land ownership — and pleaded for the establishment of a native anti-Soviet government. In a tone of despair he stressed that "the Russian fights today with exceptional bravery and self-sacrifice for nothing more or less than recognition of his human dignity" — the one thing, above all else, the Germans seemed determined not to grant him.

Harwith von Bittenfeld, an officer active in recruiting Soviet nationals for the *Wehrmacht,* has testified:

With an intelligent political policy we could have won the war in the East simply because the Russian people themselves would have overthrown the regime. Especially in the first months of the war, surrenders were on a mass scale and were *political* not *military.* At that time I would go out as a cavalry officer on a patrol and would come back with thousands of altogether voluntary prisoners.

Two German officers prominently connected with operations on Russian soil prepared for American Intelligence an extensive joint analysis of German occupation policy. Though their names cannot be given here, I am able to quote them. Herewith a few pertinent excerpts:

At the beginning of the Soviet campaign the German troops were hailed as liberators by the bulk of the Soviet population. The Soviet citizens did not fear the Germans in any way. The population stayed in the villages and towns without making any attempt to escape from the invaders. The efforts of the Soviet administration to evacuate the population from the areas under German threat were obstructed and mostly doomed to failure.

Only members of the Communist Party and Soviet officials retreated. The orders of the Soviet government for destroying the harvest and all stocks were not executed. The peasants did all they could to avoid driving off the cattle. Stalin's order to leave the occupied territories to the German invaders as scorched earth was considered a measure of despair and merely helped to increase the hatred against the dictator.

. . . A kind welcome was given to the German soldiers. Following an old Russian custom the peasants offered salt and bread to the German guests. In spite of their low standard of life they presented flowers, fruits and milk.

. . . The Soviet patriotic propaganda at first had only a very limited influence on the population and was mostly considered a dirty trick. All attempts of Stalin to make the war popular as a holy struggle for the defense of the fatherland turned out to be a failure. Especially among Red Army men and peasants there was a complete lack of patriotic feeling. Monuments of Lenin, Stalin, and other communist leaders were often destroyed by the population itself. Soviet citizens and soldiers willingly gave all military information without any pressure being put on them.

. . . The mass of the population not only in the rural districts but also in the towns was willing to collaborate with the Germans. Artisans and shopkeepers hoped for the reopening of individual enterprises and the restoration of private property. The Soviet citizens were prepared to contribute to the overthrow of the Stalin system by fulfilling even far-reaching German demands. They were ready to make great sacrifices for the achievement of this aim.

. . . The mass of the Red Army men did not want to fight and went over to the German lines. Soviet officers and soldiers who resented their capture were the exception. Where there was any stiff resistance it was due to the impossibility of deserting; for instance, if the fronts were stabilized or if the Red Army men were taken by surprise. The fighting spirit of the infantry was very low. They were driven forward like a herd of sheep. Prisoners stated that the commissars and some officers forced them to fight. . . . The Germans had been warned of the partisans (guerrillas). In the first month of the war, however, there was no partisan activity whatsoever.

In a move unique in military history, the Kremlin decreed the organization of special formations for deployment *behind* the front lines to block retreat. They had orders to shoot if necessary to stop unauthorized flight. But who was to block the blockers? Besides, great masses of Red soldiery "retreated" forward, in waves of desertion, as often as backward in rout.

The Stalin order on desertion, to which I have already alluded, defined everyone taken prisoner by the enemy as a deserter, to be punished accordingly if caught, his family at home to be shorn of allotments and other benefits. This measure, putting the brand of treason upon millions of uniformed men in enemy hands, amounted to a confession that the Soviet Union, unlike other belligerents, could never be sure whether its nationals had been taken by force or had given themselves up willingly. Meanwhile, in the territories held by the enemy, the people fraternized with the German soldiers and made no secret of their high hopes of a happier life without Bolshevism.

These facts add up to one of the great secrets of the Second World War. It was so well guarded at the time, and has been so slow in seeping out since then, that even yet it is not generally enough known and certainly not well enough understood.

Soviet Russia and the democracies concealed the truth for self-evident reasons of morale, though the wisdom of the democratic allies on this score is open to question in the perspective of time. But even the Nazis soft-pedaled the facts. On the whole they preferred to claim military triumphs rather than easy victories by the virtual default of the enemy. Leaders close to Hitler who were dead set against a benevolent policy toward the Eastern peoples, regarding it as error and weakness, had a special political motive for hiding and denying that the "subhuman Slavs," the *Untermenschen,* were not Bolsheviks after all. In general it went against the Nazi grain to accept "inferior peoples" as comrades at arms against communism.

A side light deserves to be noted. After the collapse of the German *Reich,* many of its military and civilian officials who had been active in the Russian campaigns and occupation were in British and American custody. The Soviets demanded their extradition as war criminals. But though Moscow pressed for surrender of many men of lesser rank and importance, it seemed curiously disinterested in the group of prisoners who knew most about the collaboration of Soviet nationals with the invaders. It never sought to bring Braeutigam, von Bittenfeld, and their kind to "justice."

Evidently the Politburo had no wish to give men of this stripe the opportunity to disclose to the world the truth about the initial popular welcome met by the invaders, the dimensions of Soviet enlistments in the German forces, and the nature of the Nazi blunder in spurning the outstretched hand of Russian friendship. Above all else, it is clear, the Kremlin was anxious to protect its bitter secret.

3. Hitler's Fatal Blunder

It is altogether consistent that the pressures for more humane policies toward the conquered Eastern populations, for converting them into allies against the Kremlin, came almost entirely from Germans basically out of sympathy with the Hitlerite philosophy and in particular with its racial obsessions. They were able to urge "political concessions" to the "liberated" Soviet masses precisely because they rejected the Nazi mirage of a Russia converted into a vast colony slaving for the *Herrenvolk*.

From the vantage point of the free world today it is significant that the most active and outspoken opponents of anti-Slav policy were Germans who had lived and worked in Soviet Russia before the war. Their judgments were thus based not alone on observation of popular attitudes under the occupation but on personal familiarity with the people under normal Soviet conditions. Prominent among them, besides those whom I have quoted, were Count Friedrich von der Schulenberg, the German ambassador to Moscow who had negotiated the fateful Hitler-Stalin alliance, and General Ernst Koestring, who had served as military attaché in his embassy.

Like nearly all foreigners who know Russia at first hand, they had learned to distinguish sharply between the rulers and the ruled. They had outgrown the error of mistaking popular opposition to the Soviet regime for endemic lack of national patriotism. In short, they had ceased to be "anti-Russian" and become specifically anti-Soviet, anti-communist. The reaction of the Soviet peoples to war did not surprise them; they had expected it, even as the Kremlin itself had expected it.

But their advice was ignored and in some cases punished, and in the end the Stalin clique reaped the benefit of Nazi insanities. They emerged from their country's catastrophe, these Germans who were best informed on Soviet realities, firmly convinced that victory in the

East might have been achieved with the co-operation of the Russian population.

This conviction was shared by many military commanders, by men like Major Count von Stuaffenberg and Lieutenant Colonel von Altenstadt, who early realized that their victories in the field were being lost in the occupied territories. Reports by Germans while the struggle was under way, and the considered judgments of German generals after their defeat, emphasize the view that the sprawling Russian continent could never be conquered in war *without the help of its inhabitants*. They learned the hard way that Russia was an arena of psychological and political warfare even more than military warfare.

General Koestring, the German Army's chief adviser on volunteers in the East, fell into American hands in the final stage of the conflict. "We Germans," he said bitterly to his captors, "through ignorance, greed and inefficiency, squandered our great capital in the struggle against Bolshevism. . . . "* To the interrogating officers his words sounded like gibberish, his bitterness seemed without point. They could not grasp that he was referring to his government's blind blunder in insulting and terrorizing the Soviet population, leaving them little alternative but to fight the invader. The "capital" squandered was the peoples' hatred of Bolshevism and yearning for justice.

In the perspective of time it should be obvious that Koestring's statement touched the very core of the Russo-German war. The fact is that the Soviet regime, tottering under stunning military blows, mass defections of its troops, panic, defeatism, and the general hostility of its subjects, was saved in the nick of time by Hitler, Himmler, Rosenberg and their cohorts. Had these Nazis deliberately planned to salvage Stalin's government and bolster his moral authority, they could scarcely have behaved any differently.

The *Wehrmacht* treated the conquered Eastern areas with some tact, if only because it recognized the decisive value of their support in military terms. Without waiting for permission from headquarters, and subsequently in defiance of orders from Hitler himself, local commanders accepted proffers of Russian help.

* Jurgen Thorwald, *Wen Sie Verderben Wollen*.

Thousands, and in time hundreds of thousands, of Soviet nationals were drawn into service as scouts and guides, helpers in the field kitchens and commissaries, drivers of wagons and chauffeurs, mechanics in field workshops. Officers in sore need of reinforcements readily put Russians into uniform. Soviet volunteers handling munitions often took the place of machine gunners who were killed, and then remained in the units.

By the spring of 1942, some eight months after the start of hostilities, an estimated two hundred thousand volunteers were spread through Germany's Eastern forces. After the first cruel Russian winter, German military leaders were grateful for local recruits; they felt lost on the boundless frozen steppes without the support of natives. But Hitler would have none of this. He authorized formation of special units of Armenians, Georgians, Turkomens, and other minor nationalities but was adamant against putting arms into Russian or Ukrainian hands.

His commanders in the field, while obeying the letter of the command, ignored its intent. They went ahead with recruitment, not for special units but for integration with their major forces, specifying that up to 10 or 15 per cent of every division be made up of Soviet volunteers and permitting replacement of casualties by local recruits. In practice it thus happened that fully half of some divisions were Soviet. Before the end of the war it was estimated that every tenth "German" soldier was a Soviet citizen!

But military authority covered only the narrow zones of actual operations. Behind the *Reichswehr* came the Nazi fanatics, the SS Black Shirts and civilian Brown Shirts, with their savage theories and lust for loot. They came armed with orders to strip the people of their last food, to exercise the prerogatives of an arrogant *Herrenvolk,* to squelch all illusions about ultimate national independence or even human equality under German rule. They succeeded in checkmating the efforts of more enlightened officials to set up even rudimentary local self-government.

At the start of the invasion Hitler in an address to the troops declared: "We do not come as enemies or oppressors of the peoples of Russia but to free them from the yoke of Bolshevism." This thought was repeated in millions of leaflets. With pathetic eagerness and credulity the population seized upon the promise. Portraits of the *Fuehrer* inscribed HITLER — LIBERATOR were posted everywhere in the wake of the conquering troops. The promise seemed at first corroborated by the relatively mild policies of the military forces.

But quickly enough the real nature of the conqueror became manifest: his brutality, his racist arrogance, his undisguised plans for exploiting the occupied areas permanently as colonies. Disillusionment set in. Even the best of the occupation bureaucrats flaunted their sense of race superiority, addressing everyone with the patronizing or insulting *"du."* They slapped and struck Russians as a matter of course, and openly preached the Hitler doctrine that Slavs were a lesser breed who should be thankful for the privilege of serving Germans.

As the armies moved eastward, the political and economic Gauleiters and Himmler's security commandos took over, and these knew no weapons but contempt and force. The great Jewish population was massacred, the non-Jewish population was decimated. Corpses hanging from trees and lampposts became a common sight. Peasant yearnings for a distribution of the collectivized land were largely frustrated on the excuse that "organic changes were not to be considered during the war." Actually, of course, agents of the Ministry of Agriculture were concerned only with maximum crops and utterly scornful of the economic preferences of *Untermenschen.*

The Nazis put their authentic stamp on the occupation and succeeded magnificently in turning the early friendship into skepticism, caution, and finally fierce hatred of the invader. What began as a war against the Soviet *Machtapparat* resolved rapidly into a war of annihilation against the Russian peoples. The men in the Kremlin could afford to smile again — Hitler was doing their work with frenzied efficiency. The *Fuehrer,* as a Soviet refugee has phrased it, "played his greatest trump, the peoples' trust, into Stalin's hands."

It is interesting that many Russians believed that the worst of the occupation personnel, Nazis like Koch and Saukel, were really Soviet agents cleverly carrying out Stalin's assignments. As far as the political consequences of their conduct were concerned, they might as well have been just that.

Schulenberg, a serious student of Russian history, saw more clearly than most of his countrymen that in the Soviet Union Nazi Germany was perpetrating its own demolition. Endlessly he pleaded for a modicum of political common sense to offset the mischief being done by terror and economic exploitation. He urged the creation of an anti-Soviet Russian government in the "liberated" areas. Though he believed that the Great Russians were the key ethnic element and must play the leading role in a post-Stalin nation, he supported self-determination as a solution of the minorities problems. He swung enough personal influence with Foreign Minister von Ribbentrop to get a hearing for his views, but both together did not succeed in budging their government from its know-nothing colonial stance.

The essence of the matter was that Hitler did not want allies in the East but colonies and objects of exploitation. It is likely that he knew as well as the Koestrings and the Schulenbergs that the collaboration of the Russian peoples could be had for the asking, but unlike them he believed that he could win the war by military means alone. The very idea of being beholden to lesser breeds was distasteful to him. Hitler and his intimates, until the last year of their reign, would not settle for what seemed to them an ambiguous, watered down victory in the East. They gambled for a clear-thousand-year conquest. A telltale detail was Hitler's boasted plan to evacuate all of Crimea, resettle the peninsula with Teutons and establish a proud "German Gibraltar" on the Black Sea.

Even before the invasion was launched, Alfred Rosenberg had been appointed Minister for the East. A Balt by birth, he was filled with a consuming hatred of all Russians. In an address to his officials on the eve of the attack he laid down ideological guidelines for what, despite some verbal camouflage, amounted to extermination of the people and great evacuations of areas suitable for German colonists. "This is a harsh necessity, bare of any feelings," he explained.

The German Supreme Command was no less candid in proposing cold-blooded starvation as standard technique. Its order of November 27, 1941, enjoined the troops to live off the land as far

as possible: "Particularly in enemy cities a large part of the population will have to go hungry. Nevertheless, nothing which the
homeland sacrificed itself to contribute, out of a misguided sense
of humanity, is to be given to prisoners or to the population. . ."

A document sent to German personnel assigned to occupation
duties in Russia recommended "the harshest and most ruthless
measures." "Above all," it cautioned, "do not become soft and
sentimental. . . . Maintain a distance from the Russians — they
are not Germans but Slavs. . . . We do not want to convert the
Russians to National Socialism, but to make them our tools." The
document, frank enough in its savagery, is part of the Nuremberg
record.

4. Nazi Weapon of Self-Destruction

The first to suffer the deadly lash of such thinking were the
hordes of prisoners, including deserters. Despite courageous protests
by the military leadership, hundreds of thousands of men were
crowded behind barbed wire under the open skies, without food
or shelter or medical help, to sicken and die. That it was not simply
a matter of inefficiency but of genocidal design is attested by the
fact that the local inhabitants were barred from sharing their
meager food with the unfortunates.

A secret German report to the Supreme Command of the Armed
Forces dated February 28, 1942, told part of the grim story:

The fate of the Soviet prisoners of war in Germany is . . . a tragedy
of the greatest extent. *Of 3.6 millions of prisoners of war, only several
hundred thousand are still able to work fully.* A large part of them has
starved, or died because of the hazards of the weather. Thousands also
died from spotted fever. . . . In the majority of cases, camp commanders
have forbidden the civilian population to put food at the disposal of the
prisoners, and they have rather let them starve to death.

Even on the march to the camps, the civilian population was not
allowed to give the prisoners of war food. In many cases, when prisoners
of war could no longer keep up the march because of hunger and ex-

haustion they were shot before the eyes of the horrified civilian population, and the corpses were left. In numerous camps, no shelter was provided at all. They lay under the open sky during rain or snow. Even tools were not made available to dig holes or caves. . . . Utterances such as these could be heard: "The more of these prisoners die, the better for us."

The report adds:

It was a basic mistake that no difference was made between real prisoners of war and deserters. It is known that German propaganda deposited millions of leaflets beyond the lines and encouraged the Red soldiers to desert, whereby good treatment and sufficient food was specifically assured to them. These promises were not kept. The deserters were beaten and left to starve the same as so many prisoners of war.

News of the heartless treatment of prisoners spread like wildfire through the length and breadth of the Soviet empire. The Kremlin saw to it that the terrifying tales brought by escaped prisoners and civilians crossing the fighting lines became widely known. They were too convincing to be dismissed as propaganda.

The German report concluded:

It can be said without exaggeration that the mistakes in the treatment of prisoners of war are to a great extent the cause of the stiffening power of resistance of the Red Army, and therefore also cause for the death of thousands of German soldiers.*

The flow of deserters naturally dwindled and before long practically dried up. The earlier resort to the white kerchief gave way to an animal dread of falling into German hands. Great masses of soldiery cut off by the rapid German advance, fearing capture, reorganized into formidable partisan formations, often under officers parachuted or infiltrated across the fronts by the Red Army. The guerrilla ranks swelled by disillusioned or simply frightened civilians fleeing Nazi terror from towns and villages.

Though many, and possibly the great majority of the partisan forces, had little love for Stalin, they were stirred by a new patriotic zeal against the foreign oppressors. In the Soloviev novel

* Quoted in *The Choice,* by Boris Shub.

already cited there is an episode that aptly mirrors the tragic mood of the *Waldmaenner,* the men of the forests, as the Germans came to call them.

Commander Mark Surov had heard that Russians were collaborating with the Germans. He "realized that it was only to be expected. The people hated Stalin and the Soviet regime and were ready to help anyone attempting to get rid of them." Now he was deep in the woods on the German side of the front, addressing the shabby, nondescript partisans under his command. "Comrades," he began, "the enemy has set foot on Russian soil, and the enemy must be driven off. That is the order of our government, the order of Stalin himself!"

But looking into the eyes of his men, he sensed that he was saying the wrong thing, that he must yield to his impulse to speak frankly:

"Friends . . . brothers!" he began again. "I'm not going to tell you that we shall fight for Stalin, for the Party, and all the rest of it. That's the sort of thing they're writing in the papers. But our aim is clear and simple: we're going to fight for our country, for our people. Nobody knows where this war will lead us, but there's only one way ahead of us: the way of struggle. . . ."

"But the German isn't our only enemy; the enemy is nesting in Russia itself and won't let the people live," somebody shouted from the rear.

"I know!" Mark replied. "We've grown many weeds on our native soil; but after all, it's our soil, and we can always pull up the weeds. The war itself will burn down many of them, and those that are left we'll pull up ourselves afterward. Isn't that so, comrades?"

There was an oppressive silence in the ranks. His words evoked no response. But then a single, hoarse voice called from the left flank. Mark knew it as the voice of Sergeant Demin, a great fair-haired giant who could hardly get into an outsize military uniform.

"You're right; there's no denying it. We'll chase the Germans out and then we'll deal with our own and treat them in the same fashion. And we'll give our own a double dose, till they shiver in their boots, and the Kremlin will be too small for them." *

* *When the Gods Are Silent,* by Mikhail Soloviev.

Jurgen Thorwald puts maltreatment of prisoners first in his indictment of Nazi policies which, as he demonstrates in a thick book thoroughly and Germanically documented, saved Bolshevism from destruction. Second, from all accounts, was the forcible seizure of men and women for slave labor in Germany. At the head of this enterprise was one Saukel, a barbarian who might have learned his methods directly from African slavers two hundred years before.

At first the recruiting was voluntary. Then accounts began to filter through on how the forced laborers were being exploited. The promises of equality with German workers turned out to be a cynical lie. The Eastern recruits were jammed into dirty barracks, kept on low rations, paid insulting wages for long hours, and, most galling of all, forced to wear odious badges of servitude. They were isolated from the local inhabitants, barred from restaurants, movie houses, and other places open to German workers.

As was to be expected, free enlistments all but ceased. And that was all right with the sadistic Saukel. He instructed his officials to meet fixed quotas notwithstanding, with no questions asked about the methods used. Men and women, even adolescents judged capable of work, were simply captured on the streets or dragged from their beds at night. There were instances when churches and movie theaters were secretly surrounded by SS commandos under Saukel's agents and all grownups shanghaied in waiting trucks.

In theory Rosenberg's *Ost-Ministerium* was committed to dismemberment of Russia through encouragement of national separatist tendencies among the non-Russian peoples. But truly self-governing non-Russian states, too, did not fit into Hitler's dream of a gigantic colonial empire. While Rosenberg mumbled vaguely of self-government under beneovolent German hegemony, he would not or could not make a forthright commitment of full independence for the Ukraine, Byelorussia, Georgia, and other ethnic territories.

Thus whatever political leverage there might have been in separatist propaganda was dissipated. Galicia — the area of the Western Ukrainians who had never been under Russian rule — was

arbitrarily annexed to the Polish Protectorate. No genuine organs
of autonomy were set up in any of the non-Russian reigons, any
more than in Russia proper. As High Commissioner for the Russian Ukraine, Berlin designated Koch, a fanatic racist who boasted
of his "tough" colonial methods. What Rosenberg seemed to promise in mealy-mouthed phrases, Koch canceled out in unambiguous
action.

An American journalist was talking to a prominent member of
the former German general staff after the war. "Do you know
where we lost the war in Russia?" the German asked.

"In Stalingrad," the journalist answered promptly.

"No, we lost it long before that — in Kiev, when we hoisted
the swastika instead of the Ukrainian flag!"

Independence leaders fled to the forests to avoid arrest, and effective Ukrainian contingents were soon fighting against both Reds
and Browns. Some of these formations survived for years beyond
the end of the main war, and desperate remnants (though hardly
as large as claimed by some Ukrainian spokesmen abroad) were said
to be holding out even in 1953.

Determined to cut down the Ukraine in both physical and intellectual stature, Koch decreed the closing of all schools above the
fourth elementary year. Germany, he said, had no earthly use for
an educated class of Ukrainians. Incredible as it sounds to a normal mind, he even forbade measures for the protection of children
and pregnant women, or general hygienic measures. He would let
nature take its course in reducing the numbers and weakening the
fiber of a population whose one virtue, as the Germans saw it, was
to be meekness. Koch was one who readily agreed with Hermann
Goering's remark: "The best would be to kill all men over fifteen
years in the Ukraine and send in SS stallions."

Conditions differed, if at all, only in detail in other parts of conquered Russia. In the summer months of 1942, the German Army
took advantage of its temporary authority in the newly captured
territories of the North Caucasus to demonstrate the advantages of
political sanity. Troops quartered there were ordered to respect
local customs and to bear in mind that the people were anti-Soviet

and therefore in effect allies. Local self-rule was organized under German guidance. Peasant committees met with German farming experts to plan dissolution of the collectives. The Saukel raiders were forbidden to do any coercive recruiting. Winds of hope blew through the North Caucasus and lifted men's spirits. But soon the Gauleiters came to undo the Army's work.

Superimposed on the physical outrages and atrocities there was constant and systematized humiliation. In their utter madness the occupation bureaucrats did not scruple to disseminate Goebbels's tracts on race, in which pictures of the least attractive Russians, Ukrainians, Asians, were contrasted with slick and smartly dressed Teutons.

"The Germans," as Boris Shub has summed it up, "had in fact devised a weapon for their own self-destruction." Thousands of them realized that the weapon of murder must in the long run turn into a weapon of suicide. But these were unheeded, helpless. Here and there, even as in the North Caucasus, some officials tried to mitigate the horrors in the hope that their easy successes in winning popular loyalty might bring the Hitler mob to its senses. But the Kochs and the Saukels complained to Berlin against such insubordination and — at least until the climactic stages of the war, when defeat loomed — they were invariably sustained by the *Fuehrer*.

In the postwar years a Soviet writer got himself into hot water by a literary indiscretion. "It is true," he wrote, "that millions of Soviet people answered Stalin's call, girded their loins for battle, and stopped the Germans at Stalingrad. But the question is, how could the Germans reach Stalingrad at all?" The Kremlin suppressed the question because it knew the answer: the Germans had even more millions of ardent accomplices in the Soviet population.

These are the accomplices whom Hitler deliberately sacrificed to his racial obsessions and territorial ambitions. The Nazis, it cannot be too emphatically repeated, saved the Soviet regime in its most desperate hour. In effect they imposed upon the reluctant Soviet peoples *a reconciliation with the communist power* for the duration. In the heart of Russia they managed to ignite a fire of patriotism in which Germany's war machine and colonial plans were destined to be consumed. They aroused a pride of nation and history such as the Kremlin propaganda unaided might never have achieved, and it was spelled out in resistance unto death.

The average Soviet citizen, whether in uniform or not, was given only the sad choice between his own and foreign despots, and for the most part chose his own. The fighting zeal in time turned the tide of war from defeat to victory. The heroism and self-sacrifice of the Russian peoples left an incredulous world gasping with admiration. But let there be no mistake about it today, as the free world wrestles with the Soviet menace: this resistance was the creation of German National Socialism — its crowning masterpiece of self-annihilation.

"The tens and hundreds of thousands of Russians who joined the German army," Stefan Osusky, a Czech political leader, has written, "bear out the opinion that, had Hitler not treated the Russians as inferior beings, the Russians would not have defended the Soviet regime, but on the contrary would have helped the German army to overthrow it." The sooner that opinion is assimilated by the free world, the better equipped it will be to meet the Kremlin challenge.

The story that the Soviet peoples rallied to defend the communist government is a fairy tale. Rally they did, but only to defend their soil, their honor, their human dignity. The slogans under which the partisans harassed the invaders were "For the Russian People," never "For the Soviets."

A large part of the Soviet population, especially the younger people, consoled themselves with the promise of a better and freer life after the victory — the promise implicit in the Kremlin's new accent on "democracy" and its democratic allies. The publication in the Soviet press of the Atlantic Charter, though without comment, seemed a portent of the big change to come. Every tin can of American food fed not only stomachs but hopes of freedom.

"The Russian people, deeply generous and patriotic, infuriated by the barbarities of the invaders, needed a miracle of faith," Alexander Kerensky wrote after the war. They chose to believe that the

Kremlin gang had experienced a change of heart. As for the more mature and skeptical, they assured one another and themselves that they would be strong enough to "pull up their own weeds" after the German locusts had been cleared away.

Despite the kidnapings for forced labor, despite the maltreatment of prisoners and the piled-up insults, nearly a million prisoners donned German uniforms: the only large-scale armies Hitler could muster among the hundreds of millions he conquered. These armies, as we shall see, could have numbered more than two million had not Nazi fear of their strength after victory intervened to limit the recruiting. There we have a clear and startling token of the popular detestation of the communist masters.

The truth about the Russo–German war, as distinct from the legend elaborated by Soviet and Allied press-agentry, must not be relegated to history. It is infinitely pertinent here and now. It may well prove to be the most important element in the current world crisis. "For the lesson of the German experience in Russia," in the words of Wallace Carroll, "is simply this: that the decisive element in a war against the Soviet regime can be the Soviet people."

XIV. Soviet Nationals in German Uniform

1. The Unknown Army

Defeatism is in the revolutionary tradition. Though Alexander Herzen was ardently Russian, he had no qualms about urging organized desertions in the Crimean War as a protest against Nicholas I. He proclaimed that England, France, and Turkey, in fighting his beloved native land, were in "a struggle of mankind (without distinction of nations) against the arrogant disturber of the peace in Europe," and his reputation for patriotism was not hurt thereby. During the Russo–Japanese War, then again in the First World War, the extreme left in Russia and the Bolsheviks in particular cheered every defeat of their own country as a blow to the autocracy and, more to the point, an opportunity for rebellion.

The doctrine that patriotism is a class rather than a national concept was dominant in Soviet propaganda until the middle thirties. The tale of how the Leninists attained power by grasping the opportunities of their country's defeat in war was told in pride. Defeatism, aimed to convert international into civil conflicts, is still part of the communist creed outside the Soviet sphere. It is at the heart of Cominform as it was of Comintern preachment.

Only in the Soviet Union and the countries under its heel has the doctrine been outlawed, on the theory that the rules change once a nation has come under communist dominion. But millions of Soviet nationals have not yet forgotten the earlier thesis that defeatism is not in itself disreputable. In 1941, that view was still fresh and without doubt helped provide the moral justification for desertion, sabotage, and actual enrollment in the enemy's armed forces. Lenin and his confreres, in accepting the help of their country's enemy, Germany, to overthrow the Provisional Government in 1917, set a precedent and a pattern of rationalization.

Judgments on the myriad Soviet citizens who joined the Germans against the Soviets should be tempered by comprehension of this background. "Revolutionary defeatism" was a familiar and ethically respectable idea to a generation reared on Bolshevik theory and history. Those who long before the war had looked forward eagerly to a chance to end their communist ordeal had no sense of treason in seeking to "make use of the Germans." Secretly, as already noted, millions looked upon the war as a European crusade against communism — and therefore *their* crusade too. Survivors now in exile do not count themselves quislings but defeated patriots. If Stalin did not scruple to join hands with the Nazis to safeguard his regime, why hesitate to do the same to destroy that regime?

Hitler understood this quite well. He was aware that the teeming Soviet recruits were not his friends but only the enemies of his enemy. Most Nazis resisted pressures to create formidable anti-Soviet forces out of the Soviet population precisely because they believed that, once Bolshevism was canceled out, those forces would fight against subjection of their country to Germany. "We will never build up a Russian Army," Hitler exclaimed in June 1943; "that's a phantom of the first order."

That phantom did materialize to some extent notwithstanding. And the ambivalence of the Germans — increasingly tempted to employ Soviet manpower but frightened of its Frankenstein potential — is the key to the pathos of the so-called Vlassov movement.

Among the prisoners swept up by the Allied advance from Normandy to Central Europe there were hundreds of thousands of Soviet nationals in German uniform, usually but not always distinguished from the rest of the German troops by the letters ROA on shoulder patches. These initials summed up one of the great, profoundly significant and strangely neglected episodes of the war.

ROA identified members of the *Russkaya Osvoboditelnaya Armia,* the Russian Army of Liberation. The more popular designation, then and especially in the postwar years, the Vlassov Army, was a misnomer. General Vlassov stood at the head of only a portion of the Soviet recruits, probably under 250,000, and even there his authority was circumscribed and at times nullified by German fears and duplicities. ROA was a generic name for all Russian volunteers, spread through the width and breadth of the *Wehrmacht,* and sometimes extended to cover also special national formations (Georgians, Turkomens, Cossacks, and others) not formally a part of the ROA concept.

Everything conspired to veil the massive Russian participation in the German military effort in mystery. Today, though one book about it has appeared in English and several in German, it still remains the "unknown army" of World War II, its true dimensions, motivations, and military role distorted by rival propagandas.

Why the Kremlin chose to ignore the ROA is obvious: the implications of a large anti-Soviet army composed of Soviet men were not exactly pleasant. The Kremlin thundered against traitors and quislings in general but carefully avoided mention of specific formations or leaders. On Soviet soil Vlassov was a forbidden word, uttered fearfully and hopefully only in whispers. That silence has remained unbroken to date. Inside the USSR the Vlassov drama has become an illicit rumor inflated by wishful thinking, never uttered in public.

Why the Germans played it down is less obvious. In normal logic it should have been trumpeted as a political triumph over the enemy. But logic was no part of the Nazi equipment. Russian patriotism, even of the anti-Bolshevik variety, was too sharply at odds with the Nazi conception of Slavs as barbarians. In any case, German propaganda soft-pedaled and at times blacked out information about its own creature, the Vlassov Army. Allied propaganda of course took its lead from the Soviets and avoided embarrassing mention of the whole phenomenon.

Thus the only large-scale fighting forces Hitler was able to mobilize among conquered peoples became a shadow army whose very existence was only vaguely known to the world. It developed into the most tragic, frustrated, and embittered foreign legion on record. Its personnel, from top leaders to plain soldiers, swung desperately between patriotic exaltation and conscience-stricken despair. They fought with the Germans whom they hated, against the democracies whose understanding they quixotically counted upon, and went down to oblivion in the general German debacle.

After the war, tens of thousands of these men lost themselves in the Central European population or were herded into DP camps, where many of them assumed new names and bogus nationalities to evade forcible repatriation to death in their native land. For years they lived in the dread shadows of a huge and ruthless Soviet man hunt, often aided and abetted by the American and British military authorities. Only in more recent years have they dared to emerge into the daylight, in a number of Vlassovite organizations: the survivors of a wartime adventure compounded of patriotism, heroism, and pathos.

What developed in Soviet Russia in the initial year of war, as we have seen, was a disorganized, un-co-ordinated anti-Soviet movement. Its armed formations, in part spontaneous and in part fashioned by the invaders, were used at the outset mainly against Soviet guerrillas and NKVD troops operating behind the German lines. Then, as Berlin began to feel the pinch of manpower losses, they were employed increasingly as integral elements in the general military machine. What most of them were rigidly denied, as a matter of Nazi policy, was that which they most craved: the chance to fight against the Bolshevik regime directly and openly in their own name.

The idea of merging the scattered Soviet volunteers into an organized anti-Soviet army took shape in the summer of 1942. Its leader and spokesman was a lieutenant general in the Red Army, with a brilliant and until then unblemished record of loyalty to the Moscow government: Andrei A. Vlassov. This man had stood so high in the Kremlin's favor that Allied intelligence at first refused to credit reports of his collaboration with the enemy. The news of his activities was treated gingerly as a possible propaganda hoax. But before long the seriousness of the movement around him became apparent.

Born into a peasant family in the Nizhni-Novgorod (now Gorki) district in 1900, Vlassov plunged into the revolutionary stream in 1917. He had been studying for the priesthood, but now transferred his spiritual zeal to what he regarded as service to his country. Throughout the civil war he fought with the Red armies, occupying an important post at the age of twenty in the storming of Perekop. He joined the Communist Party, graduated from the Frunze Military Academy, and came to enjoy the confidence of the highest government circles. In 1928 Stalin sent him to China as one of the Soviet military advisers to Chiang Kai-shek.

Only a handful of the officers' corps survived the blood purges of 1936–1938. Vlassov, then a colonel, was in this select company. By 1940 he was commanding the 99th Infantry Division in the Kiev military district; the division was cited as the best-led and best-disciplined in the country. After the German onslaught, he led the 4th Mechanized Corps in Pzemyszl and Lvov, and defended Kiev. Then, by personal order of Stalin, he was directed to organize the defense of Moscow, as head of the 20th Army.

"The formation of the 20th Army," Vlassov himself said later, "was accomplished in the most difficult conditions. I did everything that depended upon me to defend the capital of the country. The 20th Army stopped the offensive against Moscow and then passed into the offensive itself. It broke through the German front, took Solnechnogorsk, Volokolamsk, Shakhovskaya, Sereda, etc., and, assuming the offensive along the whole Moscow front, came to Gzhatsk."

His men, he explained, were not defending Sovietism but their country — "for that Motherland they withstood unnumbered sufferings and sacrificed everything." Unquestionably he played a leading role in halting the Nazi offensive on the capital. The press gave him formal credit, along with six other generals, as "saviors" of the city, and on January 2, 1942, he received the Order of the Red Banner from Stalin's hands with the usual fanfare of publicity.

A number of American correspondents interviewed General Vlassov in his headquarters outside Moscow on December 17, 1941.

Miss Eve Curie, daughter of the famous Polish-French scientists, talked to him several weeks later. They all described him as a strong, tall man, studious looking, wearing glasses, and they reported his confidence in ultimate victory. Miss Curie was especially impressed by his devotion to the country and his hatred of the Germans. In Vlassov she saw "a man who waged war with something more than courage: he waged it with passion."

A few months later the 2nd Assault Army, which was his next command, was cut off in the Volkhov encirclement to the east of Leningrad. Though Stalin offered to send a plane to rescue him, Vlassov chose to remain with his decimated troops — already thoughts of liberating his country from the regime he had gradually come to distrust and then to hate filled his mind. For a month Vlassov and his dwindling followers hid in the forests and swamps, then they too were caught.

This time of concealment was fateful for Vlassov. He was to tell often of the problems that agitated him: "Would it not be a crime to shed more blood? Is not Bolshevism, and in particular Stalin, the chief enemy of the Russian people? Is not the first and holy duty of every Russian to rise against Stalin and his clique? There, in the forest and the moors, I came finally to the conclusion that my duty is to call the Russian nation to struggle for the overthrow of Bolshevik power . . . the creation of a New Russia where every man could be happy."

The Germans had been deeply impressed by Vlassov's courage and skill. To those who were speculating on the possibilities of a Russian anti-Soviet army his capture seemed a godsend. One Russian expert in the Foreign Office in Berlin wrote: "I have not the least doubt that this man was sent to us by fate at the decisive moment and that his employment can turn the course of the war in our favor." Another reported that "General Vlassov is inspired by a burning hatred of the Bolshevik system and Stalin personally." A third touched the essence of Vlassovism. "He is not . . . a mere seeker after political glory and accordingly will never become a purchasable hireling and will never be willing to lead hirelings."

* * *

Toward the end of June, 1942, Vlassov announced his liberating role with an appeal to all "Russian patriots" through the press in the German-held area. It was the first of a number of statements which today form a kind of testament to his remaining followers. Vlassov emphasized that though he had prospered personally under the Soviet system, he supported the aspirations of his countrymen for freedom.

"How do I imagine the New Russia to be?" he was to ask in a pronouncement in Prague in 1944. "History does not walk backward. I do not call the people to the past, either. No! I call to the bright future, to the struggle for and achievement of the national revolution, to the struggle for the creation of the New Russia — the motherland of our great nation. I call it to the path of brotherhood and unity with other peoples of Europe, and in the first place, to the path of cooperation and eternal friendship with the great German nation.

"My call has met sympathy not only in the widest circles of the prisoners, but also in the wide masses of the Russian people, where Bolshevism still reigns. This compassionate response of Russians, who declared themselves ready to place themselves under the banners of the Russian Army of Liberation, gives me the right to say that I have taken the right course, and the task which I undertake is the righteous task, the action of the Russian people."

Vlassov's headquarters was established at Dabendorf, a Berlin suburb. A school for political instruction was there set up under General Trukhin: more than seven thousand students, mostly officers, had passed through its courses by the end of the war. In August and September, 1942, Vlassov was allowed to tour the Leningrad, Byelorussia and Pskov occupied areas. The response to his personal appeals was overwhelming. Tens of thousands of letters from civilians and captive Red Army men poured into Dabendorf.

The great majority of volunteers came from the prisoner-of-war camps. However they may have rationalized it, these wretched Russians no doubt were also influenced by the chance of escaping the hunger and horrors of those German hellholes. Surviving volunteers, however, reject this material explanation in anger. Had they retained faith in the Soviet regime, they insist, they would not have donned German uniforms under any conditions, any more than Americans in Japanese hellholes would have consented to become Japanese soldiers.

Moreover, and this argument is impressive, the flow of volunteers did not decline after somewhat more decent conditions came to prevail — in part at least through Vlassovite pressures — in the German camps. After I had written the first article on the Vlassov Army to appear in America, in February, 1948, I received a personal letter from the council of an Association of Youth of the Russian People in Munich, which contained many Vlassovites. It took exception to my suggestion that volunteers joined ROA "to save their skins" from German camps.

It said in part:

The facts are very eloquent. In November 1944 when the defeat of the German armies and the end of the war were obvious to anyone, in the Officers' Camp situated in the Norwegian Islands, a call was made for volunteers to join the army. At that time nobody died in the camps any more. However, only 15 of the total of 500 Soviet prisoners did not join. In the course of two months the Germans released only 65 men. It should be particularly noted that the more obvious became the end of the war, the nearer the Red Army approached, the greater was the entry list of the Vlassov ranks, and at the war's end, in February–March, the Enlistment Bureau of the Vlassov Army had in its files over two and a half million applications for volunteers wishing to join the ranks.

As many as 800,000 at one time or another wore the ROA insignia, though probably less than a third of them were acknowledged by the Vlassov leaders as belonging to their formation. The most significant fact, however, is not the actual but the potential scope of the movement. The statistics on applicants, according to pro-Vlassovite reports, come close to the 2,500,000 mentioned in the letter from Munich. This could have been the magnitude of the armed force under the ex-Soviet general, that is to say, if the Nazis had not obstructed and sabotaged their own creation.

We cannot know to what extent the Kremlin was frightened by the Vlassov Army; the so-called Free Germany Army under General von Paulus, organized after the Stalingrad victory, was Mos-

cow's counterpart. But there is ample evidence that the Nazis were
continually scared of their handiwork.

2. *The Vlassov Movement*

Almost from the start a deep contradiction developed between the
Russian patriotism of the *Vlassovtsi* and the ambitions of their
foreign sponsors. The ROA was caught, mauled, shoved around,
and humiliated in a continuous tug of war between the *Wehrmacht,*
concerned with purely military purposes, and the Nazi ideologists,
concerned with keeping all "Eastern barbarians" in their place.
Pressures upon Vlassov and his staff to glorify Hitler and Hitler
doctrines, including the anti-Semitic insanities, were unceasing.

That some of them, though apparently not Vlassov himself, now
and then yielded to this duress was inevitable. Vlassovite statements
with an anti-Semitic flavor have been found and brought together
in an effort to smear the Vlassov movement as simply a Nazilike
formation. However, compilations of an opposite order, in favor
of race equality, have also been made and, considering the time
and the place, are more impressive.

In justice to the gallant Vlassov movement, it seems to me, it
should be judged by its formal organization pronouncements, such
as the Prague Manifesto and Vlassov's own speeches, rather than by
the words of individual members dependent for their very lives
upon the Germans. The mere *absence* of anti-Semitic nonsense in a
statement drafted in Nazi captivity came close to an act of defiance.

In public declarations and in the Dabendorf indoctrination
courses, Vlassov spokesmen always insisted upon the sovereignty
and inviolability of Russia as the basis of their movement. Collaboration, they insisted, was governed by necessity — it was a means to
an end and involved neither political nor territorial commitments
to Germany. They did proclaim the necessity for friendly relations
with Germany but were revealingly careful always to refer to "the
German people" rather than their current regime; moreover, that
friendship was promised no less to all other European peoples.

Privately, expressions of national patriotism went much further. It went, in fact, to the point of envisioning possible military action against the Germans should the security and honor of a liberated Russia require it. Nazi fear that a resurgent Russian nationalism of their own nurturing might boomerang against Berlin's colonial plans was not unfounded by any means.

By the end of 1942, the opponents of ROA in the German hierarchy had won their point: that the military and propaganda value of the Russian formation was not worth the risks and the doctrinal compromises involved. The German High Command itself showed signs of nervousness over the expansion and the fervor of the Vlassov movement. Upon orders from the highest quarters, the German-controlled Russian-language press therefore ceased to publicize the ROA or gave it only grudging notice. Recruiting was blocked. The movements of ROA leaders were sharply restricted.

As guerrilla warfare increased in occupied Russia, the theory that the Slavs were unregenerate and must be softened by master-race terror gained in favor. This was naturally reflected in a deterioration of relations with Hitler's Soviet recruits. There were more and more outbreaks of anti-German feeling among the volunteers. Arrests and executions of insubordinate ROA officers became commonplace. The scope of Vlassov's activities was narrowed and the blanket of silence around his movement was drawn more closely. If his effectiveness organizationally was thereby reduced, his moral authority among his followers was enhanced. German harassment tended to take the edge off the "made-in-Germany" label, which was his biggest moral handicap.

That more sagacious men in the Nazi leadership questioned the wisdom of their government's anti-Vlassov line may be surmised from an entry in his diary by Goebbels, on April 29, 1943:

The Russian General Vlassov, who is fighting on our side in the Separatist Army [sic], has been pretty much shelved by the Ministry of the East. He wrote a report that rather grips at one's heartstrings. One cannot but be astounded at the lack of political instinct in our Central Berlin Administration. If we were pursuing or had pursued a somewhat cleverer policy in the East, we would certainly be further along there than we are.

At best it was an unhappy, mutually suspicious Russo–German marriage of convenience. Symptomatic of the strained atmosphere were the constant rumors that General Vlassov had been arrested or killed. It has since been established that in at least one period he was taken into custody and held incommunicado. Early in 1944 the Germans were obliged to take cognizance of the rumors by announcing officially that "General Vlassov is alive and well," though his whereabouts, they added, could not be disclosed for military reasons.

The fundamental Nazi aversion to Vlassov can be tasted in an SS proclamation of October 14, 1943, in which Himmler declared:

The Slav people have never been able to settle their own affairs. . . . In this connection I would like to mention openly the name of General Vlassov. Great hopes were set on this General Vlassov. As many will have foreseen, these hopes were not justified. . . . With a conceit characteristic of the Russian and the Slav, Herr Vlassov began to tell a tale to the effect that Germany has never been able to conquer Russia, that Russia can only be conquered by Russians.

It is to be hoped, as a matter of Russian honor, that Himmler was not misquoting.

The whole story of the ROA composes in retrospect into a pattern of Nazi double-dealing. The original bargain has assumed the establishment of a provisional Russian governing committee to administer occupied areas. Vlassov continually demanded what he had been promised: a homogeneous army under independent Russian command with its own fighting sectors on the Eastern fronts. He had exacted promises of more humane treatment of Russian prisoners and labor deportees. The Nazis violated every promise in full or in substance, and reneged on every understanding. In self-defeating arrogance, they restricted ROA propaganda in conquered Soviet areas.

And at all times Vlassov was importuned to consent to postwar frontiers deep inside his country. This he consistently refused even to discuss, maintaining that he had no authority to deal with matters within the competence of the future "free Russia." With the same stubbornness he defied Nazi demands that he make forthright anti-Semitic commitments.

By the beginning of 1944 the bulk of the Russian Liberation troops had been transferred to the Western front and deployed along the Atlantic Wall from Holland to the Spanish frontier. For the *Vlassovtsi* this was the most disillusioning blow of all. They had enrolled to fight against the Red Army. At every opportunity they had stressed that they had no quarrel with the Anglo-Americans and French. Now that Allied victory was in sight, they were being deliberately placed in the path of the democratic Allies!

ROA morale began to crack. Russian officers were increasingly superseded by Germans; more and more of them were arrested or simply disappeared. Vlassov and his top associates were not permitted to go to the West, where most of the forces theoretically under their command were concentrated. Only his associate, General Malishkin, made one brief visit to France.

ROA survivors today claim almost unanimously that their leaders instructed them secretly to surrender and turn their arms against the Germans. Many of them joined the French Maquis before the invasion of Normandy; others joined afterwards. Some succeeded in joining the Resistance in northern Italy. The majority were kept in line by their German commanders and retreated with the formations to which they were attached.

With total disaster around the corner, the Nazis finally permitted Vlassov to organize above the battalion level. Five divisions were authorized but only three began formation — ill-equipped and below standard strength — and only two came into real being. Curiously, Himmler, the most emphatic of the opponents of independent Russian forces, became the instrument of this futile last-hour change in policy. Through the pleading of German military and political leaders who thought it was possible even at that last moment to exploit the potential of anti-Soviet emotion, he had agreed to meet Vlassov. He came away convinced, as Goebbels had been, that Germany had blundered.

3. A Heroic Legend

In this new climate of impending German defeat, Vlassov was also allowed to organize politically, as he had demanded from the outset. The decision was taken at a Berlin meting in October, 1944. On November 14 the *Vlassovtsi* therefore held their first and only general convention, in Prague. It established a Committee for the Liberation of the Peoples of Russia, in which, it is well to note, there were more civilians than military men; and it adopted a manifesto, made public four days later, signed by Vlassov as chairman and about fifty officers, intellectuals, former Soviet officials, workers and peasants.

Despite impassioned oratory and fervid dedication to the "new free Russia," it was a sad and quixotic occasion. There was a desperate self-delusion in the way delegates argued vehemently over details of the political and social patterns of their "liberated" fatherland; in the way Vlassov, Malishkin, Maltzev and other generals invoked a tomorrow which they knew in their hearts would not dawn for them as individuals.

As for their brave manifesto, it was a stillborn document. Again in violation of solemn promises, the Germans sabotaged its distribution. The convention's acceptance of "the assistance of Germany on condition that the honor and independence of our country shall remain unprejudiced" must have seemed a piece of Slav impudence to the Nazis even in their twilight hours. Its refusal to embrace Nazi racial obsessions must have seemed a deliberate affront. The German press and radio either ignored the Prague meeting or damned it with faint notice. Only vague echoes of the gathering and its pronouncements were allowed to reach Russians outside or inside their country.

But as a systematic expression of Russian anti-Soviet aspirations, the manifesto constitutes a vital national document. History has many surprises up its capacious sleeve. What the anti-Soviet Russians set down on paper in Prague may one day be regarded as a Declaration of Independence by a liberated nation.

The manifesto began with a reminder of the democratic freedoms for which the Russian peoples had struck in March, 1917, and a denunciation of "the outlived czarist regime, which did not wish and could not abolish the causes of social injustice, the remaining elements of serfdom, economic and cultural backwardness." The Bolsheviks, it charged, had "usurped the power conquered by the people . . . throwing the people into a permanent state of misery, lawlessness and most shameless exploitation."

The energies of all the Russian peoples, it went on, "should be directed to the destruction of the monstrous machine of Bolshevism, granting to every man the right to live and create freely, in the limits of his strength and potentialities, for the creation of an order assuring the defense of man against the arbitrary will of others and preventing the appropriation of the products of his labor by anyone else, including the state." The manifesto dedicated the liberation movement to the overthrow of the Red tyranny and "restoration to the peoples of Russia of the rights won by them during the national revolution of 1917." It called for an end to the war and "an honorable peace with Germany," and "creation of a new, free, national state government without Bolsheviks and exploiters." A fourteen-point program of principles to govern reorganization of the country pledged, among other things:

Equality of all the peoples of Russia and their right to national development, self-assertion, and state self-existence along democratic lines.

Friendly relations with all countries and universal promotion of international co-operation.

Measures for the strengthening of the family and marriage, with genuine equality of rights for women.

Liquidation of the collective farm system, with free distribution of land as the private property of peasants.

Restoration of labor as an inviolable private property and full scope for labor organization; the opportunity for private initiative in the economic life of the nation.

Social justice and the protection of the workers against exploitation, regardless of their origin or past activities.

Attainment of genuine rights to free education, medical aid, rest, and old age insurance.

Abolition of the system of terror and oppression; and in particular the liquidation of the exile and concentration-camp systems, plus guarantees of free speech, press, assembly, religion, thought, and true equality of all under law.

Release of the political prisoners of Bolshevism, but "no revenge and persecution of those who will desist from struggling for Stalin and Bolshevism."

A hastily drawn and not always felicitously worded document, but essentially democratic in the Western sense, it was to be assailed as too left by the rights in the emigration, and too right by the lefts. Soviet sympathizers of course denounced it as "reactionary." At the start of the Vlassov movement, it assuredly would have rallied millions of Stalin's unhappy subjects, given them a goal and a feeling of cohesion. Coming at the end of the war, almost within earshot of Stalin's mighty armies rolling inexorably westward, it was a monument to German political ineptitude.

In high-pitched rhetoric the Committee for Liberation summoned "tens of millions" inside and outside Russia to greet "the hour of liberation." Few ever heard the call. The golden opportunity had been squandered.

ROA officers were again stymied in renewed recruiting efforts. Fleeing before the Red tide, Soviet nationals who sought to join up with Vlassov were forced instead into SS divisions — and deserted, of course, at the first opportunity. A plan for ROA airborne leaflet-dropping units collapsed when Vlassov insisted on full control over the contents of the leaflets.

At the very end the *Wehrmacht* did allow a few independent operations by the *Vlassovtsi*. One of these, though trivial in extent, is politically impressive. As the Red Army approached the Oder River, a tiny force of ROA men under a Colonel Sakharov was sent to the Eastern front. It fought a successful engagement in the course of which a great many Soviet soldiers passed over voluntarily to the ROA side. On surrendering they declared that they did so solely because they were faced by Vlassov forces.

This astonishing incident at the end of the war, when Stalin's total victory was a certainty, was reported by Russian prisoners to American interrogators. Somehow it points up the romanticism that marked the death throes of the Vlassov enterprise and its mystery army. It suggests also what might have been, had the anti-Soviet potential among the Russian peoples been given full play and encouragement.

Another telltale episode took place in the Balkans. The German forces under General von Panwitz, fighting against two Red Army divisions, included a number of Cossack units. So many of the Soviet troops refused to shoot, or went over to the Cossacks, that the divisions were hastily withdrawn and replaced by Bulgarian troops.

In the rising flood of defeat the ROA general staff solemnly labored to elaborate plans for penetration of the Soviet lines and an uprising against the communists. But in the hour of final German collapse the Vlassov Army achieved a moment of glory — in Prague and *against* the Germans. Its First Division under General Bunichenko — the only real division it possessed — came to the rescue of the hard-pressed Czech Resistance and saved the city from German destruction. In its death agony the ROA was thus able to demonstrate, for history, where its sympathies really lay. Overnight the *Vlassovtsi* became heroes in the eyes of the Czechs.

The salvaged capital was immediately thereafter invested by the Red Army, which scooped up all the *Vlassovtsi* who had not managed to escape and shot them, officers and men alike, in wholesale lots. The ROA remnants surrendered to the United States Army in Czechoslovakia and Austria, all of them under the pathetic delusion that they were putting themselves into friendly custody. The belief that the Allies, having disposed of Hitler, would now turn against Stalin was widespread not only among Soviet nationals in German uniform but among millions of their countrymen. It helps explain why tens of thousands flocked to Vlassov even in the final

months, when the defeat of the Germans was an absolute certainty.
There is still some lack of clarity about General Vlassov's last
days in freedom. With a number of his closest associates, he fled
to Austria. As they approached Pilsen, grateful Czechs of that area
greeted the Russians with a parade and flowers as the saviors of
Prague. At an open-air meeting, Vlassov was decorated with
flowers and cheered wildly. American officers in Pilsen, apparently
in the belief that the man being feted was a Red Army general,
joined in the celebration and drew their share of the joyous cheers.

But in the next few days, while presumably being transferred
from one American headquarters to another, Vlassov and a batch
of his followers were turned over to the Soviet military on a high-
road. The indications are that the transfer had been prearranged.
There is no margin for uncertainty that many of the leading Vlassov officers and thousands of the ROA rank and file were surrendered to a Red doom by their American, British and French
captors.

Two Vlassov generals, Meandrov and Maltzev, slit their wrists
in suicide attempts when apprised that they were being turned
over to Stalin. Both of them were rushed to hospitals, given the
best care available, restored to approximate health — then forcibly
handed over to the Soviet executioners.

Nothing was heard of Vlassov for about fifteen months after his
surrender. Then the mystery was ended with a Moscow announcement — published in tiny type among the miscellaneous news items
in the Soviet press — that ten traitors, one of them named Andrei
A. Vlassov, had been executed after a secret court-martial. About
the nature of their treachery the Russian people were told exactly
nothing.

As far as the public record inside the USSR is concerned, there
never was any Russian Liberation Army. But among Soviet nationals outside Russia, especially the hundreds of thousands of wartime and postwar *émigrés* raised under the Soviet system, Vlassov
is remembered and the movement he headed luxuriates as a heroic
legend. For many of them his name has become a banner. They
do not doubt that one day the label of traitor stuck on his corpse

will be removed and that he will rank among the great heroes of the free Russian spirit.

These homesick exiles reject the quisling ingredients in the story, in their inner certainty of its basic patriotic motives and inspirations. For all its mistakes and confusions, the ill-fated liberation movement provides additional proof that there is "another Russia," deeply opposed to Bolshevism and its works — a Russia that awaits an opportune moment to assert itself, weapons in hand if necessary, in the name of national freedom.

XV. Fugitives from Bolshevism

1. The Nonreturners

Scattered through the world today there are between five and six hundred thousand former Soviet citizens for whom no precise name exists in standard dictionaries. They are neither *"émigrés"* nor "exiles" in the conventional sense; in the great majority they did not deliberately emigrate and were not deliberately exiled. They simply found themselves, through the exigencies of the great war, beyond their native frontiers and chose not to re-cross them as long as the present political system endured in their homeland.

They do have a long, tongue-twisting word for themselves: *nyevozrashtchentzi,* literally "nonreturners." That describes the physical fact of their self-exile accurately and also carries the proper political overtones of renunciation. It is a word the world would do well to learn and ponder, for it sums up a most dramatic historical event, unprecedented in its scale.

At the end of the war the word defined several million men, women, and children. Since then so many of them have been repatriated by brute force and moral coercion, so many others have succumbed to panic fear of the Kremlin's ubiquitous police agents, so many have surrendered in the hope of saving relatives and friends back home from reprisals, that the numbers have dwindled.

But the significance of the phenomenon is not primarily in its statistics. It is inherent in the event itself. Consider the facts:

A great mass of people, mostly prisoners of war and slave laborers of an enemy nation at whose hands they have suffered persecution and humiliation, find themselves outside their native country at the climax of a world war. Their country has emerged as the winner, haloed in glory and enhanced in power. One naturally expects them to embrace the liberating victory in joy and hasten back to their homeland. But to the utter amazement of the other victors, they resist repatriation, in hundreds of cases even to the death, preferring suicide to returning. Only their own government is not at all astonished by this unnatural behavior of its displaced citizenry; on the contrary, having foreseen everything clearly, it has cagily involved other governments in an obscene scheme for forcible repatriation.

An American can realize the strangeness of all this only by imagining that vast numbers of American prisoners, released through victory, had fought desperately to remain in Japan or Germany.

The best informed guesses indicate that at the time of Germany's capitulation over ten million of the Kremlin's subjects (aside from its fighting forces) were dispersed in Europe west of the Soviet borders. They comprised military prisoners, forced-labor contingents, Soviet nationals in the defeated German armies. They included also great numbers who had followed the retreating Germans rather than await their own armies — in itself an extraordinary circumstance, a case of "voting with their feet" against the Soviet regime.

Millions of these displaced people, of course, were overrun by Stalin's forces in the East European countries now under Moscow dominion and had no alternative except repatriation. The luckier and more energetic among them managed to outrace the Soviet westward advance: some Russian families in primitive *telegas,* peasant cars, somehow got as far as France. For the rest, the dream of sanctuary in Poland, the Baltic and Balkan lands, or in Germany east of the Elbe, was washed out by the onrushing Red tides. "If the Red Army had not taken Poland and Czechoslovakia the number of Soviet fugitives might have reached possibly ten million," one escapee, T. N., has written.

Those who fell under the authority of the Western Allies are usually estimated at some six million, though one official American figure was over seven million. It should not be supposed that this Soviet humanity had a really free choice on remaining or going home. To begin with, most of them were under a simple human constraint to return to wives, children, parents, and other loved ones inside the USSR. Others, having served in the enemy ranks, were aware that they faced execution and did not dare go back. Most important, there was the undertaking by Roosevelt and Churchill in Yalta to repatriate Stalin's subjects by force if necessary. Though this agreement was secret, knowledge of it spread quickly; the Soviets saw to that. Additional millions decided that since they would be shipped back in any case, they were better off to go voluntarily, with a show of enthusiasm.

Had the Allies let it be known that the democratic principle of political asylum would be honored, that force would not be employed to drive people home against their will, the world would have seen a remarkable plebiscite. It is altogether likely that three or four million would have opted for freedom in exile as against a resumption of their old life under the hammer and sickle. This judgment is supported by the fact that despite the multiple pressures more than a million *tried* to evade repatriation — and more than half a million succeeded.

One should pause to savor the implications of this fact. The magnetic pull of home, however wretched and oppressed the home may be, is terrific. It is no easy thing for men and women to give up their country, careers, friends, lifelong associations, almost their human identity, for the uncertainties of life in a strange and inhospitable world, without a language or a job or a firm legal status; to do so in the awareness that at best they would be unwelcome wards of foreign nations and hunted like animals by the implacable agents of their own government.

That prospect would be frightening even to educated and exceptional persons. To the simple uprooted Russians it must have been appalling. For the most part they were provincials to whom any spot beyond their native region had always seemed alien and crammed with terrors. Yet more than a million of them "chose freedom," a precarious freedom as virtual outlaws in countries where they were not wanted and told so without inhibitions. Clearly only fears and revulsions of the first order could account for their decision. They asserted in action their profound opposition of the communist system in their native land.

"They love Russia and yearn for Russia," Louis Fischer wrote after interviewing a lot of the nonreturners. "They are political fugitives. . . . The hundreds of thousands of Russian DP's in Central Europe . . . demonstrate that when Soviet Russians had a choice they voted against the Bolshevik dictatorship. This is the most revealing fact I know about Soviet Russia." *

In other words, the refusal of these Soviet millions to go back revealed to one American more than some fifteen years' residence in the USSR had done. Unfortunately the world at large has barely begun to catch up with that great revelation.

The nonreturners were not lured into self-exile by capitalist fleshpots. They were under no illusions about the hardships they faced in an alien environment. They knew that a dislocated postwar Europe could not absorb them and that emigration to the United States or some other more normal country was only a faint hope; that meanwhile they would be held in overcrowded and unhygienic barracks in displaced persons' camps. They knew that Stalin's recent allies did not begin to understand their plight and their motives and regarded them as a first-class headache. How, indeed, could the ordinary American or British military functionary comprehend this bizarre preference for a foul camp or even death to returning home?

Figures on camp inmates are not a sufficient indication of the extent of the nonreturner community. For every one who ended up in a DP enclosure, there to be screened and badgered endlessly with sticks and carrots, probably two or three just lost themselves in the population. Throughout Germany and Austria, and to a lesser degree Italy and France, there are today Russians who have somehow merged with the local citizenry. Besides, both inside and outside the camps, tens of thousands pretended to be Poles or

* *Look*, November 23, 1948.

Czechs or Yugoslavs in order to cheat the Yalta repatriation plans.
By this time only a few thousand remain in the DP centers. The
rest have found new homes in many countries or continue to live
in a half-illicit condition on false documents or without any legal
papers in Central Europe. As late as 1947, when the American authorities finally announced that forcible repatriation would cease,
most of them lived in dread of denunciation, ambush, kidnapping
— enough such episodes of terror having been publicized to keep
them in a ferment of worry.

2. *Old and New Émigrés*

Russian *émigrés* of the early 1917–1920 vintage had little to fear
once they were beyond their native frontiers. The fledgling communist regime was inclined to take a good-riddance view of runaway subjects, and the democratic world was still loyal to liberal
theories of political asylum. But the new wartime and postwar
fugitives defied a powerful and vengeful government, served by
legions of secret police and plainly determined to use every pressure within or without the law to make them go back.

There are other important differences between the two waves of
migration. Fugitives in the first period of the Russian revolution
represented fairly distinct social, economic, and political elements.
Most of them were upper- and middle-class people, monarchists,
landlords, businessman, czarist officers. A minority were radicals
of the anti-Bolshevik persuasions — Mensheviks, Social Revolutionaries, and the like. With few exceptions they were *untypical* of
their countrymen who remained to mold and be molded by the
new events.

The nonreturners are on the whole typical of entire Soviet population. They represent every class and group, from the humblest
peasant to five-star generals. They add up to a fair and impressive
sampling of the new, Soviet-made citizenry: a larger sampling than
scientific opinion testers consider adequate in polling a nation on
any subject.

To be sure, some correctives are in order. A considerable number of nonreturners had let their anti-Soviet passion involve them in military or other kinds of collaboration with the Germans, and to that extent are not typical emotionally of the mass of peoples back home. But after all the discounts are made, the intense opposition of the nonreturners to communism comes close to providing a "poll" of Soviet popular opinion.

The nonreturners were largely young people. Their spokesmen in exile say that the average age in 1945 was probably around thirty. This is a telltale fact. It refutes the easy assumption of those who insist that the new generation, without memory of the past and completely indoctrinated by the Soviets, is forever lost to decency and the idea of freedom. The self-exiled masses are products of the Soviet period. The refugees of an earlier period ran away from something they feared, something they saw coming, but the precise nature of what they dreaded was not yet clear. The new recruits to their ranks have all been raised under the Leninist-Stalinist dispensation. They know exactly what it is they are rejecting, though they are not always capable of conveying that knowledge to unsympathetic interrogators.

One more distinction from the older refugees deserves mention. It is their optimism about the future of Russia. The 1917–1920 runaways are by this time aging people, surfeited with disappointment. Most newcomers by contrast are full of hope, amazingly sure that the Soviet regime is rotten ripe and doomed to fall. They write and argue among themselves about the kind of government and social system that should take its place; they draw up detailed programs and constitutions for tomorrow's Russia. At the root of their hopes is their certainty that those whom they have left behind feel as they do about the regime.

I have talked to a great many of them, both in Europe and in the United States. They are a homesick lot, eager to convince foreigners that they have not renounced their country but only its government. Many of them seem obsessed by anxiety not to be mistaken for "reactionaries." Their quarrel is not primarily with the new ideology but with Soviet terror and oppression, the denial of elementary human rights. A few, indeed, talk of Stalin's "betrayal of the revolution." It is not the lure of capitalism as such that is keeping them from their homeland but a kind of hunger for personal dignity, a revulsion against the police state.

Few among them, I believe, are under the delusion that the Soviet economy can be unscrambled or have any hankering for a private-enterprise society in the American sense. Their mental vision of the Russia of tomorrow, on the economic side, is closer to the pattern of the Nep period, with heavy basic industry, transport, communications, and banking nationalized and private economy dominant in small enterprises.

But a curious and psychologically revealing quirk appears in their politics. Even when they propose a more or less socialist program, they avoid words like "Marxism" and "socialism." These have evidently become repellent symbols of suffering. The social-democratic groups in the Russian emigration have been remarkably unsuccessful in attracting the new refugees; less, I think, because of their program than because of their nomenclature. The *émigré* monarchists have been even less successful. Reference to a restoration of czardom merely amuses the newcomers, though many of them believe that "strong" and "disciplined" government will be needed in the post-Bolshevik Russia, on the basis of law and civil liberties.

3. Democratic Bayonets for Stalin

Not until late 1946 did the world at large learn in some detail about the hush-hush bargain in Yalta under which Allied bayonets and machine guns were enlisted in the noble task of driving Soviet citizens back into their prison land. Even today thick layers of reticence still cover the subject; we must hope it betokens a bad conscience. Those who have essayed to defend other phases of Yalta ignored this one. There are no extenuating circumstances.

Vatican sources were, I believe, the first to alert the world to the crime. A Chicago *Tribune* dispatch from Paris by Henry Wales, on December 17, 1946, gave some detail. Wales had come into possession of a confidential UNRRA memorandum, the notorious Order No. 199. This not only instructed DP camp officials to effect "speedy return" of Soviet nationals to their homeland in accordance with the Yalta agreement, but outlined pressures and hinted at punishments toward that end.

Among other things UNRRA, then under the direction of Fiorello La Guardia, ordered that DP's too active in opposing repatriation be transferred to special camps for the incorrigibly anti-Soviet, so that they would not infect others with their views. It provided that Soviet publications, films, posters, and so on, be made available to inmates, although anti-Soviet propaganda materials were strictly prohibited, and that in general "UNRRA employes must try to persuade the DP's to agree voluntarily to proceed to Russia." That the document was less naïve than it seemed was indicated in its article 8, which warned:

"The advisability of holding mass meetings to consider repatriation or confer with Soviet liaison officers is questionable as such meetings provide an opportunity for dissidents, hecklers, and antipatriation organizers and may result in emotional mob action."

Translated into plain English this meant that anti-Soviet persons must be prevented from asking embarrassing questions or reminding their countrymen of conditions at home under a terror regime. Somehow, by virtue of Yalta, "dissidence" — meaning hostility to Bolshevism — had become a crime in American eyes!

The role of UNRRA in riding herd on Stalin's enemies, both under Herbert Lehman and La Guardia, was hardly one to make Americans proud of their statesmen. La Guardia in particular showed himself insensitive to the fears and grievances of the Kremlin's runaway subjects. Since UNRRA was widely infiltrated by communists and fellow travelers in any case, the plight of would-be nonreturners was far from enviable.

Did President Roosevelt and Prime Minister Churchill realize that they were compounding a moral obscenity in their secret agreement with Stalin? One prefers to believe that they did not quite grasp the implications of their act — that they were not consciously violating precepts of humanity, let alone political wisdom. It was not a pretty spectacle: democratic leaders, with miles of speeches about freedom and human rights to their credit, making that sanguinary and repulsive commitment.

Stalin at least knew what he was doing. He demanded forcible repatriation precisely because he took it for granted that his subjects, having accidentally escaped his clutches, would not willingly return for more. No doubt he was as astonished as he was gratified by the lighthearted readiness of the Western Allies to serve as his hunters of fugitive slaves.

Immediately after hostilities ceased, mixed repatriation teams of Soviet and Allied officers began the process of sorting, questioning, intimidating, and coercing displaced Soviet citizens. Communist propaganda had the right of way in all DP camps and anticommunist materials were strictly barred. Soviet officers ran the show, American and British military men stood by to enforce their decisions. Every type of inducement, including extra rations, and every type of threat, including reprisals against relatives, was employed to break the will of the reluctant.

Americans who entered innocently upon the assignment soon discovered that it was not the routine job of screening they had visualized. They found themselves at the heart of a tragedy of Homeric scope and often beyond their understanding. Still under the spell of wartime slogans about "our great democratic ally," they were baffled by the whole business. Themselves pining to get home to America, they could not at first grasp why so many Russians pined to avoid going home to Russia.

"Hundreds of faces passed daily before the table at which we sat with Soviet representatives," one American, Ginghis Guirey, was to write. "Almost without exception these people were frightened of one thing: returning to the Soviet Union."

Mr. Guirey, born in Turkey, the son of a father who had fought the Reds in the Caucasus during the civil wars, had been brought up in an anti-Soviet tradition. Yet even he was apparently shocked by the violence of the anti-Soviet feelings of these displaced products of Bolshevik life. A passage from his book suggests the ugliness of the chore we were doing for the Politburo:

> A number of DP's spoke to me of an incident which had occurred in May when about 5,000 Cossacks and Adigays, men, women and children who had run from the Soviet Union, were at Kaernten in Austria. The British, allegedly under a certain General Arbuthnot, followed orders to repatriate them. One-third killed themselves rather than return to Russia. Eyewitnesses I spoke to said fathers shot their children and then themselves, mothers threw themselves into rivers, over cliffs. Why? There must be something wrong with things like that to happen, we told ourselves.
>
> The most unpleasant aspect of this unpleasant business was the fear these people displayed. Involuntarily one began to look over one's shoulder. I heard so many threats to commit suicide from people who feared repatriation that it became almost commonplace. And they were not fooling.*

Vivid descriptions of the frenzy of self-destruction that overwhelmed Soviet citizens faced with repatriation have been given by eye witnesses of the macabre scenes in Dachau, Plattling, Weibling, Kempten, Regensburg and other assembly points in Central Europe, as well as in France and Italy. It's a theme made to order for a modern Dante. They tell how wounded, bleeding, scorched men and women who had not quite succeeded in killing themselves were dragged to waiting American or British trucks; how sympathetic DP's of other nationalities threw themselves prone across roads to block the trucks.

A Russian, describing how American MP's herded sixteen hundred of his countrymen with clubs, rifles and machine guns for delivery to the Soviets, ends his tale with an ancient cry: "Father, forgive them, for they know not what they do." American soldiers naturally found the task humiliating and on occasion revolted against performing it. A *Christian Science Monitor* dispatch from Frankfurt, dated September 10, 1945, tried to indicate this. Of twenty-five men

* *The Shadow of Power,* Bobbs-Merrill, 1953.

assigned to one such raid, it said, twenty-one reported sick, obviously wishing to evade the onerous duty.

A Russian priest in touch with the situation wrote to friends in America on December 3, 1946:

> Displaced persons of Soviet citizenship . . . are oppressed by the continuing illegality of their situation, by the need to hide their real identities and pretend they are *émigrés* of 1920 or Poles or Baltic citizens. The inhuman Yalta agreement not having been revoked, they go on living in a harrowing atmosphere of uncertainty, dread and enervating rumors . . .

When it comes to repatriation, truly horrible scenes occurred. In Dachau, where there were no prisoners of war but just ordinary deportees, *Ostarbeiter,* Americans ordered them handcuffed in order to turn them over more conveniently. The unfortunate men, driven to desperation, smashed window panes with their heads and cut their throats with glass. They managed somehow to set fire to one of their barracks and threw themselves into the flames, having first soaked themselves in spilled gasolene. Ten of the men were burned to death. There were 275 cases of suicide or attempted suicide.

Another such scene was enacted in a camp for Russian DP's at Kempten, Southern Bavaria, on August 2, 1945, a Sunday. I shall let William Henry Chamberlin, who obtained the facts from eye witnesses, tell the story:

> American troops drove up to the camp and ordered the inmates, who were mostly at church, to board the trucks for transportation to the nearest Soviet assembly point. When the Russians unanimously refused, the troops broke into the church, overturned the altar, manhandled the priest, dragged out men, women and children, clubbing them with rifle butts and throwing them into the trucks.

Some of the women, to save their children, tossed them into a neighboring camp for Baltic refugees. The latter offered detailed testimony about this horrible incident. When I was in Germany last year [1946], a high American officer told me that the Kempten affair created such a scandal that General Eisenhower decided to stop forcible repatriation. I learned from another source that the officer responsible for the Kempten brutalities (whether he was a fellow traveler or just a man who would have offered the familiar Nazi excuse that he was merely "obeying orders" I do not know) was shunned and boycotted in his mess.*

Whether or not General Eisenhower did in fact order a halt at the time, officially the Allies continued to honor the Yalta slave-hunting commitment. Not until early in 1947 did General McNarney formally announce the end of forced repatriation. But incidents as shocking as those in Dachau and Kempten took place even after that. In Italy, for instance, several hundred Soviet nationals were delivered against their will to the Soviet Command from a camp in Rimini, under British control, and another in Pisa, under American control, in May of that year. Many of the refugees committed suicide, many more were killed and wounded in endeavoring to resist, and a lot of serious casualties were suffered by the British and American troops in the melee.

A fine but neglected novel, *Green Boundary*,** offers an incidental glimpse of the sordid business. The author, Boris Ilyin, an American of Russian origin, served as military interrogator and interpreter in Germany after the war. Though his account is fictional, it is self-evidently based on intimate observation.

The hero, Major Radonov, like the book's author an American of Russian extraction, had befriended a nonreturner couple, the Melnikovs. They had been picked up and taken to an American camp, where some two thousand of the unfortunates were being processed for repatriation. Radonov rushed to the camp that night in the hope of helping his friends.

"You can't see anybody, Major," the lieutenant in charge told him. "We've got them all locked up in their barracks under guard. We had trouble with them today. . . . I'm not going to send one of my men into any barracks for them. The goddam DP's will tear your guts out if you go in."

Radonov pleaded some more.

"We've got forty barracksful of them," said the lieutenant. "If

* The *New Leader,* August 23, 1947.
** Houghton Mifflin, 1949.

you started walking in hunting for these friends of yours, you'd
start another riot for sure, sooner or later. We had enough trouble
with them. Did you see that man's face? I've got two other men
hurt."

"And there are three stiffs in the back room," a soldier inter-
jected. "DP stiffs. Three of them."

"Yeah, but not from the riot," the lieutenant said. "Suicides. They
all cut themselves with pieces of glass. You wait. By tomorrow
morning there'll be a lot more."

At another point the lieutenant exclaimed: "Major, maybe you
think it's a great pleasure for me on this job. Maybe you think
we *like* batting these DP's over the head, and shipping them off. . . . "

The despairing Radonov then looked up the UNRRA official in
charge. But there was nothing this man could do — orders were
orders. They had two thousand Soviet men and women there, he
explained, and "of course none of them wanted to go home."

A personal *émigré* account by a former Red officer throws light
on another aspect of the tragedy. All repatriates, even those returning of their own free will, were regarded by the Kremlin as tainted
with treachery or, at best, corrupted by contact with the non-Soviet
world. This officer not only was returning voluntarily but looked
upon those who stayed behind as "ungrateful and erring sons of
our country." He was put in command of four hundred men bound
for the Soviet Union. His disillusionment came *after* he had turned
his charges over to the Red Army.

Instead of being greeted as returning heroes, they were met with
curses and accusations. Sixty of the four hundred were shot after
the initial Soviet interrogation. The rest were packed into cattle
cars destined for the forced-labor zone in the Omsk region of
Siberia. The officer was one of several who managed to escape
en route. He ends his story with a cry from the heart:

With a feeling of pain I reflect on my shattered life. . . . And now
do I not still love my country? At the first call of my people I shall
return to serve it — the people, but not those who cling to their power
and are ruthlessly destroying our helpless misguided people. Judge me!
Pass judgment on me and tell me what I am guilty of! My conscience is

clear and, despite everything I have been through, I have enough strength left in me to fight for the real liberation of my enslaved and terrorized but still magnificent people.*

Back in 1950 a young Ukrainian called on me. A tall, clean-cut fellow recently arrived in the United States, he was working as a dishwasher in a Brooklyn restaurant and happy to be alive in freedom. His story remains fresh in my memory because of an unusual feature. The very NKVD officer who was interrogating and threatening him at an assembly camp deep behind the Soviet lines later the same night risked his life to help him escape. Even the Kremlin's Praetorian Guard may be less totally devoted than is generally assumed. The bluster had been a show to conceal this NKVD man's secret sympathy with the victims.

4. Man Hunt in Europe

Over and above the organized repatriation on the basis of Yalta, beyond the propaganda pressures and legalized use of force, the Kremlin was conducting a Europe-wide man hunt on its own. In the nature of the case comparatively little can be known about its methods and accomplishments. But its existence was an open secret which struck terror to the heart of all nonreturners, especially those in hiding outside camps.

Beria's goon squads ran loose from the Elbe to the Atlantic. But their happiest hunting ground was probably in France, where strong communist influence in the government and virtual control in portions of the police system gave the Moscow head hunters a perfect area of operations.

According to Soviet data there were about 180,000 Soviet citizens in France at the war's end and the NKVD got busy retrieving them. It set up shop in Paris at 4 Rue du Général Appert, under the name of Mission Militaire Soviétique, with hundreds of its agents enjoying diplomatic immunity. "The building," Ruth Fischer learned, "was

---

* From statements collected by David J. Dallin.

equipped with special electric devices and fortified with cement cellars. Intruders were discouraged by doors of solid steel and other comparable security measures. An underground was dug to a neighboring building, 49 Rue de la Faisanderie, which houses the Soviet Commercial Legation." *

The world will never know what crimes were perpetrated in the concrete cellars of those buildings, and in the section of the camp at Beauregard, near Paris, assigned to the Soviets for their repatriation activities. The NKVD engaged in systematic abductions, murdering runaways who could not be kidnaped. A few Russians, having escaped from Beauregard, told the French press tales of horror. From all parts of the country, it appeared, kidnaped Soviet men and women were dragged to the camp to be "processed" as the first stage in their journey to the "socialist fatherland." Abuse, beatings, and tortures were routine procedures.

I have before me the statement of a Red Army officer, now a nonreturner, who was at one time himself engaged in the man hunt. He refers to conditions in 1945–1946 which may have been amended, for better or worse, later:

Several NKVD men are assigned to the tracking of a single man, often for weeks on end. This group of hunted men is under no illusions as to the fate which awaits them. After their arrest, in spite of the extensive precautions which are taken to guard them on their journey to the Soviet Zone, they attempt most desperate escapes.

For instance, if 15 men escape, 10 or 11 are recovered and slain, but 3 or 4 escape and this is considered too much by the NKVD. For some time now this class of escapee is no longer transported to the USSR. After interrogation they are liquidated either in the basement of the Military Mission or the Embassy or at Camp Beauregard on the outskirts of Paris.

Some of the more interesting prisoners, who have to be interrogated in Moscow, are shipped by plane. But we have received strict orders that if any of these offer resistance they are to be shot immediately if it can be done discreetly.

* Ruth Fischer's *Special Reports,* news letter.

Informers as well as those who made the arrests, he attested, were at that time getting cash rewards, so much per head depending on the importance of the victim.

The gruesome details of one of the "desperate escapes" to which he alluded were given to me by a woman who had them directly from a survivor. N.X., as she calls him, joined a repatriation group voluntarily. Though he detested the Soviet regime, he was intensely homesick for his mother. It was in the Soviet camp behind barbed wire, learning of what happened to others, that he changed his mind.

He succeeded in escaping. But soon the French police caught up with him and, on the pretext that he had no documents, turned him over to the Soviet military. He was confined in Beauregard. From there he was loaded with seventeen other men into a sealed freight car for the journey "home." All eighteen decided on a desperate scheme. With great exertion they broke a hole in the floor of the car, and one by one slid down to the tracks under the speeding train.

"A certain number were killed," the woman told me. "N.X. described to me the horrible tension of the moment when he slid down and pressed flat against the ground. He was drenched by hot blood and saw parts of a torn body on the nearest wheel. Those who waited their turn to escape heard the anguished cries of comrades who perished. But all of them preferred the nightmarish kind of escape to repatriation."

One NKVD exploit in the man hunt made headlines in the French papers for a while. The young Red Army lieutenant and communist Palchinsky had a brilliant war record. Escaping from German captivity, he succeeded in joining the French Maquis. After the liberation he decided not to return to the Soviet Union. Knowing that he was being sought by the man hunters, he hid in the apartment of a prominent *émigré* family, the Prince Galitzins, on Rue Erlanger.

On March 6, 1946, he was at home alone. A limousine drew up, and three men were seen entering the house. A while later they emerged, dragging a fourth man to the car. When the police arrived, they found that the apartment door had been broken down. Spattered blood and smashed furniture gave evidence of a terrible struggle. Neighbors had noted the license number of the limousine; it turned out to be phony. Neither the police nor the Paris press had any doubt that this was another Moscow-directed job.

The Galitzins, frightened for their own fate, fled to the United States. The night before his abduction, young Palchinsky had been writing an article about the nonreturners. He had ended with these words:

> We appeal to the public opinion of the world to grasp the significance of the problem of Soviet citizens in Europe and request the legalization of the new emigration. The war is ended, the fascists are defeated. But the blood of thousands of innocent victims, opposed to the Soviet regime, is still flowing. We are faced by a new and terrible aggressor. History will never forgive the perpetrators of these sacrifices — nor those who can but will not stop them.

By this time the man hunt is over. But Lieutenant Palchinsky, who has doubtless paid with his life for trying to "tell the West," has not yet been heard or understood. The Moscow dictatorship is so anxious to bring the Palchinskys home precisely because it wants to seal their lips, because it does not want the free portion of humankind to find out how the Russian peoples feel about their regime.

Their sacrifices will have been in vain unless we take the lesson of the nonreturners to heart and study its political import. The fact that the world is still largely indifferent to the whole phenomenon of the new Soviet emigration suggests that the anesthesia of wartime indoctrination has not quite worn off. This mass rejection by its citizens of a country they love is unique in history. Soviet and communist propaganda may dismiss them as "bandits," "war criminals," "quislings." Soviet-infected Westerners may echo these smears. It still remains to be explained why the Kremlin breeds "traitors" and "bandits" on such a scale among people brought up under its own regime.

The nonreturners themselves burn with zeal to make us understand the Soviet realities. Singly and in groups they have written statements, appeals, articles, books, all but a few of which remain unpublished. A collective statement declares: "The people of Russia will have their say one day; and as long as their mouths are closed by force, *we* will talk for them." So far, few will listen. The writers are confused, frustrated, at a loss to understand why a world gearing for struggle with the Soviet threat seems to ignore them.

A girl born and raised under the Soviet regime writes: "I am proud that by refusing to return to the land of Stalin's autocracy I have become morally purer."

A former officer in the Red Army Medical Corps writes: "I have refused to return to the USSR not because of personal fear, but because I have become an enemy of the regime."

A Leningrad worker explains: "I have been torn away from my country by circumstances independent of my will. But since I have been in Europe and learned the true meaning of freedom, I shall never return to my country, whatever my fate may be, before it is freed from Stalin's tyranny."

A collective declaration asserts: "When the hour strikes, every one of us voluntary exiles will be ready to serve the cause of the Russian people and perform his duty with honor."

A Soviet citizen of Tatar extraction, Kolumbayev by name, in an article in the New York monthly *Rossia,* states:

"They [the Soviets] want us because they are afraid of us and want to destroy us. We are much more dangerous to them than the old emigration — because we were all born and bred in the Soviet Union; because we lived and worked there and were witnesses of all the infamy of the Soviet government."

Another declaration printed in *Rossia* says: "My life is all ahead of me. I am healthy and strong and my spirit is likewise strong, my resolve unbroken. And one day in the not distant future I will be in the fore of the great fight that will bring freedom and happiness to the oppressed peoples of Russia."

5. *Betrayal of Natural Allies*

The flow of Soviet fugitives did not cease with the end of the war. Great numbers of officers and enlisted men in the victorious armies, suddenly faced by the sobering prospect of a return to their old

Soviet life, preferred freedom. The same was true of men in the Red occupation forces and in the civilian occupation ranks.

They had had a look at the world beyond their communized homeland. Despite the poverty and the political oppressions in the lands they had traversed, the contrast with what they had left behind at home shattered their preconceptions. Many a German, coming in friendly contact with Soviet occupation officials, was shocked to discover that he, the defeated, was being envied by his conquerors.

Red Army deserters between 1945 and 1948 probably exceeded twenty thousand. No half way accurate count could be made. Because Allied occupation authorities in Austria and Germany, especially in the first period, were under orders to hand them back to the Soviets, few of the runaways announced themselves. For the most part they destroyed their documents and uniforms and lost themselves in the local population or faded into the mass of nonreturners. Had they been assured of political asylum, the twenty thousand would very likely have been quadrupled.

And by every test of common sense these men, mostly between twenty and thirty-five years old, *were* political refugees. "The reason that they deserted from the Russian army," as George E. Sokolsky wrote at the time, "is that they hate communism and love liberty. They assumed that liberty-loving human beings would be welcomed by liberty-loving countries. But a deserter is a deserter and we are still a friendly ally of Soviet Russia; so, we hand them over to be killed."*

This surrender of our natural allies for instant execution by our natural foes is another unsightly blot on the Allied record. Usually their units were assembled to witness the executions, as an object lesson. "Don't fool yourselves that the American and British will protect you," the propaganda said in substance. "They will hand back all traitors who desert their posts." Despite Allied blindness, the fugitives kept coming.

The Kremlin took panicky measures to stem the tide of defection. Demobilized soldiers and officers were transported to the Soviet borders in locked cars under police convoy, like criminals. Military and civilian personnel in the occupation forces were forbidden to

* New York *Sun,* June 16, 1947.

mix with the local population and subjected to rules that made them virtual prisoners in their camps and barracks. Officers who were bachelors were replaced by married men whose families back home served as hostages. Moreover, units were rotated with increasing frequency, to reduce the incidence of "bourgeois infection." Despite these and other precautions, defections continued on a large scale until 1948, and in driblets since then.

Early in 1948 Joseph and Stewart Alsop wrote in their column:

A Russian who deserts from the Soviet occupation forces in Germany knows that he will be shot if he is caught. He knows that the ruthlessly efficient Soviet secret police, the MVD, is more than likely to catch him. He knows that his family in the Soviet Union will almost certainly suffer as a consequence of his desertion. He knows that the dreary half-life of a man without a country is the best he can hope for if he succeeds.

Yet it can now be revealed on undoubted authority that each month more than a thousand Soviet soldiers and civilian officials are risking death to flee to the American zone of Germany.

The astonishing total of deserters in the last twelve months is just over 13,000. Of these about 4,000 were officers, including two generals, one a lieutenant general on Marshal Sokolovsky's staff. Approximately 6,000 were enlisted men, and 3,000 were Russian workers and civilian officials.

Earlier a New York *Times* story from Berlin* reported that seven thousand Soviet army deserters were confined in a single camp in Guestrow, Eastern Mecklenburg, "and patrols are scouring the forests and villages for others." It was estimated, the dispatch continued, "that as many as 10 per cent of the occupation troops were deserting, some becoming bandits and others, it was suspected, filtering into displaced persons' camps."

While on a visit to Munich in May, 1952, my wife and I met and talked with a dozen or so new Soviet defectors: Russians and a few Ukrainians. The scene was a Friendship Center set up in that city by the American Friends of Russian Freedom, a private organization with offices in New York. All but two or three of the men were under thirty, most of them in their early twenties.

One of the youngsters, a stocky lad of perhaps twenty-two, attracted

* March 26, 1947.

my attention because he seemed so typically peasant in looks and demeanor. But it was hard to break through his shyness. "The others will tell you," he would say in answer to questions, blushing. "It's the same for all of us soldiers." I insisted and finally he began to talk.

"When did you desert the Red Army?" I asked.

"About a month ago."

"And how long were you in Germany before making the break?"

"Also about a month."

"You mean that a few weeks in a foreign country were enough to decide you to renounce your native country?"

"Oh no, it's not that all. I always wanted to escape but got the chance only when I was brought to Germany."

"But why, why?" I asked.

At that he looked at me with most unflattering eyes, and shook his head sadly. His silence was more eloquent than the speeches of his more articulate companions. "These crazy foreigners," it seemed to say, "asking why a Russian wants to run away! Like asking a convict why he wants to escape from prison!"

So here through the years we have had another case of thousands of Soviet nationals, from ordinary soldiers to high-ranking officers, "voting with their feet" against the Kremlin regime as soon as that franchise was opened to them. Considering the obstacles put in their way, the deadly risks they ran, the policy of forcibly handing them back adhered to by the Allies long after the war, these defectors may reasonably be accepted as representative of hundreds of thousands who would vote as they did if given the chance under less dangerous conditions.

The Soviets could not take the loyalty of their occupation forces for granted. Rainer Hildebrandt, a German who was boldly fighting the Reds in Berlin, was convinced that this was a vital factor in restraining the Kremlin's aggressive urges. Any new war, he wrote in 1949, "would have to be begun by the 300,000 soldiers and officers of the Soviet Army stationed in the East Zone of Germany. And Stalin has little reason to believe that they have any desire to fight for him against the democracies. For this army, although its personnel has been shifted many times, has become the least reliable factor in all

of Stalin's calculations. It is perhaps the army Stalin fears most." *
An American aviation writer, Gill Robb Wilson, happened to be on a military air base near Stockholm the evening of May 17, 1949, when a Soviet airman brought down his plane and begged for political asylum. He listened in while the refugee from the skies was questioned by officials on the field. Reporting the episode in a newspaper dispatch, Mr. Wilson wrote in part:

The wife of the Soviet airman had been taken to Siberia — he knew not where. His brother was dead. His children were gone. The politicians in Moscow wore the medals and the people had the diet of sweat and grief. Every one was spying on every one else. There was nothing to live for as far as he was concerned. Enough was enough. . . .
The young Russian in his conversation conveyed a distinct impression that it was the regime from which he fled rather than his country. Judging him uneducated beyond the school grades and patently a son of the soil, it was yet apparent that he was intelligent and thoughtful. He carried himself as a soldier and not without a sense of dignity.**

Only a few of the more dramatic escapes, like that of flyers Pirogov and Barsov, ever got into the news columns. Indeed, as Marguerite Higgins estimated in 1949, "only 15 per cent of all Russian deserters ever contact the American officials," since "our officials have never publicly given assurances that Russian deserters would be granted a haven in our zone." *** For a variety of reasons, runaways from Czechoslovakia, Hungary and other satellite countries have received more attention than those from the Soviet Union proper.
But politically the self-exiles of Soviet origin are vastly more meaningful. The satellite fugitives come from areas where communism is a new visitation and still in process of solidifying power. They are all products of precommunist times, their memories of the past fresh and insistent. But Soviet escapees have been raised under communism and have no direct personal knowledge of the past. Having been born and raised in the Soviet Union, the pre-Bolshevik times are for

* The *New Leader*, September 17, 1949.
** New York *Herald Tribune*, May 26, 1949.
*** *Saturday Evening Post*, June 4, 1949.

them just history. Their revolt is not *for the past* but clearly, sharply, consciously, *against the present.*

Our failure to understand this revolt, our years of actual connivance with the Kremlin in apprehending and returning the rebels, stands like a grim wall between the West and the peoples of Russia. It has done more than all of Moscow's anti-American and anti-British propaganda to generate distrust of our intentions and our protestations of a love of freedom. "Bitter memories of early postwar compulsory repatriation," in the view of Edmund Stevens, a former *Christian Science Monitor* correspondent in Moscow, is among the reasons for the decline in defections after 1948. Soviet propaganda, he reported to his paper from Munich, "has exploited to the utmost" the fact that "for an extended period in the first postwar years deserters from the Soviet Army who sought sanctuary in the West were handed back."

That our persecution of nonreturners and deserters was a blunder of the first magnitude should by now be sufficiently obvious to thoughtful observers. It was part of, and the consequence of, the larger blunder: the failure of the democracies to recognize and address themselves to the peoples of Russia.

The very fact of finding themselves on the same side with free nations heartened those peoples, gave them the sense that their long isolation from civilized mankind was drawing to an end. The publication of the Atlantic Charter and other Allied pronouncements in the Soviet press, with their references to freedom and justice and self-determination, sent a thrill of hope through their hope-starved hearts.

But as if deliberately determined to douse those hopes, the democracies ignored the people and dedicated themselves instead to flamboyant glorification of Stalin and his regime. They gave credit to the dictatorship rather than its subjects for the heroic war exploits. Thus the Russian peoples were driven reluctantly, with heavy hearts, to the conviction that America, Britain, France were not on their side after all, but only on the side of the hated Kremlin gang. Any doubts in this connection were wiped out by the ease with which the democracies scrapped the Atlantic Charter and all the other lofty documents in their anxiety to please and appease and buy off the Soviets. Then, to clinch their conviction, came forcible repatriation and surrender of military fugitives. Millions of Russians who had direct knowledge of these Allied mistakes and political crimes carried it back to their cities, towns and villages, probably even exaggerated by their bitterness.

We may plead ignorance in mitigation of those policies. But unfortunately there are too many evidences that this ignorance persists, that the Kremlin need only make a few gestures of conciliation to revive the old moods of appeasement, the old delusions of coexistence. There have been democratic professions of friendship for the Russian peoples, even indications of a desire to liberate them rather than to trade them for the shadows of security. But these new attitudes are still made of cobweb stuff that crumbles under the prod of Soviet diplomacy.

If we wish to make allies of the Russian peoples — as ultimately we must, as a matter of our own survival — there is a record to be explained and expunged. A record splotched with Russian tears and blood. The free world, and the United States in the first place, must find the moral courage to repudiate and apologize for war and postwar blunders vis-à-vis the Soviet citizenry. They must acknowledge past mistakes and confusions. They must convince the Russian peoples that the talk of friendship and liberation is genuine, not a piece of hypocrisy to improve their bargaining position in relation to the Kremlin.

XVI. The Lost Peace

1. Contaminated by the West

The alliance between regime and people for struggle against the foreign invader was never complete, always tenuous. As defeat of the Germans became more assured, the old civil conflict was resumed. By the time that hostilities with Germany ended, hostilities between the Kremlin and its subjects were again in full swing.

The wartime reconciliation was unstable from the start because it rested on a big lie. It had been made largely on the people's terms, to meet popular yearnings and preferences: a retreat from Bolshevism, revival of old-style patriotism, renunciation of world-revolutionary meddling, legalization of the Church hierarchy, and so forth. The country was encouraged to believe that these and other concessions were for keeps, that they reflected a change of heart in the Kremlin. And that was the big lie.

For Stalin had acted grudgingly, under the duress of military necessity, and was biding his time to withdraw every concession. Party "activists" were never left in doubt that it was only a "tactic," that the people would be cheated of the fruits of their sacrifices as soon and as thoroughly as possible. The word passed down to the faithful was not to take the new line too seriously but to gird their loins for revolutionary struggles to come.

Stalin and his chief associates, in fact, were very careful not to burn their ideological bridges behind them. They never repudiated the Bolshevik essence forthrightly, in so many words; they never asserted that the new policies would endure. The seeming surrender to popular will was just another communist ruse.

The deception was especially raw with respect to the *rapproche-ment* with the capitalist democracies. That was a temporary expedient, a bitter pill to be regurgitated at the first opportunity. By 1944, we have learned from Soviet fugitives, closed meetings of trusted comrades were chewing on a directive handed down from the highest levels: "The war on fascism ends, the war on capitalism begins."

This, incidentally, is the best answer to those who pretend that it was the conduct of the Allies, and America in particular, which precipitated the cold war. Actually Moscow had issued its fighting orders and prepared its cadres for the postwar contest long before the Allies had done any of the sinful things charged against them by attorneys for the Kremlin. Already the wartime contacts with free nations, though held to an absolute miniumum by the Soviets, had ignited "dangerous thoughts," and these had to be stamped out resolutely before they burst into a general conflagration. The Soviet rulers, as Churchill was to say a few years later, had good reason to fear the friendship of the West more than its enmity.

A certain laxness and liberalism had crept into the totalitarian system under war conditions. For the sake of fighting morale, Stalin had allowed hope of greater freedom to flourish unchecked. He had given tacit approval to old-fashioned national — as distinct from Soviet — patriotism; to books and plays and movies in which ordinary Russians rather than accredited communist officials were the heroes; to cordial feelings for the democracies and Western culture. The regime had closed its eyes as millions of peasant families enlarged their private plots at the expense of the *kolkhoz* acreage.

The people were thus permitted to assume that the nightmarish past was over, that a new era would be ushered in by victory. It was not exactly a promise, rather a subtle suggestion to nourish wishful thinking. Young people in particular were buoyed up by the belief that with the war's end there would be less pressure, more concern for the well-being of ordinary folk. Even those empty phrases about "free and unfettered elections" which Stalin had to accept in Teheran and Yalta helped fertilize illusions: If enemy peoples were being guaranteed some democratic rights, surely the victorious Russian peoples could expect no less. . . .

"The people of the home front were sick with a chronic psychosis," a former Soviet army officer has stated. "They were filled with an unshakable conviction that the day of victory, the day marking the end of the war, would not only bring deliverance from all the fevered nightmares of wartime, but would bring something bigger and better than had existed before the war. . . . The Leader would thank the people for their faithful service to the fatherland. The Leader would not forget!" *

In short, moods and tendencies had developed which, if allowed to deepen, might doom the dictatorship. The Soviet leaders acted promptly and ruthlessly to crush liberal delusions and restore the *status quo ante*. They were determined at all costs to turn back the clock to 1939. Some six years of experience had to be rewritten or blotted out. The awesome authority of the party and the government had to be restored and fortified. As always, physical force and the force of propaganda were counted upon to do the job.

There are those who argue that the Kremlin lost a great opportunity to make peace with the people. I doubt this. Had it permitted the wartime expectations to grow, had it allowed the new sense of friendship with the non-Soviet world to prosper, the Soviet *vlast* would have been mortally endangered. To safeguard its power, the Politburo had little choice but to haul down an iron curtain and resort to iron discipline. A totalitarian regime cannot too long relax its pressures without courting an accounting with its victims.

The postwar screenings and purgings, the new mass deportations and the liquidation of entire "autonomous regions," were not senseless bursts of dictatorial distemper. From the vantage point of the Kremlin they were indispensable measures to bulwark their absolute power, doses of totalitarian medicine for a restive population.

About sixty-five million Soviet people had lived for longer or shorter periods under German occupation — or, more to the point,

---

* *The Terror Machine*, by Gregory Klimov.

outside the control of the Soviet regime. The psychological impact of that vacation from Bolshevism cannot be overestimated.

The conqueror was brutal and did not endear himself to the masses. But he did not have enough personnel or means to enforce the kind of total surveillance and thought control which had been normal before his arrival. The shield of language itself gave the people a certain freedom of expression. Besides, there was one exciting privilege the Germans did not deny them — the privilege of cussing and discussing the Soviet system.

For the first time in their mature lives millions of men and women tasted the incredible experience of talking freely about their grievances; about purges, concentration camps, and assorted Soviet crimes. They knew these things in a general way, of course. But it was quite another thing to compare notes with neighbors, to confirm dreadful suspicions, to hear the horrendous details from the mouths of victims. The Germans published about seventy newspapers in the occupied areas, devoted to glorifying Hitlerism — and exposing Stalinism. Articles by former inmates of forced-labor camps, eyewitnesses of atrocities, former communists with chilling stories to tell, were standard journalistic fare.

More than that, the Germans threw open the bloodstained Soviet execution cellars to public inspection. They organized exhibitions of torture implements gathered in local NKVD headquarters. They found secret police burial places and dug up the corpses for identification by relatives. They released documents from captured archives which gave their new subjects concrete information on the knavery and sadism of their whilom bosses. In many cities the fleeing communists, unable to evacuate prisoners, had simply sealed and set fire to the prisons; these sickening funeral pyres were opened to the public.

In the Ukrainian town of Vinnitsa, near the Rumanian border, the residents had long wondered what transpired in a neglected pear orchard behind thirteen-foot walls, always heavily guarded. The sign over the gates read "Special Construction, NKVD." After the arrival of the Germans, the enclosure was opened. People were horrified to find that it was a cemetery of mass graves. Hundreds of bodies were dug up by the Vinnitsa population, and the Germans later went at the job systematically. The exhumed bodies were those of inhabitants of the town and the region, presumably exiled to Siberia, who had in fact been murdered and buried.

Nearly four hundred victims were identified by their relatives, from their clothes or from half-decayed documents found in their pockets, all dated 1937 and 1938. The Germans put recovered letters, snapshots, party and trade-union cards on display in shop windows. Several other secret burial places were found, and in all close to ten thousand corpses were disinterred and reburied. The macabre funerals went on for more than three months.* Exhibits of this sort became familiar in scores of towns and cities.

Those sixty-five million, the Kremlin could be sure, would never be the same again. They had learned too much. They had had a taste of comparative freedom, and a chance to appraise Bolshevism without inhibitions. It was no secret to Stalin that thousands of his subjects, obliged to use books as fuel, had first of all consigned communist literature, including his own and Lenin's works, to the flames, often making a joyous ceremony of the symbolic incineration; that they had demonstratively destroyed tons of pictures and statues of Soviet leaders. It was a taste of vengeance the flavor of which lingered on the palate.

In addition, there were the approximately fifteen millon who, as soldiers or slave laborers, had actually seen the "outside world." Even under chaotic war conditions that world seemed amazingly rich and free compared to the desolations and oppressions at home. In Poland, Rumania, Germany, the Red troops saw towns and villages and farmsteads which recalled the life of which their parents or grandparents had spoken so nostalgically. They saw working-class homes more luxurious than those of high officials back home, well-stocked shops, newspapers that expressed clashing opinions. They made personal contact with a world of free farmers, free artisans, prideful personal possessions. Their government, they real-

* Details provided in an article by an eyewitness, Constantin Sibirsky, a Soviet writer now in exile, and by others.

ized, had lied to them about the supposed horrors of capitalist existence.

Nearly half the population, in short, had been pulled out of its Soviet rut. Appetites for simple human comforts and simple human rights had been aroused. The Kremlin faced a formidable task of brainwashing and reconditioning nearly its entire citizenry. This task it tackled with its accustomed energy once victory was certain.

2. Brainwashing a Nation

There was no more soft talk about "the imperishable image of eternal Russia." The czars and their generals were for the most part sent back to the doghouse of history. The Komsomols (Communist Youth) were ordered to renew the campaign against the "superstitions" of religion. In general there was an end to "rotten liberalism" and pampering of the masses.

In the Kremlin's eyes everyone who had come in touch with Germans or other foreigners was contaminated and suspect: as a possible collaborator in act or thought, or possible victim of democratic contagions. This meant screening of all returning citizens and, within the limits of physical possibilities, all who had lived under the occupation. It was a political laundering of gigantic scope.

The Volga Germans had been uprooted and scattered at the start of the war. At its finish the government revealed that a number of other autonomous regions and "independent Soviet republics" had been summarily dissolved, their populations in largest part deported to Central Asia, Siberia, the Far North. Some were consigned to labor camps, others were resettled in distant areas in need of manpower for agriculture, mining, or industry. Those affected were the Kalmyks, the Crimean Tartars, the Chechens, and the Karachevs, all adjudged to have worked with the Germans against the Soviets.

These five national areas had a population of 2,800,000. Which is a lot of "traitors," even for a population as huge as the Soviet Union's.

Where wholesale vengeance on all inhabitants was physically impossible — in the Ukraine, Byelorussia, Georgia, sections of Great Russia itself — hundreds of thousands were rounded up and transported to forced-labor colonies. NKVD agents in the occupied areas had been industrious in recording the names of persons too friendly with the invader or too frank in damning the Bolsheviks. Mutual denunciations, here as in France after the liberation, also provided hordes of victims.

At the same time the returning millions from enemy prison and labor camps, willing or coerced repatriates, demobilized soldiers, were all put through the wringer of interrogation. Thousands were shot. Hundreds of thousands considered unreliable or infected by the capitalist-democratic viruses went directly from Europe to Siberia and other exile points. There is reason to believe that close to half of the returning soldiers and civilians were not allowed to go back to their original homes. The theory was that their accounts of the glamorous outer world would find too ready acceptance in their native areas, where people knew them personally.

For the Kremlin the basic imperative was, of course, to remold the history of the war years in its own image. A lot of disagreeable truths had to be erased: that the enemy had penetrated a thousand miles, that the Soviets had been on the sheer brink of defeat, that millions had collaborated with the Germans, that the regime had been forced to soft-pedal or disown fundamental Bolshevik views.

So the best sellers of the war period went one after another into the garbage cans, sometimes the authors along with them. There had been no retreat, but only a strategy of exhausting the enemy by luring him eastward. The Communist Party, not "the people," had saved the country. Indeed, there was never any doubt of victory: How could there have been under the "wise leadership of Generalissimo Stalin," whose military genius made Napoleon, Alexander the Great, and Hannibal look like bunglers?

Though old-fashioned patriotism had been invoked by the government itself, it was made a crime retroactively. How *could* so many mischievous novelists, playwrights, journalists, scenarists, have forgotten the difference between Soviet patriotism, class pa-

triotism, and the decayed patriotism of the imperialist past? Off
with their heads!

A certain Panferov was bold enough, or foolish enough, to write
an article upbraiding those who seemed to have forgotten the defeats and hardships of the war. "How can we forget about it?"
he exclaimed. "Can we forget that the Germans were at Stalingrad,
at Mozdok, near Moscow? How can we forget the burdens shoul-
dered by our people during the war? Did not these heavy burdens
at times make our joints crack. . . ."

Poor Panferov was made an object lesson for others who dared
remember too much. *Pravda* in June, 1946, assailed him without
pity for having divided the war into defensive and offensive phases
— "for his irresponsible ridicule of the correct historical statement
that during the period of retreat the Red Army was wearing out
the enemy's strength." The ability to forget, or to pretend amnesia,
became indispensable to survival.

The communists also concentrated on wiping out the memory
that American aid had been a vital factor in winning the war. The
revised line was that the USSR had triumphed *despite* the duplicities of false allies. The people could now be told the simple truth:
that Soviet Russia had beaten Germany and then Japan singlehandedly . . . well, almost singlehandedly. The double-dealing
democracies, and America especially, had conserved their strength
and developed an atom bomb for their coming aggressions against
the USSR and the "people's democracies" in Eastern Europe. The
West was wicked and vicious, the habitat of imperialist warmongers and mad fascist dogs. Anyone who doubted this was self-
evidently a traitor ripe for liquidation.

The nostalgia for the West must have been terribly strong to
compel the Kremlin to go to the irrational lengths it did to beat
it down. The virulence of the disease was implicit in the vigor of
the therapeutic countermeasures. Professors were attacked for quot-
ing foreign books. Foreign plays which had been on the boards for
years were outlawed. Their staging, it was officially stated, was an
attempt "to reawaken survivals of capitalism in the minds and in
the everyday life" of the Soviet masses — three decades after the

revolution the masters were still afraid of arousing desires for capitalism! A candidate for a doctoral degree was liquidated for saying a good word about the International Red Cross. A writer faced treason charges for stating that a foreigner named Fleming had discovered penicillin, when "everyone knows" that it was a Soviet discovery. A movie producer was ruined for remarking that David Wark Griffith was "the father of world cinema." Sports writers, circus performers, movie directors, composers of symphonies, were lambasted for "kowtowing to the West" in their work.

Yet after two years of this egregious nonsense the disease apparently had not abated. *Pravda* complained, on November 17, 1946, that "one still encounters so-called intellectuals who, having returned home, are ready to fall into ecstasies before everything, without exception, that they have seen abroad. . . ." It remained a standard complaint in the years that followed.

3. Postwar Purges

The formal postwar purge was launched with a noisy offensive in the domain of culture, against writers, artists, musicians, scholars. The Leningrad boss and Politburo member, the late Andrei Zhdanov, then widely regarded as Stalin's likely heir, led the assault. Those years, indeed, came to be known as the era of Zhdanovism, a word that denoted know-nothing xenophobia. The assignment of Zhdanovism was to turn back, by force, the consciousness and even the psychology of a nation to 1939; to pluck from its mind and soul the knowledge and insights acquired in wartime.

Inveighing against traffic with "rotten" Western ideas, Zhdanov demanded a return to revolutionary zeal: "Does it suit us, the representatives of the advanced Soviet culture, to bow before bourgeois culture or play the role of its disciples? Our job is to scourge boldly and to attack bourgeois culture, which is in a state of miasma and corruption!" Why miasmic and corrupt culture held such a powerful appeal for men and women raised under the Soviet aegis he did not try to elucidate.

It is perhaps symbolic that to exemplify the evil addiction to cultural corruption Zhdanov concentrated his verbal fire on a humorist and a poetess. He was serving notice that there was to be no more margin for laughter or poetry in Russia. A new time of communist intransigence, of pitiless collectivism, was beginning.

The fat, mild-mannered Zoschenko, who had been writing the same sort of satiric sketches for twenty-five years, Zhdanov denounced as "a literary swindler," and the aging Akhmatova, who wrote soulful poems, he told off as "a fornicatrix and nun who mixes fornication and prayer." These became the keynotes for esthetic criticism on the same elegant level which has filled the Soviet press ever since.

Boris Pasternak, a truly sensitive poet, was denounced in venomous terms, as was the late Sergei Eisenstein, the top Soviet cinema director. In the milder climate of the war Eisenstein had made a few superb pictures, but now he was again charged with the dread crime of "formalism," of "art for art's sake." Anything that was freely creative, joyous, overflowing in the arts came in for the same stultifying labels. Shostakovich, the outstanding composer, who had weathered an attack in the 1930's, was subjected to another.

Nor was the campaign limited to the arts. Philosophy was declared to be a "party science," and professors who took cognizance of "bourgeois philosophers" were treated as dangerous deviators. Historians were branded as enemies of the state for an outmoded concern with "objectivity." Some of the foremost architects were denounced for "slavish toadying to decadent American architecture." Even in geography and map making the censors managed to unearth "depraved tendencies." The genetics theory associated with the name of Lysenko, which claimed that enduring biological changes could be produced by environment and not only by heredity, was made official dogma, and all dissenters branded as traitors.

There followed a nationwide epidemic of confessions by writers, composers, journalists, scientists. Many of them hastened to accuse themselves before someone else got around to it. Contritely they acknowledged shocking crimes like aping the West, putting entertainment above the party line, succumbing to objectivity in science and formalism in art — wicked indulgences unworthy of the Soviet epoch.

They begged for the party's forgiveness for "bourgeois national" lyrics, plays, stories, symphonies, canvases — never alluding, of course, to the fact that they had been praised and rewarded for those very creations during the war. Above all, the badgered brethren of the arts and sciences abused the capitalist world for its degenerate emphasis on people, truth, beauty, and lofty emotions, rather than harsh revolutionary tasks.

A curious facet of the cultural purge was the expressed or implied admission that Soviet culture was utterly sterile. The country was not yet producing any of the noble arts, superior to the West's, demanded by its bureaucrats. Even Zhdanov went no further than to insist that "the new socialist society . . . is *capable* of creating the most advanced literature." He did not dare claim that it was actually doing so, since he could not point to a single convincing proof.

Having set up shop as critics, the bureaucrats castigated the cultural community for total failure to come through with any of the wonderful works, superior to those of the degenerate West. It did not occur to them that the barrenness of Soviet art since the rise of Stalin might be due to Soviet conditions. The dastardly artist or scientist was at fault and must be chastised, not for lack of talent but for lack of loyalty. The bureaucrats really had no alternative. They could scarcely admit, in the words of Dwight Macdonald, that "this drying up of all the springs of artistic creation is the surest indication of the real quality of the Soviet social system."

The intensified provincialism, intended to cure the people of their wartime love affair with the democracies, found expression also in a drive against something called "cosmopolitanism." The culprits, it turned out, were mostly Jews. Though they were not attacked and liquidated frankly as Jews, the anti-Semitic stench of the campaign was too strong to be missed.

Anti-Semitism, one of the foul legacies of the *ancien régime,* was fought by the Soviets in their first twenty years as a tangential expression of opposition to the regime. The prominence of Trotsky, Zinoviev, and other Jews among the founding fathers of the Bolshevik state fed existing prejudice against their race; Jews were convenient scapegoats for the crimes of the government and the hardships of life. Anti-Semitism in Soviet Russia tended to rise and fall almost in direct ratio to the sufferings of the population.

The irony of this fact is that on the whole the Jews had been more brutally hit by the Bolshevik innovations than any other group in the country. Having been barred from agriculture, they were necessarily shopkeepers, peddlers, artisans employing a few apprentices. This made them "capitalists" and "bourgeois elements" by Bolshevik definition, subject to persecution and virtual outlawry. When private trade was restored under Nep, they naturally went into it with great zeal and often great success. With the suppression of Nep, they found themselves doubly blacklisted, as pre-1917 capitalists and as Soviet Nepmen. It was estimated that in the early 1930's fully half the Jewish families were classified as "disfranchised" — *lishentsi* — deprived of nearly all social and human rights.

Nevertheless, until about 1938 the Kremlin continued to combat overt anti-Semitism, regarding it as a symptom of hostility to the regime. Then, slowly and almost clandestinely, the government itself became anti-Semitic. Jews were quietly removed from important posts; limitations were placed on the percentage of Jews in various types of schools. This trend was deepened, and rationalized in terms of political necessity, during the twenty-two months of the Berlin-Moscow pact of friendship.

With the end of the war, all restraints were abandoned. Because the Russian Jew was basically Western-minded and in so many cases had relatives abroad, because he harbored sympathies for the sufferings and aspirations of Jews in other countries, he provided, as so often in history, an ideal object of xenophobia. In a sense he became "the Westerner within" in the anti-Western campaign.

"Cosmopolitanism" was the convenient instrument of persecution. Hundreds of writers, critics, creative artists, professors, scientists were accused of a special affinity for the West — they were declared to be "rootless, passportless" creatures with an alleged hankering for the fleshpots of Wall Street and Tel Aviv who must be "hounded out of Soviet life." That there might be no mistaking their identity, the attacks emphasized the Hebraic names and patronymics of the culprits, and where necessary stripped them of their Russianized pen names: a strange enough performance in a country ruled by men, from Lenin and Stalin down, who rarely used the names to which they were born.

The cultural purge set the tone: a return to Bolshevik orthodoxy, hostility to all non-Soviet infidels. The cleansing was quickly extended to every other department of Soviet life.

Collectivized peasants, as I have already noted, had managed to expand their privately cultivated plots. Now this was branded and punished as "theft of state property." Workers had taken unwonted liberties, such as extra rations and occasional lateness. Now they were charged with wrecking production. Factory and mine directors, engineers, accountants, foremen in all parts of the country were accused of thievery, graft, diversion of funds, falsification of figures. Local officials, including judges and prosecutors, found themselves under fire for conniving in black-market operations, ration frauds, bonuses for faked achievements. And every charge meant tens of thousands of additional demotions, arrests, exiles.

One day the target might be "embezzlers and thieves" in the retail trade organizations, the next day officials in the meat industry, Diesel plants, coal mines, automotive plants, army commissaries. "Medical racketeers" were arrested for alleged faking of certificates of illness. Editors were cleansed for tolerating "cosmopolitan" or otherwise ideologically proscribed authors. Bribery, it appeared, had become even more widespread than in czarist times, with the tariffs for different types of documents and favors fairly standardized in every region. The variety of sins and sinners seemed to be almost without limit.

Military leaders, even unto marshals of the realm like Zhukov, Timoshenko, Golovanov, Voronov, were put in their place. A history of the war appeared in which there was no mention of Zhukov! Stalin was clearly intent upon restoring the unquestioned primacy of the party. Commissars sporting high military titles were again given the right of way over professional fighting men. Though the military specialists were loaded with economic privileges, gold braid, and medals, they were made to understand that thenceforth they must play second fiddle to the politicians.

As for the party itself, membership had doubled during the war. Entry into the ranks of the elite had been made easier in the interests of victory. Now came the process of casting out those of inadequate faith and tightening of the ranks. "Mass replacement of leading party personnel" was announced in the Ukraine, where the "degeneration" seems to have been especially grievous. Half of the party bureaucrats in that "republic" were ousted in eighteen postwar months; 91 per cent of all regional Soviet chairmen were removed. The same sort of party purge, if on a smaller scale, took place in the rest of the country.

As always in the past, the exact dimensions of the *chistka* (purge) were nowhere indicated. On the basis of long experience, however, it can be assumed that for every arrest or accusation made public there were thousands without benefit of publicity. If one takes into account the screening of soldiers, repatriates and entire autonomous regions, it may be set down as the most extensive purge in Soviet history, exceeding even the Yagoda-Yezhov excesses of the late thirties.

But there are a number of significant differences between the post- and the prewar purges. In the earlier series the targets were specified social or political groups and classes: engineers or kulaks or erring communists. In 1936–1938, for instance, the cleansing was in essence political, directed against alleged Trotskyites, Bukharinites, and other dissenters from the party line. Its greatest toll was taken among the upper classes, including the new Soviet intelligentsia. The great masses were involved only indirectly; they

watched the grim spectacle from some distance — for though some
ten million were involved, it was primarily a quarrel among the
masters.

But the postwar purge spared no one. It was not simply a government or party or economic *chistka* but an all-national purge —
in the words of Ruth Fischer, "a crisis of the entire social system,
a reaction to the pressure of hungry millions beating on the iron
curtain of the state-party regime." The quarrel was not with an
identifiable segment of the citizenry but with the whole Soviet
society.

This is one telltale difference. Another needs to be carefully
noted. The crimes charged in the postwar purge were no longer
political deviation; Trotskyism was practically unmentioned. They
were crimes of *moral and cultural corruption*. Contamination by
Western ideas, a hankering for Western values, graft and embezzlement, mass collaboration with a hostile country, moral degeneration, artistic sit-down strikes — these took the place of the
"plots" and "spying for foreign capitalists" which marked previous
outbursts.

If the Kremlin's frenzied accusations against huge portions of its
own population were even half true, they would connote an extraordinary degree of national demoralization. In justice to the Russian people the Kremlin's verdict must be discounted. The likely
truth is that the average Soviet citizen during the war had begun
to reach out for the sweets of private property and even more so
the sweets of self-assertion and private dignity. He was being
slapped down and put back in his totalitarian place.

But the vital fact for the rest of the world is the magnitude of
the internal Soviet psychological distress and dislocation. For every
nonreturner now in Europe or the Americas, there are doubtless
hundreds of spiritual nonreturners inside the USSR. The more
intensive the purges, the more intensively the purged and brow-
beaten citizen thinks his own thoughts, ponders what he has seen
and learned and surmised during the war years.

A revised history of Russia prepared under Stalin's personal supervision contains a passage about Russia's war with Napoleon which has a modern ring:

The general upsurge of popular patriotism in Russia was the decisive factor in the triumph of the Russian Army. Frightened, not only by Napoleon but first of all by their own peasants and serfs, the Russian feudal lords appraised the victory as a triumph of the autocracy and serfdom. They asserted with satisfaction that the simple people had never displayed such loyalty as in 1812. Others went to the extreme of insisting that for the Russian the word liberty had no meaning; that obedience had become a habit with him.

This is almost a perfect summation of what happened in World War II. Again patriotism was the decisive element in achieving victory. Again the rulers, like the feudal lords in 1812, frightened by their own subjects, hastened to rob them of their victory. Again the outcome was appraised as a triumph of the autocracy, rather than the people, and the Kremlin gang proceeded to act on the appraisal with more ruthlessness than their predecessors were capable of applying in the milder days of the divine rights of czars.

But in 1812 Russia did not forget the peace it had lost. Thirteen years later came the Decembrist uprising upon the death of Alexander I, harbinger of a revolutionary upsurge which could no longer be repressed. Without insisting upon mechanical historical parallels, we can be sure at least that after 1945, too, Russia did not forget the peace of which it had been robbed; the pledges that had been violated; the hopes that have been washed out in terror. The story of the war has been told; its aftermath is very much an unfinished story.

XVII. Chimera of Coexistence

1. Policies of Confusion

American policy toward the Soviet Union since the war's end has been hard to define and label. It has not rested on any irreducible body of principle, either in political morality or in national self-interest. Our statesmanship has lived from hand to mouth, relying on improvisation, now under the prod of panic, now under the spur of hope.

Moscow acted, Washington reacted. The Kremlin provoked a civil war in Greece, we hastily produced a Truman Doctrine by way of answer. The Politburo blockaded Berlin, we responded with a spectacular airlift. Moscow unloosed an invasion of South Korea, we threw in our best forces to check the move. A Soviet diplomat hinted at truce in Korea, we jumped for the bait and spent a year in fruitless negotiations, while the enemy built up his forces.

Not one of our major actions has been addressed to the cause of the trouble, but only to its immediate effects. Not one of them has aimed to put the Soviets on the defensive, or reduce their monopoly of the initiative in world affairs, or curb their capacity for further ventures in aggrandizement.

The Kremlin started fires at will, and the free world, under American prompting, rushed fire brigades to the scene, first on one side of the globe, then on the other. One conflagration having been brought under control, we waited anxiously, scarcely daring to breathe, for the next outbreak at some time and place of the Kremlin's selection. This bizarre and humiliating behavior was apparently geared to the theory that the way to deal with a chronic pyromaniac is to build a huge and mobile fire department. (Sometimes, as in the case of Tibet, we did not even bother to put out the fire, and in the case of China we added fuel to the blaze.)

As policy our conduct could hardly be more to the taste of the communists if they had themselves prescribed it — which to a large extent they *did,* through the influence of their agents and sympathizers on our thinking. We have had a multiplicity of tactics, some of them admirable and effective, but no strategy. The essence of strategy is a definite plan for attaining an unequivocal decision, whereas free-world policy has been marked by evasion, temporizing, vacillation: in short, confusion.

The central concept of the improvisation, with a permanent stalemate in view, was "containment." That doctrine, of which Dean Acheson was the dedicated instrument, calls for a holding operation to maintain the *status quo* — not as an interim maneuver but as a final goal. Its utmost objective is an armed truce. In the specific case it is a policy of trying to block Soviet expansion while forswearing any dynamic measures to reduce Soviet power and empire. Containment is thus negative, defensive, and defeatist; not a solution but a fatalistic assertion that we consider the problem insoluble. James Burnham has rightly called it "the bureaucratic verbalization of a policy of drift."

After Korea, containment was not often mentioned by those who labored under its debilitating spell. It had become so obviously futile and shabby, so degrading against the background of swelling casualty figures, that our statesmen were overcome by embarrassment. At the very time when containment psychology was crippling both our diplomacy and our military strategy in Korea, some publications announced its death. With the election of General Eisenhower, its demise was made official. "We shall never acquiesce in the enslavement of any people in order to purchase fancied gain for ourselves," the President declared in his first State of the Union address: as terse and exact a repudiation of the containment idea as one could wish.

But while the word has been buried, the spirit of containment persists. It is manifest in a tremulous avoidance of the initiative, a dread of "provoking" the enemy, an inclination to pay him some more blackmail for the boon of an armistice. It is evident in the eagerness with which any gesture of moderation by the Kremlin is still received by the non-Soviet world. A few kind words in Russian, a few minor concessions, and we are off on another binge of wishful thinking, ready to forget Kremlin crimes, the hundreds of millions of victims of those crimes, and — most important — the nature of the Soviet regime.

As long as this state of mind continues, the Kremlin bosses can relax, knowing that there will be no serious blows directed against their own survival. In fact, the more individual actions of containment they manage to impose upon us, the more scattered they are geographically, the better the picture becomes from Moscow's standpoint. Without staking its own major forces, without involving risks for its own sphere of dominion, it creates a continuing emergency for the non-Soviet world.

The thermostat governing the degrees of cold and hot war is still on the Kremlin wall, under exclusive Kremlin control. The Soviets can continue to manipulate not only our emotions, propelling us at will between the extremes of pessimism and optimism, but our economy and the character of our military preparations.

Economically, as we are acutely aware, containment siphons off our vitality on an ever more dangerous scale. Strategically — and of this most Americans are still blissfully unaware — containment obliges us to build all conceivable types of military force, to subsidize all kinds of allies, so that we may be prepared for flareups in an infinite number and variety of possible theatres of conflict.

Even opulent America does not have inexhaustible resources and productive capacity; its manpower is sharply limited. The endless diversity of force demanded by containment therefore prevents us from concentrating on the military means best suited for action against the instigator of all the mischief. Greece yesterday, Korea today, Iran or Thailand tomorrow, are for the Kremlin a species of insurance against the development of the kind and quantity of American force specifically calculated to deter Soviet Russia or to defeat it if a showdown is forced upon us.

To put the matter another way, containment commits the free world to dealing with symptoms while ignoring causes. In the cold war it limits us to fighting and winning battles while precluding victory. In the measure that it diverts our energies, substance, and technology to isolated and indecisive enterprises, it squanders potentials that should be husbanded for a rainy day, the day that is when it rains atom bombs.

As national policy containment is a good deal lower than appeasement in the scale of futility. Its very purpose, in fact, is to bring about a condition of balanced strength in order to induce the Soviets *to accept appeasement.*

The Kremlin is today roughly in the same position as Hitler was in 1940–1941. By cunning diplomacy, promotion of civil strife, and sheer grab it has achieved a territorial expansion much larger than Hitler did by military action. Suppose America and Britain in 1940–1941 had chosen to apply the doctrine of containment. In that case the Nazis would have been permitted to retain their conquered empire in return for a promise — a Nazi promise! — not to conquer any more; the peoples overrun by the Brown scourge would have been written off permanently, condemned to Nazi thralldom in perpetuity as payoff for our supposed security.

In relation to Hitler that kind of bargain sounds immoral, monstrous. As a practical proposition, moreover, it could not have survived the test of time and Nazi dynamism. Yet this is at bottom the bargain set as the goal of "successful" containment applied to the current totalitarian empire builder. I submit that it is no less monstrous and immoral and offers even less prospect of a stable solution. And it would consign the peoples of the satellite states, China, and the Soviet Union proper — a third of the human race — to permanent servitude in payment for the highly illusory stabilization of a half-free, half-slave world.

What would we get for our tremendous investments if containment were "successful"? At best what former Secretary Acheson in earnest and the late Joe Stalin with tongue in cheek called "coexistence" of the Soviet and non-Soviet worlds. This would mean a nervous equilibrium for as long as, but no longer than, Moscow is willing to desist from upsetting it again. Far from tapering off our military expenditures, we would have to step them up continually to keep pace with the enemy's growing might in order to maintain the crucial balance. Unless we kidded ourselves into a sense of false security, dropped our guard, and in due time "woke up dead" in an all-Soviet world.

Meanwhile we would have lost what remains of faith in the West among the Russian and satellite peoples. And what remains cannot be too much. Year after year they have listened in anguish as our statesmen and press begged the Kremlin to please "live and let live" — to keep the slaves already in its stockades on condition that it make no more slave raids. They heard Mr. Acheson reassure Moscow endlessly that we had no desire "to subvert the Soviet Union," although the Soviet Union was busily subverting all other countries. They watched us do handsprings of delight every time Stalin, and after him Malenkov, said with a broad wink, "Sure . . . we can coexist."

What conclusions could the humanity behind the Soviet curtains draw? Only that the West stood ready at all times to consign them to communist perdition in a cynical bargain for coexistence.

During and after the war we spit on the Atlantic Charter and all other idealistic goals to please Stalin. We surrendered hundreds of millions of people to Bolshevik torments, frankly acknowledging that it was blackmail to protect our own freedom. The Poles, the Balts, the Czechs, finally the Chinese were turned over to the Kremlin as down payments for "peace." After which, under the drooping banners of containment, we kept asking plaintively, "Now comrades, haven't you got enough yet? Can't we be friends now?"

This was scarcely calculated to inspire trust in the courage or wisdom of the democracies, least of all in their political morals, among the millions who hoped against hope that we would make common cause with them. After all, the West did not even pretend that it was concerned with *their* freedom, provided their ordeal could safeguard our own a little longer.

In 1951 the United States Senate solemnly affirmed American friendship for the peoples of Russia. But amazingly, its fine declaration of love wound up with assurances that we were always prepared to come to terms with their dictators! The chief sponsor of the friendship resolution, the late Senator Brien McMahon, then went about the country advocating a fifty-billion-dollar payoff to the Soviets if only they would refrain from further aggressions.

Friendship for the captives coupled with a live-and-let-live proposal to their captors! There we have something like a record in confusion, on the moral and practical planes alike. There are ample reasons in common sense and common humanity for a show of fellow feeling to the Kremlin's victims. There may be reasons of expediency or desperation for seeking a *status quo* arrangement with the Kremlin clique. But the combination of both overtures in the same document by the same statesmen is hypocrisy or stupidity or both.

We cannot have it both ways. If our offer to split the world forever into free and slave sections is genuine, then the expressions of affection for the slaves is phony. Worse, to the victims it must look like plain trickery: an attempt to jockey the Kremlin into agreement by threatening to make a united front with its subjects.

2. *Coexistence Is a Trap*

The fallacy at the heart of our confusion is the assumption that the Soviet Union is a national state like other states, which can be placated, bought off, or contained. President Roosevelt's Great Design, envisaging the USSR as a senior partner in a world based on law, rested on that tragic misapprehension. So did the postwar appeasements and the improvisations of containment after Roosevelt.

They all left out of reckoning the fact that the Soviet Union is not a conventional nation, moved by ordinary national purposes, abiding by normal rules of foreign intercourse — but an *inter-nation,* nucleus of the one world of communist dogma, a world dictatorship in embryo. They all chose to brush aside the fact that the Kremlin is the powerhouse of world communism, whose paramount objective is the annihilation of noncommunist civilization.

These are not guesses. They are facts. Their reality has been attested by Soviet conduct through all the Soviet years. They have been set forth fully, candidly, in boring repetition by all Kremlin leaders, in books available at your public library. Wide variations may be found in communist methods at different times, but the main theme — war to the death against capitalist states — has remained fixed and implacable.

In negotiations with the Soviet Union, the representatives of nations confront the representatives of an inter-nation, a conspiracy. There can be no common political currency acceptable in both camps. When the Kremlin talks of "peace" it does not mean what we do; it refers to the pursuance of its permanent offensive without open military action. When it speaks of coexistence it does not mean what we do; it refers to a breathing spell during which it can better prepare to cut our throats.

How contain an entity that in sober fact has no fixed frontiers in the ordinary sense? The Huks in the Philippines, the Viet Minh in Indo-China, the Red-held areas in Burma and Malaya, communist undergrounds in a dozen countries, legal Red parties and their fellow-traveling adjuncts in the free nations — these are as truly a part of the Soviet empire as Bulgaria or China. Call it a movement, a secular religion, a world conspiracy or what you will, it can be contained only by fighting it everywhere. And fighting is doomed to failure unless it is geared to complete victory. How coexist with a force frankly (and from its own viewpoint inevitably) dedicated to destroying us?

"Conflicting great powers," William R. Mathews, editor of the Arizona *Daily Star* writes, "have lived in coexistence since the beginning of time." True, but they were all powers of the same political species, with clearly defined frontiers, populations, national interests. None of them was committed by its innermost nature to world hegemony: a commitment it could drop only by ceasing to be itself. None of them commanded the allegiance of vast numbers throughout the world, or disposed of potent organized forces, including military and para-military formations, within the confines of other powers.

Coexistence is a two-way street. Great powers could exist side by side despite disparate systems and ideals because all of them accepted the principle of coexistence, not in words but in fact, as if it were a law of nature. What remained to negotiate, or to establish by force of arms, were the terms for living together. Russia therefore was able to find a *modus vivendi* with other powers in the past; it will have no trouble finding it in the future, after the elimination of the Bolshevik regime.

But the present Russia does not and *cannot* abide by the principle of coexistence. When it evokes the chimera, it is deliberately practicing verbal deceit, since it does not and *cannot* renounce its role as spearhead of communist world revolution. Any engagements it enters into with "the enemy," for disarmament let us say, must be fraudulent. Communists will disarm, Lenin said, "only after we have completely forced down and expropriated the bourgeoisie of the whole world . . . after disarmament of the bourgeoisie by the proletariat."

George F. Kennan, credited with chief authorship of the containment doctrine, has stated that the "thesis of a basic antagonism between the capitalist and socialist worlds" has been "canonized in Soviet philosophy . . . and is now anchored in the Soviet structure of thought by bonds far greater than those of mere ideology." He called that antagonism a "fiction" — but a fiction which governs the conduct of an aggressive police state is very real. The ideas which fueled the Mohammedan drive for conquest may have been fictions in the cold light of logic; that was small consolation to communities in Asia, Africa, and the Iberian peninsula which wished only to coexist but were overrun notwithstanding.

The notion that the Soviet rulers may have a change of heart some balmy morning, and decide at last to live and let live, is a shocking naïveté. Where the heart of their creed is involved they are not free agents but captives of their whole history. The "fiction" of capitalist encirclement provides the motive power of their ideological machine. It is the supreme alibi for their savagery. "If a hostile world did not exist," Peter Viereck wrote recently, "Stalin [today read Malenkov] would need to invent it." He *did* invent it at the end of the last war.

Writing in *Collier's* a few years ago, Winston Churchill went to the core of humanity's current plight: "Greater divergencies have

opened among men than those of the religious wars of the Reforma-
tion, or of the political and social conflicts of the French Revolution,
or of the power struggle just concluded with Hitler's Germany. The
schism between communism on the one hand and Christian ethics
and Western civilization on the other is the most deadly, far-reaching
and rending that the human race has known."

It is pathetic self-delusion to assume that explosive elements of
this sort can be contained through conventional alliances, live-and-
let-live settlements, divisions of the world into neat spheres of influence. Or that the crisis they represent can long be evaded by European neutralism or American isolationism.

The circumstance that Mr. Churchill under the pressures of
British politics seems to have forgotten his own words does not
diminish their truth. Coexistence with the Soviet inter-nation is a
mirage of wishful thinking. Its partisans would have us treat a plague
as if it were an orthodox country, when already there are few spots in
the anatomy of this globe that have not been to some degree infected.

Containment has not worked. While it was official free-world policy, Czechoslovakia fell, China fell, Tibet fell, Guatemala succumbed
to a limited extent; the ravages of communism weakened large areas
in the Near East and in Southwest China; a neutralism whose effect
is to enhance the relative power of the Soviets gained ground in
Western Europe and seems to have conquered the minds of Britain
and India.

The one saving grace of containment, as a matter of fact, is that it
hasn't worked. Therefore, despite the doctrine in theory, we have
been driven in practice to dabble in political warfare; to make gestures of friendship to the Russian peoples; to encourage some types
of resistance in the satellite countries; to extend some help to the
Chinese Nationalists and to bar Red China from the United
Nations.

The "success" of containment — more plainly, a general settlement
for coexistence — would in the long run prove more calamitous than
its failures. For it would guarantee the Kremlin a free hand for as
long as it wished to consolidate its power and vitalize its forces — in
our sphere as well as its own — for the next big push. Such powers of

resistance as we have generated in the last few years would be quickly dissipated. We have seen how even the dim prospect of a settlement, following Stalin's death, operated to expose and sharpen the differences among the free nations. An actual settlement, bringing the illusion that the common danger has passed, would fragmentize the non-Soviet world beyond easy repair, possibly forever.

The advantages of coexistence for the Kremlin and its dangers for us are so striking that one wonders why the Soviets have been so slow and coy in agreeing to be "contained."

3. Containment Equals Surrender

The most ambitious presentation of the containment thesis came from England in 1951, in a book called *Policy for the West,* by Barbara Ward. I propose to consider it here in some detail, only because it provides a useful close-up of the mental processes of a large and still influential segment of so-called liberal public opinion. Miss Ward belongs to those anticommunists whose minds somehow cannot compass a world without the Soviet regime — who elaborate formulas to conceal, especially from themselves, this psychological surrender.

It was symptomatic of the fatuous political climate in the book reviewing trade that the opus was hailed as a messenger of "inspiration" and "hope." What was Miss Ward's thrilling message? Only that if the West makes itself supremely strong and supremely "good" (cleaning its own house, raising living standards in backward areas, and so on), it *might* "deter the Soviets from further aggressions and persuade them to negotiate or at least to live as they did in the twenties and thirties, primarily concerned with their own affairs." The *primarily* is a disingenuous touch. As for making the communists disgorge their conquests and retreat to their positions of the twenties and thirties, let alone relaxing their cruel grip on Russia itself — nothing so bold or decent seems to have entered the lady's head.

The policy for the West she recommends "is not to drive the enemy to defeat but to secure a settlement with him." In other words, acceptance of the communist regime in Russia and all the satellites and all the fifth columns as permanent afflictions to be permanently endured! The eight hundred millions already in chains to be abandoned without a sigh of regret, in return for the chance — she doesn't claim it is more than a chance — that the rest of us may remain unbound! In order that readers make no rash discounts of this tough position, Miss Ward explicitly consigns China and implicitly also Korea to the fenced-off world to be conciliated and contained. Such is the "hope," such the "inspiration," discerned by keen-eyed book reviewers.

Before the war, Miss Ward argues, the Soviet Union did not constitute a threat because the West was relatively stronger and would presumably have slapped down aggression. Therefore, "the Western task is . . . to secure conditions in which the Soviet Union is prepared to wait." Wait for what? Obviously an opportunity to crush its patient containers.

This reasoning slurs over the fact that even in the twenties and thirties Moscow was not exactly a passive waiter, as witnessed by its conquest of Georgia, the Central Asian principalities, Outer Mongolia, Tannu Tuva; the initial Soviet intervention in China; the undeclared war on Manchuria in 1929; the swipes at Sinkiang, Rumania and other regions. It overlooks the indirect aggressions by communist fifth columns in all countries. And, of course, it evades the other half of its own logic, which is that another and on the whole easier way to make the West relatively stronger is to devote ourselves to *making the Soviets weaker.*

Even in its period of "waiting," the Kremlin spared no energies, resources and ingenuity to undermine and if possible overthrow the non-Soviet civilizations. If we compel negotiations and settlement, through heroic exertions and bankrupting expenditures of the kind Miss Ward outlines, such activity certainly will not cease. The Soviets are not famous for carrying out their bargains. But while the Kremlin continues to dig under the foundations of the free world, no Western action aimed frankly at weakening and ultimately overthrowing the Soviets has any place in Miss Ward's blueprint for self-bleeding and moral surrender.

Her policy for the West falls into two main categories: the development of military vitality and the accomplishment of a long array of social and political reforms. Militarily, the Western Powers should prepare to deal "with the problem of defending the gigantic periphery of the free world, knowing all the time that they, as defenders, cannot pick the scene of action. Their only expedient is, therefore, to create small, highly armed police units which can be dispatched with sufficient speed to any point of conflict in time to reinforce the resistance by local forces."

Translated into reality, this means unlimited preparedness to fight endless Koreas at times and places of Moscow's choosing, while guaranteeing in advance that the real aggressor would not be discommoded in his home fortress.

At the politico-social end, Miss Ward's program is so huge, exorbitant and controversial that I cannot attempt to summarize it here. There are weaknesses and inconsistencies in Western society, "cracks and fissures" in its social setup. (Does she know any system in all mortal history without them?) We have sinned and are sinning against underprivileged classes and areas. Hence, we must dedicate ourselves forthwith to atonement, universal justice, and universal prosperity.

"Universal" perhaps overstates the case, since she is wholly indifferent to suffering and injustice in the Soviet third of the globe. Why Greece and Italy and Ethiopia must be "saved," but not Eastern Germany, or Bulgaria, or Tibet, remains unexplained. Miss Ward's zeal for freedom is neatly selective. We are all against depressions, famines, disunity, and sin. But to assert, as she does repeatedly, that our "only hope" lies in self-perfection makes defeatist nonsense. Since perfection will assuredly not be attained, containment is by her own logic doomed to failure.

Even in its present sorry state, Miss Ward concedes, the Western segment is infinitely better off, more humane and successful than the Soviet segment. But apparently this great differential is not great enough to immunize us against communist subversion. At what point, precisely, the blessed state of immunity will be reached is not clear.

And how long must we devote ourselves to the assorted military and social tasks, each of them gigantic, which add up to our "only hope" of inducing Moscow to wait? "The next twenty or thirty years" or "for a generation to come" are her more optimistic answers. A less comforting estimate is given on page 203: "The holding of the frontiers of freedom — which is the essence of defense policy under containment — may last as long as Britain's 'Eastern Question' lasted. It may even have to endure as a permanent feature of our civilization — as the Roman frontier endured through hundreds of years."

Prodigious sacrifice and effort and armament for a generation, perhaps for centuries, which *if* effective will gain us — what? Communist consent to being appeased and reappeased! The privilege of sharing this good earth forever with barbarians, without lifting a finger to throw off their yoke! Denuded of "liberal" trimmings, such plans for coexistence do have a Gilbert and Sullivan flavor.

If she is aware that there are alternative courses, Miss Ward fails to acknowledge them. At no point does she take cognizance of possible policies aiming to capture the initiative for the West, to exploit the "cracks and fissures" within the Soviet sphere, to forge a united front with the peoples oppressed by Sovietism, and ultimately to liberate those peoples and ourselves from the incubus. Characteristically, it does not occur to her to distinguish between the Kremlin and its unhappy subjects, in the way she distinguishes, for instance, between the ruling shifts and the masses in the Near East or Africa. She does not even draw a line, in any genuine sense, between the Soviet puppet regimes and their restive populations.

Whatever doubts she may have about the hostility of Russians to their tyrants, there are none at all about the hostility of the satellite peoples to their Red proconsuls. Whether those hostilities will at the proper time be converted into overt resistance depends, in decisive measure, upon the encouragement, understanding, and support of the outside world. But these Miss Ward's blueprint rules out by definition. Containment, as she describes it, comes close to perpetual incarceration, so far as Stalin's victims are concerned.

Nowhere in her three hundred mellifluous pages, indeed, is there a word of simple compassion for the tormented peoples of the Soviet prison state, nowhere even a prayer for their eventual deliverance. She does not seem aware that the multitudinous Kremlin victims are part of the human race, entitled to some of the freedoms and decencies and material comforts she is so concerned to preserve for Anglo-Saxons and confer on lesser breeds not yet in Soviet keeping.

Miss Ward describes communism as "one of the most tremendous fakes ever perpetrated on bewildered humanity," resting on doctrine "profoundly and terrifyingly reactionary." Here is a central truth on which she might have based her analysis and policy counsel. Instead, she focuses in a guilt-conscious spirit on the lesser faults in our free societies! Kennan, in his writings on containment, at any rate held out half a hope of "an erosion of despotism" from within, despite our undertaking not to do anything to accelerate that erosion. But Miss Ward is more hard-boiled; she does not hold out any such hope for centuries to come. It is the *reductio ad absurdum* of coexistence.

An underestimate, if not complete dismissal, of the Russian and satellite peoples is generally the hallmark of containment thinking. Kennan himself, curiously, is an exception to this rule. He knows the Russians too well and values them too highly for an offhand dismissal. In his celebrated "X" article in *Foreign Affairs* he declared that the free world "will never prevail in any struggle against the destructive workings of Soviet power *unless the Russian people are our willing allies."*

Obviously it is quite a feat to square that conviction with a policy of containment. We cannot make allies of people by solemnly promising to recognize their continued enslavement, to do nothing to help liberate them, and to deal only with their slave masters. And this contradiction gets Kennan into a lot of forensic trouble. The whole passage is worth a closer look:

If it should fall to us to take up arms against those who today dispose over the Russian people, we can try not to give that people the impression that we are their enemies, or consider them ours. . . . We can give them the feeling that we are on their side, and that our victory, if it comes will be used to provide them with a chance to shape their destiny in the future to a pattern happier than that which they have known in the past. . . .

It would be tragic if our indignation over Soviet outlooks and policies led us to make ourselves the accomplices of despotism by forgetting the greatness of the Russian people, losing our confidence in their genius and their potential for good, and placing ourselves in opposition to their natural feelings. The vital importance of this becomes even clearer when we reflect that we in the outside world who believe in the cause of freedom will never prevail in any struggle against the destructive working of Soviet power unless the Russian people are our willing allies. This goes for peace, and it goes for war. . . .

He begins, let us note, by indicating that we must make friends of the Russian people if we have to go to war with their rulers — and ends by asserting that we must make allies of them *whether in peace or war.* Yet this conclusion — logically inescapable — appears in an essay which sets the rules for containment. And rule number one is under no circumstances to commit ourselves to the liberation of those friends and allies — thus making ourselves the very thing he warns against: "accomplices of despotism." He tries and fails to square the circle of strict neutrality in the struggle between the Kremlin and its subjects without forfeiting every chance of turning the latter into "willing allies."

In a speech in Scranton, Pennsylvania, on January 16, 1953, soon after he was expelled from Moscow, Kennan further compounded the inherent confusion of the containment thesis. In sharp dissent from his own earlier words, he now stated that "the problem . . . is not one of our relations with the Russian people or the other peoples of the Soviet Union." He said further:

The Russian people, with whom it has been my privilege to come more closely into contact, are a great people — differing from ourselves, to be sure, in many ways — embracing, like every other great people, light and dark sides to their national character — but a people full of feeling and humanity, affected by and large by the same impulses that animate people and give life its meaning in this or any country.

Most of them, I am sure, have the same sort of inner awareness we do of their affinity with the rest of mankind — an awareness of the fact that in the long run we human beings must learn to be charitable with one another and to stand together or face the suicidal destruction of our entire civilization.

After such words one expects a plea that we build bridges to this great people, in defiance of their hated government; that we turn those "impulses that animate people" and their sense of "affinity with the rest of mankind" into weapons against the common enemy. But nothing of the sort! The Russian population, alas, is cut off from us by a humiliating Iron Curtain, and hence he concludes: "Our problem is not with these common people but with the men who contrived to command their obedience — the Soviet leaders." Telescoping his thoughts, we have approximately the following: "We can never win against the Soviet power without an alliance with the Russian people. We must sedulously avoid positive action to bring about that alliance. Consequently we can never win." Such is the defeatist essence of containment and coexistence.

Mr. Kennan is quite as knowledgeable and brilliant as he is reputed to be, besides being a talented writer. There is no doubt of his sensitive sympathy for the Russian peoples "in their long and excruciating subjection to the power of human evil," to use his own words. His fault as a political guide, I venture to suggest, is a kind of temperamental distaste for doing, for intrusion. For him all roads seem to lead to inaction — to letting history take its course. He is like a splendid diagnostician who knows no therapy other than the healing of time. But time, alas, considering the tempo of communist successes, is a medicine in dangerously short supply.

Of course, advice which dispenses with bitter medicines and precludes the risks of action has a strong appeal — the appeal to "a kind of sophisticated, armchair moderation that relies on history to do America's work for it." The characterization is from an editorial in *Life,* March 24, 1952, which went on to say:

> *That* kind of "moderation" is a betrayal, first, of the principle that freedom under law is everybody's right and America's mission. It is a betrayal, second, of those 500,000 exiles from the Soviet Union whose

hatred of Stalin reflects the suffering of the Russian people. If we try to "wait out" communism, their hope of freedom will wither. And with it our strength and self-respect will wither too.

The U.S. has minimum requirements of Russia, but they are irreducible and mandatory: liberation. Our problem is to achieve this with the least risk of hot war. It will call for many plans and campaigns; but the very first plan can't be drawn until we have a clear objective, are determined to win it, and know our enemy's name. The name isn't Russia; it's the Kremlin gang.

Suppose "it happened here," and a totalitarian gang captured control of the United States. Would Americans see nothing wrong in free-world statesmanship which began by abandoning them to the usurpers of their freedom, ignoring the people and considering only the gang in power? Would they not wish the democracies to examine whether the gang does in fact "command the obedience" of the population as totally as claimed? Whether the Iron Curtain could be breached?

It happens that more than a million former Soviet citizens in exile, and tens of millions within the Soviet frontiers, are thinking along these lines. We can make them our friends and allies only by aligning ourselves openly and unambiguously on their side. To write them off as utterly without influence is to betray them and ourselves.

In the light of what transpired during the Russo-German war, the labors of his successors to win popular approval after Stalin's passing, the flow of fugitives across the Iron Curtain, defeatism of the Ward-Kennan order is unjustified and indecent. It is not enough for the free world to express a pallid and ineffective friendship for the Kremlin's victims. It must demonstrate and deserve that friendship through policies geared, without equivocation, to eventual liberation: policies calculated to make the Russian and satellite populations "our willing allies." And that, in Kennan's words, goes for peace, and it goes for war.

XVIII. Imperialism: Communist or Russian?

1. A Mischievous Theory

By the end of World War II, the heroic sacrifices of the Russian people had built up an immense capital of good will, admiration, and even affection for the USSR. The Politburo could have drawn on it for years and decades to come, to help restore its war-torn economy and to bolster Russia's position in the world.

The weary and grateful Allies were pathetically eager to let bygones be bygones; no allusions were ever made to the two years of Soviet-Nazi collaboration, or to the twenty years of communist subversion that went before. The democracies had their arms wide open to welcome the prodigal country into the family of nations, their purses wide open to speed up Russian rehabilitation.

Stalin did not hesitate to squander that capital. Purposefully and with diabolic skill he proceeded to turn the good will into fear, the affection into hate. The wartime alliance having been smashed with a few swift blows, he swung his party-state back to the dogma of irresistible conflict between his own and the "bourgeois" worlds. Communist parties everywhere were ordered to throw off their sheep's clothing of local patriotism and take up their old lives as revolutionary wolves. The Iron Curtain was rung down and the cold war was under way.

No one was threatening the Soviet Union. On the contrary, the democracies were dismantling their victorious war machines, unilaterally, and pleading for Soviet friendship and collaboration at almost any price. Every reasonable and a lot of unreasonable demands by Moscow were being met. As token of trust, we handed over bleeding chunks of European and Asian territory to the Kremlin, betraying devoted allies like Poland and China, and doing mayhem to our democratic conscience in the process. American and British military police were put at the Kremlin's service in driving back its runaway slaves. As late as the launching of the Marshall Plan, provoked by Soviet aggressiveness, the USSR and its hand-tooled "peoples' democracies" were offered a share in the American bounty and a voice in its management.

The interests of Russia as a nation would have been best served by co-operation with the West. Of this there can be no logical doubt. The country needed time and loans to heal its wounds. Already it had acquired vast new territories, resources, manpower, and reparations: more booty than had ever before fallen to a victor in war. As for the Russian peoples, they had demonstrated clearly enough their deep distaste for foreign adventuring; they craved only a chance to live normal lives at home.

But the Politburo rejected the proffered friendship, violently and insultingly. It unloosed instead a hysterical scare of new wars, forcing its subjects to gird for struggle with imaginary foes. The dream of an interlude of genuine peace, improved living conditions, normal intercourse with a world cleansed of Hitlerism — the dream that had animated the Russian masses through the dread war years — was buried in propaganda about "imperialist warmongers."

Soviet Russia faced a clear choice: between a dominant role in a stabilized world, virtually on its own terms, and a resumption of communist hostilities. Its masters chose the latter. In truth no genuine choice was involved. Stalin had never seriously considered the peaceable alternative; his preparations for renewed ideological warfare on a global scale had been perfected long before the war was finished. The prospect of a fixed and stable pattern, indeed, alarmed the Kremlin, now burning to make the most of the possibilities opened up by postwar tensions and dislocations.

This automatic sacrifice of national interests to communist purposes is of critical importance in understanding Soviet foreign policy and the nature of mankind's present predicament. *It knocks the props from under the superficial theory that Soviet aggression is just the old Russian imperialism in a new form.*

That theory is infinitely mischievous. It mistakes an ideological offensive for old-fashioned national expansion. It converts a great historic struggle between freedom and totalitarianism into a geographical "East-West" struggle. It is false, unrealistic, and therefore a dangerous foundation for policy. Its most dangerous feature is that it deliberately crowds "the East," and in particular the peoples of the Soviet sphere, into the wrong corner by identifying them as "the enemy."

The essence of garden variety imperialism is the promotion of national self-interest. It aims to expand the wealth and power of a country in order to assure its security and raise the well-being of its citizenry. By this test, communist imperialism is an animal of an altogether different order. For it operates in defiance of, and largely at the expense of, Russia's intrinsic interests.

Where national interests *seem* to be served by Kremlin policy, it is a coincidence. The operational base of world communism happens to be located on a national entity called Russia. The fortification of that base therefore involves the strengthening of Russia. But national interests are advanced only to the extent that they are consistent with the larger communist objectives.

The Soviet people, their preferences and creature comforts, their very lives, are expendable in pursuit of specifically Red goals — goals to which they are fundamentally opposed. The Kremlin is not an instrument in the hands of a nation for the achievement of national purposes; to the contrary, the nation is an instrument in the Kremlin's hands for the achievement of international party purposes. This distinction is all-important.

A normal Russia, czarist or democratic, would as a matter of course have taken a potent and honored place in the Great Design projected by President Roosevelt, even as the Russia of 1815 did after the elimination of Napoleon. The present plight of the world

cannot be attributed to the character of Russia or its people. It is
related to the character of the current party-state, engaged in activities only superficially comparable to ordinary imperialist and expansionist ambitions.

2. *Russians as Imperialists*

The assumption that imperialism is a peculiarly Russian disorder
— that Russians are somehow more inclined to absorb weak neighbors and fill void spaces than other peoples — is racist drivel. Every
great power in history, without exception, waxed big and strong
through the centuries by exactly the same methods of colonization,
intimidation, and outright conquest as Russia did in its time of
growth.

Until recently the English were looked upon as the typical imperialists, and before them the Spaniards and the Dutch. The
Swedes had their century of empire, dominating the Baltic and
taking big bites out of Russia until Peter the Great stopped them.
In the Napoleonic era France seemed the aggressor par excellence,
until curbed and tamed by Britain and Russia; its armies marched
clear across a continent into the heart of Russia. From 1870 to date,
the Germans have been regarded as insatiably expansionist in their
very genes.

It was only in recent times, of course, that imperialism got its bad
name. Before that it was taken for granted as the way of mankind.
In Russian expansion from the Duchy of Muscovy to the sprawling
nation of 1917 there is little if anything that does not have its replica
in the history of other great powers.

Professor Michael Karpovich of Harvard has written:

With the formation of the Muscovite empire, the experience of
the Russian state not only parallels, but is concurrent with the growth
of national states in the West. The Vassilys and Ivans who unified "the
Russian lands" were contemporaries of Ferdinand and Isabella in Spain,
Louis XIV in France, the Tudors in England. In essence, they all pursued
the same methods and sought similar "ideological justifications" for their

policies. . . . The foreign policy of the czars was the customary policy of a national state. The Romanoff autocracy, unlike the Soviet Union, was neither an "ideocracy" nor an insurrectionary-totalitarian state, and it is impossible to find a parallel with "Marxism-Leninism-Stalinism" in its foreign policy.*

The defeat of Hitler by the Soviets has a close historical parallel in the defeat of Napoleon by Alexander I in 1814. But Alexander, unlike Stalin, did not grab any lands or try to Russianize the world. Having captured not only Berlin but Paris, he soon withdrew his forces to his own country. The peace he dictated to Europe was one of the most generous in history.** It was England that helped itself to Malta and a number of French colonies. Nor did Russia, after defeating Turkey in 1878, annex any enemy soil.

The Russian imperial impulse, no different in kind from that which moved England or France or Japan, spent itself before the end of the nineteenth century. The mood of the country, certainly so far as its influential liberal and progressive elements were concerned, was increasingly anti-imperialist. Further ventures in expansion, such as the one that led to the Russo-Japanese War, aroused vigorous popular opposition. Far from feeding some built-in imperialist appetite in the Russian heart, these ventures helped to turn the people against the dynasty.

As the First World War ground to a close, the demands for a peace "without annexations or contributions" on the basis of self-determination in disputed regions came from the Provisional Government in Petrograd, which for itself had renounced all imperial claims. Russian public opinion on this issue was so intense that even the Bolsheviks were compelled to disown expansionist intentions and cancel out some of the czars' conquests.

Russian imperialism was less colonial on the British pattern than continental on the American pattern. It was not sparked by any

* The *New Leader,* June 14, 1951.
** M. Rimbaud, the French historian of Russia, writing about the Vienna Congress of 1815, declared: "It is an incontestible fact that of all the allies, Russia showed herself the least grasping. . . . Her skilful leniency toward France finished the work begun by the war."

flaming imperial idea or theory of race superiority. In fact, some of the conquered areas were granted political privileges and economic advantages denied to people in the homeland; Russian Poland enjoyed a large degree of autonomy until the 1860's, and Finland to the very end.

The absorption of the vast Siberian spaces was made through exploration and settlement of areas inhabited only by aboriginal tribes: a process not unlike the settlement of the American West. Except for the southeastern fringe of largely Moslem regions overrun in the later stages of Russian expansion, the peoples embraced by the empire were predominantly of the same Slavic stock: Great Russian, Little Russian (Ukrainian), and White or Byelorussian — the differences among whom were not as sharp as those between Catalonian and Andalusian in Spain; Bavarian and Prussian in Germany; Scotch, Welsh, and English in Great Britain. Russia rarely reached out overseas in search of colonies to exploit, but continually stretched its own frontiers in search of natural boundaries and outlets.

I am not "defending" the historic process called Russian imperialism, but merely asserting that it was not exceptional or unprecedented or endemically Russian. Its faults, its crimes, its justifications were those of parallel processes throughout the world. To explain the drive for an all-communist world — a drive to which Russia's native interests are being ruthlessly subordinated — as "Russian imperialism" is to distort and falsify the present crisis.

Mankind could deal easily enough with a conventional Russian urge to expand; that has its natural limits. The problem today is to deal with a fanatical and unlimited communist drive. That drive is already almost as much Chinese as it is Russian and, so far as American or British communists are concerned, as much American or British as Russian. Red imperialism in Indo-China, the Philippines, Korea, is not being implemented by Russians or even by Soviet nationals. Its largest conquest, in China, was attained by Chinese forces and does not require Russian occupation or policing. Should Italy or France be added to the Soviet empire, it is as likely to be accomplished by Italians and Frenchmen as by the Red Army.

To equate this sort of expansion with ordinary national imperialism is to misjudge our times. It is an error that would convert the world-wide political contest — which is as intense inside as outside the USSR — into an old-style struggle against Russia and the Russian people.

What choice does such an approach leave to those people but to rally around the regime they hate? As little choice as Hitler left them when they were convinced that he was not warring against communism but against Russia. The strange insistence that Soviet aggression is a continuation of the deeply national and patriotic imperialism of the past permits the Kremlin gang to pose, with some justice, as champions of the traditional Russia. It enables Malenkov and Molotov to warn that the West, like Hitler, pretends to be fighting communism but actually aims to cut up, destroy and dominate Russia.

In effect it pins the guilt for Kremlin foreign policy on the Russian peoples. In another dimension, it is the familiar fallacy of blaming the worst victims of Bolshevism and its most consistent opponents for all Bolshevik excesses; of finding in Russian history the explanations and alibis for Soviet conduct. No matter how thickly it is cushioned with curses on communism, the whole thesis of Red imperialism as a revival of Russian imperialism is anti-Russian (as distinct from anti-Soviet) propaganda. It raises an insuperable wall between ourselves and the Russian peoples. Should war come, it would tend to give the Kremlin insurance against what it most fears: the angers of its subjects.

Unfortunately that thesis has been propagated by free-world statesmen, most of whom certainly do not understand the implications of their attitude. Dean Acheson, testifying before a Senate committee on June 26, 1951, explained that the problem was simply "Russian imperialism," to which the Politburo has added "new weapons and new tactics — the weapons of conspiracy, subversion, psychological and ideological warfare, and indirect aggression." He failed to understand that these weapons are the result of a totally new species of imperialism; that they represent a far-reaching break with the past rather than its continuation.

"It is clear," Secretary Acheson went on, "that this process of encroachment and consolidation, by which Russia has grown in the last 500 years from the Duchy of Muscovy to a vast empire, has got to be stopped."

But does not every great nation on earth, when viewed in the perspective of many centuries, present the same picture of growth through "encroachment and consolidation"? How did a small island off Northwestern Europe blossom into the vast British empire? For that matter, how did a narrow fringe of Atlantic coast expand into the continental United States?

In the final analysis, there is nothing Mr. Acheson said of Russia that could not be said with equal justice of other empires. Substitute for the Duchy of Muscovy the original core of other countries, and precisely the same strictures apply to every great power extant. Less than a century ago, when both the United States and Russia were in the throes of "manifest destiny," the New York *Herald* could write of these countries as "two young giants, engaged in the same work — that of expansion and progression . . . the interests of both demand that they should go hand in hand in their march to empire."

At best the wisdom of raking up and challenging five hundred years of any country's history is open to question. It is on a par with the suggestion that we give back America to the Indians. I think we have our hands full enough with the history of the last thirty-five years without taking on five centuries. At worst this indictment of a nation's entire history must operate to force an artificial patriotic solidarity upon the peoples of Russia and their dictatorship.

The Acheson statement and others like it amount to a declaration of hostilities against Russia as a nation and its people. The fact that the statements are not so intended is small comfort. They obscure and basically deny the ideological essence of the present-day struggle, reducing it to a traditional fight for land, ports, colonies. The concept vitiates every attempt to establish friendly relations with the Soviet people over the heads of their despots. Unless quickly exposed and repudiated, it promises a virtual repetition of the political insanity which cost Germany the support of the Russian populace against the Kremlin.

This is not academic speculation. It is directed to the very heart of our problem vis-à-vis world communism. If Soviet aggression were in fact merely Russian imperialism, the Soviet peoples would have a direct stake in its success. Why should the Achesons work so hard to convince them that they do have such a stake?

3. The Nationalities Problem

No doubt the last five centuries of history could stand a lot of revision — and not alone in Russia — if human affairs could be unreeled backward. Perhaps Siberia should be returned to its aboriginal tribes, Bokhara restored as an independent emirate, Georgia given full independence. Perhaps the Ukraine, though its history and culture have been so long and so densely interwoven with Russia's that no one really knows precisely where one ends and the other begins, should be cleanly severed from Russia.

These are serious problems, particularly for the peoples involved. No one in his senses can make light of them. We can only pray that some day they will be solved without bloodshed and recrimination by democratic means. But they are ethnic and territorial problems in the same category as the Serb-Croat struggle in Yugoslavia, the Bavarian independence movement in Germany, Breton national aspirations in France. *They are not inherently a part of the communist problem with which mankind is called upon to wrestle.*

The issue of Ukrainian statehood, to take the sorest of the sore points in Russia's mosaic of races, existed before the advent of Bolshevism and will continue after Bolshevism has become an evil memory. Its injection into the world-wide communist challenge can only divert attention and emotion from the larger and primary problem.

No genuine democrat would support any solution short of full Ukrainian independence within a Russian federation of equals. Neither would he question the natural right of Ukrainians to self-determination under adequate democratic safeguards. Whether they choose to remain as an equal partner in a free Russia, or prefer to go it alone as a sovereign state is hardly a decision that foreigners, however well-meaning (or Ukrainian *émigrés,* for that matter), can take upon themselves. The people themselves must make those internal decisions, and they will be able to do so only after the Soviet regime ceases to exist. Whatever the ultimate solution, whatever one's private view of the most just and desirable solution, it is without intrinsic relevance to the struggle of free men — in concert with their kind within the USSR — against the communist menace.

It would be presumptuous for outsiders to give answers to the thousand-and-one thorny domestic questions which will have to be answered after the fall of the Soivets. Our rights and obligations, I believe, are limited to the problem we have *in common* with *all* the inhabitants of the Soviet sphere: namely, how most expeditiously to free them and the rest of the human race from the abominations of Bolshevism.

We can labor for the liberation of all of Czechoslovakia from its Red fetters without becoming involved in the domestic issue of the ultimate relations between the Czechs and the Slovaks. We can undertake to help overthrow the Red regime in Hungary without prescribing specific solutions for the minority problems in that country. It is within our competence, in the interests of the survival of the civilization we cherish, to shield Germany against being Bolshevized; but it surely is not within our competence to rule on Bavarian independence or Austro-German union.

By the same logic free men, in committing themselves to the liberation of the entire USSR from its Soviet chains, do not acquire the right to blueprint the size and shape of the successor state or states. Any such attempt could only complicate and perhaps wreck the alliance for the common objective we have in view.

Were the free world to champion sovereign statehood for the Ukraine, Byelorussia, Georgia, Azerbaidjan, Turkestan, a dozen or two dozen other areas, it would risk the alienation of (1) Great Russians believing in the unity of the empire; (2) non-Russians who prefer a federated system like Switzerland or that of the United States; (3) ethnic groups omitted from the list of future independent countries. On the other hand, were the free world to champion an undivided Russia, it would risk the enmity of millions of non-Russians who crave separate statehood.

We have no alternative, in sober fact, but to avoid meddling with these secondary problems. As Professor Burnham has underlined, it would not "be proper at any time for America to prescribe in detail the political and social arrangements that will replace the Soviet state system." What applies to America applies to its associates in the free world. Whether any or all of the hundred-odd national areas will remain as equal members in a union of equals, or will begin a separate and sovereign existence, is for the people themselves to decide. It is pertinent to the larger struggle only in the sense that liquidation of the Bolshevik power is the precondition for *any* popular democratic decisions.

It is sometimes argued that we should help inflame racial and national antagonisms within the Soviet empire as a tactic of political harassment: to add to the internal tensions plaguing the Kremlin. This is expediency carried to the most immoral extreme. Morals aside, it would assuredly backfire, as Rosenberg's dismemberment policies backfired during the war. For one thing, dissensions among the subjects can only strengthen the power of the regime. For another, the threat of arbitrary dismemberment might operate to rally one hundred million Great Russians and tens of millions of non-Russians around the Kremlin. Most important of all, the free world would be guilty of invading a vital area of internal affairs, in which no self-respecting Russian citizen can tolerate outside pressures and dictation.

This seems to me the common sense of the complex ethnic problem in Russia, so far as fighters against the whole Soviet system are concerned. When Americans speak of friendship for the Russian people, they refer not only to those who are Russians racially but to all the inhabitants of that country. To us they are equally citizens of the geographical entity known before 1917 as Russia and thereafter as the Soviet Union, and equally victims of the Soviet usurpers. This admittedly may not be scientifically accurate, but it avoids a lot of divisive semantics.

Americans, Britons, and others who make sovereignty for the Ukraine or Slovakia or any other area a precondition for common struggle against the Kremlin seem to me to be unwittingly playing the Kremlin's game. If Slovak or Ukrainian nationhood is for any reason close to their hearts, they have every right to advocate it, precisely as they might advocate Basque, Walloon, Breton, or Macedonian nationhood. They do *not* have a right to confound that issue with the unrelated task — so much larger and more pressing that it must have priority on the agenda of mankind today — of canceling out the Soviet regime and all its extensions beyond the Soviet borders.

Among the dispersed *émigrés* from the Soviet Union there are extremist Russian chauvinists who reject the principle of self-determination. They regard Russia as eternally "one and indivisible." Any analysis which concedes the possibility of secessions seems to them proof that the analyst is a "dismemberer of Russia."

They are more than balanced by non-Russian extremists who also reject self-determination, demanding an advance pledge of absolute sovereignty for their particular area. In their partisan emotion, they proclaim that "the Russian people proper, the Muscovites, could scarcely be interested in the collapse of Bolshevism and a change in the totalitarian regime." * If the Kremlin, too, believed this, its commissars assuredly would sleep more easily. Millions of "Muscovites," sharing the blessings of prison camps with Ukrainians, Azerbaidjanians, Mongolians, and so on, would be horrified by that judgment in exile. In any case, in the eyes of such non-Russian chauvinists my analysis will presumably be damned as "Russian imperialism."

Perhaps the two sets of intolerance cancel each other out. In six years of residence in the Soviet Union, I came into close contact with men and women of all the principal ethnic groups in the

---

* *Ukrainian Information Service,* London, 1951. The recurrent assertion by certain non-Russian *émigrés* that ethnic Russians have not resisted Bolshevism is a sample of know-nothing partisanship and has been amply refuted, I trust, in the foregoing pages. They forget the White Guards, the army of the Constituent Assembly, the Kronstadt rebellion, the Vlassov Movement, indeed the permanent civil war in its entirety.

country. Moscow is a cosmopolitan city, and I came to know also cities like Kiev, Kharkov, Odessa, Tiflis. I had occasion to discuss politics frankly (so frankly that they were risking their freedom if not their lives) with Ukrainians, Georgians, Armenians, as well as Great Russians.

Yet at the end of those years I was not especially conscious of the "nationalities problem," except as a quite secondary and for the time being almost irrelevant area of thought and emotion. I listened to complaints about "Russian arrogance," against Moscow's iron control of supposedly "independent Soviet republics." The theoretical autonomy of "autonomous areas" was the target of endless jibes, as was the bogus "freedom of national culture," which in practice amounted to the privilege of mouthing the official inanities in your own language.

But not once did I hear anyone argue fervently for sovereign statehood for the Ukraine or Azerbaidjan, as the case might be. If a passion for secession from Russia existed in any of these men and women, it was certainly submerged in deeper anti-Soviet emotions. Against the colossal infamies, degradations, and sufferings to which the entire population was subjected, talk of "national independence" would have seemed trivial if not obscene. Those with sufficient psychic reserves and courage to protest at all protested against the denial of simple *human* independence.

My own impressions on this score are certainly not conclusive. I submit them for what they are worth. Having compared notes with others who lived long in the Soviet Union, I know that my experience in this respect is not unique. Only when we came into contact with certain non-Russians in the *émigré* world did we realize that the nationalities question held primacy in their emotions, even above their hatred of communism. This was true especially of non-Russians who, having emigrated before the revolution or at the start of the Soviet era, had not suffered its cruelties on their own bodies and souls. More recent *émigrés,* whether Great Russian or not, are in the main too keenly aware of the common travail of their countrymen of all races to be totally obsessed by purely national grievances.

In the ruthless minority which strapped Russia into its Soviet strait jacket, there were more non-Russians than Russians, in proportion to the country's ethnic ratios. Lenin was partly of German descent on his mother's side, Stalin was a Georgian, Trotsky a Jew, Antonov-Ovseenko a Ukrainian, Djerzhinsky a Pole. Of Djerzhinsky's successors as chief of the terror machine, only two, Yezhov and Kruglov, were Great Russians; Lavrentia Beria was a Georgian. The great dividing line through all the thirty-five Soviet years has not been racial or regional but ideological: between those who have been devoted to the regime and the great mass which has opposed it, if only silently in its heart.

Foreigners, American Congressmen included, who set themselves to juggling the Russian ethnic map are, I fear, far beyond their depth. The crazy-quilt pattern of minorities and minorities within minorities, complicated by intermarriage and colonization tides through the centuries, has been made more chaotic by trends since the revolution. Vast shifts in population have occurred, in utter disregard of ethnic patterns, as a by-product of industrialization and urbanization, and through huge forcible resettlement. Millions from all parts of the country have been transplanted to common slave-labor camps, creating a community of wretchedness stronger than any race feelings. During and since World War II millions more have been evacuated, deported, scattered.

There has been a mighty blending of blood and dispersal of peoples that will not be easily unscrambled, no matter how easily this is accomplished in *émigré* newspapers. Enemies of Bolshevism should not be diverted from their dedication by this issue. Their appeal to the Soviet people must be geared to their common cause: to the things that unite the victims of the police state, rather than the things that divide them. This view assuredly does not imply hostility to a separate national existence for any ethnic component. If the view is misunderstood, or distorted for partisan purposes, that is a risk we must take. No outsider has any inherent right either to oppose national separation or to insist upon it. Earnest foes of the Kremlin do have a right to oppose fragmentation of the anti-Kremlin forces on any postponable issue, and to insist that first things come first in a common front against the common challenge.

Not long ago a minor American official, addressing a Ukrainian mass meeting, spoke movingly of "the fate of the Ukraine under the domination of the Bolsheviks," reciting the litany of mass killings, exiles, forcible collectivization, suffered by Ukrainians. He was wasting breath, turning his good intentions into a travesty, by implying that only Ukrainians or especially the Ukraine were victimized. He forgot that all the peoples of the Soviet Union are in the same prison state and that they will remain there unless they force its walls *together*.

We must leave no margin for doubt that the fight, in alliance with the Soviet people, is not against "Russia" but against the Kremlin dictatorship; not to settle all of the country's problems in one fell swoop, but to provide a climate of freedom in which those problems can be tackled by the people themselves.

4. On "Provoking" the Kremlin

Free-world policy has been colored and at times paralyzed by the curious assumption that Moscow is itching for a final showdown — that it will unleash a world war the moment it is "provoked," if not sooner. The image behind this dread is of an idiot juggling explosives: He must not be rudely shocked or angered or he will drop them, despite the certainty of blowing himself to pieces.

It is not exactly flattering to the common sense of the Kremlin. Its bosses would have to be in a mad and suicidal mood deliberately to set off World War III. But they happen to be crazy as foxes, and far from courting destruction are interested above all else in safeguarding their power. Since it gives them the initiative, they make the most of our jitters. They hold the threat of war over our heads — and their own. But actually, there is no room for doubt, they are as terrified of war as we are, if not more so.

The Soviet leaders will not risk an all-out conflict until they are certain of victory, and they are much too realistic to think that vic-

tory is in the bag. War is a possibility in the present world crisis
whether anyone wants it or not. But there is no reason to scare ourselves with the specter of a touchy, trigger-happy, and supremely
self-confident Kremlin.

The low morale of its people, the dubious loyalty of its satellites,
its chilling memories of the last war, its backward economy and
transport as compared with ours — these argue against the notion
that the Soviet Union would knowingly ignite a war. Its overseers
know that the occupation of Europe, if they could accomplish it,
would not be the end but the beginning of the contest — as it was
for Nazi Germany. They know that *they* may be destroyed even if
Russia is not defeated: that Russia, in fact, might evade defeat by
throwing its Soviet regime to the capitalist lions.

Had the Politburo been looking for a convenient excuse to release
its juggernaut, at a time when its power in relation to ours was
greater than it is now, it had plenty to choose from. There was the
Truman Doctrine, the Marshall Plan, the Berlin airlift, UN intervention in Korea, NATO, to mention a few. Besides, dictatorships
are expert in rolling their own "provocations" when they need
them.

There was a period when the Soviet Union could easily have
overrun Europe; probably it could still do so. It could have swallowed Finland, which dared to kick the communists out of its
government, or seized Iran, or reinforced communist guerrillas in
Greece to the point of victory, or smashed the Berlin airlift. It could
have stamped out the deadliest challenge to Soviet authority in its
own bailiwick by crushing Tito's Yugoslavia.

It did none of these things. Why? Plainly because each of them
packed the risk of a war to a decision.

For years Western statesmen and pundits practically invited
Stalin to march to the Atlantic by proclaiming that he could do it
at will in a few weeks. He did not accept the invitation. Instead,
the Kremlin limited itself prudently to actions safely short of the
ultimate challenge, avoided overt military ventures, and, when
things seemed too hot, managed to retreat under some face-saving
pretext. Its one large-scale and overt use of military force, the

Korean invasion, was undertaken only after the withdrawal of American troops and only after repeated assurances by Washington that we had written off the peninsula as indefensible. And even then Moscow's role was kept as veiled and indirect as it could manage.

The great achievements in expanding the Soviet empire, it is well to bear in mind, were brought about by crafty exploitation of favorable conditions rather than by frontal attack. The Kremlin's aggressions have always been directed against small, helpless neighbors like the Central Asian principalities, Georgia, Mongolia, the three Baltic republics. Its one outright military adventure was the invasion of Finland in 1940; but that certainly seemed a sure thing.

For the rest, Stalin got half of Poland by a deal with Nazi Germany, as a bonus on duplicity; he grabbed the present satellite countries with the tacit consent of his wartime allies; and he conquered China from within by default of democratic statesmanship. The very success of these methods doubtless has confirmed Moscow's preference for indirect methods. A real, undisguised aggressive war against the free world — on the order of Hitler's offensive — is not in the character of Kremlin behavior.

Dictators in general do not lightly risk their hard-won power. Even the Nazi fanatics counted on quick and easy blitz victories, a deal with a Munich-minded England, and American neutrality. The communist bosses are aware that, whatever the final outcome, war would begin with the destruction of their industrial centers, fuel sources, communications — the very foundations of their power. The supposition that they would deliberately invite another installment of the kind of destruction and carnage they had in the last war, but with atomic trimmings, risking their own total extinction, runs counter to logic. The fate of Hitler and Mussolini surely cannot be far from the minds of Malenkov and Company.

As they look back on the Russo-German war, these men are conscious of facts which the non-Soviet world seems somehow to have forgotten. The most terrifying of these, from where they sit, is that Soviet Russia was quickly crowded to the sheer brink of defeat. More territory was in enemy hands than ever before in

Russian history, and popular morale was near the vanishing point before the comeback began. In the end, and only with overwhelming help from American industry, victory was snatched from the very jaws of disaster, at a ghastly cost. Had not the mighty Allied air offensives sapped Germany's vigor, Russia would very likely have fallen to the invaders despite American aid.

In the light of their hairsbreadth escape, Soviet leaders today can hardly be too optimistic about another and more terrible struggle, this time without first-class allies, and with America aligned *against* them. China and the restive East European satellites are not adequate substitutes for Great Britain and the United States. In the light of the violent disturbances throughout Red Europe in June and July of 1953, they would be unmitigated fools to base excessive hopes and plans on the military forces and manpower of their puppet states; whether East German, Czechoslovak, Polish, and Hungarian guns will be pointed eastward or westward in the hour of decision is certainly a wide-open question.

They remember, too, the facts about the German invasion set forth in this book. They can have no doubt that a showdown with the free world would involve a showdown with the Russian peoples and the other captive populations. They cannot count on the absolute loyalty of their armed forces. A peacetime army can be kept comparatively well fed, indoctrinated, and more or less isolated from the temper of the population at large. A vast army for war, mobilized quickly from the farms and mines and factories, is another matter. It reflects the discontents and muffled aspirations of the masses.

These masses were deliberately *rejected* by the Nazis. The picture might have been quite different had the invaders come to liberate Russia, not to dismember and colonize it. The Malenkov crowd has cause to fear that the picture *will* be different in a war with democracies — the one test to which its regime has not yet been subjected — fighting the Bolshevik tyrants rather than Russia and the Russians. The more clearly and emphatically we can drive that difference home now, in advance of hostilities, the more fearful the tyrants will be of touching off hostilities. *Far from "pro-*

voking" a war, an alliance with the Russian peoples is the best in-surance against the catastrophe.

At best, despite our failure to differentiate between the regime and its subjects, the Politburo would have to earmark a large part of its military forces and millions of security personnel just for holding down the lid at home. The civil war that has been going on since 1917 would be intensified, making a two-front conflict — with the foreign entente and internally — inescapable from the start. The disillusionments since the victory in 1945, the tens of millions who remember their glimpse of life without Soviets — these are elements the shrewd manipulators in the Kremlin cannot omit from their calculations. The country has seen the rulers too close to ignominious defeat, dependent on capitalist allies for survival, to believe in their invincibility.

Every one of the factors that made the population tolerant of, and even enthusiastic for, the German invaders is still operative. The Russian people "are discontented to the point of hatred for the Soviet system," a Red Army officer told official American interrogators. "It will take ten to twenty years for the Soviet regime to regain the control of the people's minds it had achieved before the war." And we know how limited that control really was. A New York *Times* dispatch from Berlin dated May 13, 1953, began with this statement:

"Five former Soviet officers, who deserted the Soviet army, said yesterday the West should regard the Soviet army as a potential ally in the liberation of the Soviet Union from Bolshevik domination."

Such *émigré* military opinion, of course, must be discounted. But the fact remains that Malenkov can be no more certain of the unequivocal loyalty of his fighting forces than we can be of their unequivocal hostility to him. It is another serious hazard — one that it is within our power to enlarge and intensify — which acts as a brake on Soviet war-making propensities and capacities.

Free-world jitters have been expressed, in another dimension, in a tendency to exaggerate Soviet Russia's physical might, even after leaving political and morale considerations out of the reckoning. The country is rich primarily in manpower. But that superiority is not decisive without the economic and industrial sinews for the attrition of a long war. The Soviets' one hundred eighty millions were helpless against Germany's eighty millions until American supplies began to pour in.

Soviet productivity is being enormously expanded, it is true. But in comparison with the democracies it is still sharply inferior. How much of its vast manpower could the Kremlin keep adequately armed and supplied in a war of several years' duration?

Food is as vital for victory as guns and planes. We shipped two million tons of it to Russia during the last war, to which Great Britain and Canada added another 300,000 tons. An escaped Red Army officer recently wrote that, in his opinion, Stalin might have squeezed through without American military equipment, but certainly not without American food. Soviet Russia is chronically on short rations in peacetime; all-out war would remove every able-bodied male farmer from the land.

It is misleading to think of the Red Army, immense and formidable as it may be, without reference to the immensity of the country. The Soviet frontiers are not only long but continents apart. In relation to the colossal spaces involved, the Soviet railroad system is pitifully small — there is a single line across the whole of Asia, for instance. Transfer of forces from one area to another would be slow and difficult. One expert has estimated that Russia could not afford to commit more than half its ground forces to an operation in Western Europe; the rest would have to be deployed in the Far East, the Near East, and other exposed segments of its huge periphery. The Kremlin cannot know where danger lurks, and must spread its available strength to defend nearly the whole of its frontier.

Meanwhile the major and probably decisive phase of war — attrition through the skies from every point on the compass — would gather deadly momentum. In that telltale contest Moscow's chief advantage, its numbers, would cease to be relevant. But its major disadvantages — domestic morale, rebellious foreign populations, inadequate productive capacity — would become sharper, and cumulative in their effects.

The overwhelming portion of Soviet industry is packed into a triangle from Leningrad and the Ukraine on the west to the newly industrialized regions of Central Siberia. It is an extremely vulnerable air target. What is dispersal in terms of ground action is not always dispersal in the equation of air warfare. Malenkov could hardly hope to transfer his industrial base to Europe. The Ruhr, Lorraine, and other industrial centers may fall into his hands — but surely not intact; and their effective restoration could be prevented by air power.

Against this background, the Moscow masters can hardly view the prospect of a final world struggle with equanimity. To suppose that they would rush into it if angered or insulted is to assume that they have lost all sense of self-preservation. Returning from a careful study of European defenses in 1951, General Carl Spaats expressed confidence that "we could win a world war and, even more important, *the Kremlin shares this conviction.*" When, in addition, the picture is appraised from the political and psychological vantage points, this judgment is strongly reinforced.

Soviet Russia is a great military power. There is no intention here to blur or underrate that fact. Maximum rearmament by the free world is imperative — all other measures are futile without that basic guarantee. But it is far from the overwhelming, almost invincible power conjured up by propaganda and our own state of mind. In its most sanguine hours the Kremlin cannot count on a better than fifty-fifty chance of victory, and those are not the odds on which it can be expected to stake its life.

Cold war — which is just another name for good old communist methods of troublemaking — is more in the Soviet line. That has paid off handsomely, and it is a field in which communists have no peers. Why should they ever abandon it for the risks of a shooting war? We may be sure they will continue to cook up peppery "incidents" and "civil wars." They will commit puppet forces while conserving their own. They will do everything they can to deepen the miasma of fears and confusions so congenial to their revolutionary talents. They will provide ingenious diversions to scatter American military power and drain American resources and economic vitality, bleeding and badgering us without letup. They will use war threats and "peace offensives" alike to keep us off balance.

But they will avoid taking the irrevocable step that would bring atomic destruction and domestic turmoil — perhaps to the point of insurrection — to the citadel of their dictatorship. The prevailing fear of the Soviets by the free world is a crucial triumph for the Kremlin in the war of nerves. It has forced us to play the game of world affairs from weakness, when we have every reason to play it boldly from strength.

Stalin, General Douglas MacArthur declared when the Soviet leader was alive, "has been engaging in the greatest bulldozing diplomacy history has ever recorded." That diplomacy, he added, "has found its success not so much in his own military strength or, indeed, in any overt threat to commit it to battle, but in the moral weakness of the free world."

In retrospect it should be clear that a firm stand from the start would have saved the non-Soviet world from its present plight. We could have used force to keep the corridors to Berlin open without the slightest risk of an all-out war — and thereby headed off the Korean adventure, prepared while the Berlin crisis diverted our attention and our strength. We could have pursued communist planes to their Manchurian nesting places and cut off the flood of Chinese "volunteers" on the northern side of the Yalu, without precipitating a world war. Indeed, our failure to do such things presents the greatest hazard of all — because it may lead the Kremlin to misjudge our will to resist and therefore to attempt one bluff too many.

America must take courage for the future, keep itself supremely strong militarily and economically, and leave no doubt that we would be prepared to use our power to the limit if no other alternative were left to us. We must make Moscow afraid of provoking *us*. That will be proof that we have heeded the sound advice of General William J. Donovan to "put aside our own fear and create fear in the mind of the enemy." We must play our cards, I repeat, from strength. And our trump is not the atomic bomb. It is the permanent civil war in the USSR, where our secret allies wait for our recognition, support, and leadership.

XIX. The Kremlin's Anti-Russian Friends

1. *Vicarious Sadism*

In his time of moral collapse, Maxim Gorki was once implored to intercede with the Kremlin, where his influence was great, for literary friends rotting in GPU dungeons or awaiting execution. Not only did he refuse but he used the occasion to express publicly his sympathy for the prison wardens and executioners. "People whose historical duty it is to kill some beings in order to save others," he declared, "are *martyrs,* and my conscience will never allow me to condemn them."

It was a degrading spectacle: The champion of the denizens of the "lower depths," in his twilight years, championing the secret police and the firing squads! He who had spoken so eloquently for the lowly and persecuted now viewing life strictly from the vantage point of those in power! The fact that he was in due course crushed by the monstrosity he was defending does not affect the pathos of his surrender to totalitarian thinking.

In his own person Gorki supplied a sample and a symbol of the hideous thing that was happening to men's minds and hearts everywhere in relation to the Soviet state. For millions of the "progressive," the high-minded, and well-meaning in all countries had chosen, like the great Russian writer, to side with the Kremlin terrorists against their victims. They had identified themselves psychologically with the masters against their slaves, with the oligarchs against the masses.

Gorki, up there on the heights with the potentates, sharing their heady privileges, having streets and cities named in his honor, had at least the excuse of human frailty. But what of those hordes of Soviet admirers beyond the Soviet frontiers, identifying themselves with a faraway omnipotence in which they had no direct share? Their obsession is hard to explain.

Yet it is, I believe, of the same order as Gorki's. In spirit, if not in fact, they too joined the engineers of a "new society" ruthless enough to shrug off pity. They too partook of unlimited power. At the bargain price of a new allegiance, they bought the illusion of being bold revolutionaries, released from the bonds of fellow feeling and moral scruple — Nietzschean men superior to the squeamish rabble.

It is not true that they supported the Soviet setup *despite* its brutality. They supported it *because* of its brutality. *We* are not milk-and-water reformers, they told themselves, but men of action, capable of any crime and no conscience to plague us. In spirit they stood with the almighty hierarchs on the ledge of Lenin's tomb as the gray masses marched by on Soviet holidays. They associated themselves inwardly with godlike decisions that doomed millions, and stood ankle-deep in blood in execution cellars pulling official triggers.

The phenomenon of vicarious sadism is still with us, though on a diminishing scale, and still preens itself in the shoddy feathers of liberalism. A strange, perverse sympathy for the Red killers in Russia and its satellite areas, in Korea, and in fifth-column formations in their own countries, can still be found among otherwise normal men and women. It is a phenomenon that bears examining today, in the context of a world held at bay by the industrious "martyrs" of the Kremlin.

The high point of stupefied, know-nothing admiration for everything Soviet in the non-Soviet world was probably reached in the early 1930's. The world-wide economic depression at the time happened to coincide with the launching of a Five-Year Plan in the USSR. The hysterical hopes of millions, born of their despairs, found a focus in mysterious and faraway Russia. They needed to believe that someone somewhere had the answer. A cheerful and "broad-minded" tolerance of Kremlin depravities therefore became standard equipment of all right-thinking liberals and fashionable for nearly everyone else.

The energetic communist catchwords of the time — human engineering, collectivization, social planning, and so on — were being spelled out in bottomless anguish for the whole Soviet population. But in the foreign propaganda they glowed with the ardor of men's yearning for a better world. Stuart Chase, writing in 1932, concluded a treatise on economic planning for America with the stirring challenge: "Why should the Russians have all the fun of remaking a world?" They were having fun in strange ways, those Russians!

André Gide, recalling his state of mind before the journey to Utopia that cured him, wrote: "Who shall say what the Soviet Union has been to us? More than a chosen land — an example, a guide. What we have dreamed of, what we hardly dared to hope, but towards which we were straining all our will and all our strength, was coming into being over there. A land existed where Utopia was in process of becoming reality." In 1934, another American and I traveled to Switzerland especially to meet Romain Rolland, because we both so admired him, to tell him some truth about the Russia we had just left. The frail old man refused to listen, begged us with stricken eyes not to disturb his faith.

The long-distance cheering squads would have no truck with sordid facts. Their eyes were fixed trancelike on wondrous statistical goals in the dim future. Their joyous noises drowned out the weeping of the wounded and the moans of the dying and, of course, the nagging reports of dissenters.

Understanding and pity for the sorrowing Russians? They renounced such things for themselves and denounced it in others as bourgeois sentimentality. As one correspondent — their favorite because he pandered to their illusions — put it, "I am a reporter, not a humanitarian." After all, they told one another, you can't make omelets without breaking eggs. Their sanctimonious password was, "What if a few more millions die?"

With dazzling courage these Americans and their fellows in other lands were ready to fight the good fight to the last Russian. The woes of sharecroppers in our South or of oppressed masses in Patagonia absorbed so much of their compassion that they had none to spare for the Soviet peoples. Injustice and denial of human rights elsewhere stirred Stalin's partisans to fervid protest; the same things in the Soviet Union stirred them to applause.

The Russian desolations seemed in some strange fashion transfigured for the faithful into noble "sacrifices" for their cause. The very magnitude of the torments seemed to them a measure of the "firmness" and "devotion" of the tormentors. It was all "scientific" in the vivisectionist sense, and its essence was a cruel indifference to the martyrdom of the Soviet peoples. In effect these were excluded from the human family, tagged for the honor of Bolshevik scalpels.

To raise hard currency for industrialization needs, the Politburo had opened its operating theaters to foreign spectators. Tens of thousands of them, chiefly from the United States, swarmed over the stricken Russian land under the auspices of Intourist, the Soviet travel bureau, or shepherded by left-wing professors and clergymen and Kremlin press agents. Year after year I watched the cavortings of the pilgrims among the muffled miseries. Amazingly, they found great squalor not only picturesque but inspiring. The worried, unsmiling faces all around them were just a national characteristic, or even proof of popular concentration on Great Historic Tasks.

The visitors babbled excitedly about the lovely "birth pangs of a new world" and the splendid "sacrifices." They got an emotional kick out of every cemetery and abattoir. Nor would they permit anyone who knew the facts to spoil their fun. How many times was I assured by newcomers that I couldn't see the forest for the trees; that I had been too close to the picture; that I wasn't taking the long view. However phrased, their real point was that I was allowing compassion for the immediate victims to blur my vision of the glories to come.

I was present once when an earnest tourist tried to make conversation through his guide with a sullen-faced woman in a queue outside a food shop. He wanted to be able to say, on returning to Brooklyn or Hollywood, that he had talked with the plain people.

"Tell her," he commanded, "that I find everything here so very *interesting.*"

The woman frowned. She examined his ruddy countenance and American clothes in silent deliberation. Then she muttered:

"Yes, it's interesting to watch a fire . . . but not to be in it."

Now and then some of these visitors were swept into the flames. These were men and women who, having decided to settle in their dreamland, made the terrible blunder of renouncing their citizenship; or people of Russian birth whose American passports were confiscated by the too hospitable police. Trapped, scared, embittered, they then wept for their lost freedom and became obsessed by a new dream: a dream of escape.

This, on the whole, was also the experience of foreigners who sojourned in Stalin's vivisectionist laboratory for long periods, as engineers or correspondents or diplomats. Their tolerance of the regime faded and in the end turned into loathing. It is not an accident that nearly all former sympathizers with the Bolshevik cause who turned against it after living in the Soviet Union — William C. Bullitt, Max Eastman, William Henry Chamberlin, Leon Dennen, Fred E. Beal, Edmund Stevens, Louis Fischer, to mention a few — admire the Russian peoples almost to the same degree that they abhor the Soviet regime.

I count myself among their number. My imported enthusiasm for the Great Experiment soured as the men, women and children around me ceased to be statistical digits and became sentient human beings. I came to feel as they did. There was ample evidence that they hated the regime. But somehow I no longer needed conventional "proofs"; the proof was in my own emotions, once I had begun to react as they did. I could at last gauge their sentiments by my own. I was now viewing the scene through Russian eyes, appraising it through Russian hearts.

2. Legends, Old and New

Uncritical and orgiastic support of "the Russian revolution," meaning the governing clique, subsided somewhat in the following years. It became more circumspect and defensive. The man-made famine of 1932–1933; the blood purges, and then the pact with Hitler had their effect. The apologists, after all, lived in dread of waking up some morning to a new chapter of Bolshevik trickery or horror needing to be justified to a fed-up world opinion. The standard excuses were wearing thin, and adoration had to be diluted with "ifs" and "buts."

Revivified Stalin worship in the war years, when the Kremlin magically became a freedom-loving ally, was different in quality. It had in it less of the earlier pristine faith in the millenium via execution squads.

In the 1930's the pro-Soviet legend had revolved around a system that was different, unique, a dictatorship ennobled by godlike cruelty beyond the petty judgments of mere mortals. But the revised legend fashioned by the comrades of the OWI, the BBC, and other Allied agencies celebrated a regime not too different from our own — democratic and liberal in its own inscrutable way. Under the earlier concept the Kremlin was changing the world. In the OWI fairy tales the world was changing the Kremlin. The USSR was now presumably moving closer to our way of life. A hundred experts explained that Soviet Russia was moving closer to capitalism, the capitalist world was moving closer to socialism — and soon the twain would meet and embrace midway.

One can imagine how Stalin and his gang writhed under this insult; how they ached with impatience to disprove it. The notion that they had been tamed by time and transformed, as it were, into Soviet Rotarians, was intended as a compliment; but to self-respecting communists it was a deadly affront. They could barely conceal their impatience to throw the bourgeois moralizings of the Atlantic Charter into the "dust bin of history."

There was another difference. The earlier glorification had been largely spontaneous, kindled by wishful thinking and fanned into flame by eager hopes. The new pro-Soviet sentiment had to be pumped up by sweating propagandists working in relays around the clock. Communist Russia had to be "sold" to the world through appeals to wartime team spirit, bolstered by elaborate falsehoods. It was fitting that so many members of the public relations and advertising professions took part in that enterprise. On the air and in the press, the eagerness to give Stalin the benefit of every doubt became the hallmark of political savvy. In time it became downright unpatriotic to doubt that the Georgian butcher was a kind of Russian Roosevelt, beloved by his cattle and throbbing with a newly acquired love of the Four Freedoms.

The illusions persisted in the last year of the war and even the years that followed, when the Kremlin seemed to be taking pleasure in making its adulators look foolish. According to Robert Sherwood, Harry Hopkins, whose influence on American policy was enormous, "had nothing but contempt for those jittery Americans who were forever looking for communists under the bed." If only they had really looked! After Yalta, Hopkins wrote:

"The Russians had proved that they could be reasonable, and far-seeing, and there wasn't any doubt in the minds of the President or any of us that we could live with them and get along with them peacefully for as far into the future as any of us could imagine. . . ." Not that Hopkins closed his eyes to the difficulty of coexistence of clashing systems in a shrinking world. "We do not want the people of the world enslaved with any more totalitarian governments," he wrote in his political testament. "I simply think that the Western world is not big enough for the kind of democracy we have and, for instance, *Mr. Franco in Spain*."

Said Churchill, in the House of Commons at the end of 1944: "Marshal Stalin and the Soviet leaders wish to live in honorable friendship and equality with the Western democracies. . . . I feel also that their word is their bond. I know of no government which stands to its obligations, even in its own despite, more solidly than the Russian Soviet Government. I decline absolutely to embark here on a discussion about Russian good faith." He embarked on it later, in Fulton, Missouri. President Roosevelt, too, had a lot to tell Congress and his fireside audiences about the credibility of the Kremlin's word.

Sir Stafford Cripps, in an interview after his mission to Moscow, said: "The Soviet government has no intention, and of this I am certain, to demand anything more in the way of territorial agression . . . This I can say with certainty as I have had it direct from Mr. Stalin himself and it has been stated publicly by the Soviet government on more than one occasion recently: The Russians do not want to interfere with the internal affairs of other countries. They wish to live and let live."

In 1945, when bright schoolboys knew better, Henry Morgenthau, Jr., Secretary of the Treasury, could write that "there has never been advanced any reasonable grounds for supposing that America is really menaced by Russia or the spread of communism." That should make a fitting epitaph on American graves in Korea.

Ralph Ingersoll, ex-publisher of the pink *PM*, wrote a whole book lambasting the British for doubting Soviet motives and maneuvering for positions of strategic advantage at the war's end, in contrast with Generals Eisenhower and Marshall, who entertained no such low suspicions of an ally. "Russia has only one primary interest," Ingersoll opined, "and that is to be let alone." To which one reviewer, Edgar Ansell Mowrer, gave the perfect riposte: "Let alone as a hermit or as a safecracker?" Late in 1945 a book entitled *We Can Do Business with Russia* was published, and favorably reviewed; Eric Johnston, then president of the United States Chamber of Commerce, was indiscreet enough to write the foreword.

These are random samplings of the addiction to know-nothing "friendship" for the Kremlin. Since then, of course, a lot of blood has flowed under the bridges. The Soviet conquest of one East European country after another, the unsuccessful Politburo adven-

tures in Greece and Iran, the cold-blooded attempt to starve Berlin
into submission, the subjection of China, and finally the Korean
aggression have helped awaken millions of the starry-eyed to
reality. More to the point, communism ceased to be exclusively a
Russian affliction. It had become a direct, immediate and tangible
threat to the civilization most of us happen to cherish. What had
passed as liberal tolerance of an "experiment" emerged more clearly
as a species of treachery to mankind.

But legends of the old and the wartime brands alike have survived in varying proportions. The tribe of fellow travelers, vague
sympathizers, and "liberal" apologists is still numerous, articulate
and influential. In all the free nations it continues to colonize every
department of life, from government to churches, from schools to
labor unions.

On the whole these folk are not as candid as they used to be. The
direct, full-throated hosannahs are confined to Communist Party
members and party press organs. The auxiliary forces must content
themselves with rhetoric about peace, one world, coexistence, and
the atomic age as affected by American "imperialism," "cartelism,"
and the like. In many places it poses as neutralism, as if freedom
and slavery were both abominations to be equally evaded by a
middle and neutral indifference.

What the current tribe has in common with the Intourist pilgrims of yore and with hired Soviet boosters is *their deep disdain
for the Russian peoples*. The ordeal of the Soviet millions doesn't
touch them. They resent being reminded of it. Their concern for
human rights and decencies, so lively when Spain or Argentina is
on the agenda, expires abruptly at the borders of Russia itself. The
sentimental-libertarian approach suitable for other dark areas is
abandoned in the Soviet sphere, where only hard-boiled criteria of
"historical necessity" apply.

3. *Who's "Anti-Russian"?*

For a long time now I have been observing the attitudes of foreigners to the Soviet Union. I think they can be fairly stated in the

form of a law of behavior: *The greater the tolerance for the Soviet regime, the greater the contempt for the Soviet peoples.* Friendship for Soviet Russia in the Moscow-sponsored sense of the sentiment always turns out, on analysis, to be insulting to the Soviet population.

How could it be otherwise? Obviously it is not easy to be friendly to a ghoulish regime and its victims, to a vivisectionist and the doomed animals, at the same time. Dedicated admirers have little choice, therefore, but to convince themselves that the Russians are a lot of subhumans anyhow, and probably enjoy being pushed around, engineered, terrorized, and liquidated.

The contempt for the people shows up in the familiar statement that Bolshevism, though unsuited for Americans or Britons, is quite all right for the coarse-grained Russians. It is manifest in the readiness of the official "friends" to kill off any number of Soviet people for the cause. Often enough, in fact, the derogation is unconcealed and loud.

Walter Duranty, of course, offers a convenient case study. He doesn't even try to conceal his low estimate of the despicable rabble among whom he lived. He has no patience, he wrote in his autobiography, with reporters who "prate of ruthless methods and the iron age and lament the brutality which drove through to its goal regardless of sacrifices and suffering." After all, he shrugged, the Stalinist methods "were most fitted to the Russian character and folkways in that they established Asiatic absolutism."

In effect the apologists ask us to believe that Russians and the other races of the USSR are wholly without the sensitivity to pain, humiliation, and outrage which God implanted in Westerners. The blunt fact is that all the nonsense about a Russian relish for absolutism is farfetched rationalization. Most of those who squeeze out complex excuses for the Kremlin's despotism at the same time demand freedom for other peoples and races, some of which have had less experience with the blessing than the Russians. Glorification of the Soviet overlords makes a contemptuous and condescending attitude toward their subjects inevitable; all the rest is a matter of form.

The cream of the cruel jest is that those who hold such insulting opinions of the Russians consider themselves honestly, even with a touch of exaltation, friends of Russia. Which in turn, by current definition, makes them liberals and progressives, as distinguished from reactionaries and crypto-fascists who suppose that Russians not only desire and deserve freedom but would recognize the thing and could take it without ill effects.

The sad fact, of more than thirty-five years' duration, is that the peoples of Russia have been denied the moral support and humane understanding of the non-Soviet world. Democratic public opinion, so sensitive to the fate of freedom elsewhere, has been indifferent to its fate in Russia. The opponents of the Soviet dictatorship have none of the solace and encouragement from free men and women upon which fighters for freedom have been able to count in almost all other times and places. The foreigners whom the Soviet masses have been permitted to see have been almost exclusively individuals and delegations come to pay homage to the dictators. The only words from outside to reach the Soviet citizenry (until the recent and belated intrusions of anticommunist broadcasts) have been paeans of praise for the Kremlin demigods. Democratic countries have not only treated the Red regime as an equal among governments but have begged for the privilege of "normal relations" with that abnormal government.

In the czarist period, enemies of the autocracy drew strength from the knowledge that they had understanding friends in the outside world. Even their acts of terrorism, they knew, would be condoned by millions who recognized their desperate plight. As George F. Kennan has rightly pointed out, "the Russian revolutionary movement . . . had enjoyed warm sympathy among the American public for fifty years prior to the Bolshevik seizure of power in 1917." The same was true of every other democratic public.

In 1903 Nicholas II announced his intention of visiting Italy. Fearful that an attempt might be made on his life, the Italian government arrested the better-known Russian exiles in the country, among them Michael Gotz. This act aroused such a storm of indignation in Italy that Gotz was immediately released, and the czar canceled his trip.

Eminent Europeans and Americans rallied as a matter of course to the support of the czar's internal enemies. Petitions in behalf of condemned revolutionists were almost routine, from men like Gerhart Hauptmann in Germany, Anatole France in France, Bernard Shaw and Wickham Stead in England, George Brandes in Denmark, Maurice Maeterlinck in Belgium, Mark Twain and William English Walling in the United States. Men of this caliber placed themselves at the head of committees, inspired by Russian exiles who appealed to them for help.

Henry Nevinson described how, in 1907, reports of the ordeal of Maria Spiridonova, a twenty-one-year-old girl who had killed General Lushenovsky, stirred all London; a great mass meeting called by the "Friends of Russian Freedom" filled Trafalgar Square to overflowing and funds were raised to help the assassin escape from Siberia. Nevinson speaks of the "outburst of pity" for the girl and the "invective against the Russian tyrants" on that occasion.

In the 1880's when George Kennan exposed political persecution in his two-volume *Siberia and the Exile System,* he was instantly hailed as a valorous liberal and, of course, a self-evident friend of Russia. Russia still meant its people, not its government. But in recent years, when journalists have reported the unadorned facts about terror in the same country — a terror incomparably more odious — they have been promptly labeled "anti-Russian" and denounced as reactionaries to boot.

After a meeting at the Lowell Institute at which Kennan reported on political conditions in Russia, Mark Twain arose and in a choked voice exclaimed: "If such a government cannot be overthrown otherwise than by dynamite, then thank God for dynamite!" In 1890 Mark Twain was one of the founders, along with Julia Ward Howe, Thomas Wentworth Higginson, William Lloyd Garrison, and others, of a Society of American Friends of Russian Freedom. A similar society existed in England.

Where are the friends of Russian freedom today? For the most part in communist "front" organizations manipulated by the

Kremlin's intelligence agents. In the time of the elder Kennan and Mark Twain the Russian peoples rated as human beings. Russian history was no different than it is today. The record of agelong subjection was clear enough. But it did not occur to foreigners to consign the nation to eternal servitude, or to discount their sufferings as investments for a future justified in terms of historical necessity. The feelings of mankind had not yet been corrupted by communist propaganda and totalitarian-liberal obfuscation; its capacity for simple compassion had not yet been anesthetized by slogans.

An *émigré* Russian historian, the late Professor G. Fedotov, writing in 1946, made a penetrating comment: "Coming together with foreigners, the Russians of the Empire had to blush for their autocracy and slavery. Had they everywhere met obsequiousness to the Russian Czar similar to that now shown by some Europeans and Americans for Stalin, it would never have occurred to them that something was wrong in their own home." *

The sadistic Vishinsky, as Stalin's chief prosecutor, was directly and personally responsible for murdering thousands of innocent men and women. But democratic statesmen do not refuse to shake his bloody hand. On the contrary, after his exertions in lambasting the United States, Comrade Vishinsky once hurried to the yacht of an American ex-diplomat for lunch, relaxation and the admiration of twittering ladies.

As a theory of social reorganization, as an economic blueprint, Bolshevism has been a ghastly failure. But as propaganda it has been magnificently successful. And in large measure this victory has been semantic. Communists and their fellow travelers have managed to corrupt and to corner the vocabulary of progress, liberalism, idealism. For every ugly fact they have provided a beguiling label. Systematic exploitation of labor is "economic democracy," and feudalization of peasants on government estates is "collective farming."

Though revolted by Soviet realities, many people cannot work

* *Review of Politics,* Notre Dame University Press, January, 1946.

up the courage to break with the nomenclature. They will swallow almost any atrocity if the alternative is to risk being called a "Red baiter" or "reactionary." They are intimidated by the noble verbiage in which ignoble facts have been clothed. But here I want to emphasize a specific aspect of that semantic conquest: the Muscovite miracle whereby opponents of the Soviet tyranny are called "anti-Russian," while those who contemn the Russians and condemn them to the role of guinea pigs are hailed as "pro-Russian."

The generations of Russian foes of autocracy who fled abroad to continue their fight, from Herzen and Bakunin to Lenin and Plekahnov and Trotsky, were universally respected as exiled patriots and spokesmen of their countrymen at home. No one sneered at them as anti-Russians or deserters. The present generation of exiles is a thousand times more numerous. Its zeal for the liberation of their country is, if anything, more intense because the provocations are so much greater. Yet even those who sympathize with the fugitives are inclined to refer to them as anti-Russian.

In truth those who fly the official flags of friendship for Russia are profoundly anti-Russian, whether they know it or not. They are not pro-Russian but pro-Soviet, pro-dictatorship. Insofar as the average Soviet citizen is aware of their antics through his press, and through occasional contact with foreign delegations of the devout, he despises them for the dupes and lickspittles of a despotic regime. However they may fool themselves and the world, they are callous enemies of the Russian population. In the ultimate reckoning of history they will be thus judged by the liberated peoples of the Russian lands.

In the nature of the case only those who oppose and expose the Soviet dictatorship can have genuine fellow feeling for its victims. Despite the false labeling, they are truly pro-Russian. In many cases they came to their present political position the hard way — through a process of disillusionment with the communist system and its claims.

Many of them have recorded the process in print; with others I have discussed their experience personally, Invariably, it appears, their "cure" dates from the time when they sensed the tensions, amounting to deadly enmity, between the Soviet masters and the people. It usually began with moral revulsion against the iniquities visited on the Soviet masses. The dawn of wisdom and balance on the Soviet issue was marked by realization that the Kremlin regime and its subjects are not merely different but irreconcilable entities.

For the world at large as well, I am convinced, wisdom will begin when it learns this great lesson.

4. A Trend to Be Nurtured

Americans who have lived in the Soviet Union or have studied it deeply have tried to teach that lesson. Our first ambassador to the Soviets, William C. Bullitt, repeatedly makes a distinction between relations with the Kremlin and relations with the Russian people.

"We have a community of interest," he writes in *The Great Globe Itself,* "with all the peoples of the world, including the peoples of the Soviet Union, our mutual interest in peace and freedom. . . . We may find peace if we have the courage to stop the aggressions of the Soviet Government now, and the goodwill to hold out, again and again, a hand of friendship to the Russian people, saying: 'March with us — for your freedom and ours.'"

James Burnham in *The Struggle for the World* cautions that the Russian people "must on all occasions be so carefully distinguished from the Soviet regime," for "they are the primary victims of the regime, as they may prove to be the chief immediate instrument of its downfall." We must "let the subjects of the communist dictatorship know," he writes, "that the United States is aware of their misery and is their ally against their tyrants. The present automatic identification of 'Russia' with the communist regime permits the regime to solidify its hold on the Russian people, to persuade them that they must stand together against the 'bourgeois world.' The people must be allowed to know that it is not them but their oppressors whom the world condemns, and that the world is ready to rejoice with them when they break their chains."

Christopher Norberg, who came in direct contact with the Soviet challenge as an official of UNRRA just after the war, strikes the identical note in *Operation Moscow*:

"The tragic paradox of the postwar era lies in the fact that there are two Russias: The one is the monumental and long-suffering Russian people. By temperament and outlook, it is filled with a deep hunger for true and lasting peace and, therefore, politically our great and sympathetic ally for a just world order.

"The other is the imperialist Stalinist oligarchy of the Politburo, whose exploitation of the Russian people reveals the true character of a totalitarian system that makes the men on the Nuremberg gallows look like the sad victims of their own dilettantism. . . ."

R. Gordon Wasson, a financier who has been a dedicated student of Russian affairs, has warned: "It ought to be an invariable rule among us, in all our utterances about Russia and in shaping our policies toward that country to distinguish between the Russian rulers and the Russian people. . . . I have talked with some of the young Russian refugees who have lately come out of Russia and it is breathtaking for me to see that the communist jargon and ideas seem to have taken no hold on them at all. . . . The Soviet rulers can only be gainers when by careless expression we imply an inner solidarity between the regime and the people it rules — a solidarity that neither the regime nor the Russian people feel, and that can only lead us into grievous mistakes of policy as we gradually succeed in communicating with the Russians." *

In a series of articles in the *Christian Science Monitor* in January, 1950, shortly after he returned from his correspondent's post in Moscow, Edmund Stevens wrote in part: "In the coming years, the strongest and most determined foes of the police state are likely to develop east of the Iron Curtain, where not even forcible indoctrination can neutralize the lessons of immediate experience. There are in Russia today legions of thinking, intelligent people who chafe under the omnipotent police state and long with their whole

* *Toward a Russian Policy* (pamphlet), Overbrook Press, Stamford, Conn., 1951.

being for freedom. . . . It is essential that the West learn to distinguish between the police state and the Soviet people, for if the former are implacable foes, the latter, unless stupidly antagonized, are potential friends and allies. And it is they who eventually will decide their country's destiny."

This dualism — regime and people, communists and Russians — seems so clear to most students of the problem that they are inclined to take it for granted. It is implied where it is not formulated in the writings of William Henry Chamberlin, W. L. White, Malcolm Muggeridge, Louis Fischer in his more recent books, a dozen others. It is the *leitmotiv* of books by runaways from the Soviet paradise like the Tchernavins, Koriakov, Klimov, Barmine, Kravchenko, Gouzenko, Kasenkina. Indeed, only those who are firmly committed psychologically to the Kremlin power system fail to understand the dichotomy or, at any rate, to face up to it.

Fortunately an awareness of this central factor has been growing in recent years. It is increasingly evident in the press and in pronouncements of political leaders. When Winston Churchill, in his Boston address in April, 1949, declared that "we have no hostility to the Russian people," he summed up a deepening sense of the dualism. President Truman reflected the same insight earlier. Alluding to Kremlin violations of treaties, he said that we would have no such troubles "if the Russian people had a voice in their government."

In one of his principal campaign speeches as Presidential candidate in 1948 Governor Thomas E. Dewey declared:

"The people of the United States have no quarrel with the people of the Soviet Union. Our firm faith in the fundamental dignity of man and his aspirations for freedom gives us only the deepest sympathy for the oppressed Russian people. We know they are not the authors of the Kremlin's aggressive ambitions. They're its victims.

"We do not retract a single word of the admiration we expressed for the people of Russia during the war. We shall make every effort to tell the people behind the iron curtain, and tell them day after day and month after month by every means at the command of your government, that we know that they want peace just as much as we do, and that they can get it by their actions in helping us."

Clare Boothe Luce, when she was in Congress, said one day:

"We must understand that the plain people of Russia live in a vast concentration camp, the prisoners of their own leaders. When we remember this, we will never act or speak as some people do, as though the great Russian people were our enemies. The Russian people are and must continue to be our friends, for the peace of the world depends on that friendship."

James F. Byrnes, writing after his retirement as Secretary of State, declared that at present the mass of Russians are helpless to affect policy. "But," he added, "in considering the future policy, we must not ignore them. They are, I believe, our hope."

Ernst Reuter, the socialist Mayor of Berlin, has had exceptional opportunities for contact with Russians, both fugitives and those still in Kremlin livery. Speaking in New York in the course of a visit in May, 1949, he pleaded with his audience never to confound "innocent" Russians with the Soviet regime. He had no doubt, he said, that if the Soviet population had freedom of expression "they would have been on our side against their masters."

The press, too, here and there provides heartening proofs of this revised estimate of the Russian situation. "It is significant," Anne O'Hare McCormick wrote, "that there is more emphasis now than ever before on the distinction between the Russian people and the Soviet government." Rodney Gilbert, then the perspicacious columnist of the New York *Herald Tribune,* found it possible to say: "It is not unlikely that the Russian people are our most potent allies in the cold war for peace." As early as December 16, 1946, a *Life* editorial on relations with the USSR began with the thought that "we must distinguish between a hostile government and a neutral nation from a friendly people," and ended with these words:

"Yet the Russian people love freedom, and they love their fellow man with a passion almost unique among all peoples. They swarm easily but they are not barbarians; they are poor but they are not tramps. They are victims of a system under which their only weapon is patience and their incorruptible humanity. They need our trust. Let us never answer their need with anger or scorn."

A *Saturday Evening Post* editorial a few years ago was titled "Our Enemies Are the Red Tyrants, Not Their Slaves." And it concluded: "Rekindling the hopes of true freedom in the ordinary Russian is a weapon worth a hundred atomic bombs. It may be our best hope of survival for ourselves."

Those tyrants, we may be sure, are doing their best to keep their subjects from learning that the world begins to draw a line between them. The Churchillian assurances that "we have no hostility to the Russian people," the United States Senate resolution of friendship for those people, the messages of fellowship for them above the heads of their rulers at last being beamed to the USSR by American and British radio stations — these are portents to terrify the Soviet hierarchy. *For they aim at the weakest and most vulnerable spot in their defenses.*

By the same token, nothing gratifies the Moscow government more than the routine and indiscriminate denunciations of "the Russians" still so much in evidence. Every such attack is seized upon by the Kremlin to convince its subjects that they are in the same boat with the dictatorship; that they have been abandoned by the rest of the world and have no choice but to make common cause with the communist regime.

In the United States, a number of citizens' organizations have arisen, with the aim of cementing friendship between the Russian and American peoples, and encouraging common action against the communist barbarians. One of these is the American Committee for Liberation from Bolshevism, of which I had the privilege of being the first chairman and which at this writing is headed by Admiral Leslie E. Stevens. Its primary objective is to provide material and moral aid to *émigrés* from the Soviet Union in their struggle against the Kremlin; it supports Station Liberation in Munich, run by Soviet exiles and Americans in co-operation and aimed at radio listeners inside the USSR. Another, American Friends of Russian Freedom, has taken upon itself the dual task of helping recest political fugitives from Russia and promoting better understanding of the Russian peoples among Americans.

These are symptoms of a growing appreciation in America of the nature of the Soviet challenge and the role of the Russian peoples. Will the world crisis be resolved in atomic horror, or through the inner weakening and ultimate overthrow of the Soviet regime? These, in the final analysis, are the only genuine alternatives. The answer depends in large measure on whether the views and sentiments of such organizations prevail in terms of free-world policy.

XX. The Fateful Choice

1. Toward a New Approach

Inside the Soviet Union it is impossible for the normal foreigner to be at the same time on the side of the regime and on the side of the people. The few who accomplish it, by dint of cheating their intelligence and drugging their conscience, become moral schizophrenics. The healthy-minded observer may postpone and rationalize and squirm, but in the end a choice between loyalty to the rulers and loyalty to the ruled becomes inescapable.

Slowly the non-Soviet world is beginning to duplicate that experience. It senses the great cleavage between the people and the dictatorship, and therefore the necessity of a fundamental choice between them. Ever more sharply journalists and statesmen betray an uncomfortable recognition of their long guilt in having treated the Russian peoples as the authors rather than the victims of Bolshevik infamies abroad and at home. With increasing frequency we hear allusions to the Soviet masses as allies, rather than enemies, of a world harassed by Politburo ambitions and obsessions.

That is all to the good. The shift in thinking may prove to be the most fruitful development since World War II. Should the idea of friendship for the Soviet people, looking toward collaboration with them, become dominant, a new confidence in the future will come with it. More and more possibilities for the stimulation and release of anti-Soviet pressures within the USSR will then be opened up. The free world will begin to throw off its feeling of helplessness.

Those who appreciate this trend and its significance must seek to deepen and accelerate it. The inertia of past policies and the assumptions on which they rest will not be overcome easily. But once the choice is made, once we cease to bemuse ourselves with the mirage of a Kremlin miraculously transformed and co-operative and begin to concentrate on fostering a united front with its subjects, appropriate policy will follow as a matter of course. *The new approach will impose its own logic upon international affairs.* When we decide to base our conduct on a firm allegiance to the people, in defiance of their police state, the initiative will at least be in our hands, not only politically but morally.

The wishful thinking and wishful maneuvering in the never-never land of coexistence which now bedevil our diplomacy will be canceled out. The Kremlin's unilateral ability to tease, distract, divide, and confuse the democracies by dangling "deals" before their eyes — deals which, however disguised, always demand the barter of the freedom of others for our own — will finally be ruled out. A whole dimension of Soviet political strategy will thus be shut off.

At the same time, our emphasis on human freedoms and moral imperatives will no longer sound hollow; they will no longer seem to be political devices, for they will have become living facts. We shall be engaged in a crusade for liberation worthy of the sacrifices that mankind in this crucial era cannot evade in any case, and the spirit of man on both sides of the Iron Curtain will be fortified for all eventualities. The impact of free-world power, which now stops short at the rim of the Soviet realm, will at last be felt throughout Russia and its captive countries, even as communist power is felt inside non-Soviet nations.

The so-called cold war is not a postwar phenomenon; only the label is new. Actually that struggle has been with us from the night the Bolsheviks hijacked power in November, 1917, and will remain with us until the day their power collapses. It has been manifest not only in international affairs but within every country, through the activities of local communist movements. World communism is an octopus, its head and heart in the Soviet Union and its tentacles gripping other nations. It does little good, in the final analysis, to hack away at the tentacles while leaving the heart immune to blows. Only when the strength of the Kremlin ebbs will its foreign extensions weaken and in the end go limp.

Must the collapse of Bolshevism be preceded by a terrifying global war? Yes — unless we head off this supreme calamity in the only way it can be headed off, which is by *winning* the cold war. Let there be no mistake about it. There is no genuine alternative to World War III except a clear-cut victory in the struggle already under way, and that in turn can be attained only in open alliance with the Kremlin's subjects.

The indispensable first step to victory is the forthright decision to win, to settle for nothing less than the elimination of the Soviet regime. The second is to make the decision known to all mankind, communicating it clearly especially to the peoples of the Soviet empire.

Moscow is inflexibly committed to the annihilation of the civilization we cherish. A commitment of the same order and the same firmness on our part with respect to Soviet barbarism can end the confusions in which the free world has been floundering for so many years. It would lift the great historic duel of our time from the swamps of make-believe to the plane of clean-cut ideological confrontation. We — and our secret allies — would know at long last what we are fighting against, and what we are fighting for.

To be effective our decision must be as sharp-edged and uncompromising as the Kremlin's; it must be spelled out as unequivocally as the communists have done in the works of Lenin and Stalin and the programs of the Comintern and Cominform. To accomplish its relentless purpose, Moscow has been consistently building fifth columns in our midst and promoting tacit alliances with millions of its sympathizers throughout the world. Having dedicated ourselves to destroying communism root and branch, we must likewise focus our energies and ingenuity upon expanding *our* fifth columns and generating ideological support within the enemy domain.

Those who urge a policy of liberation are asked, "But how will we reach the Russian peoples?" The question touches the lesser and easier half of the problem. The greater half is how to reach the peoples of the free world, how to clarify their conception of the challenge and their grasp of the opportunity.

The masses behind the Red curtains will know our new viewpoint precisely as they have known our old viewpoints. It will be manifest in words, acts, and emotions too immense in their totality to be hidden from them. We need but identify the enemy properly and pledge ourselves courageously and convincingly to his defeat to win more ardent allies — and allies more strategically placed for our common objectives — than we can purchase with Marshall Plans and Point-Four Programs, desirable as they may be.

"No iron curtain, no terror measures adopted by the Soviet regime, will be able to hinder the long-distance effect of *an inner change in the Western world's attitude to that country*." This is the opinion of Ernst Reuter, who lived among the Russians for years, and for more years, as Mayor of West Berlin, fought the Kremlin's minions at close range. If we are clear in our own minds that the Soviets and their terrorized subjects are distinct and mutually hostile entities, that Russian interests and Bolshevik interests are different and normally contradictory things, our sense of this dualism will in time be recognized by the beleaguered Russian peoples.

With regard to the Red satellites, the psychological posture of the non-Soviet world is still relatively sound and realistic. The record of their conquest and enslavement has not yet been smeared out of recognition by totalitarian-liberal double-talk. Not even far-left journals of opinion pretend that the population of Poland or Hungary or Czechoslovakia is solidly and enthusiastically behind its regime. No one argues that we are locked in cold combat with those populations. An American or British pundit who values his reputation as a democrat would not dare proclaim that *any* Pole or Czech or Chinese is "the enemy."

In short, we still think of the satellite peoples as part of *our* humanity, as captives who will sooner or later be liberated. They have not been written off like the Russians. Some tendency, in line with fatalistic containment attitudes, to give them up as irretrievably lost to the communists, has been arrested, one must hope, by the convulsions of resistance, particularly in Eastern Germany, which electrified the free world in the summer of 1953.

As a result, policy geared to the liberation of these peoples, predicated upon their collaboration with the free world when favorable conditions are created or arise spontaneously through the chemistry of events, does not sound farfetched. *That attitude need only be extended to embrace Soviet Russia itself to bring an invigorating clarity to our relations with the Kremlin.*

The Western mind still balks at liberation policies vis-à-vis Russia proper chiefly because the record of its conquest and enslavement has been blotted out or concealed, because the history of its consistent resistance to Bolshevism has been largely ignored. If the facts which I have attempted to set forth in these pages are understood and given their proper weight in our thinking, startling new horizons for action will be opened up.

The imagination of the free portion of mankind has been paralyzed by the assumption that the Kremlin and its victims have been successfully welded into an indissoluble whole. That assumption is false, fatalistic, and implies an ultimate war to the death with the Russian peoples; if adhered to stubbornly, it will operate to bring about the very solidarity it assumes.

"We should make it clear," John Foster Dulles wrote before he became Secretary of State, ". . . that United States policy seeks as one of its peaceable goals the eventual restoration of genuine independence in the nations of Europe and Asia now dominated by Moscow and that we will not be a party to any 'deal' confirming the rule of Soviet despotism." *

And General Eisenhower, in one of his campaign speeches, talked in the same vein: "Our government . . . must tell the Kremlin that we shall never recognize the slightest permanence in Russia's position in Eastern Europe and Asia. The day must come when the peoples of the enslaved lands will have the opportunity . . . to choose their own paths into the future." **

Both of them unfortunately failed to specify, beyond danger of

* *Life,* May 19, 1952.
** Address in New York, August 25, 1952.

misunderstanding, that their statements applied to Russia no less than to its satellites. Yet a policy of liberation which stops at the Russian frontiers, which makes a meaningless technical distinction between countries conquered by communism before and after 1945, remains simon-pure containment; it merely narrows the area to be contained without disowning the principle.

As long as we accept the permanence of communist rule within Russia, we cut all psychological-political and moral bridges to the Russian peoples. We have nothing to say to them. We remain, as heretofore, neutrals, if not enemies, in their unceasing struggle against the Red regime.

Whether American forces are committed to Europe and Asia is of secondary importance to the hundreds of millions under the hammer and sickle. What they watch for is proof of a basic change in our attitude to the whole system of Soviet power. The only Western goal that has any personal relevance for the captive populations is one that holds out a promise of eventual elimination of the Kremlin *vlast*. Those people crave reassurance of ultimate release, without which they cannot be expected to keep alive the flame of hope.

They crave reassurance, too, that they will not be punished as a nation for the sins and aggressions of their Red usurpers — that after the end of the Soviets the historic Russia will occupy a place of honor and influence in our world commensurate with its natural greatness and genius. The principle of "collective guilt" established in Nuremberg and Japan hangs as a threat over the heads of millions of Soviet citizens, operating to tie their personal destinies into the fate of the dictatorship. To that extent it imposes upon them a loyalty they may not feel. So far as the USSR is concerned, that principle must be disowned. In its fourth decade, there are few if any who have not "collaborated" with the regime. Even party members often join out of necessity or under the goad of ambition; thousands of others, having entered the fold with enthusiasm, are rapidly disillusioned. Both Russia as a nation and its citizens as individuals must be helped to grasp the identity of their interests with those of the free world.

We must leave no doubt that we have learned, as Walter Lippmann phrased it (though in a quite different polemic context), "to distinguish clearly between the Stalinist regime and the Russian nation, to treat the one as an ugly, intolerable and transient phase and to recognize the other as representing the enduring and vital national interests of Russia. We should make it plain that the Russian people will not have to sacrifice, will not put in jeopardy, their legitimate national interests if they liquidate the Bolshevist system, and agree to withdraw their armies from Eastern Europe." *

2. *Geared to Love, Not Hate*

If the West were today engaged in a full-scale shooting war, it would have neither reservations nor inhibitions in seeking by all means to enlarge the gulf between the enemy government and its citizenry. The need for allies behind its lines would be too urgent to squander time and energy in soul-searching speculation as to whether the gulf is as wide as some people claim, whether the Russian is capable of understanding freedom, whether we have a right to "meddle" in his country's internal affairs. Whatever the costs in money and in life, however uncertain the results, we would proceed with the job of weakening and if possible springing the Soviet system from within. By the same token, we would move boldly, uninhibitedly, to expose and neutralize the enemy's fifth columns in our midst; we would acknowledge that tolerance for them makes as little sense as tolerance for native Nazis would have made during World War II.

Well, we *are* at war. We are destined to remain at war until one side or the other is defeated and expunged. The need to weaken the enemy is, if anything, more compelling than it would be in a "real" war, since it offers the best hope of preventing the "real" war. The greater its domestic tensions, the less certain the Soviet government is of the allegiance and obedience of its subjects, the more anxious it will be to avoid a showdown. Every day we lose in

* New York *Herald Tribune,* July 14, 1953.

launching a policy of liberation is therefore a gift of time to the Kremlin. Every thoughtless attack on "Russia" and "the Russians," when the targets are the Soviets and the communist minority, makes an alliance with our secret allies that much harder to achieve.

Writing of the Russia of his time, General von Clausewitz declared:

"She can only be defeated by her own weakness and by effects of internal dissension. To hit these weak spots of her political existence, a shock going right to the heart of her government will be necessary."

Whatever validity his judgment had when it was pronounced, it applies a hundredfold to Soviet Russia today, in cold and hot war alike. Had the Hitlerites, who admired the purely military precepts of Clausewitz, taken to heart this political aspect of his doctrine, the story of their struggle with the USSR might have had a different ending. Neither Napoleon nor Hitler, be it remembered, could defeat Russia — and in both cases because they were up against boundless Russian patriotism. *That patriotism can and must be enlisted on the side of freedom.*

A great deal of debris remains to be cleared away. The Russian people burned their fingers on the Germans, who promised liberation and delivered a new species of slavery, made more onerous by racial contempt. It was inevitable that they should hold the sins of the Germans against the West as a whole. Then they watched, incredible and heartsick, as the victorious Allies supinely yielded to every wish and whim of their tyrants, turned over patriotic Russian enemies of the regime to Stalin, then begged abjectly for a permanent division of the world. They noted in despair that our interest in the freedom of the free was coupled with a strange indifference to the freedom of the unfree.

The timidity of the West, its anxiety to do business with the Politburo, its years of kowtowing to Moscow, have done more than all the communist propaganda to convince the Soviet people that the free world is flabby, decadent, hopelessly devoid of principle, and above all, completely disinterested in their travail and aspirations. With our own hands we undermined confidence in our good will and faith in our democratic pretensions. A job of rehabilitation should be undertaken without delay.

The United States, and the other democratic powers, should face up to their political blunders and moral failures. They must repudiate the past insofar as it blocks an understanding with Russia over the heads of its internal occupying forces. When that is done, we shall be in a better moral position to persuade its people that we are not *against* the Russians but *with* them against their autocracy; that the fateful conflict is not between East and West, not for territory and loot as the communists charge, but for human dignity and decency.

Only with and through the Russian peoples can atomic warfare be postponed and perhaps obviated entirely. Another world war is by no means inevitable. But the possibility cannot be ignored, regardless of what policies we follow. Should that war be forced upon us, every investment now in furthering better relations with the Russian peoples will pay off by shortening the road to victory and saving millions of lives on both sides. Popular disaffection in the USSR will then be worth more than atom bombs in hastening the defeat of the communists. Bonds of friendship with the Soviet people, established *before* the cold war bursts into hot conflict, hold the only genuine hope of short-cutting such a struggle.

There are those who, denying the possibility of disturbing the Soviet Union internally under peacetime conditions, contend that a consistent policy of liberation could yield results only "in case of war." Why do anything now, they ask, when we are seeking to prevent war? But even if its premise were correct, the argument ought not to dissuade us from the course of liberation. After all, we have been devoting our diplomacy and pouring out our substance to gain allies in the West "in case of war." Why, in plain logic, is not a comparable effort to gain decisive allies within the Soviet sphere equally justified? Under our present policy, however, we have not even carried out the wishes of Congress, which appropriated one hundred million dollars to implement an ally-winning program behind the Iron Curtain, while spending billions to win over Western Europe.

One does not have to share his political philosophy to acknowledge the wisdom of this statement by Grand Duke Vladimir, pretender to the Russian throne:

> There is only one effective way of limiting the horrors of a war against communism, and at the same time achieving a rapid victory, namely, to secure the active and willing co-operation of the Russian people in the common cause. For inevitably the Russian people must be the deciding factor in this fight to the death, which has already begun.
>
> To win the confidence and obtain the assistance of the Russian people, the latter will have to be convinced that the Western Powers are fighting communism, not waging a war on Russia. The vast majority of the Russian people, and of the soldiers of the Red Army, is certainly anti-communist. The Russian, however, has been so often deceived that he is bound to be suspicious, particularly at first, of foreigners and their promises. Experience with the Germans and later the Allied Powers, who so inhumanly handed over anticommunist volunteers to the Soviet Union, make it unlikely that large numbers of Russians will voluntarily come over and join the anti-Soviet forces as they did at the beginning of the German campaign.*

If we wait to allay those suspicions until war breaks out, it may be too late. That assignment cannot be tackled too soon or too vigorously. The United States certainly has no territorial or economic ambitions in Russia. Its sole aim, even on the level of self-interest and expediency, can only be the emancipation of Russia and its entry as an equal and honored member into the family of nations. Not only do we not want anything from a free Russia but we stand ready to give of our substance, our technological genius, and our spirit to help rehabilitate the country materially and politically.

Simple truths and pledges of this character can be made self-evident to the Kremlin's subjects. When they are fully convinced that our objective is not the defeat of Russia but its liberation — and therefore coincides with their own innermost desires — the people will flock to us. They have been famished for friendship and understanding and will reach out for it avidly.

---

* *Nasha Strana*, No. 121, February, 1952.

At a time when few other American journalists had such insights, David Lawrence wrote:

We must approach the Russian people directly, making it plain to them that we are sincere believers in the dignity of the individual and in the Judeo-Christian concept of human brotherhood. . . . We must explain to all the world, not only our friendliness to the Russian people but our willingness to use our material resources and make sacrifices in their behalf. We must offer concrete plans of economic and financial aid that are designed to improve the standard of living not only of all the people of Russia but of the peoples of all the satellite countries whom we wish to liberate from the Kremlin's domination. . . . In short, the time has come to appeal to peoples instead of drifting along on the mistaken assumption that the leopards in the Kremlin will change their spots. . . .
We can have a people's peace — and it can be a peace without appeasing any of the despotic governments now lined up against us in the cold war. It can be a peace of liberation for the human beings now under the yoke of tyranny. They can be liberated by the moral force of mankind which alone can direct and mobilize the material resources of the world and bring enduring peace.*

His words, as far as we know, fell on barren soil. I am not too sanguine, in all conscience, that the thesis I have tried to elaborate in this book will fare any better — though I am convinced it must prevail ultimately. Such optimism as I can muster rests only on the belief that the ground is by now more fertile. It has been plowed up by a few more years of failure and frustration, years marked by the final loss of China, the Red seizure of Tibet, the continued vitality of communist movements in France and Italy, the spread of neutralist-defeatist sentiment in the West, and especially the terrible and largely useless bloodletting in Korea. More of the delusions of containment and coexistence have been exploded. The granite of the communist determination to smash our world, which is under all the shifts in Kremlin policy, has become more apparent than ever before.

The search for a different, a better, a morally more inspiring

* *U.S. News and World Report,* June 23, 1950.

answer to the predicament of mankind has become more intense, the logic of a commitment to liberation more compelling.

It is not the contention of this book that the peoples of Russia are "in revolt," that there are secret societies and underground resistance movements. Should such implications have been left anywhere in these pages, it was no part of my intention. If these things existed, indeed, they would not necessarily be too significant: Isolated pockets of hostility in a nation that is basically loyal to its established order are meaningless; but general hostility, with only isolated pockets of loyalty, is a mortal threat to that order. The significance is in the vast, pervasive, and continuous resistance which we have examined.

Possibly there are miniscule revolutionary cells, particularly among Soviet youth. Without doubt there is a freemasonry of the like-minded — unspoken understandings among small anti-Soviet groups in all departments of life — too nebulous to be exposed and dispersed by secret police. But none of this, we may be sure, is on a scale to alarm or endanger the regime.

We are concerned with *potentials* for insurrection, with states of mind, with deep-running but unarticulated protest. A few million of the most politically conscious Soviet citizens, largely in the upper brackets of the system of power including the ruling party itself, may have translated their recalcitrance into specific hopes and plans. For the rest the opposition is amorphous and unchanneled: an elemental response to physical and psychic distress. There is no fire, but the inflammable stuffs for a conflagration are piled high against the time when internal or external events may apply the match.

In the book by Major Klimov which I have already cited, he paints a vivid portrait of his friend "Andrei," an MVD officer, a cynical, embittered, and deeply unhappy man. Outwardly Andrei is the staunch Chekist, part of the Kremlin's stern shield against its multitudinous foes, but inwardly he hates the machine in which he is caught. In talking to Klimov, whose lack of fervor for the regime he senses, Andrei was brutally frank:

"If it's a question of ideological enemies," he said, "then all the nation is our ideological enemy. Those who fall into the hands of the MVD are only victims of a lottery. Out of every hundred charges brought by the MVD, ninety-nine are pure inventions. We act on the principle that every man is our enemy. To catch an enemy red-handed you have to give him the opportunity to commit a hostile act. If we wait, it may be too late. For their name is: million. So we seize the first at hand and accuse him of what you will. Thus we liquidate a certain proportion of the potential enemy and simultaneously paralyze the will of the others."

Referring to a stubborn prisoner then in his hands, undergoing interrogation by torture, Andrei says: "He is dangerous chiefly because he is one of the millions. Throw a lighted idea into that powder barrel and the whole lot would go up!" *

Such is the nature of the opposition, unplanned, unorganized, without apparent leadership, yet limitless. The Andreis in the MVD know that it is there, that "every man is our enemy," and wait nervously for the "lighted idea" that will touch off an explosion. This is the potential which the free world thus far has denied or ignored — to which we can address ourselves, after we cleanse our own hearts of the illusions of containment and the temptations of appeasement. Because it is a potential, it must be carefully nurtured, before it is choked and withered by the dusts of neglect and despair. Our obligation, in the simplest terms of self-interest as well as in the loftiest terms of mankind's redemption, is to keep alive internal Soviet opposition, to break down the terrifying sense of isolation from free men under which the Kremlin's foes at home have lived, to convince them that the conscience of the West has been thoroughly aroused at last.

I have suggested in other contexts that a revision of basic attitudes, one that makes us devoted partisans rather than aloof onlookers in Russia's permanent civil war, will dictate new policies. The elaboration of those policies is not in the pattern of this book. My purpose has been primarily to present the philosophy of alliance with the Kremlin's internal opposition, to establish that we have friends and

* *The Terror Machine.*

allies within the Soviet Union whose numbers can ultimately embrace nearly the entire population.

There is little reason for making contact with the Russian peoples until we have ceased to consider them expendables in negotiations with their dictators. Before that point is reached, discussion of techniques of communication and tactics of psychological offensive is so much flailing of water. It will become realistic only when we have a clear message to deliver: a message that will be delivered not alone in words but in deeds.

"What could more enhearten the subject peoples or more dismay their rulers," James Burnham has asked, "than news of a representative of free Poland sitting in the councils of NATO; free regiments marching under the flags of Rumania, Esthonia, Russia; a free Ukrainian unit capturing a hill in Korea or wiping out one of Ho Chi Minh's detachments in Indochina; a class of a thousand young East Europeans graduating with degrees in administration, agriculture, and engineering; 20,000 East European, Chinese, and Russian exiles combining military training with agriculture in North Africa; a NATO destroyer manned by Baltic seamen; free spokesmen of all the captive nations received with honor in Whitehall, the Quai d'Orsay, and the Department of State?" *

Possible demonstrative undertakings of this type crowd to one's mind as soon as it is freed to think along these lines. A ring of broadcasting stations capable of penetrating the whole Soviet empire could be built up, including peripatetic stations designed to foil jamming. Hundreds of thousands of tiny individual radio receivers, capable of picking up "liberation" stations, could be scattered by balloon and planes and smuggled into Soviet occupation centers in Germany and Austria; we have the assurance of General David Sarnoff, the foremost authority in this field, that such instruments can be built. Special projects suggest themselves for infiltrating both civilian and military personnel stationed outside the Soviet Union. Already some experimental newspapers, prepared by émigré groups, find their way mysteriously into Soviet-controlled

* *Containment or Liberation?* Viking, 1953.

regions; the possibilities in this regard have not been sufficiently explored.

But the heart of the matter is not in such enterprises. It is in the basic change of policy, as reflected in day-to-day dealings with the Kremlin and other political developments; in the more confident posture of the free world, its alertness in exposing Soviet crimes and championing the victims always and everywhere. A new political climate would become manifest in ways too numerous to be inventoried.

The Kremlin's subjects have felt themselves cut off from the living community of free men. The enemies of Sovietism under the hammer and sickle in particular have felt themselves in bleak isolation, without tangible prospect of moral let alone material support from the outer world. The hundreds of thousands of Soviet fugitives passionately dedicated to unshackling their native land have been made to feel like intruders in the Western world rather than welcome and valued recruits to a common cause.

All that can be changed — not overnight to be sure, but slowly and inexorably — by pledges at the highest levels, backed by an aware public opinion, that there will be and can be no truce with communism; that we shall never consent to the permanent sundering of the world into slave and free areas, even if that were possible. The pledges must have behind them as much weight as there has been behind the corresponding communist commitments to the final destruction of free societies.

Political-psychological warfare is not a substitute for military vitality; on the contrary, military strength of the right kind is the indispensable background for effective nonmilitary action. But political action must be on a scale for victory. It will be waste effort if conceived as an extra, rather than a main enterprise, on a par with military preparedness and closely integrated with our military planning. Physical strength, and the certainty that it will be used as a last resort, will be the guarantee that all other efforts can continue without interruption, until the Kremlin's power has been whittled down to the point where our secret allies can deal with it.

Our dominant emotion toward the satellite peoples, coloring our thinking and influencing our actions, has been compassion — a compassion diffused by anger at their tormentors and touched, too, by some feeling of guilt for our contribution to their ordeal. But compassion, alas, has been absent, or at best a pallid and inhibited thing, in our relations with, and our thinking about, Russia proper.

There we have allowed ourselves to be guided largely by hate for the communists and their works. I submit that a better guide is at hand, more effective practically and more satisfying morally. That guide is love: an abounding love for the Russian peoples which will gradually open up a thousand paths to their hearts and their minds. We Americans shy away from words like love and nobility. Yet in meeting the communist challenge the way of love would be more noble, even if it were more arduous, which fortunately it is not. Our secret allies wait to hear from us.

3. *Homo Sovieticus*

In the spring of 1931 Boris Pilnyak, who had been under heavy political clouds only a few years before, was granted a visa to travel abroad. It was the literary sensation of the season. The tacit question was whether the novelist would really return to the Soviet Union. One night, in New York, I broached that question. "No," Pilnyak answered thoughtfully, "I must go home. Outside Russia I feel like a fish out of water. I just can't write, or even think clearly, except on Russian soil."

It was this kind of hunger for Russia that drew Ilya Ehrenburg back from emigration. No one who has read the novels of his Paris period, with their satiric anti-Soviet overtones, can accept his subsequent communist ravings at face value. Nostalgia for the homeland also moved Prince D. S. Mirsky to give up a pleasant life in London for the uncertainties of a Soviet existence; a few months after reaching Moscow the poor fellow, forever trapped, was already filled with melancholy self-reproach.

But in the case of Count Alexei Tolstoy, novelist, playwright, and *bon vivant,* I do not need to guess. I know.

Having failed to adjust himself to life as an *émigré* immediately after the revolution, he returned. Frankly addicted to comfort and money, he deliberately chose to play the profitable role of sycophant, and in time became the writer-laureate of the Kremlin, successor to Gorki in Stalin's court.

When Tolstoy died during the war, he was accorded a grade-A state funeral, with all the ceremonial trimmings reserved for loyal servants happily removed from the temptations of future disloyalty. His huge ghost (assuming that ghosts are roughly the shape of their originals) must have chuckled, its multiple chins quaking, at the exquisite irony. For the ghost knew — as did a few of Tolstoy's trusted friends — that he despised the Bolshevik system and its leaders, looking upon them as criminals and interlopers. His too-loud hosannas for Soviet culture and "achievements" were part of a charade of contempt, and his tragedy was that the contempt was directed in the first place against himself. A Faustian tragedy it was, in which a gifted man served the devil for the reward of fleshpots.

Almost alone in all Russia, Tolstoy was allowed to live in the old baronial manner. In Dietskoye Selo, outside Leningrad, he occupied a spacious house, its walls hung with tapestries and paintings borrowed from the Hermitage Museum. His friends called him "Count." The night my wife and I were there he had some thirty guests, among them the young composer Shostakovich, at his lordly table, this in a time of general food shortage. In the midst of the drinking and hilarity, Tolstoy suddenly motioned me to follow him upstairs to his library.

He locked the door behind us. He had become very serious, his face clouded by pain. It was a large gabled attic chamber, lined with books, a massive worktable in the center. At the gabled end opposite the door a small window framed a typically Russian pastoral scene in that twilit northern night: a tiny wood church in pastel shades, cows browsing in the foreground, several peasants at work.

First Tolstoy showed me a death mask of Peter the Great, one of three extant. He was then at work on the second volume of his great Petrine novel, and I grasped that he wanted me to see the mask as a symbol. Then he pointed beyond the window.

"Gene," he said quietly, "this is the real Russia, *my* Russia. The rest is a fraud. When I enter this room I shake off the Soviet nightmare, I shut out its stink and its horror. For a little while I am myself, with Peter the Great. I can tell *them,* the *merzavtsi* [scoundrels], to go to hell. . . . Some day, believe me, all Russia will send them to hell. . . . That's all — I wanted you to know — now let's join the company."

Though he never again mentioned his real feelings to me, it remained a silent secret between us. And always thereafter, when I heard it argued that the traditional Russian is dead, that he had been replaced by a robotlike *Homo Sovieticus,* that incident in the library came to my mind. It was one of innumerable experiences which together convinced me that the crust of Soviet conformity can be very thin. A hundred times, under the touch of vodka or the greater intoxication of a confidential mood, I saw that crust break. And after a while I ceased to be astonished when men who seemed outwardly the very models of faithful communists suddenly began to damn everything Soviet.

Tolstoy's obsession with the age of Peter was in a sense an escape from a hateful present. There were others who tried to hide out in the past, in historical works of art, to avoid lying about the current scene. The masters sensed this subtle treason: The author of a fine novel about the slaves in ancient Rome was soon himself transformed into a concentration camp slave. Even the civil war period, which Sholokhov and others made their literary demesne, was an area of escape: at least it gave some play for emotion beyond the frozen party-line patterns of the novels and plays dealing with the immediate scene. There were other, more desperate devices. One day a popular novelist, whose works were strictly machine-made propaganda, confided to me that he was secretly writing a "real book," one that told the truth — and hiding the manuscript in the rafters against the future.

Nor was this clandestine life under the Soviet masks limited to artists. I sensed it in the contempt with which a handyman, fixing something in my office, kept referring to *nashi noviye bari,* our new masters. A raised eyebrow, a helpless shrug of the shoulders, a

touch of whimsy in referring to some news item, could be tip-off
enough that hot resentments bubbled under an impeccably Soviet
exterior. On occasion, too, there were outright explosions of subversive sentiment that shocked me by their passion. Despite the
danger — sometimes, I suspected, because of the danger — Russians
talked. In their pressing need for expression and human sympathy
they endowed this or that acquaintance with the necessary qualities
of discretion, sometimes with sad consequences for both of them.

I am not suggesting that thirty-five years of life in the strait jacket
of communism have not affected the individual. Of course they
have. Those who know the totalitarian society only by hearsay
cannot even imagine what it means to be eternally immersed in
fear, dependent on the tricks of protective hypocrisy, pretending
joy and enthusiasm when the soul is convulsed with despair. A man's
natural instincts and impulses are repressed and deformed. The need
to bridle one's tongue and control one's facial expression and
counterfeit one's deepest feelings can be psychologically crippling.

Under the Soviets schizophrenia is almost a way of life. There is
the outer and public self conforming with the official rules, and
under it another self revealed only to trusted friends or hidden
even from them and from yourself. There is the moral attrition involved in concealing your past — not a guilty past, but such innocent
accidents as a priest or czarist police officer in your ancestry. There
is the erosion of personality caused by the shock of denunciations by
your close friends or relations; or worse, by the conscious or accidental betrayal of others in the process of saving your own skin.

The Soviet man steps warily in a world of traps and pitfalls. An
incautious remark or a new acquaintanceship may reduce his life to
ashes. He must not only be on the party line, but be there at precisely the right time, neither too soon nor too late. He must be alert
to denounce himself before others denounce him. The late Dr.
Hermann Borchardt, who taught German in a Soviet university for
a year, once asked a Russian friend to define communism. "Communism," the man replied, "is the art of speaking unnaturally." *

Among recent escapees from the Soviet Union one constantly

* From an unpublished manuscript in the author's possession.

meets men who are passionately anti-Bolshevik, yet Bolshevik to the core in their own psychology. They are suspicious and conniving, self-centered and materialist, in the grip of a kind of greed for survival. For the most striking effect of "socialism" of the Soviet variety has been to attach men more grimly to private property and personal advantage, to their little possessions and little careers. Some of the fugitives never lose the stigmata of their Soviet crucifixion, others require many years of freedom to restore them to psychic health. To buy what you will, to speak your mind, to move about without "documents," to take full responsibility for your own life and conduct — these are things *Homo Sovieticus* must learn from scratch, as a child learns to walk.

This is not remarkable. What is remarkable is that men and women of the Soviet generation, once they inhale the air of freedom, for the most part do thaw out and throw off their Bolshevik masks. The inner Russian, it appears, has survived: the Russian of the *shirokii natura,* the broad nature, with his primordial leanings to the spiritual and idealistic.

The communist "engineers of the soul" have sweated to uproot these qualities, leaving only a totalitarian robot, and they have succeeded in individual cases. But they have failed with the population as a whole. There is a fine Russian word for a fine Russian characteristic: *vynosslivost,* meaning a patient and hopeful endurance, "lasting a thing out." The country and its people have demonstrated it in the last thirty-five years.

Again and again the traditional Russian breaks through the *Homo Sovieticus,* dramatically, startlingly. Some communist being put through the paces of a public purge has acquitted himself splendidly, but cannot repress a final remark that costs him his career. "Which will finally triumph, socialism or capitalism?" he is asked, and in a blinding moment of honesty he shrugs his shoulders and says, "Who knows? who knows?" An old man being interrogated is asked how he fared under the old capitalist system. He knows the "right" answer well enough, yet he is impelled by something deeper than common sense to reply, "To tell the truth, very well. My employer was kind and generous."

In the thirties Moscow, Leningrad, and other centers were swept by a veritable craze for the phonograph records, strictly forbidden, of a refugee Russian composer and singer, one Vertinsky. His were sentimental ballads, full of exotic flowers and tender emotion, nostalgia and heartbreak. A cracked Vertinsky record fetched fantastic prices in the black market, and people risked arrest to hear those croonings. The hard-boiled, unfeeling "new man" is a propaganda fiction. Given the least official leeway on this score, and the people rush to hear gypsy music; writers rush to write on simple, human subjects; even communists rush to baptize their children.

In the fourth decade of his subjection, the Soviet man is still skeptical of what he reads in the Soviet press and cynical about the official propaganda. Let a thing be sufficiently repeated in *Izvestia* and on the radio, and the Russian begins to suspect that it's a lie or a trick. "What are *they* trying to put over? What's *really* behind their slogans?" When I lived in Moscow the press was so full of the depression in the United States and the capitalist world that I had a job of it convincing my Soviet friends that there *was* a depression.

Many if not most of the characteristics we ascribe to *Homo Sovieticus* are neither Soviet nor Russian, but plain human. Given an equivalent total oppression, any people would develop the same set of traits. Most of what the communist citizen does for the state he regards as drudgery, as a sort of tax in kind. He brings personal love and interest only to his own plot of ground, his own family, his own belongings. He places an exaggerated value on these things through what one fugitive Soviet writer calls a "thirst for more personality," for some tokens of individuality to distinguish him from the gray mass of which he is a part.

One of the most acid descriptions of the deleterious effects on character worked by Bolshevism has been written by Mikhail Koriakov; so much so that he exposed himself to attack on this ground. Yet he is himself a living proof that the Russian core has not been corrupted beyond redemption.

"I was exactly the same in Russia as I am today," he declares.

"And I left friends in Moscow who think and speak as I do — with the only difference that they are unable to express themselves as freely. It seems to me that Russia may be compared to a lantern with soot-covered walls. It is true that the glass is sooty. But, somewhere within, the light still burns. And it is a strong light, for it still breaks occasionally through the smoky glass." *

According to Koriakov that unquenchable light is Orthodox Christianity. Probably he is wrong in identifying it so narrowly as a specific religious denomination. But he is right, I believe, in relating that light to a religious essence — to the thirst for righteousness, the respect for the human spirit, which have informed Russian thought and emotion through the centuries. Behind the soot there is still the celebrated Russian soul.

The fanatic faith in Bolshevik tenets which was generated in the earlier period has crumbled under the blows of later years, and no permissible new faith has arisen. The original aspirations and motivations have been emptied of everything but a bleak and unappetizing careerism. The *élan* of communism, the appeal to young imaginations which it still enjoys in noncommunist countries, has all but expired in the Soviet Union itself. Soviet youth finds no outlet for its idealistic urges except in dreams of freedom.

It is to be expected that young Soviet men and women of ability should try to enter the Communist Party, as the shortest road to preferment and respectability. Private ambition is as strong a driving force as in any other place under any other system. What is almost miraculous, however, is that thousands of them *avoid* joining the party, resisting pressures and even threats, in order to save a few crumbs of personal independence, some margin of inner freedom.

Similarly, it is easy to understand why young men, though deeply religious in temper, cannot bring themselves to embrace a career in the church. They know it means penury, abuse, persecution. Nevertheless, throughout the Soviet years, thousands have prepared for the priesthood despite the certainty of martyrdom.

"The statistics of concentration camps," Koriakov writes in the

* "The Faith of the Soviet," in *Thought,* Fordham University Quarterly, December, 1950.

essay I have already quoted, "would show a tremendous percentage of young people among the inmates. . . . The students, whom I knew very well, are in a ferment of the most varied and contradictory searchings and strivings. Recoiling from Marxism-Leninism, they grasp at Leibnitz, Nikolai Kuzansky, Schelling."

Virtually all who have written from personal knowledge of the concentration camps and political isolators underline that youth was well represented and often predominant among the prisoners. It is mathematically demonstrable, in fact, that this has to be so: that in the fourth decade of Soviet *vlast* there could not be enough millions of "enemies of the people" of the prerevolutionary generation to fill the camps and the prisons. And among the escapees from the Soviet Union and deserters from the Red Army, too, as I have pointed out elsewhere, the young are in the majority. Hostility to the Soviet regime is not a carry-over from the past but a contemporary phenomenon.

This gives us the right to believe that the inner Russian man is still whole. The scars inflicted by Soviet upbringing and experience are big and ugly, but they are largely on the surface. When the whole story is told, as one day it must be, we shall have reason for pride in our secret allies. Let us hope that they, in turn, will have reason for pride in our understanding of their plight and our determination to co-operate with them for the overthrow of the Soviet regime.